Cape Town

timeout.com/capetown

Published by Time Out Guides Ltd, a wholly owned subsidiary of Time Out Group Ltd.
Time Out and the Time Out logo are trademarks of Time Out Group Ltd.

© Time Out Group Ltd 2004

10 9 8 7 6 5 4 3 2 1

This edition first published in Great Britain in 2004 by Ebury
Ebury is a division of The Random House Group Ltd,
20 Vauxhall Bridge Road, London SW1V 2SA

Random House Australia Pty Limited, 20 Alfred Street, Milsons Point, Sydney, New South Wales 2061, Australia
Random House New Zealand Limited, 18 Poland Road, Glenfield, Auckland 10, New Zealand
Random House South Africa (Pty) Limited, Endulini, 5A Jubilee Road, Parktown 2193, South Africa

Random House UK Limited Reg. No. 954009

Distributed in USA by Publishers Group West
1700 Fourth Street, Berkeley, California 94710

Distributed in Canada by Penguin Canada Ltd
10 Alcorn Avenue, Toronto, Ontario, Canada M4V 3B2

For further distribution details, see www.timeout.com

ISBN 1-904978-12-6

A CIP catalogue record for this book is available from the British Library

Colour reprographics by Icon, Crowne House, 56-58 Southwark Street, London SE1 1UN

Printed and bound by Cayfosa-Quebecor, Ctra. De Caldes, KM 3 08 130 Sta, Perpètua de Mogoda, Barcelona, Spain

Time Out Guides Limited
Universal House
251 Tottenham Court Road
London W1T 7AB
Tel + 44 (0)20 7813 3000
Fax + 44 (0)20 7813 6001
Email guides@timeout.com
www.timeout.com

Editorial

Editor (Cape Town) Sam Woulidge
Editor (London) Lily Dunn
Managing Editor Anelde Greeff
Copy Editor Christine Riley
Listings Checker Daniel Bugan
Proofreader Mary Lindsay
Indexer Jackie Brind

Editorial/Managing Director Peter Fiennes
Series Editor Ruth Jarvis
Deputy Series Editor Lesley McCave
Guides Co-ordinator Anna Norman
Accountant Sarah Bostock

Design

Art Director Mandy Martin
Acting Art Director Scott Moore
Acting Art Editor Tracey Ridgewell
Acting Senior Designer Astrid Kogler
Designer Sam Lands
Junior Designer Oliver Knight
Digital Imaging Dan Conway
Ad Make-up Charlotte Blythe

Picture Desk

Picture Editor Jael Marschner
Deputy Picture Editor Kit Burnet
Picture Researcher Ivy Lahon
Picture Desk Assistant/Librarian Laura Lord

Advertising

Sales Director Mark Phillips
International Sales Manager Ross Canadé
International Sales Executive James Tuson
Advertising Sales (Cape Town) New Media Publishing
Advertising Assistant Lucy Butler

Marketing

Marketing Manager Mandy Martinez
US Publicity & Marketing Associate Rosella Albanese

Production

Guides Production Director Mark Lamond
Production Controller Samantha Furniss

Time Out Group

Chairman Tony Elliott
Managing Director Mike Hardwick
Group Financial Director Richard Waterlow
Group Commercial Director Lesley Gill
Group Marketing Director Christine Cort
Group General Manager Nichola Coulthard
Group Art Director John Oakey
Online Managing Director David Pepper
Group Production Director Steve Proctor
Group IT Director Simon Chappell

Contributors

Introduction Mark van Dijk. **History** Max Du Preez (*Key events* Mark van Dijk). **Cape Town Today** Rick Crosier (*Kids who live on the streets* Sam Woulidge). **Where to Stay** Rick Crosier, Sam Woulidge, Mark Van Dijk. **Sightseeing** Mark van Dijk (*Architecture: beauty and the beast* Rick Crosier). **Southern Suburbs** Lauren Beukes, with contributions from Mark Van Dijk. **False Bay** Jeanne Davies, with contributions from Mark van Dijk. **Winelands** Lauren Beukes, with contributions from Mark van Dijk (*Stellenbosch Maties, Strawberry-picking* Anelde Greeff; *My kind of town* Sam Woulidge). **Restaurants** Lisa van Aswegen, Sam Woulidge, Anelde Greeff, Rick Crosier. **Pubs & Bars** Casey O'Neil (*Local brews; Bars for cigar buffs* Rick Crosier). **Shops & Services** Anelde Greeff, Sam Woulidge (*Say it with a T-shirt* Mark van Dijk; *Gifts that glitter* Johannie Liebenberg; *The best Cape tipple* Vaughan Johnson). **Festivals & Events** Mark van Dijk. **Children** Rene Wentzel. **Comedy** Rick Crosier (*My kind of town* Sam Woulidge). **Film** Rick Crosier (*My kind of town* Robert Whitaker). **Galleries** Melvyn Minnaar, Sam Woulidge. **Gay & Lesbian** Herman Lategan. **Music** Helen Gavera, Nils van der Linde (*Music to run countries by, The beat of the African soul* Casey O'Neil). **Nightlife** Casey O'Neil. **Sport & Fitness** Dan Nicholl, Dominique le Roux (*The way of the winds* Ami Kapilevich). **Theatre & Dance** Robyn Cohen. **Getting Started** Lily Dunn. **Whale Route** Adelle Horler. **Garden Route** Mark van Dijk. **Route 62** Mark van Dijk. **West Coast** Adelle Holler. **Directory** Lisa van Aswegen, Daniel Bugan, Alexandra Cooper, Lily Dunn, Ruth Jarvis.

Maps J.S. Graphics (john@jsgraphics.co.uk). Maps are based on material supplied by New Holland Publishing (Cape Town).

Photography Jurie Senekal, except pages 6, 11, 17 Corbis; pages 8, 9 Topham Picturepoint; page 13 Rex; pages 60, 156, 198, 218, 245 Christo Maritz; page 94 Johan Wilkie; pages 220, 221 Annelene Oberholzer; pages 223, 225, 226, 227, 228, 230, 232, 242, 246 Richard van Ryneveld; pages 234, 236, 238, 241 Mark van Dijk. The following images were provided by the featured establishments/artists: pages 15, 98, 152, 153, 155, 165, 169, 197, 202, 206, 209.

Time Out Cape Town is based on the 2004 *Cape Town Visitors' Guide* produced by New Media Publishing (www.newmediapub.co.za). With thanks to Bridget McCarney.

Contents

Introduction

Blighted through history but blessed by nature, Cape Town is a survivor city that no longer wears its scars on its sleeve. It has emerged smooth and cosmopolitan from centuries of division and oppression, flanked as ever by its world-famous natural assets. Assets like Table Mountain, which has posed a monumental challenge to years of glossy-brochure writers trying to avoid the clichés. But how else do you describe the gorgeous Winelands, and seascapes from the Atlantic Seaboard and False Bay? The good news is that Cape Town really is a beautiful city. And after long and exhausting troubles, it seems determined to kick back and enjoy itself.

One of Cape Town's main charms is its combination of the natural beauty of a provincial town with the smooth sophistication of a First World city. It feels at once like a European city with its café terraces; an African city with its boisterous street traders; and a South African city with its laid-back, tongue-in-cheek locals. For evidence of the newfound cosmopolitan vibe, just hop aboard one of the local minibus taxis and take in the cultural stew. The locals here can trace their roots from Europe, central Africa, and the ancient spice lands of the East.

'City of contrasts'? In between the leafy suburbs and lush Winelands you'll find dusty, poverty-stricken townships, where food and running water are as scarce as crime is commonplace. And a few blocks up from the modern colonial City Centre is the cobblestoned inner-city suburb of Bo-Kaap, where houses have stood untouched since the 18th century.

'Irresistible attractions'? If Table Mountain doesn't grab you, the Winelands or beaches will. And before the Cape Wine hangover or the Clifton Beach sunburn has worn off, you'll feel Robben Island's pull. This infamous isle, where Nelson Mandela spent much of his life imprisoned, now stands as a chilling reminder of South Africa's grim, apartheid-stained past.

But of course you already knew about the mountain, the island, the beaches and the bay. And you knew about apartheid, the Winelands and Robben Island.

But what you probably didn't know was that Cape Town is one of the smallest big cities in the world. A brisk walk from the Waterfront to the upper end of the Company Gardens, at the foot of Table Mountain, could take slightly more than an hour if you don't make any stops along the way. But there's a catch. Of course you'll stop along the way. You'll stop, and you'll lose yourself in the cafés, restaurants and shops on Long Street, the sights along Museum Mile, the market in Greenmarket Square or in a reverie down one of the beautiful shady paths in the Company Gardens.

And as you stroll down Museum Mile or admire the view from Table Mountain's aerial cableway you'll find that Cape Town is one of two things: it's either the place where tired old brochure clichés are born, or it's the place where tired old brochure clichés come to die.

ABOUT THE TIME OUT CITY GUIDES
Time Out Cape Town is the latest addition to the city guide series produced by the people behind London and New York's successful listings magazines. Our guides are all written and updated by resident experts who have striven to provide you with the most up-to-date information you'll need to explore the city.

THE LOWDOWN ON THE LISTINGS
Above all, we've tried to make this book as useful as possible. Transport information (where relevant), opening times, admission prices, websites and credit card details are all included in our listings. And, as far as possible, we've given details of facilities, services and events, all checked and correct at the time we went to press. However, owners and managers can change their arrangements at any time. Before you go out of your way, we'd strongly advise you to telephone and check opening times, dates of events, exhibitions and other particulars, particularly during the long and busy summer period. While every effort has been made to ensure the accuracy of the information contained in this guide, the publishers cannot accept responsibility for any errors that it may contain.

PRICES AND PAYMENT
We have indicated whether venues such as shops, hotels and restaurants accept credit cards but have only listed the major international cards, such as American Express (**AmEx**), Diners Club (**DC**), MasterCard (**MC**) and Visa (**V**). Few shops, restaurants and

attractions will accept travellers' cheques; it's advised that you change your money before heading out for the day.

The prices we've supplied should be treated as guidelines, not gospel. Fluctuating exchange rates and inflation can cause charges, in shops and restaurants particularly, to change rapidly. If prices vary wildly from those we've quoted, ask whether there's a good reason. If not, go elsewhere, then please write and let us know. We aim to give the best and most up-to-date advice, so we always want to know if you've been badly treated or overcharged.

THE LIE OF THE LAND

For convenience, we've divided Cape Town into manageable areas (such as City Bowl, False Bay, Winelands). We've used these areas throughout the guide, either to divide a chapter or in the address itself. Where possible, we have indicated a cross street as not all venues have street numbers. There is limited public transport in the city, so we have not given it in the address.

TELEPHONE NUMBERS

The country code for Cape Town is 021. Even though we have included this code in the guide entries, there is no need to use it within the city. Some listings also carry the 086 code: this tends to be a recorded information number and is not always accessible from outside the country. For more details of phone codes, *see p258*.

ESSENTIAL INFORMATION

For all the practical information you might need – including visa and customs information, disabled access, emergency telephone numbers, useful websites and the transport system – turn to the **Directory** chapter at the back of this guide. It starts on page 248.

MAPS

We've include a series of fully indexed colour maps to the city – they start on page 272. Wherever possible we give a grid reference against all venues that appear on the maps.

LET US KNOW WHAT YOU THINK

We hope you enjoy *Time Out Cape Town*. We welcome recommendations of places to include in future editions and take notice of your criticisms. Email us at guides@timeout.com with your feedback.

There is an online version of this book, along with guides to 45 other international cities, at **www.timeout.com**.

mobile phone rentals

Shana Coetzee and her dynamic team of professional consultants will ensure that you have access to a personal consultant 24/7, on our Customer Care Help Line - *084 444 0014* ensuring you piece of mind at all times

we offer you

- Free incoming calls in South Africa
- Free first 60 secs of the first call made*
- Free itemized billing - by fax or e-mail
- Free Caller ID
- Avoid high roaming charges
- Avoid high hotel telephone charges
- 24 Hour Customer Care Help Line - **084 444 0014**
- Mobile numbers can be allocated to you prior to your departure to South Africa
- Phones delivered and collected
- Fast, friendly and reliable service
- Immediate access to international dialing
- Immediate access to Emergency Services
- Our customers can order foreign exchange and have it delivered to their hotel

With every Mobile Phone rented get

Free Travel Insurance

& Free International SOS Emergency Services

contact us today

mobile
+27 (0) 84 855 5555
email
shana@cellcrentals.co.za
www.cellcrentals.co.za

cell c
rentals
for yourself

* conditions apply

In Context

THE DIVISIONAL COUNCIL OF THE CAPE
WHITE AREA
BY ORDER SECRETARY

DIE AFDELINGSRAAD VAN DIE KAAP
BLANKE GEBIED
OP LAS SEKRETARIS

History

Colonialism, conflict and eventual unity make up this city's painful but colourful story.

South Africa is an ancient land. Its rocks and plains date from the time Africa was still part of Gondwanaland, a composite continent made up of South America, Africa, Antarctica, India and Australia that existed until more than 100 million years ago. Human beings walked these plains and rocks hundreds of thousands of years ago, when the species developed along the east side of Africa. Some of the oldest fossilised remains of our pre-human ancestors were found in South Africa, in places such as the Cradle of Humankind outside Johannesburg.

The area around present-day Cape Town and along the coastlines to the west and east was inhabited by homo sapiens long before other continents were discovered. The human remains excavated in caves at Klasies River

Mouth on the southern Cape coast were between 75,000 and 120,000 years old – the oldest examples of homo sapiens to date. In 1993 it was proved that the people who occupied the Blombos Cave in the same area, at least 77,000 years ago, had a well-developed culture and produced impressive stone engravings.

It was around this time that some parties started to leave Africa, gradually moving through the Middle East, southern Europe and southern and southeast Asia. Climate, culture, diet and genetic isolation meant that those living in Europe, Asia and the Americas developed different physical features over time. Only 500 years ago did those pale-skinned humans return to 'discover' the southern part of the continent of their origin.

MEN AMONG MEN

At the time of colonisation, the indigenous people of the area were known collectively as the Khoikhoi ('men among men', or 'real people', as khoi means 'person'). The first Europeans to meet them named them the Hottentots, apparently after a word used in the Khoikhoi welcoming dance. Historians now believe the Khoikhoi derived from aboriginal hunters who lived in northern Botswana, and that they moved down the Atlantic Coast to the western Cape about 2,000 years ago, after they had switched from hunting to herding. At first they only kept fat-tailed sheep, but by the time the Europeans encountered them, they had acquired cattle, most likely from the Bantu-speaking farmers in the eastern Cape.

The Khoikhoi were closely related to a hunter-gatherer people whose ancestors probably never left the subcontinent. The first Dutch settlers called these hunters Bosjesmannen (men of the bush, later Boesmans or Bushmen) and the Khoikhoi called them Sonqua or San. They spoke a variety of languages characterised by the use of clicks or implosive consonants, very similar to the sounds of the Khoikhoi.

While the San lived mainly in caves and overhangs in small, mobile groups with a weak hierarchical system, the Khoikhoi lived in round reed huts in larger settlements. Each clan had a headman, a hereditary position, and the villages of a particular tribe fell under a chief. The chief ruled by the consent of a council of elders. They acted as a court to settle disputes and hear criminal cases. The Khoikhoi had a complex system customs such as initiation rituals, weddings and funerals, and livestock were central to much of their culture. Biogeneticists recently found that the San and Khoikhoi have genetic threads linking them to the first ever human beings.

FIRST DEFENCES

In February 1488, the Portuguese seafarer Bartholomeu Dias rounded the Cape and landed at Mossel Bay, east of Cape Town. He was met by the Khoikhoi, and when they tried to defend their precious watering hole, Dias's men killed one of their group with a crossbow. This incident could be regarded as the first act of resistance by the indigenous people of southern Africa against European colonialism, and the beginning of the struggle for land. Others point to an incident 11 years later when Dias's colleague, Vasco Da Gama, planted a cross and a *padrao* (commemorative pillar) on the Mossel Bay dunes. As they sailed away, they saw the Khoi men defiantly push the cross and the *padrao* over.

If Dias and Da Gama had travelled a little further along the east coast, they would have come across another group of indigenous people, the amaXhosa. They were part of a large family of farmers, together called the Bantu-speakers, who had migrated in stages from Africa's Great Lakes District to the south around 2,000 years ago.

> ## 'The early European settlers regarded the San hunter-gatherers as primitive beings not worth much more than animals.'

The early European settlers, and to some extent even the Bantu-speakers, regarded the San hunter-gatherers as primitive beings not worth much more than animals. Many were killed in unequal battles with settlers. Only small groups of San survive today in Namibia and Botswana, but their ancestors left an astonishing legacy in the form of rock paintings and engravings all over southern Africa, the oldest surviving examples being 20,000 years old. The paintings reflect a very complex spiritual relationship with the environment. Thousands of examples have, remarkably, survived across South Africa. Many San were assimilated into Bantu-speaking societies – the clicks in the Xhosa language are a result of this.

CAPE OF GOOD HOME

After Bartholomew Dias's 1488 visit, many European ships on their way to the East stopped at the Cape to replenish water and food supplies. Without exception, the seafarers' diaries reflect the astonishment they experienced when Table Mountain, the peaks of the Peninsula and the bay came into view. Dias himself named it Cabo de Boa Esperanca, Cape of Good Hope, although neither he nor Da Gama actually went into Table Bay. Antonio de Saldanha was probably the first European to land there in 1503. He climbed the mountain and named it 'The Table of the Cape of Good Hope'.

It was not before 1652 that Europeans settled at the Cape. The Dutch East India Company, or VOC, had decided that the mortality rate among sailors of their fleet trading with the East was too high, especially due to scurvy, and ordered Jan Van Riebeeck to establish a halfway refreshment station with vegetable gardens and a hospital at the Cape. On 6 April 1652 Van Riebeeck arrived with three ships in Table Bay. He was met by Autshomato, also called Herrie die Strandloper (Harry the Beachwalker), a Khoikhoi chief who had spent a year with the

Engraved for Moore's Voyages & Travels.

Habits of the **HOTTENTOT** Men & Women.

Hottentots: Or Khoikhoi as they were known among themselves. *See p7.*

English on a trip to the East between 1631 and 1632. Fluent in English, he was enlisted as Van Riebeeck's interpreter. Later he fell out of favour and was jailed at first in Van Riebeeck's fort and then on Robben Island, from where he escaped in a leaky boat (*see p14* **SA in an island**).

Initially the VOC had no intention of creating a colony on the Cape. But within five years it allowed a number of its employees to set up private farms around Cape Town. The presence of 'free burghers' increased quickly over the next few decades.

The new colony needed more people, and before the end of the 17th century groups of French Huguenots (1688) and German immigrants joined the Dutch settlers at the Cape. Most of them were Calvinist Protestants. The descendants of these settlers would later call themselves the Afrikaners. Most of the Huguenots were given farms in the Franschhoek

('French corner') and Paarl areas and contributed greatly to South Africa's wine-making culture. Almost from the beginning the free burghers were in conflict with the authorities, and distrusted the government. Their sense of vulnerability as frontiers people would inform their behaviour for three centuries.

The development of commercial agriculture soon threatened the Khoikhoi's way of life. As early as 1659, a group of Khoikhoi attacked the settler farms, driving off much of the livestock. Van Riebeeck tried to keep settlers and Khoikhoi apart by planting a hedge of bitter-almond on the outskirts of Cape Town. The Khoikhoi society quickly disintegrated under settler pressure. Many resorted to lives as labourers on settler farms, others moved inland, only to be displaced later by settler farmers. Many Khoikhoi died during the smallpox epidemic of 1713.

SLAVE TRADE

The VOC did not want to encourage more European labourers to come to the Cape, because they proved to be troublesome. Still, they did need more workers on the farms, so in 1658 the first ships carrying slaves arrived at the Cape. The slaves came from Dahomey, Angola and Mozambique in Africa and from India, the East Indies and Madagascar. Between the arrival of the first slave ships and the end of the slave trade in 1807, about 60,000 slaves had been brought to the Cape.

Slavery changed the basic political and social character of the Cape of Good Hope. By 1795, two-thirds of the burghers around Cape Town and three-quarters of the farmers in the districts of Stellenbosch and Drakenstein owned slaves. The burghers' European tradition dictated that the sanctity of property rights was central to their own freedom. Slave owners included their slaves on inventories of property together with their cattle and sheep. All slaves were black, and this instilled a distorted image of black people in many white minds. Add to this the perpetual fear of slave uprisings on isolated farms and it becomes easier to understand white attitudes in the following centuries, which ultimately resulted in formalised apartheid.

PURE THEORY

Apartheid, the ideology of racial separation formally adopted by the National Party government in 1948, theoretically presupposed that pure races existed in South Africa. Yet there had been thousands of 'mixed' marriages during the first century of colonialism on the Cape, the majority between settler men and slave women. Virtually all old Afrikaner families can trace a slave mother somewhere in their past.

A slave woman who married a white man was integrated into white society, together with her children. It was a female slave's easiest way to get her freedom. There were more white men than women in the colony and almost twice as many male slaves as females. On the farms outside Cape Town, the best chance male slaves had to find a wife was among the Khoikhoi. A child between a slave and a Khoikhoi would be born free, but forced to work on the farm for a period. These offspring were later called Baster Hottentotte, and they occupied a very low position on the social ladder. Descendants of white and Khoikhoi relationships outside of marriage and without formal acceptance by the church were called Basters, and they enjoyed much more freedom than the Baster Hottentotte. The Basters later formed the nucleus of the Rehoboth Basters of Namibia and the Griqua, mostly of the northern Cape.

Between the two main cultural-economic groups, those being the Christian European group and the Muslim or 'Cape Malay' group, another group existed at the Cape – some were slaves, some were freed slaves, some were Baster Hottentotte, some were the offspring of white and black liaisons but were not claimed by their white fathers. This group was later called the Cape Coloureds.

> **'In 1834 all slaves were liberated, although they had to serve four years of 'apprenticeship' before they were completely free.'**

The VOC had actively discouraged the use of French and German among the first settlers, with Dutch being the dominant language. But the slaves, the Basters, the Cape Malays and the Baster Hottentotte who worked on the farms and in the kitchens developed a simplified, creolised version of Dutch to communicate with their masters and each other. This developed into a fully fledged indigenous language later

Coloniser Jan Van Riebeeck of **DEIC**. *See p14.*

called Afrikaans – the language white Afrikaner nationalism later claimed as its own property and tribal symbol.

In 1795, Britain conquered the Cape, then returned the colony to the Dutch eight years later – only to reclaim it in 1806. It would remain a British colony for more than a century.

Under pressure from British missionaries working in the Cape and humanitarians in Britain, the British government scrapped the regulations limiting the rights of the Khoisan and freed slaves in 1828. In 1834 all slaves were liberated, although they had to serve four years of 'apprenticeship' before they were completely free. By this time, the settler farmers had expanded their operations along the interior and along the coast to what became known as the Eastern Cape, where they started to compete with another indigenous group, the amaXhosa. This conflict had the same root as the conflict with the Khoikhoi: land.

MIGRATING TIMES

Around 3,000 years ago, black farming peoples who lived in the region of the Great Lakes of Africa developed a common language that was later called Bantu. During the next 1,000 years, many of them migrated south. These farmers kept cattle, sheep and goats and grew sorghum and millet. They had an advanced social culture and mostly lived in large permanent settlements. A thousand years ago one of the main centres of power of the Bantu-speakers of southern Africa was at Mapungubwe Hill on the border between South Africa and Zimbabwe, now best known for the finely crafted gold artefacts which were found there.

The migrators split into four language groups as they moved into South Africa: the Nguni-speakers moved down the east coast, the Venda and Tsonga stayed in the north, and the Sotho-Tswana-speakers migrated down the central part of the country. The Xhosa were the Nguni-speakers who moved all the way down to the Eastern Cape, while those who spoke the Zulu dialect of Nguni settled in present-day KwaZulu-Natal.

At the end of the 18th century these black farmers (the term 'Bantu' that was used to depict them became a derogatory word during the apartheid years) were living in a number of small chiefdoms. The early years of the 19th century brought a great social upheaval. It was a period of serious suffering, but also nation-building. By the end of it, Shaka had forged the Zulu nation from several chiefdoms and Mzilikazi established the Ndebele and Matabele under his leadership. Moshoeshoe, an extraordinary diplomat and statesman for his time, had collected a number of chiefdoms

and thousands of refugees – Nguni-speakers as well as Sotho-Setswana-speakers – at his mountain stronghold in Lesotho and formed the Basotho. The Tsonga and Venda remained in their mountainous territory in the north; Sekwati built up the Pedi; Sobhuza the Swazi. In the Eastern Cape, the Xhosa developed a form of unity with smaller groups such as the Thembu, the Mfengu and the Mpondo.

A small community, the Lemba, whose individuals have great artistic skill, believe that they are descendants of black Jews from the Middle East, and they still live among the Venda. Their claim was recently proved to be correct after extensive DNA testing. Many Lemba still live strictly as orthodox Jews.

WAR TORN

The trekboers, as the burghers who had moved well away from the Cape were called, waged war against the Xhosa, but while the trekboers had firearms, the Xhosa had greater numbers. When the British Army was deployed against the Xhosa after 1811, the balance of power was tipped. During the brutal war of 1834-35 the Xhosa king, Hintsa, was decapitated. The Eighth Frontier War of 1850-52 was the most savage war against the Xhosa. Some 16,000 Xhosa were killed, and large numbers of settlements burned and cattle captured.

A great tragedy that befell the Xhosa can partly be explained by the trauma of these wars. In 1856, a young woman called Nongqawuse had a vision in which two men who were long dead told her that a great resurrection of her people was about to occur. To ensure that it happened, the people had to kill all their cattle and not plant any more crops. She convinced her uncle, a well-known seer named Mhalakaza, of the authenticity of the vision and he convinced paramount chief Sarili. The killing took place over the next year. By the end of December 1857, tens of thousands, perhaps as many as 50,000, Xhosa had died of starvation. More than 25,000 left for the Cape Colony to seek work.

RULE BRITANNIA

In 1820 the British settled some 4,000 British subjects, mostly farmers and tradesmen, in the eastern Cape. The colonial government started promoting the use of English at the expense of Dutch-Afrikaans and elevated the new British settlers into public positions. This caused deep bitterness among the Cape burghers.

Around the middle of the 19th century, developments in South Africa started to move away from the Mother City. But events in the central and northern interior would have a direct and lasting impact on Cape life.

After the 1835 war against the Xhosa, the Afrikaner trekboers in the Eastern Cape started to plan to move north into the interior of South Africa. They were unhappy about Britain's abolition of slavery, felt insecure so close to the frontier with the Xhosa, and needed more land for their cattle. Between 1835 and 1845, about 15,000 Afrikaners, accompanied by some 5,000 servants, had left the colony in convoys of oxwagons and on horseback. They were called Voortrekkers.

Their migration, which was later known as the Great Trek, would change South Africa fundamentally and ultimately lead to the formation of a formal nation-state. The Voortrekkers took with them the European convictions and traditions of white dominance and used these in structuring their relations with the black peoples of the interior.

The Voortrekkers staked out farms in what are today the provinces of KwaZulu-Natal, Gauteng, the Free State and Mpumalanga. The black societies in most of these regions were still suffering the after-effects of the great upheavals of the beginning of the century. Some of these areas were therefore not actively occupied at the time of the Voortrekker settlement, but others were and this led to violent clashes with the black tribes.

The Voortrekkers declared the Republic of Natalia in Natal, but Britain annexed it as a colony in 1843. Most of the Voortrekkers trekked further west and declared the South African Republic with Pretoria as its capital in 1843 and the Republic of the Orange Free State with Bloemfontein as its capital in 1854. With the Cape and Natal under British colonial rule, the whole country was now occupied by whites.

In 1990 **Nelson Mandela** is released from prison after 27 years. *See p16.*

From 1860 onwards, another population group was added to South Africa's ethnic diversity. Shiploads of indentured labourers from India were taken to Natal to work in the new sugar plantations. Later, Indian traders came to South Africa under their own initiative, mainly to set up shops in the towns of Natal, the Free State and the Transvaal. In 1893, an Indian lawyer arrived on a legal assignment to Indian traders in Pretoria. He decided to stay on when he suffered racial discrimination by whites and realised that Indians' rights were threatened. His name was Mohandas Ghandi, and he later became one of the most powerful moral influences in the world.

ALL THAT GLITTERS

Britain's two South African colonies were not regarded as prize possessions back in London, but this changed dramatically when diamonds were discovered near the confluence of the Gariep and Vaal Rivers in 1867 and gold outside Pretoria in 1886. But the Boers of the Free State, as well as the Griqua of Griqualand, claimed ownership of the diamond area and the gold reef fell inside the South African Republic. The diamond fields were extraordinarily rich and attracted fortune-seekers from all over the world. The town of Kimberley developed rapidly amid the abundant diamond pipes. The British declared that the Orange Free State border ran about a mile east of the richest mines, and annexed the area into the Cape Colony, together with the whole of Griqualand West.

In 1889 Cecil John Rhodes, an entrepreneur and ardent believer in British imperialism, acquired the monopoly over the four Kimberley diamond pipes. His company was called De Beers Consolidated Mines. Rhodes later became the Prime Minister of the Cape Colony. Tens of thousands of black people from all over South Africa rushed to Kimberley in the hope of finding jobs. It was De Beers who first started the practice of employing rural black men and putting them up in closed barracks. Thus a system which lasted in some form to the end of the 20th century was established. It devastated the social fabric of rural black societies: men from the rural areas were employed in the cities and put up in single-sex accommodation, only seeing their families once or twice a year. It was called the migrant labour system.

In 1886 a reef of gold, the richest deposit in the world, was discovered in the South African Republic. Once more there was a rush of fortune-seekers, but again big mining houses stepped in and within a few years eight conglomerates controlled all the mining on what became known as the Witwatersrand. Virtually overnight a city sprang up on the once open grasslands:

named Johannesburg. Black workers from across the subcontinent rushed to the mines and were employed under similar conditions to those at the diamond mines.

BOERS AND BLOOD

The discovery of diamonds and gold gave a new urgency to British plans for a confederation of the four political units in South Africa. It put such pressure on the South African Republic that its president, Paul Kruger, declared war with Britain in 1899. The Republic was joined by the Republic of the Orange Free State.

It was the fiercest war ever fought on the African subcontinent. More than 300,000 British soldiers took on the two republics with a total white population of around 300,000 and less than 70,000 soldiers. It was an uneven war, but the Boer commandos were highly mobile, sometimes using tactics that would later be called guerrilla warfare. By 1902 most Boer women and children were in diseased concentration camps and the captured men and boys in prisoner-of-war camps in Ceylon, St Helena and Burma. These practices did much to destroy the Boers' spirit, as did the British 'scorched earth' policy toward the end of the war, burning farmsteads and crops and killing cattle. In May 1902 the two republics surrendered and signed the Peace of Vereeniging.

The war, which was for a long time called the Anglo-Boer War but is now called the South African War, did not only affect the Boers and the British soldiers. Thousands of black and Coloured South Africans fought on both sides, although most fought with the British. Tens of thousands of blacks, mostly farm workers, were also put in concentration camps and 30,000 died there. Some 110,000 white women and children were put in concentration camps; 27,000 of them died. And 30,000 farms were destroyed. The war created deep bitterness and anti-British sentiment among Afrikaners for generations.

BLACK V WHITE

In May 1908, delegates from the Cape, Natal and the two former republics met at a National Convention to negotiate the establishment of a united South African state. Only white delegates were invited. Despite the fact that there were four times more black people than whites in the four regions, black people were only given a very limited franchise in the Cape alone. The South African Act was approved by the British Parliament. On 31 May 1910, the Union of South Africa with four provinces came into being. Parliament was to be seated in Cape Town. The exclusion of the majority black population from political power in South Africa was now formalised.

Voters from all races and backgrounds queue together for the general election. *See p16.*

Black intellectuals and community leaders protested against the new constitution, but when their protest fell on deaf ears in Cape Town and London, they formed the South African Native National Congress in January 1912. It was the first national body of indigenous people in South Africa and the first coordinated movement to resist white domination. The executive of 11 were all highly educated, five of them having studied in the US or Britain. The movement later changed its name to the African National Congress. The ANC stepped up their protest in 1913, after the Native Land Act was adopted, limiting black land ownership to about eight per cent of the land surface. A figure that was then increased to 13 per cent in 1936.

Two years after the ANC's birth, white Afrikaners also formed their first national political party, the National Party. In 1918, a secret males-only body, the Afrikaner Broederbond, was formed to further the cause of Afrikaner nationalism in business, education and culture. It became very powerful in later years. In 1938, Afrikaner nationalism experienced a massive upsurge with a national re-enactment of the Great Trek a century earlier. Ten years later the National Party defeated the United Party of General Jan Smuts in the general election. The party ruled South Africa until 1994.

APARTHEID YEARS

Racial separation and a denial of black South Africans' political and human rights began in 1652 and continued under British rule until 1948. But the National Party turned these practices and attitudes into a formal ideology they called apartheid, literally meaning 'separateness'. The new government spent considerable energy during its first years in power to write numerous apartheid laws. The population was classified according to race; sex between mixed couples and marriages

SA in an island

Robben Island is rather innocently called Seal Island ('rob' is the Dutch word for seal), but the story of this island is mostly a sad, and often brutal, one. But, in a sense, the story reflects the history of South Africa itself, and therefore it is not without a positive outcome.

The island was known for thousands of years to the indigenous San and Khoikhoi people, but it is unlikely that they ever went there before the first European ships arrived in the 15th century. And when they did go to the island, it was more often than not as prisoners. During the 16th and early 17th century many Khoikhoi who displeased the Dutch, English or Portuguese seafarers were left on the island as punishment. But it was also used as a post office during this period, because many of the seafarers were afraid of the Khoikhoi on the mainland and preferred to pick up their post, fresh water and seal or penguin meat on Robben Island.

In 1610, ten English criminals who had escaped the gallows and taken to work in the Cape instead, fled from the mainland and lived on the island for more than a year. The 'Newgate Men' as they were called, were eventually taken back to England and hanged.

After Jan van Riebeeck of the Dutch East India Company established a permanent refreshment station at Cape Town, many 'troublesome' Khoikhoi were banished to

Robben Island, the first being a man called Autshomato, who spoke English and was used as an interpreter by the Dutch.

When the European settlers clashed with the Xhosa in the Eastern Cape in the early 19th century, rebellious Xhosa leaders and chiefs were regularly imprisoned on the island. Later that century Robben Island was also used as a colony for lepers and those suffering from mental illness.

During World War II, the South African Navy took control of the island. It built houses and roads and installed heavy cannon to defend Cape Town from possible enemy ships. In 1961, the Prisons Department took over the island and built a new jail. From the early 1960s onwards many political prisoners were sent to the island jail, but kept apart from sentenced criminals.

Among the most famous political prisoners on the island were Nelson Mandela, Walter Sisulu and Govan Mbeki. Robben Island became 'the University' where hundreds of young activists were taught by Mandela and his older friends – and where some prisoners obtained university degrees through correspondence study.

In 1986, Mandela was transferred from Robben Island to Pollsmoor prison, but some prisoners remained on the island until 1990.

Robben Island was transformed into a museum after 1994 (see p59).

across the colour bar were criminalised; separate residential areas and public amenities were enforced; separate education was instituted; and the movement of black South Africans was regulated by the carrying of pass books.

The National Party later called their policies 'separate development', protesting that they did not discriminate, but that for the sake of peace and fairness black Africans should exercise their political rights in ten tribal states or homelands. The theory was that South Africa proper was white man's land where blacks would enjoy limited rights, but that their homelands would eventually become independent, sovereign states where they would enjoy full rights. Some of those Bantustans, like Transkei, Ciskei and Bophuthatswana, did later become 'independent', but South Africa was the only country that recognised them.

The man who championed the homelands policy and under whose leadership South Africa left the Commonwealth and became a republic

in 1961 was Dr Hendrik Verwoerd, the National Party's third prime minister who came to South Africa from the Netherlands as a child.

The ANC slowly grew as a movement and organised a successful 'Defiance Campaign' in 1952 to protest against unjust laws. In 1955 delegates from all over the country gathered in Kliptown outside Johannesburg to adopt the Freedom Charter. This document, which was headed 'The people shall govern!', remained the ANC's ideological compass for four decades. But a group of Africanists in the ANC did not like the fact that the Charter acknowledged whites as full citizens with equal rights, and in 1957 they broke away to form the Pan Africanist Congress (PAC) with Robert Sobukwe as their first leader.

In 1960, the PAC organised protests against the pass laws, forming large demonstrations. It was at one of these demonstrations, in Sharpeville south of Johannesburg, that police panicked and killed 69 people.

Later the same day a crowd of 6,000 from Langa and Nyanga just outside Cape Town marched to the city, led by a young PAC activist, Philip Kgosana. The police opened fire and killed three and injured 47.

These two events were turning points in South African history. The government banned the ANC and PAC, and both organisations went underground and formed military wings, the ANC formed Umkhonto we Sizwe (Spear of the Nation) and the PAC formed Poqo (Pure). Most of the first Umkhonto we Sizwe leaders, including the firebrand young lawyer Nelson Mandela, were arrested in 1963 and jailed on Robben Island (see p14 **SA in an island**). Some ANC leaders went into exile.

> **'In 1960, Verwoerd declared: "A psychotic preoccupation with the rights of non-white peoples is sweeping the world". He was stabbed to death in 1966.'**

It was also during this time that many African colonies gained their independence. In March 1960, Verwoerd declared: 'A psychotic preoccupation with the rights, the liberties and the privileges of non-white peoples is sweeping the world – at the expense of due consideration of the rights and merits of white people. The fundamental reality being disregarded is that without white civilisation, non-whites may never have known the meaning of idealism or ambition, liberty or opportunity.'

Verwoerd was stabbed to death in his seat in Parliament, Cape Town, in September 1966. A court declared that his killer, a parliamentary messenger named Demitrio Tsafendas, was mentally disturbed.

A CAPE WITH NO COLOUR
One of the cruelest aspects of apartheid was that over three million blacks were forcibly removed over four decades because the areas where they lived were declared 'white'. In Cape Town, this was a particularly painful experience.

District Six was a vibrant, colourful suburb situated right next to the Cape Town City Centre at the foot of Devil's Peak. The majority of the residents were Coloured – their ancestors had been living there since the emancipation of the slaves in the 1830s – but whites, blacks, Indians and Chinese also lived in the area. Between 1965 and 1967 it was declared a 'white' area under the Group Areas Act. The same fate befell Coloured residents living in Kalk Bay and Simonstown.

The residents were moved to new Coloured townships miles away on the Cape Flats and Mitchell's Plain behind Strandfontein. District Six was then razed to the ground, saving only the churches and mosques. The new townships were situated far from shops and places of work; parts of them soon developed into slums. Gangsterism and crime increased progressively.

FIGHTING BACK
The arrests of ANC leaders in the early 1960s forced the ANC into a period of near dormancy, but internally the resistance simmered. During the early 1970s a charismatic young intellectual, Steve Biko, gained a strong following with his Black Consciousness views. Early 1973 saw a series of strikes and industrial unrest. In June 1976, Soweto school children protested against the Bantu Education system and the use of Afrikaans in schools. Some were shot dead by police. Many youngsters left to join the ANC in exile, injecting the movement with new energy.

Steve Biko was detained in the Eastern Cape in August 1977. He was first assaulted in the police cells, then thrown naked into a police van for the trip to Pretoria. He died on the way.

That same year a scandal broke over the way funds for the Department of Information were misused, and a year later Prime Minister John Vorster resigned and was replaced by his Minister of Defence, PW Botha. Botha appointed General Magnus Malan as Minister of Defence. In response to internal and international opposition to apartheid, they militarised South Africa. Important decision making shifted to the State Security Council, and security forces believed they had a licence to kill anti-apartheid activists. Hundreds of young white men were conscripted into the Defence Force, which was engaged in destabilising operations in neighbour states and a full-scale war in Angola.

But Botha also tried to reform apartheid and instituted a programme of 'power sharing' with Coloured and Indian South Africans getting their own chambers of Parliament. But the exclusion of blacks provoked deep anger and was one of the motivating factors for the birth of a new national resistance movement, the United Democratic Front, which was formed in Cape Town in 1984. The United Democratic Front was ideologically aligned with the ANC, as was the new trade union movement, the Congress of South African Trade Unions (Cosatu).

PURPLE REIGN
The period between 1984 and 1990 was a turbulent one. There were regular violent protests, often put down by overwhelming force. Month after month the streets of Cape Town's townships, even the inner city,

reverberated with the stomping feet of marchers and the crackle of gunfire, while tear gas often lingered in the air. At one stage the police sprayed protestors in the city with purple-dyed water so they could be identified later. The purple stains remained on city walls for days, and then a famous graffito appeared: 'The Purple shall govern!'.

On 15 October 1985, a railway truck travelled through a crowd of protesting youths in Athlone on the Cape Flats. It turned round and drove past them again. This time they hurled stones and bricks at it. Suddenly armed men hidden in empty crates at the back of the truck leapt up and started shooting with shotguns. Three youngsters were killed and 20 wounded. The incident, called the Trojan Horse shootings, caused great anger in Cape Town. The period was also marked by strikes and mass action by trade unions that destabilised the economy, already crippled by international sanctions and financial restrictions by international banks.

POWER TO THE PEOPLE

It was in the late 1980s that the government and the ANC came to realise that neither side could win the battle and that a settlement was the only way to stop South Africa from being completely ruined. Nelson Mandela started secret talks with the government from his jail cell, and government agents had several meetings with ANC leaders in exile.

In January 1989 PW Botha suffered a stroke and in August that year FW de Klerk became president. UDF leaders in the Cape called his bluff after his first reconciliatory speech and staged a mass march through the streets of Cape Town, led by Anglican Archbishop Desmond Tutu. It led to a nationwide demonstration of 'People's Power' with marches in most cities and many towns. In October, at the request of Mandela, the first group of political prisoners, all old stalwarts of the ANC like Walter Sisulu, were released from jail after more than 25 years behind bars.

In November 1989, the Berlin Wall fell and the Soviet Union started to disintegrate. This meant the old National Party argument that the ANC had to be suppressed because they were tools of communist imperialism, fell away. A month later, Nelson Mandela and FW de Klerk had their first face-to-face meeting in the president's Cape Town office. The Old South Africa was fast unravelling.

De Klerk opened the 1990 session of Parliament on 2 February with announcements that stunned the world. He unbanned the ANC, PAC and Communist Party; lifted large sections of the emergency regulations; and announced the release of many political prisoners. And, he

declared, Nelson Mandela would be released unconditionally within a few days.

De Klerk ended his speech: 'The season of violence is over. The time for reconstruction and reconciliation has begun… I pray that the Almighty Lord will guide and sustain us on our course through uncharted waters.'

FREE NELSON MANDELA

In the late afternoon of 11 February 1990 Nelson Mandela walked out of prison after 27 years of incarceration. South Africans and the world were stunned to witness his lack of bitterness and huge capacity for reconciliation.

By April most senior ANC leaders in exile had returned to South Africa, and on 3 May the first formal meeting between the government and the ANC took place at the official state residence, Groote Schuur in Cape Town. Senior ANC delegate, Thabo Mbeki, remarked after the first day that the delegates 'quickly understood that there was nobody there with horns'. After three days the meeting issued the Groote Schuur minute that contained a commitment to negotiations and a review of security legislation and of the armed struggle.

After intense negotiations, which lasted 18 months, the Convention for a Democratic South Africa (Codesa), comprising most of the country's political parties, met on 20 December 1991 at Kempton Park to begin the task of preparing an interim constitution for a democratic South Africa.

The next two years were complicated by politically-inspired violence, especially between supporters of the Inkatha Freedom Party and the ANC, and dramatic events such as the right-wing assassination of the popular Communist Party leader Chris Hani, a right-wing attack on the Codesa building and an abortive invasion of the Bophuthatswana homeland by the Afrikaner Weerstandsbeweging. But each time, the two main sides, led by Nelson Mandela and FW de Klerk, brought the negotiators back to the table.

In the early morning hours of 18 November 1993 the parties agreed to the final text of the Interim Constitution, and two months later a parallel government, the Transitional Executive Council, was established.

UNITED TO ALL

On 17 April 1994, millions of South Africans of all races and classes queued together at polling stations for the first election of all citizens for a government in a united South Africa. The ANC won by a large majority and formed a Government of National Unity with cabinet seats for the National Party and the Inkatha Freedom Party.

On 10 May 1994, Thabo Mbeki and FW de Klerk were sworn in as deputy presidents at a ceremony at the Union Buildings in Pretoria. Then Nelson Mandela took the oath as the first president of a democratic South Africa. Six fighter planes, which had only a few years earlier dropped bombs on ANC camps in neighbouring states, flew past in a salute.

Mandela ended his inauguration speech with the words 'Let freedom reign. God bless Africa.'

The elected members of Parliament formed a Constitutional Assembly to define a final Constitution. It was adopted on 18 November 1996 and signed into law by President Nelson Mandela on 10 December in Sharpeville.

That same year the Truth and Reconciliation Commission, which was part of the negotiated settlement, started to hear evidence that came from victims of past human rights violations.

It was chaired by Nobel Peace Laureate Archbishop Desmond Tutu. The Commission also had the power to grant amnesty to perpetrators of such human rights, mostly security policemen during the stormy 1980s, who revealed all the facts of their crimes and proved that they had a political motive.

In the years that have passed since the first elections of 1994, South Africa has become a stable, progressive democracy with a vibrant economy and a strong leadership role in Africa. District Six was given back to its original owners; large numbers of other displaced communities were given their land back or were compensated for their loss; more than a million new homes were built for the homeless within the first ten years; and millions of people who had never had access to clean water, received it on their doorstep for the first time.

Truth and Reconciliation Commission: Archbishop Desmond Tutu and Thabo Mbeki.

Key events

1488 Portuguese explorer Bartholomeu Dias rounds lands at Mossel Bay, where he is met by the indigenous people, Khoikhoi.
1497 Portuguese sailor Vasco da Gama plants a cross on the Mossel Bay dunes.
1652 Jan van Riebeek and company arrives and Cape Town becomes the Dutch East India Company's mainland base of operations.
1795 The British occupation of the Cape Colony begins, and – apart from brief rule by the Dutch from 1803 to 1806 – continues uninterrupted for more than a century.
1816-28 Shaka emerges as one of Africa's greatest military leaders, his Zulu army becoming one of the most powerful in southern Africa.
1836-8 Huge groups of Afrikaners (white farmers of mainly Dutch descent) leave the Cape and British rule. These 'Voortrekkers' ('pioneers') embark on the Great Trek north.
1867 Thousands of fortune-seekers descend on the confluence of the Gariep and Vaal Rivers after diamonds are discovered in Kimberley. The British seize control of the area in 1871.
1886 A handful of people become very rich very quickly when the biggest gold discovery in recorded history occurs on the Witwatersrand in the southern Transvaal.
1887 Cecil Rhodes's De Beers conglomerate takes over diamond operations in Kimberley. De Beers confines its employees to disease-ridden, crime-riddled labour camps.
1897 Xhosa teacher Enoch Sontonga composes the hymn *Nkosi Sikelel' iAfrica* ('God Bless Africa'). The song later becomes the anthem of the ANC and – with 'Die Stem' ('The Voice') – is incorporated into South Africa's national anthem in 1994.
1899-1902 Thousands of British soldiers and Boer guerrillas are killed in the Boer War, and thousands more women and children die in concentration camps. The Boer population is reduced to less than 50 per cent and the war ultimately results in the formation of the British-ruled Union of South Africa in 1904.
1910 Britain grants independence, but the government of the Union of South Africa continues to recognise only the whites' rights.
1912 The South African Native National Congress (later the African National Congress or ANC) is founded.
1918 Nelson Rolihlahla Mandela is born in the tiny Transkei village of Qunu on 18 July.

1948 The National Party begins its domination of South African politics with victory in the all-white general election. A series of laws sees the practices of apartheid turn into official policy: ethnic groups are officially defined, separate institutions are created for each group and intermarriage is outlawed.
1960 ANC President Albert Luthuli is awarded the Nobel Peace Prize. The ruling National Party Government officially leaves the Commonwealth and later becomes the Republic of South Africa. Many are killed during anti-pass law protests in Sharpeville. The ANC is then outlawed; the government declares the first State of Emergency.
1961-2 The ANC abandons its non-violent protest and takes up arms against the South African Government. Nelson Mandela undergoes military training in Algeria, and on his return to South Africa he is arrested and sentenced to five years in prison.
1963-4 The leaders of the ANC's military wing are arrested and tried after a raid on their secret headquarters. The Rivonia Trial sees Mandela sentenced to life imprisonment.
1976 A student revolt in Soweto ignites protests throughout the country, and tensions escalate when black-consciousness activist Steve Biko dies while in police custody.
1984 Cabinet minister Piet Koornhof announces to the world that 'apartheid is dead'. To prove his point, the National Party Government attempts to legalise shebeens (black-run township drinking establishments).
1985 Township leaders launch a civil disobedience campaign to protest against apartheid (which appears to be still alive), prompting the National Party to establish South Africa's third State of Emergency. With apartheid police in guerrilla warfare with angry black youths, the government declares a National Emergency (this lasts until 1990).
1990 President FW de Klerk announces the end of the ban on the ANC and authorises the release of political prisoners. Nelson Mandela is released from prison and is elected president of the ANC.
1993 Mandela and de Klerk share the Nobel Peace Prize.
1994 South Africa holds its first free elections in late April. The ANC wins power with over 60 per cent of the vote, and on 10 May Nelson Mandela is inaugurated as the President of the Republic of South Africa.

Cape Town Today

A city that is proud of its contradictions.

Ten years into South Africa's democracy, Cape Town has changed considerably. Like New Orleans, another tourism-driven city where opulence and poverty share the same backyard, it is a city of extreme contradictions. Once considered something of a sleepy hollow, the preserve of artsy wholegrain types given to wearing sandals and extolling the spiritual virtues of Table Mountain, it has now overtaken Johannesburg as the country's focal feature. Yet despite the fact that it is now far more expensive than the second city, residents still earn considerably less. Then there's the image problem: On the one hand you have a rather vocal group who believe that Cape Town is living in denial of the fact that it's part of the African continent and is, to all intents and purposes, pretending to be 'Little Europe'. On the other hand you have an equally vociferous bunch who believes it's becoming all too African, what with all those chaps selling wire bicycles and refuse bags at traffic lights and everything. In fairness, both camps have a point. It is a city where the distance between some of the most expensive real estate in the world and some of the cheapest wouldn't cause the most unfit of walkers to break a sweat. Yes, the crime rate may be higher than in many major cities, but then so is the number of luxury cars. And while it's all but impossible to venture outdoors without bumping into a

restaurant specialising in sushi or Italian food, locating one that specialises in local fare tends to require something of an expedition. While Cape Town is certainly a city of contradictions, it is not a city with an identity crisis; rather it is a case of, as Walt Whitman put it, 'Do I contradict myself? Then I contradict myself. I am large, I contain multitudes.'

SMALL AND COMFORTABLE

While it certainly contains multitudes, Cape Town is not large, at least not geographically speaking. It is indeed possible to hoof the length of the City Centre for an hour's investment on the parking meter and return with change to spare. Driving is little different, most Capetonians exist within fairly contained comfort zones, and any destination that takes more than four songs on the radio to reach is widely considered, in Cape Town parlance, to be 'a bit of a mission'. Which is not to say locals are lazy, but rather that when the world is on your doorstep you don't really need to venture much further than that.

Given this rather insular existence it will hardly come as a shock to learn that Capetonians tend to exist in cliques – hence our ever-spreading reputation as an aloof and unfriendly bunch. Fortunately, this isolationist policy does not extend to foreigners, probably because we mostly encounter them in

establishments that the healthy tourist influx has largely rendered beyond the leap of the local pocket. As unaffordable as it may be, restaurant and café culture is still a huge part of Cape Town life; there are so many restaurants that you could eat out twice a day for upwards of five years and never cross paths with the same menu twice.

Eating, it could be said, is our regional culture: while you'd be hard pressed in a crowd to find someone who can tell you about the latest exhibition or give directions to a local museum, pretty much every Capetonian considers him- or herself a gastronaut of some seasoning and is more than happy to point you towards an establishment worth its salt.

> **'Cape Town holds the Houses of Parliament, but local politics are a bit of a dog's breakfast.'**

Another key feature of local life is the political one, yet while Cape Town holds the Houses of Parliament, local politics are a bit of a dog's breakfast with city leadership posts tending to change hands every hour on the hour and politicians crossing the floor to change parties so often the casual observer might be forgiven for thinking they were watching a ballroom dancing competition.

DRIVE TIME

While restaurants and politicians come and go, one aspect of the city that remains constant is the lack of decent public transport. Despite efforts to upgrade security, trains remain dangerous at all but the peakiest of peak hours; minibus taxis are less than salubrious; buses are slow and metered taxis can put a serious crimp in an evening's budget. That said, they're still the best bet. Driving yourself around is simple enough, unlike in Jo'burg, which went into a frenzy of re-naming streets a couple of years back resulting in a state where most map books are now hopelessly out of date. Cape Town has avoided this particular trap. The only problem with getting around under your own steam is that there are some areas best avoided, such as Cape Flats, that punctuate routes to the safer areas – you don't really want to make a wrong turn into one of them.

Which brings us to another Cape Town idiosyncrasy: in most places it's an insurance man's bet that anyone behind the wheel after midnight is probably well-to-full. Not so here: chances are we're just heading out. A far more dangerous crowd hits the road earlier in the evening, with quick after-work one-act plays

often morphing into full-blown epics. But, thankfully, the average Capetonian, if drinking, tends to keep to home ground.

GOOD SPORT

What we do do well, sometimes anyway, is play sports. However, while South Africans are known as sports fans of some note, Capetonians, especially on the tourist-friendly Atlantic Seaboard, are somewhat more subdued on this front, essentially regarding the whole face-painting and whooping-about business as a bit déclassé. Southern and Northern Suburbs residents are more enthusiastic – rugby, cricket and soccer being particular favourites. This division became keenly apparent during the city's failed bid for the 2004 Olympic Games, an event Cape Town's infrastructure was patently ill equipped to handle, battling as it does with daily rush-hour traffic, which tends to move with all the enthusiasm of continental drift. That said, Cape Town acquitted itself particularly well when hosting the rugby and cricket world cups, and the annual Cape Argus Pick 'n' Pay Cycle Tour, the largest timed event in the world with some 35,000 people taking part, is always a rousing success. There is no reason to suspect that, should our bid for the football World Cup in 2010 be successful, things will be much different.

Some of the disappointment over the loss of the Olympics was allayed by the development of the much-ballyhooed Cape Town International Convention Centre, which finally opened for business in 2003 to decidedly mixed reaction. While kindness itself couldn't describe it as the acme of architectural splendour, and some folks feel it has all the charm and ambiance of an international airport, the facilities are world class. The indoor canals, bless them, make for no small degree of amusement as absent-minded delegates drown their shoes in them on a regular basis, though the smiles fade rather quickly when it comes to paying for parking.

CRIME AND PUNISHMENT

Parking is a topic very dear to the Capetonian heart, and even dearer to the wallet. Legend has it that there was once a time when you could park without the aid of a man in a fluorescent vest waving his arms about. Nowadays you can hardly stop at a traffic light without an informal parking attendant trying to charge you. The standard tariff is R2, and while it most certainly is an extortion racket – most attendants couldn't ably protect themselves from a mild breeze, let alone protect your car – Capetonians consider it a small price to pay for preventing crime from happening elsewhere.

As to other crimes; while the Western Cape has spent considerable time troubling the Top Ten lists where violent crime is concerned, the picture is not as bleak as it might appear at first glance, the figures having been given a shot in the arm by gang warfare on the Cape Flats. This has quietened down considerably in recent years and the official crime statistics show a marked improvement. In the more affluent areas, crime prevention is almost completely the preserve of private armed response security companies, one of Cape Town's biggest growth industries in the past decade. While kidnapping and hijacking epidemics were predicted, neither of these came to pass, though the drug trade is still doing good business, as is the sex trade – the only larger section you're likely to find in the classified section of any newspaper is the one advertising used cars.

PRETTY AND PINK

Another myth is that Cape Town is the gay capital of southern Africa. There was a huge brouhaha when the former head honcho of Cape Town Tourism published a 'pink guide' to the city. In reality, while gay culture is huge the local gay population is relatively small, certainly compared to Jo'burg. What's worse, at least according to some same-sexers, is that heterosexuals are muscling in on their game – the annual Mother City Queer Project having become probably the biggest social event of the year other than the J&B Met. That said, while most establishments are extremely gay-friendly there are very few that paddle exclusively in what appears to be a diminishing pool.

COLOUR COMPLEXITIES

The Group Areas Act of the apartheid era split the various race groups into different areas and these divisions are largely still extant, with economics having replaced legislation. The result is that there is still less racial integration than might otherwise be the case. Things are changing, though, with the integration of schools in the mid '90s and black economic empowerment the most powerful forces. The current climate is one of little racial animosity, but also one in which people still tend to stick with their own. Other than in work-related situations, it is still rare to see the sort of integrated gatherings so beloved of soft-drink commercials. The 'Many Cultures, One City' slogan put forward by tourism officials some years back is uncomfortably accurate. Cape Town is still a little like New York in that neighbourhoods are divided along historical lines, except that instead of Irish and Italian, we have Muslim, Jewish, coloured, black, gay, English and Afrikaans. While these divisions are becoming increasingly porous, in many cases the stereotypes still hold true.

One positive result of this is that, in order to affirm cultural identities, most communities have placed great emphasis on their cultural heritage, thereby enriching the city through difference. And while Cape Town might be laid-back, bland it's not – a drive along the N2, for example, might well feature Xhosa youths, faces caked in white mud, undergoing the traditional circumcision initiation ceremony, or the odd bit of livestock making its way across an overhead bridge.

Kids who live on the streets

CAPE TOWN.
HOME OF TABLE MOUNTAIN, THE CABLEWAY, GREENMARKET SQUARE AND SEVERAL HUNDRED STREET CHILDREN.

The city of Cape Town is home to several hundred street children. Most organisations that deal with these youngsters advocate not giving them money as this perpetuates their self-destructive lifestyle and makes it difficult for them to be rehabilitated and reintroduced into family units. If you are approached, offer them a smile, but give no money. Instead, if you want to help, buy them some food or support the following charities who do incredible work with these marginalised children by trying to rebuild their shattered lives.
The Homestead (021 419 9763/www.home stead.org.za).
Street Universe (021 447 3583/www.street universe.org.za).
Salesian Institute (021 425 1450).

Protestors on the streets of Cape Town.

A more obvious example of this co-existence of the old world and the new is the fishing industry – much of which operates out of the Victoria and Alfred Waterfront, Cape Town's premier tourist attraction by several lengths. Within spitting distance of each other you have a working harbour, five-star hotels and the Oceana Power Boat Club, a recreational slipway that the V&A powers-that-be are currently trying to shut down in order to make way for new commercial developments.

> ### 'The biggest racial issue in Cape Town at the moment is the influx of refugees from South Africa's northern neighbours.'

Cape Town's strength is in its contradictions, and, more than that, its ability to co-exist – the fact that while you can have some of the finest fish prepared at a superb restaurant, just down the road you can purchase freshly caught snoek off the back of a pick-up truck.

The biggest racial issue in Cape Town at the moment comes, ironically, from beyond its borders – the influx of refugees from South Africa's northern neighbours. Under the impression that the Mother City will live up to her nurturing nickname, these refugees have turned up en masse, ending up primarily in the drug and parking attendant rackets. If Cape Town has to add a 12th official language to the already confusing 11 it will likely be French.

BOOM TIME

Property in Cape Town, given the average local salary, is punitively expensive, a two-bedroom flat in a good area costing significantly more than a five-bedroom house in one of Jo'burg's better suburbs. The recent rates hike, which is essentially a stealth tax on the wealthy involving some logical contortionism (depending on where you live it now costs different amounts to flush your lavatory), has forced residents out of their homes and has given developers an opportunity to reap large profits by making cash cows like Camps Bay and Clifton every bit as crowded and unpleasant as Monaco. In these areas the term 'Billionaire's Boulevard' is becoming increasingly literal.

The positive knock-on effect of this is the gentrification of formerly dreadful areas like Woodstock and Observatory where up-and-comers now share wall space with the previously disadvantaged. The handing back of District Six in the City Bowl to its original coloured residents – who had been resettled – will probably change the city a great deal, and, given the previous vibrancy of the area, one hopes and assumes for the better.

If, despite all our differences there is one thing that makes Cape Town work, it is this: no-one who lives in the city would want to live anywhere else in the world. And while, as a community, we might differ significantly on many issues, when it comes to our city we're increasingly realising that now is the time for all good people to come to the aid of the party.

Long may our contradictions sustain us.

Where to Stay

Where to Stay   26

Features

Where to Stay

From indulgent spas to hot hostels and boutique guesthouses, Cape Town has a bed for every head.

Mount Nelson Hotel.
See p27.

It was once almost impossible to find a good hotel in Cape Town, in fact the city featured some truly awful examples – even at the upper end of the bracket. But then the tourists started to swarm in and something had to change. Subsequent to the city's growing popularity, a number of new hotels have sprung up and the majority are excellent – even by international standards. Where once visiting dignitaries were forced to endure mediocre hotels seemingly decorated by a blind man on a particularly bad acid trip, they now have a grab-bag of above average hotels to choose from. That said, Cape Town does probably have more hotels than it needs, which is good news for tourists – the city's hotels have increasingly priced themselves out of the market and, as such, are feeling the pinch of unoccupied rooms.

Be prepared that a hotel's published rates are not absolute and binding, and any establishment that is inflexible on this front is either not interested in your business or likely to be out to fleece you. The better hotels know that an occupied room is better than an empty

room and will accordingly go the extra mile to accommodate your budget. Don't be shy to mention this to them. And have a sharp look at the charges before you attack the mini-bar – it is not uncommon for two fingers to cost you a third of the bottle.

For good deals you'd be well advised to look at hotel websites for special offers or to check out www.mtbeds.co.za or www.lastminute.co.za where you can find good-quality, reduced-priced accommodation if you are prepared to plan your itinerary at short notice.

The tourist boom in Cape Town also gave birth to new industry sectors: guesthouses at the upper end of the market and the slightly cheaper and more homely B&Bs. For detailed information on a variety of guesthouses and B&Bs go to www.portfoliocollection.com. It's a user-friendly website listing hundreds of accredited establishments to suit all tastes and budgets. These homes-away-from-homes have not replaced the backpacking lodges, which are still very much a part of the tourist scene and offer visitors some rather pleasant surprises.

Traditionally, backpacking is a wanderlusty way of life that sends scruffy youngsters across the world with a dollar a day and a knapsack on their back, abandoning comfort and safety to experience the bigness and wideness of the big, wide world. As a result, overnight stays at backpackers' hostels have often meant sharing a matchbox-sized room with an unwashed foreigner. Not so (not always) in Cape Town, where more than a dozen, high-quality hostels are hidden away in the Long Street area alone. Most of these provide secluded courtyards, comfortable double rooms and in-house internet cafés – all held together by regimented tagging systems. Somehow, the city's lodge owners have found a space among the roughed-up guides and scruffed-up dormitories for luxuries such as whirlpool baths, lock-up safes and e-connections – and often at prices that are too steep for rand-bearing locals.

So have hostel owners sold out? Ask the backpackers themselves, most of whom are more than happy to pay the extra dollar for a safe (and not too uncomfortable) place to crash before hopping aboard the morning overland truck to Vic Falls.

All rates mentioned in the listings are per room, accommodating two persons. All rates are subject to change and can vary dramatically from season to season. Special offers are introduced periodically. It's best to check the websites, or contact the hotels directly and negotiate the best offers.

City Bowl

Deluxe

Mount Nelson Hotel

76 Orange Street, Gardens (021 483 1000/ www.mountnelsonhotel.orient-express.com). **Rates** (incl breakfast) R5,485-R6,310. **Credit** AmEx, DC, MC, V. **Map** p282 G5.
Known as 'the Nellie', this hotel's pink buildings are its trademark. It's also renowned for its afternoon high teas, lush gardens and famous visitors. A young Winston Churchill, when he was a war correspondent during the Anglo-Boer War, was based here. More recently, Jerry Springer, Oprah Winfrey and Samuel L Jackson have all put their heads on the Nellie's pillows. An established colonial hotel, the Mount Nelson is a much-loved Cape Town landmark, frequented by locals, who, even if they can't afford to check in for a night, know that they're welcome, for either afternoon tea, dinner or a great night out at the newly launched and rather fabulous bar, Planet. Those who do stay over will be exposed to old-fashioned hospitality, friendly service and beautiful, luxurious surroundings.
Hotel services *Babysitting. Bar. Beauty salon. Business centre. Concierge. Disabled: adapted rooms.*

Garden. Gym. Internet access: ASDL/ISDN. Limousine service. No-smoking rooms. Parking. Restaurants (2). Swimming pools (2). **Room services** *Air-conditioning. Bathrobe. Hairdryer. Laundry/ dry cleaning. Mini-bar. Newspaper. Room service (24 hrs). TV: satellite/movie channel.*

Expensive

Protea Hotel Victoria Junction

Corner of Somerset & Ebenezer Roads, City Centre (021 418 1234/www.proteahotels.com). **Rates** R1,376-R1,876. **Credit** AmEx, DC, MC, V. **Map** p282 G2.
This is a slick, modern hotel, with edgy design and hip touches. If you can afford to, try and stay in one of the two-storey loft apartments. These have floor-to-ceiling windows with superlative views of the mountain and the buzz of Somerset Road. Nice extras include a hi-fi system fitted with CD player, electronic exercise bicycle and telescope. This is a stylish hotel, with great art – look out in particular for the portraits by Francine Schialom Greenblatt – and plenty of urban energy.
Hotel services *Bar. Concierge. Disabled: adapted rooms. Internet access: ISDN. No-smoking rooms. Parking. Swimming pool.* **Room services** *Air-conditioning. Hairdryer. Laundry/dry cleaning. Mini-bar. Room service (24 hrs). TV.*

The best Hotels

For backpackers
Ashanti Travel Centre (see p31) is more than just a hostel and the **Breakwater Lodge** (see p34) has great prices and a location to match.

For boutique lovers
The **Metropole Hotel** (see p29) is an Afro-glam oasis in frenetic Long Street; **Cape Heritage Hotel** (see p28) is historical, hip and plumly located in the centre of town.

For luxury
The **Cape Grace** (see p31) has elegance and delicious food, while the **Twelve Apostles Hotel & Spa** (see p32) does sexy chic. The **Mount Nelson** (see p27) is the grande dame of Cape Town high society.

For a swish hotel bar
The **Cape Grace**'s La Bascule (see p31) offers over 400 types of whisky and a view of the yacht basin; Planet at the **Mount Nelson** (see p27) is a sophisticated newcomer; and the outside deck at the **Raddisson** (see p33) is as close to the sea as you'll get with a cocktail in your hand.

Metropole Hotel. *See p29.*

Moderate

Cape Heritage Hotel

90 Bree Street, City Centre (021 424 4646/
www.capeheritage.co.za). **Rates** R1,000-R1,600.
Credit AmEx, DC, MC, V. **Map** p282 G4.

This gorgeous hotel is part of the stylish Heritage
Square, home to some fabulous restaurants and hip
drinking spots set in an 18th-century courtyard.
This boutique hotel occupies part of some carefully
restored buildings dating back to 1771. Each room
is individually and stylishly decorated – a refreshing antidote to chain hotels and striped bedcovers.
Its proximity (due to the shared courtyard) to good
restaurants and all the sights of the city make this
a winner. The breakfast room is worth noting for
being both personal and chic, and the smallish size
of the hotel means attentive, personal service.
Hotel services *Bar. Beauty salon. Concierge. Gym.*
Internet access: ADSL. Limousine service. No-
smoking rooms. Parking. Restaurants (6). **Room**
services *Air-conditioning. Hairdryer. Laundry/dry*
cleaning. Mini-bar. Newspaper. TV: satellite/VCR.

Cape Milner

2A Milner Road, Tamboerskloof (021 426 1101/
www.threecities.co.za). **Rates** R1,230-R2,040. **Credit**
AmEx, DC, MC, V. **Map** p282 F4.

This tranquil hotel in the City Bowl offers visitors
stylish living at competitive prices. The decor is contemporary minimalist and certain rooms have magnificent views of Table Mountain. The hotel also has
a swimming pool and a sundeck/outside bar area
where you can relax and catch the last rays of sun
setting over the mountain. It also has a small restaurant if you don't feel like leaving the hotel. The hotel
is also small enough to ensure personal attention
and a comfortable bolt-hole if you don't like crowds.
Hotel services *Bar. Beauty salon. Disabled: adapted*
room. Garden. Gym. No-smoking rooms. Parking
(R20). Restaurant. Swimming pool. **Room services**
Air-conditioning. Hairdryer. Room service (24 hours).
TV: satellite/in-house movie channel.

Cape Town Lodge

110 Buitengracht Street, City Centre (021 422 0030/
www.capetownlodge.co.za). **Rates** R895-R1,450.
Credit AmEx, DC, MC, V. **Map** p282 G4.

In a rather ugly building on a busy street is where
you'll find this central hotel. But, if you manage to
stay in the Table Mountain Suite, you'll have one of
the most incredible views of the mountain in the
whole of Cape Town. The common parts of the hotel
are lovely, as is the rooftop swimming pool.
Hotel services *Bar. Beauty salon. Concierge.*
Disabled: adapted rooms. Gym. Internet access: ISDN.
No-smoking rooms. Parking (R35). Restaurant.

Swimming pool. **Room services** *Air-conditioning. Hairdryer. Laundry/dry cleaning. Mini-bar. Room service (11am-11pm). TV/in-house movie channel.*

Ikhaya Lodge

Dunkley Square, Wandel Street, Gardens (021 461 8880/www.ikhayalodge.co.za). **Rates** (incl breakfast) R840-R1,480. **Credit** AmEx, DC, MC, V. **Map** p282 G5.
Boasting great mountain views and situated on the trendy Dunkley Square (with its numerous restaurants and cafés), this African-themed lodge will appeal to those wanting comfort and a flavour of rural Africa in an urban setting.
Hotel services *Bar. No-smoking rooms. Parking. Restaurant.* **Room services** *Fan. Laundry/ dry cleaning. TV.*

Metropole Hotel

38 Long Street, City Centre (021 423 7247/ www.metropolehotel.co.za). **Rates** (incl breakfast) R1,326-R1,950. **Credit** AmEx, DC, MC, V. **Map** p282 G4.
Afro-glam is how the Metropole describes its style. This 29-room, privately owned hotel is the new flavour of the month. Set right in the heart of Long Street, it offers calm, minimalist bedrooms, a vibrant red bar with original Versace couch and an elegantly simple restaurant (Veranda serves great food at excellent prices) with views of frenetic Long Street.

The hotel is all about contrasts – entering the cool foyer you escape a street filled with odd shops and harassed pedestrians. This is one for those with a sense of style and a yearning to experience the energy of the city centre. The hotel is also gay-friendly.
Hotel services *Bar. Concierge. Garden. Internet access: ASDL. No-smoking rooms. Parking (R40). Hairdryer. Mini-bar. Room service (7am-11pm). TV: satellite.*

Walden House Guesthouse

5 Burnside Road, Tamboerskloof (021 424 4256). **Rates** (incl breakfast) R950-R1,280. **Credit** AmEx, DC, MC, V. **Map** p282 F4.
The Walden House offers guests a choice of seven elegant en-suite rooms in the colonial style: white-cotton bed linen, mosquito netting, white-painted wooden floors and ceiling fans for hot African summer days. All provide a tasteful base from which to explore the city.
Hotel services *Garden. Gym. No-smoking rooms. Parking.* **Room services** *Fan. Hairdryer. Laundry/ dry cleaning. Mini-bar.*

Welgelegen Guesthouse

6 Stephen Street, Gardens (021 426 2373/ www.welgelegen.co.za). **Rates** (incl breakfast) R1,200. **Credit** AmEx, DC, MC, V. **Map** p282 F5.

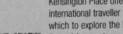

Guesthouses have come a long way since merely being a room or two in someone's home rented out to tourists. These days, many of them are more like very beautiful, small hotels and Welgelegen leads the pack with its eclectic and contemporary design and superb finishes. This beautifully renovated guesthouse, consisting of two houses joined by a peaceful courtyard with a plunge pool, will appeal to those wanting attentive personal service. The en-suite bedrooms are all lovely.

Hotel services *Bar. Garden. Gym. No-smoking rooms. Parking. Swimming pool.* **Room services** *Air-conditioning. Hairdryer. Mini-bar. TV: satellite.*

Budget

Ashanti Travel Centre

11 Hof Street, Gardens (021 423 8721/021 423 8790/www.ashanti.co.za). **Rates** R55/person camping; R85/person in a dorm; R320/en-suite double room. **Credit** MC, V. **Map** p282 F6.

If ever proof were needed that backpackers don't really want to 'rough it' when they're bedding down in Cape Town, Ashanti would surely be earmarked as a prime example. Situated in Gardens (in Cape Town but not quite *in* Cape Town), the hostel's many facilities include an excellent on-site bar and restaurant, a gorgeous swimming pool, internet access, a laundry service and fax and mail holding services. What's more, your possessions are safeguarded by the hostel's security-tagging system. Ashanti's rates are a little higher than some of Cape Town's other hostels, but if you want to indulge in a few home comforts before you hop on a dusty truck and head off into the desert for a month, Ashanti is definitely the place to stay.

Hostel services *Bar. Café. Garden. Gym. Internet access: ASDL. No-smoking rooms. Swimming pool. TV lounge: VCR/satellite. Payphone. Laundry.*

Backpack & African Travel Centre

74 New Church Street, City Centre (021 423 4530/ 021 423 0065/www.backpackers.co.za). **Rates** R85/ person in a dorm; R360 en-suite double room. **Credit** AmEx, DC, MC, V. **Map** p282 G3.

While most backpacker lodges will at least help you to organise overland trips and tours from Cape Town, the Backpack actually has a tour centre on site. So once you've settled into one of the comfy and secure rooms, the African Travel Centre will provide you with free and comprehensive info to help you arrange your trip out of Cape Town (day trips, overland safaris, wildlife expeditions or car and intercity bus services). Enjoy the weekly barbecues.

Hostel services *Bar. Café. Internet access: ASDL. No-smoking rooms. TV lounge: VCR/satellite. Payphone. Laundry. Self-catering facilities.*

Castle Street Backpackers

57 Castle Street, City Centre (021 424 7524/ 021 424 7524/www.castlestreet.co.za). **Rates** R70/ person in a dorm; R190 double room. **No credit cards. Map** p282 G3.

As far as location is concerned, you'd be hard pressed to beat Castle Street Backpackers. Situated only a block away from Cape Town's Tourist Information Centre (in Burg Street), the hostel is within walking distance of anything you'll need in Cape Town. Modestly proportioned and clean, this is a hostel that offers a rare blend of intimacy and big-city convenience.

Hostel services *Bar. Internet access: ASDL. Laundry. No-smoking rooms. Payphone. Self-catering facilities. TV lounge: VCR/satellite.*

Long Street Backpackers

209 Long Street, City Centre (021 423 0615/ 021 423 1842/www.longstreetbackpackers.co.za). **Rates** R70/person in a dorm; R180 double room. **No credit cards. Map** p282 G4.

The first hostel to open on Long Street (back in 1993), Long Street Backpackers is deservedly one of the most highly-rated lodges in Cape Town. Situated in the middle of Long Street's backpacker district, the hostel has established a hard-earned reputation for comfort, convenience and hospitality. Despite also being located slap-bang in the middle of Long Street's clubbing area, it offers its guests almost unrivalled security: this is the only hostel in Cape Town that has a 24-hour police camera set up right outside its door.

Hostel services *Bar. Internet access: ASDL. Laundry. No-smoking rooms. Pool room. Self-catering facilities. Swimming pool. TV lounge: satellite/VCR. Payphone.*

Atlantic Seaboard & Waterfront

Deluxe

Cape Grace

West Quay, V&A Waterfront (021 410 7100/ www.capegrace.com). **Rates** (incl breakfast) R4,200-R10,600. **Credit** AmEx, DC, MC, V. **Map** p283 H2.

The elegant, understated Cape Grace boasts an outstanding restaurant, one.waterfront (*see p106*), and La Bascule (*see p122*), a whisky bar boasting a selection of 400 whiskies from all over the world. Situated at the water's edge of the V&A yacht basin and overlooking the gleaming yachts and the working harbour, this award-winning hotel offers classic style with friendly, yet discreet, service. The recent addition of a spa further enhances an already superb array of services. Simply called the Spa at Cape Grace, it is exclusive to hotel guests and is inspired by the people and cultures of southern Africa and traditional African remedies.

Hotel services *Bar. Beauty salon. Business centre. Concierge. Disabled: adapted rooms. Garden. Gym. Internet access: ISDN. Limousine service. No-smoking rooms. Parking. Restaurant. Swimming pool.* **Room services** *Air-conditioning. Hairdryer. Internet access (56k dial-up). Laundry/dry cleaning. Mini-bar. Newspaper. Room service (24 hours). TV: satellite.*

Where to Stay

Twelve Apostles Hotel & Spa

Victoria Road (021 437 9000/www.12apostleshotel. com). **Rates** (incl breakfast) R3,760-R12,000. **Credit** AmEx, DC, MC, V. **Map** p284 B8.

The Twelve Apostles is something of a plaudit magnet (it was recently named by *Condé Nast Traveler* magazine as one of the Top 100 new hotels worldwide), and frankly it's not difficult to see why. The service and accommodation are predictably excellent; the decor is elegant and seductive. The setting itself is stunning – the sea and magnificent mountains surround the hotel, and the view from the terrace is breathtaking. Special extras include a luxurious private cinema and the recently opened spa (*see below* **Looking for good chi?**). The Leopard Lounge has been decorated with perhaps a tad too much enthusiasm, so head for the balcony and sea views instead. The hotel pays great attention to detail and guests are completely pampered and spoilt. It's fairly pricey by local standards, but then it is a case of getting what you pay for.

Hotel services *Babysitting. Bar (2). Beauty salon. Business centre. Cinema. Concierge. Disabled: adapted rooms. Garden. Gym. Internet access: ISDN. No-smoking rooms. Parking. Restaurant (2). Spa. Swimming pools (2).* **Room services** *Airconditioning. Bathrobes. Hairdryer. Laundry/dry cleaning. Mini-bar. Newspaper. Room service (24 hours). TV: DVD/satellite/VHS.*

Expensive

Bay Hotel Camps Bay

69 Victoria Road, Camps Bay (021 430 4444/ www.thebay.co.za). **Rates** (incl breakfast) R2,960-R8,140. No under-12s. **Credit** AmEx, DC, MC, V. **Map** p284 B8.

In the heart of the hugely fashionable Camps Bay strip is 'the Bay'. It overlooks one of the most loved Cape Town beaches (leave the lobby, cross the road and hey presto you're on the beach) and its neighbours are some of the most popular restaurants in

Looking for good chi?

There is a plethora of spas in the Cape, or at least a plethora of places calling themselves spas. A proper spa is for more than just a massage and a whiff of lavender oil. It is a place where you can wallow in therapeutic waters and pad gracefully from treatment room to treatment room clad in fluffy white robes, smiling serenely while fighting the good fight against cellulite and stress. Sounds unrealistic? Here are two places that come close to the ideal.

Santé Wellness Centre

At Winelands Hotel & Wellness Centre. See p40.

The elegant simplicity of the Santé Wellness Centre provides the good life in a modern African setting. Despite the Italian-inspired design of the hotel, the spa pays tribute to the mountains and vineyards that surround it. Dark woods, mosaic treatment rooms and the soft smell of vanilla candles will soon have you feeling indulged and gorgeous. It's best to check in for a night (or two or three) and fully experience this world-class facility, where the emphasis is on soul rather than slimming. Specialities? Three curved mosaic 'experience showers' give you options such

as 'tropical rain' – releasing fruity aromas – and 'cold mist', which envelops you in a soft haze of water and mint fragrance. The mosaic steam room could easily claim to be one of the best of its kind. Imagine lying on shiny blue tiles benches, surrounded by steam, while you look up at the ceiling where tiny lights change from purple to blue to green, listening to the soft rhythmic sounds of the small stones bubbling in a clay bowl. There are those who swear by the chakra-blancing rainbow bath, but the more indulgent will no doubt opt for the three-hour long vinotherapy treatment. Here, instead of just imbibing the wines of the region, you also get to loll around in it. There is a 'wine-casket' bath the Mother City. The hotel itself is well designed and casually elegant – chic enough for those accustomed to five-star treatment, but informal enough to get away from it all. Sandy B, the hotel's cocktail lounge, is great for winding down after a day on the beach. **Hotel services** *Babysitting. Bar. Beauty salon. Business centre. Concierge. Disabled: adapted rooms. Garden. Gym. Internet access: ASDL/Wi-Fi enabled. No-smoking rooms. Parking. Restaurant. Swimming pool.* **Room services** *Air-conditioning. Hairdryer. Laundry/dry cleaning. Mini-bar. Room service (24 hours). TV: satellite.*

Cape Cove Guesthouse

11 Avenue Deauville, Fresnaye (021 434 7969/ www.capecove.co.za). **Rates** (incl breakfast) R1,810-R2,530. No under-12s. **Credit** MC, V. **Map** p281 C4.
Set in the very desirable location of Fresnaye, this place is actually less of a guesthouse and more of a small, exclusive hotel. The minimalist structure features stone, wood, water and glass, while the interior

decor is rich and bold, with African tribal influences. The six en-suite rooms are all beautifully decorated and the owners' attention to detail and luxury is evident. There are two swimming pools; one overlooking the ocean and the other a sensually lit courtyard pool, perfect for night-time dips.
Hotel services *Bar. Beauty salon. Concierge. Disabled: adapted rooms. Garden. Gym. Internet access: ISDN. No-smoking rooms. Parking. Restaurant. Swimming pools (2).* **Room services** *Air-conditioning. Bathrobe. Hairdryer. Laundry/dry cleaning. Mini-bar. Newspaper. Room service (24 hours). TV: satellite.*

Radisson Hotel Waterfront

Beach Road, Granger Bay (021 418 5729/ www.radissonsas.com). **Rates** (incl breakfast) R2,240-R3,020. No under-12s. **Credit** AmEx, DC, MC, V. **Map** p282 G1.
The Radisson boasts one of the best sundecks and drinking spots in the whole of the city. Literally on the water's edge at Granger Bay (next to the V&A

using wine and grape pulp, a Chardonnay cocoon wrap and a Cape Classique massage. The sort of treatments Bacchus would certainly approve of.

Twelve Apostles Sanctuary Spa

See p32.
This decadent spa (*pictured*) is fabulously over the top. A haven of cavernous proportions, it is situated in an underground grotto on the slopes of Table Mountain, only a few metres from the Atlantic. The spa incorporates the surrounding natural elements in new ways – fantasy and sensuality are the key principals here. Modern elements such as coloured light therapy are a standard feature. A Buddha bathed in green light fronts the spa waterfall and lends an air of serenity. A floating glass staircase leads you to a brine pool (with a faux-starlit ceiling) and transports you to another world. If it's sensuality you're after, this is where you'll find it – you can hide away from the world while reclining on loungers in the candlelit cave, and the beautiful Rasul Chamber was designed to inspire meditative calm. When the sea air and

mountain views beckon, you can have your massage in one of the private outdoor gazebos, where the ocean breezes and soft aromas of the indigenous flora fynbos lull the pamperees into a calm cocoon. It's difficult not to be seduced by the ambience of this intimate spa. The indulgence is carried out by expertly trained therapists who understand that a cold glass of white wine is sometimes so much better than a fruit shake. A couple of hours here will have you plotting get-rich-quick schemes to pay for regular check-ins. This is an idyllic retreat where opulence and zen calm makes for blissful indulgence.

Natural highs at the **Radisson Hotel Waterfront**. *See p33.*

Waterfront), this hotel's bar/drinks deck is hugely popular with Capetonians, which means that guests who check in here for a couple of nights will find themselves mixing with the locals, who wish that they too could lounge around the gorgeous infinity pool. (You won't get closer to the sea without getting into it.) Modern and slick, the hotel has bedrooms arranged around an atrium, but it's worth forking out extra for the sea-facing suites. Within walking distance from the V&A and 15 minutes' drive from the centre of town, the Radisson offers its guests a glimpse of the laid-back lifestyle that Capetonians are wont to enjoy, without having to sacrifice first-world efficiency.
Hotel services *Babysitting. Bars (2). Beauty salon. Business centre. Concierge. Disabled: adapted rooms. Garden. Gym. Internet access: ISDN. Limousine service. No-smoking rooms. Parking. Restaurant (2). Swimming pool.* **Room services** *Air-conditioning. Bathrobe. Hairdryer. Laundry/dry cleaning. Mini-bar. Newspaper. Room service (24 hours). TV: satellite.*

Moderate

Whale Cottage Camps Bay
57 Camps Bay Drive, Camps Bay (021 438 3840/ www.whalecottage.com). **Rates** (incl breakfast) R250-R600. **Credit** AmEx, DC, MC, V. **Map** p284 B9.
Part of the Whale Cottage portfolio (go to the website for details of their other properties), this guesthouse offers visitors personalised service in a tranquil home environment. The sea views are gorgeous and there are four en-suite bedrooms, each tastefully decorated in shades of blue and white. The highlight of the amenities are two swimming pools, which are much needed during the summer months. There is no single surcharge.

Hotel services *Bar. Garden. Internet access: ASDL. No-smoking rooms. Parking. Swimming pools (2).* **Room services** *Air-conditioning. Hairdryer. Laundry. Mini-bar. Newspaper. TV: Satellite/DVD.*

Budget

Breakwater Lodge
Portswood Road, V&A Waterfront (021 406 1911/ www.breakwaterlodge.co.za). **Rates** R630. **Credit** AmEx, DC, MC, V. **Map** p282 G2.
The Breakwater Lodge offers some of the best value for money in the city. Set in the V&A Waterfront, in the 19th-century Breakwater prison, now also used as the University of Cape Town's Graduate Business School, this functional hotel, with its reasonable rates, high standards of cleanliness and central location is a great place from which to explore the city. The 268 rooms are clean, functional and even offer a nod to some rather basic but pleasant interior decorating. Stonebreakers, the self-service restaurant, offers nourishment at sensible prices.
Hotel services *Bar. Business centre. Disabled: adapted rooms. Internet access: ASDL. Laundry (self-service and service). No-smoking rooms. Parking. Restaurants (2). Swimming pool.* **Room services** *Air-conditioning. Hairdryer. Laundry. TV.*

Cape Town Ritz Hotel
Main Road, Sea Point (021 439 6010/ www.africanskyhotels.co.za). **Rates** R690. **Credit** AmEx, DC, MC, V. **Map** p282 E2.
What was once an elegant modern hotel (whose claim to fame was, and perhaps still is, a revolving restaurant that offered panoramic views of the Atlantic Seaboard) is now looking slightly tired in what has become a somewhat dodgy part of Sea Point. However, if you're only looking for a hotel to

use as a base while you explore the rest of the city and peninsula, the central location and these affordable rates will leave you with enough change to indulge in some retail therapy. The 222 rooms all look pretty much the same: some are rather small and dark (choose carefully) and those higher up in the building offer some good views.

Hotel services *Bar. No-smoking rooms. Parking. Restaurant. Swimming pool.* **Room services** *Air-conditioning. Hairdryer. Laundry/dry cleaning. Mini-bar. Room service (24 hours). TV: satellite.*

City Lodge Waterfront

Corner of Dock & Alfred Roads, V&A Waterfront (021 419 9450/www.citylodge.co.za). **Rates** R820. **Credit** AmEx, DC, MC, V. **Map** p283 H2.

This is the flagship hotel in the affordable City Lodge hotel group. It has recently been revamped, so as far as moderate hotel accommodation goes, this is probably as good as you'll get. Decor-wise it's ordinary but nice and staff are helpful. There's also a pool and internet café. It's perfectly situated if you want to spend your money on sightseeing and shopping rather than expensive luxury hotels. It's centrally located and since its revamp, is looking rather good. This is not a shabby address.

Hotel services *Bar. Disabled: adapted rooms. Gym. Internet access: ISDN. No-smoking rooms. Parking. Swimming pool.* **Room services** *Air-conditioning. Internet access: ISDN/telephone line. Hairdryer. Laundry/dry cleaning. TV: satellite.*

Victoria & Alfred Hotel

Corner of Dock & Alfred Roads, V&A Waterfront (021 419 6677/www.vahotel.co.za). **Rates** R2,140-R2,940. **Credit** AmEx, DC, MC, V. **Map** p283 H2.

Although bathed in the exciting bustle of the Waterfront, this hotel maintains a comfortable and elegant atmosphere. Alongside the Alfred Basin, overlooking Table Mountain and the harbour, lies the hotel's Waterfront Café, perfect for early-morning coffees or late-night dinners, with the lights of the yachts twinkling only a pavement away.

Hotel services *Bar. Concierge. Disabled: adapted rooms. Gym. Internet access: ISDN. Laundry. No-smoking rooms. Parking. Restaurant. Free shuttle to the swimming pool at sister hotel, the Ambassador.* **Room services** *Air-conditioning. Hairdryer. Mini-bar. Newspaper. Room service (24 hours). TV: satellite/DVD.*

Southern Suburbs

Expensive

Sérénité Wellness Spa and Hotel

16 Debaren Close, Constantia (021 713 1760/www.serenite.co.za). **Rates** R2,100-R3,500. No under-15s. **Credit** AmEx, DC, MC, V.

Sérénité is a destination hotel spa in the Constantia Valley that has 14 luxurious suites ideal for visitors who need to recharge their batteries. In a quiet

Victoria & Alfred Hotel: not such a shady character.

" In the heart of Cape Town sits the independently run Cape Heritage Hotel. Four star comfort emerges from the beautifully restored 18th century townhouse that plays neighbour to a wide selection of leading restaurants in historical Heritage Square. The hotel's team specialise in providing colourful Capetonian advice whilst lovingly tending to the oldest grapevine in South Africa which still thrives in the square's courtyard. "

CAPE HERITAGE HOTEL
1771

90 Bree Street, Cape Town 8001
P.O.Box 4475, Cape Town 8000, South Africa
Tel: 27 (021) 424 4646 Fax: 27 (021) 424 4949
E-mail: info@capeheritage.co.za
Website:www.capeheritage.co.za

setting, forest walks, healthy gourmet cuisine and specialised treatments are the order of the day. While close enough to the city, this isn't the place to stay if you want to explore Cape Town. It's much better as somewhere to stay and hibernate for a couple of days, or to end a busy holiday in a relaxed and peaceful fashion.

Hotel services *Bar. Concierge. Garden. Gym. Sauna. No-smoking. Parking. Restaurant. Swimming pool.* **Room services** *Air-conditioning. Hairdryer. Laundry/dry cleaning. Newspaper. Room service (24 hours). TV: satellite.*

Moderate

Courtyard Cape Town

Liesbeek Avenue, off Liesbeek Parkway, Mowbray (021 448 3929/www.citylodge.co.za). **Rates** R770-R880. **Credit** AmEx, DC, MC, V.

Offering the visitor far more than the reasonable rates indicate, this hotel was originally built as a private residence in 1661. The historical Cape Dutch Manor House has been converted into a hotel and is situated near the N2 motorway, so while it's not exactly based in the centre of things, it isn't too far away from all the sights and it does provide easy access if you've rented a car and are keen to travel. **Hotel services** *Bar. Concierge. Disabled: adapted rooms. Garden. Internet access: ISDN. No-smoking rooms. Parking. Restaurant. Swimming pool.* **Room services** *Air-conditioning. Hairdryer. Laundry/dry cleaning. Room service (24 hours). TV: satellite.*

Vineyard Hotel

Collington Road, Newlands (021 657 4500/ www.vineyard.co.za). **Rates** R1,055-R2,855. **Credit** AmEx, DC, MC, V.

Good value for money, this hotel was first built as a private residence for Lady Anne Barnard in 1799. The property has now been converted into a four-star deluxe hotel, set in beautiful, wide expanses of landscaped gardens bordering the Liesbeek River. New to the property are fitness facilities; a luxurious spa is due to open in late 2004. **Hotel services** *Bar. Concierge. Cottages (2) with kitchenettes. Disabled: adapted rooms. Garden. Gym. Internet access: ASDL. No-smoking rooms. Parking. Restaurants (2). Swimming pool.* **Room services** *Air-conditioning. Bathrobe. Hairdryer. Laundry/ dry cleaning. Mini-bar. Newspaper. Room service (24 hours). TV: satellite.*

Budget

Green Elephant Backpackers

57 Milton Road, Observatory (021 448 6359/ 021 448 0510/www.capestay.co.za/greenelephant). **Rates** R75/person in a dorm; R250 en-suite double room. **Credit** AmEx, DC, MC, V.

Situated in the lively and bohemian student Observatory suburb, the Green Elephant is within staggering distance of the area's famous clubs, pubs and restaurants. Because it's not in the city centre,

it has a more laid-back set of neighbours – and (like Obs itself) the hostel's atmosphere falls somewhere between city sass and suburban safety. The mod-cons are all in place: guests have access to a solar-heated swimming pool, hot whirlpool bath, satellite television, international phone/fax service and inter-net facilities. There are also double rooms with (somewhat implausibly for a hostel) four-poster beds. It's fun and friendly, like most of its kind. **Hostel services** *Bar. Café. Internet access: ASDL. Laundry. No-smoking rooms. Payphone. Self-catering facilities. Swimming pool. TV lounge: satellite/VCR.*

Northern Suburbs

Moderate

Protea Hotel Dolphin Beach

Marine Drive, Tableview (021 557 8140/ www.proteahotels.com/dolphinbeach). **Rates** R1,095-R2,095. **Credit** AmEx, DC, MC, V.

Ever fancied an apartment overlooking the sea, with a long stretch of sandy white beach on which to walk in the early mornings? For a fee, you can realise your dreams. The Protea Hotel offers luxury suites for those wishing to stay on this side of the Atlantic Ocean. Less crowded, and slightly less fashionable (it's more family-oriented) than its Atlantic Seaboard neighbours, the area does offer the best place for those wanting to kite-surf. If it's not sport you're after, this is still a very good place from which to explore Cape Town. You'll need to hire a car though, as it is slightly out of town and at a remove from the major tourist attractions. **Hotel services** *Bar. Beauty salon. Gym. No-smoking rooms. Parking. Restaurant. Swimming pool.* **Room services** *Air-conditioning. Hairdryer. Internet access: ISDN/telephone line. Kitchenette. Laundry/dry cleaning. TV: satellite.*

Budget

Blue Peter Hotel

56 Popham Road, Bloubergstrand (021 554 1956/ www.bluepeter.co.za). **Rates** (incl breakfast) R470-R600. **Credit** AmEx, DC, MC, V.

The Blue Peter is an old-fashioned hotel. Privately owned, this property with its beautiful sea views has a charm all of its own. If you're not fussy about stay-ing in slightly dated accommodation, you'd have dif-ficulty finding more charming accommodation at such reasonable prices. So the rooms are a bit tired, but they're spotlessly clean. The main attraction: The sea views, once again, and the legendary Lower Deck, where locals gather in the restaurant or on the grass in front of the hotel, order great pizzas, drink beer, soak up the sun and watch the waves. The Blue Peter is an informal, jolly place. **Hotel services** *Bars (2). Garden. Parking. Restaurants (2).* **Room services** *Air-conditioning. Hairdryer. Laundry/dry cleaning. Room service (18 hours). TV: satellite.*

Pool positions at **La Couronne**.

Town Lodge Bellville

Corner of Willie van Schoor Avenue & Mispel Road, Bellville (021 948 7990/www.citylodge.co.za). **Rates** R500. **Credit** AmEx, DC, MC, V.

Part of the City Lodge hotel chain, this place is fine if you see a hotel as a purely functional thing. In the heart of the Northern Suburbs, near a fair number of shopping malls, the Town Lodge Belleville is spotlessly clean and as good a base as any. It's important to note that you'll need a car to get around, as the location is slightly out of the way. But the prices are great, and the Lodge often operates even better special deals. It's an ordinary place, the carpets are dead ugly and the rooms smallish, but it really is great value for money. There is even a swimming pool for when the African sun gets too much.

Hotel services *Bar. Disabled: adapted rooms. Garden. Gym. No-smoking rooms. Parking. Restaurant. Swimming pool.* **Room services** *Air-conditioning. Hairdryer. Internet access: ISDN/telephone line. Laundry/dry cleaning. Room service. TV: satellite.*

Winelands

Expensive

La Couronne

Dassenberg Road, Franschhoek (021 876 2770/ www.lacouronnehotel.co.za). **Rates** R1,800-R5,000. **Credit** AmEx, DC, MC, V.

This luxurious boutique hotel is situated on a working wine estate and is the sort of place from that, even if you're dying to explore Franschhoek, you simply can't drag yourself away from. The rooms are beautifully decorated, with magnificent views overlooking rose gardens and rolling vineyards. The swimming pool is glorious and great for those hot days when the sun bakes down on the valley. The lounges are of the leather, cane and dark-wood, old-colonial style and the restaurant is one of the best in the region. An utterly romantic hotel with wonderful staff who will gladly help you with your sightseeing plans and offer interesting ideas to experience the best that the region offers.

Hotel services *Babysitting. Bar. Business centre. Concierge. Garden. Gym. Limousine service. No-smoking rooms. Parking. Restaurant. Swimming pool.* **Room services** *Air-conditioning. Bathrobe. Hairdryer. Laundry/dry cleaning. Mini-bar. Newspaper. Room service (24 hours). TV: satellite.*

Lanzerac Manor

Lanzerac Street, Stellenbosch (021 887 1132/ www.lanzerac.co.za). **Rates** (incl breakfast) R1,350-R4,030. **Credit** AmEx, DC, MC, V.

Set on a 300-year-old, enormous country estate, Lanzerac Manor is an excellent example of Cape Dutch architecture. It is also located on a working wine farm which produces award-winning wines. This means that you'll be able to walk in the vineyards, see how they make the stuff and then indulge, before retiring to elegant bedrooms or suites. To complete the rural idyll, squirrels can often be spied playing in the oak trees. This is an ideal place from which to explore the other wine farms in the region. **Hotel services** *Bar. Concierge. Disabled: adapted rooms. Garden. No-smoking rooms. Parking. Restaurant. Swimming pool.* **Room services** *Air-conditioning. Bathrobe. Hairdryer. Internet access: ISDN. Laundry/dry cleaning. Mini-bar. Newspaper. Room service (24 hours). TV: satellite.*

Spier

Spier Estate, R310, Lynedoch, Stellenbosch (021 809 1111/www.spier.co.za). **Rates** (incl breakfast) R1,290-R1,950. **Credit** AmEx, DC, MC, V.
Spier is the quintessential one-stop shop for the winelands experience. Some may argue that it is Disneyland of the winelands, but having said that, few places can beat it for sheer scale and selection of activities. Where else can you see a show, eat at

Doing it your way

If you're planning a longer stay and want to make Cape Town your base for a couple of weeks or even months, your best bet would be to consider self-catering accommodation or even long-term rentals. The following agencies are worth considering, and we have included two properties that are highly recommended for tight budgets.

Channel Estate

65 Arthur's Road, Sea Point, Atlantic Seaboard (021 424 2308/www.channelestate.co.za). **Rates** R1,200-R5,000 per unit/day. **Credit** AmEx, DC, MC, V. **Map** p281 D3.
Channel Estate specialises in short- and long-term rentals on the Atlantic Seaboard. Flats and homes are all fully furnished, allowing you to drop your bags and feel quite at home. If you're looking to rent during peak season, you'll need to contact the agency well in advance, since the best properties are inevitably taken first.

Foot of Table Mountain

Oranjezicht, City Bowl (021 852 4626/ www.capestay.co.za/table-mountain). **Rates** R600-R900 per night/4 people. **Credit** AmEx, DC, MC, V. **Map** p283 H2.
Nestled between the slopes of Table Mountain and the city centre is this luxurious and spacious two-bedroom apartment. It sleeps four comfortably (there's no need to bunk on one of those dreaded sleeper couches) and offers all the amenities you could require, including a coffee-espresso machine, TV and CD player as well as a cash mini-bar stocked with South African wines. There's a free basket of traditional Cape goodies upon arrival. It's well within walking distance or a short drive of most Cape Town sights.

Green Point Cottage

8 Dysart Road, Green Point, Atlantic Seaboard (021 424 2090/www.capestay.co.za/dysartfick). **Rates** R450-R750 per night/4 people. **Credit** AmEx, DC, MC, V. **Map** p282 F2.

This lovely cottage, full of old-fashioned charm, is decorated with wooden floors and natural fabrics in earth tones. It has easy access to the V&A Waterfront, Green Point's vibrant nightlife, restaurants and the Sea Point promenade. Perfect for extended stays in Cape Town.

Icon Villas & Vistas

Tamboerskloof, City Bowl (021 424 0905/ www.icape.co.za). **Rates** R450-R350 per unit/day. **Credit** AmEx, DC, MC, V. **Map** p282 F4.
This company specialises in providing private, self-catering accommodation for visitors who prefer to do their own thing while on holiday. Homes can by rented on a daily, weekly or monthly basis. The accommodation varies from villas and penthouses to small cottages and stylish apartments. All are carefully selected to ensure high standards – rest assured you will be living in a well-maintained and clean setting. Part of the extended service is to provide you with information relating to all activities in and around the city, which is great even for the more independent traveller, as it's always insightful to have locals' recommendations.

Village & Life

(021 422 2371/www.villageandlife.co.za). **Rates** R600-R3,600 per unit/day. **Credit** AmEx, DC, MC, V. **Map** p282 G4.
Village & Life offers luxury, self-catering accommodation in Cape Town, with unique hospitality villages in De Waterkant, Camps Bay, Mouille Point and the Waterfront. The homes are all beautifully decorated, fully equipped and maintained by friendly staff. Each 'village' has a tourist information desk, assisting visitors with bookings and all manner of queries. To stay in beautiful surroundings, but to enjoy a greater degree of independence than a hotel can offer, this may well be your best bet.

Peaks of luxury: **Lanzerac Manor**. *See p38.*

four different restaurants, pat a cheetah, go for a wine-tasting, ride a horse, picnic alongside the river, play a game of golf, go for a facial and sleep in luxury? Go if you have the energy.
Hotel services *Bars (4). Beauty salon. Concierge. Disabled: adapted rooms. Garden. Internet access: ISDN. No-smoking rooms. Parking. Restaurants (5). Swimming pools (7).* **Room services** *Air-conditioning. Bathrobe. Hairdryer. Laundry/dry cleaning. Mini-bar. Newspaper. Room service (24 hours). TV: satellite.*

Winelands Hotel & Wellness Centre

Simonsvlei Farm, Klapmuts (021 875 5357/ www.santewellness.co.za). **Rates** (incl breakfast) R2,645-R3,000. **Credit** AmEx, DC, MC, V.
One of the newest additions to the hotel scene, this boutique hotel and destination spa is certain to set some pulses racing and hearts aflutter. It's a fabulous place, set in vineyards surrounded by mountains. This small hotel has a wonderful spa where visitors can relax in holistic, yet luxurious, surroundings. The design of the hotel and spa is Italian-inspired, but the decor is modern African. Dark woods, Persian carpets, burnt reds and ochres blend with the environment. The hotel boasts the largest private collection of Walter Batiss works and their presence throughout the hotel is much admired. Bedrooms are large and elegant, and the bath tubs are obscenely large, with Aveda bath products adding a classy touch. The spa is aimed at holistic health, indulging guests with world-class treatments

(see p32 **Looking for good chi?**). Two restaurants – one preparing gourmet spa cuisine and the other pure gourmet magic, vie for attention. The entire hotel is designed to relax its guests, and the attentive and friendly staff will make you feel at home. In fact this is much better than being at home. This is a good base for exploring the region.
Hotel services *Beauty salon. Concierge. Disabled: adapted rooms. Garden. Gym. Parking. Restaurant. Swimming pool.* **Room services** *Air-conditioning. Bathrobe. Hairdryer. Laundry/dry cleaning. Mini-bar. Newspaper. Room service (24 hours). TV: satellite/DVD.*

Moderate

D'Oude Werf

30 Church Street, Stellenbosch (021 887 4608/ www.ouwewerf.com). **Rates** (incl breakfast) R500-R1,390. **Credit** AmEx, DC, MC, V. **Map** p278 Q3.
This family hotel is the oldest inn in South Africa. It has recently been refurbished and, while it is now more sophisticated, it has lost none of its charm. The hotel has a very good restaurant, 1802 (the year the inn was established), as well as a swimming pool for those sweltering hot days. Traditional and intimate, it is situated in the middle of the historic Stellenbosch quarter and a good jumping-off point for exploring other parts of town.
Hotel services *Beauty salon. Concierge. Garden. No-smoking rooms. Restaurant. Swimming pool.* **Room services** *Air-conditioning. Bathrobe. Hairdryer. Laundry/dry cleaning. Mini-bar. Room service (18 hours). TV: satellite.*

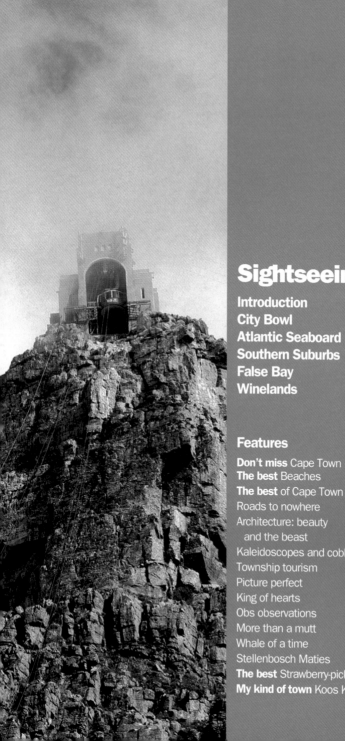

Sightseeing

Introduction

With beaches on all sides, stunning Winelands and a bustling City Centre, there's something different for every day in Cape Town.

CITY BOWL

Boxed in on four sides by the choppy waters of Table Bay, the towering Devil's Peak, the majestic Table Mountain and the rolling Lion's Head (with its 'rump', Signal Hill), Cape Town's **City Centre** is squeezed into the City Bowl, the tiny space between its northern slopes and the waters of Table Bay. This must have seemed like a good idea for the early settlers (who knew they'd eventually run out of space in the valley?), and – although it's a nightmare for car-bound commuters – it makes the centre of the Mother City a dream for sightseers: the various neighbourhoods and their many attractions are all within easy walking distance of each other.

Typically for a city centre, the main museums and historical sights are here, many of which are clustered along **Museum Mile**. The surrounding City Bowl is more residential and encompasses the areas of **Bo-Kaap** (meaning upper Cape), which is situated at the foot of Signal Hill, as well as the trendy suburbs of Tamboerskloof, Gardens and Oranjezicht.

Don't miss **Cape Town**

● Make sure you see the two oceans meet at Cape Point and enjoy the privacy of the clean and secluded beaches of the **Cape of Good Hope** (*see p78*).
● **Franschhoek** is the self-professed Cape capital of food and wine, so an essential stop for any foodie (*see p80*).
● Stroll through the fynbos and fauna at **Kirstenbosch Botanical Gardens**, one of the most beautiful gardens in the world (*see p65*).
● You can't visit Cape Town without taking in its political history: make a pilgrimage to Nelson Mandela's former jail cell on **Robben Island** (*see p59*).
● Take a hike or alternatively take the cableway, but make sure you get to the top of **Table Mountain** (*see p56*).
● Do some shopping at **V&A Waterfront** (*see p58*), or wander along the harbour and watch the fishing boats come in.

Watching over the city is the iconic – and instantly recognisable – **Table Mountain**, flanked on either side by Lion's Head and Devil's Peak, with the Twelve Apostles stretching behind it. A trip to the top is a must-do, particularly on one of the hiking trails. Surrounded by forests, you'll soon forget that you're slap-bang in the middle of the city.

ATLANTIC SEABOARD

On the other side of the mountain, at the foot of the western slopes, you'll find the famous Atlantic Seaboard, where multimillion dollar real estate clings to the ragged rocks overlooking the golden, Riviera-like sands of **Clifton** and **Camps Bay**.

At its northern tip is the huge **V&A Waterfront** complex, whose Nelson Mandela Gateway (near the old Clock Tower) is the embarkation point for trips to **Robben Island**, which housed many of South Africa's anti-apartheid icons, including Mandela and Walter Sisulu, and now has a fascinating museum.

SOUTHERN SUBURBS

South of the City Bowl, extending towards the point of the Cape Peninsula, the Southern Suburbs include bohemian **Observatory**, studenty **Rondebosch**, sporty **Newlands** and affluent **Constantia**. Here you'll find some hidden suburban treasures, as well as **Groot Constantia** – the grandest of the old Cape Dutch wine estates, and the **Kirstenbosch Botanical Gardens**.

FALSE BAY

Continuing south, the greater city moves through the seaside suburbs of **Muizenberg**, **Fish Hoek** and **Simonstown** until it eventually runs out of land, and the peninsula tapers off to **Cape Point**, the dramatic meeting place of the chilly Atlantic and the warm Indian Ocean waters of False Bay.

WINELANDS

To the east of the city, the beautiful valleys and vineyards of the Cape Winelands stretch out invitingly, offering excellent wine in gorgeous setting. **Paarl**, **Stellenbosch** and **Franschhoek** may be a bit of an excursion from Cape Town, but they are very much considered a part of it by locals.

SIGHTSEEING TIPS

What with its Winelands, beaches and warm, sunny days, Cape Town just can't help being the most laid-back city in South Africa. But the easygoing atmosphere can be deceptive: while Cape Town may feel safe, it's still a big and bustling city – and an African city at that. So while paranoia isn't required, a bit of traveller's common sense certainly is. For advice, *see p251 and* **Directory: Safety & security**.

In the blazing heat of the African summer, this can be one hot town. Always wear sun protection and preferably a hat, and avoid the midday heat by ducking into an air-conditioned museum or restaurant.

Guided tours

For some interesting takes on the Mother City, go on one of the many guided trips and tours around town. A visit to one of the tourist offices *see* **Directory: Tourist information** is the best bet for joining a group tour or to get information about your options. From here you can take a trip on the **Cape Town Explorer Topless Bus**, which departs every hour between 10am and 4pm daily. The tour is two hours long and costs R90 (R40 for concessions). The more fit and adventurous can try **Cape Town on Foot** – a two-hour walk through town and history, led by Ursula Stevens. Walks start at the City Centre tourist office at 11am, Monday to Friday.

By air

Sport-helicopters

V&A Waterfront, Atlantic Seaboard (021 419 5907/ www.sport-helicopters.co.za).
Sport-helicopters offers an array of scenic tours around Cape Point, Hout Bay and the Winelands.

NAC

021 425 3868/www.nacmakana.com
Scenic flights or hot air balloon rides along the Winelands and the West Coast.

The best Beaches

Bloubergstrand

Perfect for an evening stroll, Blouberg offers some of the best views of Table Mountain across the bay (*see p63*).

Boulders

Avoid the False Bay winds and spend some time swimming with the penguins near Simonstown (*see p75*).

Camps Bay

Just as trendy as Clifton Fourth (but friendlier), this stunning beach is the heart of the Cape 'Riviera' (*see p62*).

Clifton Fourth

Park your bottom next to the gorgeous swimsuit models and watch as they peer over their designer sunglasses at their perfect tans (*see p61*).

Fish Hoek

With its warm and shallow waters, this is the best family beach and one of the safest in the Cape (*see p74*).

Wineland Ballooning

Paarl, Winelands (021 863 3192).
Wineland Ballooning offers early-morning balloon flights from Paarl, followed by a champagne break-fast. Phone for details of packages.

By boat

Circe Launches

Hout Bay Harbour, Atlantic Seaboard (021 790 1040/www.circelaunches.co.za). **Tours** hourly 9.30am-4.30pm daily.
This is the only glass-bottomed boat in South Africa. Tours in Hout Bay depart every hour, every day between 9.30am and 4.30pm.

Sightseeing

Sea Point beachfront. *See p61.*

Tigresse Cruises

Table Bay Harbour, Northern Suburbs (021 424 1455).

Tigresse Cruises offers one-hour sails and sunset cruises of the bay area. This company has one of the Cape's fastest catamarans.

Nadita Boat Charters

Gordon's Bay, False Bay (083 654 0662/083 653 8012).

If you want a little more action than merely sipping a drink and staring at the choppy sea, Nadita Boat Charters organises deep-sea game fishing trips, including all the gear and snacks.

Townships

Grassroutes Tours

021 706 1006/082 951 1016/grassroutes@iafrica.com.

Grassroutes offers half-day and full-day township tours, with the latter including a visit to Robben Island (*see p59*). Other activities offered include visits to craft markets and shebeens. *See also p61* **Township tourism**.

Our Pride Tours

021 531 4291/082 446 7974.

Half-day and full-day tours of the townships, with the added option of a traditional lunch.

New World Inc

021 790 8825.

New World Inc is a specialist in township music tours. A typical tour may include an interactive music workshop, traditional dancing, African storytelling and an African meal. This company also offers custom-made tours, so you can arrange an itinerary best suited to your interests and timetable. Phone in advance to find out more.

The best of Cape Town

Insider experiences

● Buy fresh fish straight from the boat at **Kalk Bay** harbour (*see p74*).
● Gawk at the city's unintentional urban artwork: the unfinished highway (*see p49* **Roads to nowhere**).
● Explore the dusty sprawl of a shanty town on a guided **township tour** (*see p61*).
● Watch out for the whales from the walkway below **Muizenberg** station (*see p73*).

Encounters with nature

● Fancy a bird with long legs? Ride an ostrich at one of **Oudtshoorn**'s ostrich farms (*see p241*).
● Trade grooming tips with the svelte and sophisticated simians at **Monkey Town** (*see p78*).
● Admire the impeccable dress sense – and convincing Charlie Chaplin imitations – of the jackass penguins at **Boulders Penguin Colony** (*see p75*).
● Get up close and personal with some fearsome jaws during a shark dive at the **Two Oceans Aquarium** (*see p60*).
● Dodge the squirrel monkeys and get intimate with the raptors at Hout Bay's **World of Birds** (*see p63*).

Breathtaking views

● Photograph the famous Table Mountain silhouette from **Milnerton** beach (*see p62*).
● Survey the peninsula from MacLear's Beacon, the highest point on **Table Mountain** (*see p56*).

● Take in the spectacular view of the rambling Southern Suburbs from the steps of **Rhodes Memorial** (*see p69*).
● Watch the City Bowl disappear into the distance as you go up the **Table Mountain** cableway (*see p57*).

Wild experiences

● If you've got the guts, take an **abseiling** flight from Table Mountain on what is thought to be the highest commercial abseil in the world (*see p202*).
● Go diving among the sharks at the **Two Oceans Aquarium** (*see p60*).
● Young adrenalin-seekers can roar across the sky in a supersonic jet at **Thundercity** (*see p156*).
● You'll get the biggest thrill by jumping off the world's highest **bungee** jump at Bloukrans Bridge (*see p203*).

Amazing drives

● There are few drives more stunning than the seaside ride of the **West Coast Road** (*see p242*).
● Sir Lowry's Pass from Somerset West to Bot River takes you up the mountains that overlook **False Bay** (*see p71*).
● Take a trip from **Camps Bay** to Hout Bay along Victoria Road, at the foot of the Twelve Apostles (*see p62*).
● Stop your car on **Boyes Drive**, which leads along the mountainside between Muizenberg and Kalk Bay, and see if you can spot a whale (*see p72*).

City Bowl

Table Mountain, Museum Mile and a bustling and beautiful City Centre.

Cape Town is blessed with a stunning setting. Located on a slither of land (much of it reclaimed) between the waters of Table Bay and the towering quartzite granite cliffs of Table Mountain, the city boasts gorgeous beaches and unspoilt natural gardens, all within a few miles of the bustling City Bowl.

It's the oldest city in southern Africa, seeing its first European settlers in the mid-17th century. Because of the sheltered bay and the strategic location at the foot of Africa, the Dutch East India Company established Cape Town as a refuelling post – a halfway stop on the well-travelled sea route to the East. The City Bowl architecture reflects Cape Town's various historical influences, taking in Cape Dutch, Victorian and Georgian styles, as well as a few towering Art Deco gems (like the General Post Office building on Darling Street), *see p50* **Architecture: beauty and the beast**.

The City Bowl makes up the heart of the city, between the bay and at the very foot of Table Mountain and the neighbouring Lion's Head and Signal Hill. It covers the entire area between the sea, the mountains and the Onder-Kaap (the old District Six), encompassing neighbourhoods such as Gardens, Tamboerskloof, Zonnebloem and Foreshore, as well as the City Centre.

The City Centre is the heart of the City Bowl. It starts at Oswald Pirow Street and runs between the Foreshore and Buitensingel Street (at the foot of Table Mountain) to Buitengracht Street (directly below the Bo-Kaap at the foot of Signal Hill) and Annandale Road (which later turns into De Waal Drive and the M3). It is Cape Town's engine room, containing the legal district, Museum Mile, the Houses of Parliament and other civic buildings, and the central business district. Here business people, lawyers, judges and parliamentarians dash about, armed with briefcases and takeaway coffee, while mounted police officers clip-clop around the commercial areas, and map-wielding tourists wander along Museum Mile.

A bustling commercial and civic area, the City Centre is not a residential area (it's simply too small), and Cape Town's central residential suburbs are found on the lower slopes of Table Mountain and Signal Hill.

The City Centre is home to most of South Africa's 'firsts', including the country's first places of worship (the Groote Kerk, St George's

Bustling **Greenmarket Square**. *See p48.*

Cathedral, the Great Synagogue and the Auwal Mosque) and its first (and only) castle (the Castle of Good Hope). It's also home to the national Houses of Parliament, which are located in Parliament Street, backing onto the lush Company Gardens.

Cape Town may be one of Africa's most important cities, but its centre is relatively tiny. This is good news for visitors: a walking tour could take only a morning, or the best part of a day, depending on stops.

City Centre

With the City Centre being so small, each street has taken on a significance and a character of its own. Keerom Street is home to the city's legal district, with the imposing Cape High Court building at the northern end, near Wale Street. Wale Street, in turn, leads up from its legal and financial southern end to the more homely western end in the Bo-Kaap.

Adderley Street (named after a British parliamentarian who successfully campaigned against the Cape becoming a convict colony) is

TAKE A TOUR DE FORCE

Experience a world-class destination. Visit Africa's largest manufacturing showroom where you can enjoy these exciting options:

DIAMOND TOUR · GOLD TOUR · GEM TOUR · AFRICAN ARTS

To go somewhere you've never been before, call us on:
+27 (0)21 424 5141 · a/h: +27 (0)82 658 8712 · www.jewelafrica.com
Cape Town · South Africa
Free shuttle service available

Cape Town's main road, and it also happens to be one of the few mountain-to-foreshore streets that isn't one-way. This is where you'll find – moving north from the Foreshore end – statues of early European traders Bartholomew Dias and Jan van Riebeeck, the railway station, and – at the northern end – the Slave Lodge and its Museum Mile neighbours.

While Adderley Street is busy and traffic jammed, Long Street and the pedestrian-only St George's Mall are much better streets for wasting time. **Long Street** (*see p48*) is the main artery of Cape Town's cosmopolitan culture: at the northern end you'll find businesses, cafés and the odd indoor African art market, the best of which is the **Pan African Market** (*see p49*). The street's southern end (closer to the mountain) never seems to sleep: this stretch is packed with antique stores, bookshops and quirky local fashion boutiques, as well as backpackers' lodges and all-night restaurants and nightclubs. Whether during the day or night, Long Street's mountain end is the most vibey part of Cape Town, and the best place to have a good time.

St George's Mall (*see p54*) is a pedestrian-only, daytime-only, bricked walkway of coffee shops, jewellers and souvenir stores. It's the safest part of the city during the day (mounted cops are on constant patrol), and the buskers and street entertainers make it well worth a leisurely hour's stroll.

As you explore Cape Town's multicultural streets you'll find that one landmark is located only a few doors down from the next. Take Church Street (leading from the steps of the Groote Kerk up to the Bo-Kaap): in the space of a few dozen metres, traditional African arts stores and the cutting-edge **Association for Visual Arts** (*see p168*) overlook specialist antique stores and cosmopolitan coffee shops, while the breeze from the Bo-Kaap blows the dust off trinkets and early-edition books at the bustling outdoor antiques market.

Cape Town Holocaust Centre

88 Hatfield Street (021 462 5553/www.museums. org.za/ctholocaust). **Open** 10am-5pm Mon-Thur, Sun; 10am-1pm Fri. **Admission** free. **Map** p282 G5.
The main function of the Holocaust Centre is to be a place of remembrance for the six million Jews who died at the hands of the Nazis, but it has sensibly and sensitively placed itself within a wider South African context. It's a sobering reminder of the disastrous consequences of prejudice and racism, with its displays including photographs, artefacts, archived documents and multimedia displays. While its message is perhaps a little too sombre for the casual holiday visitor, the Holocaust Centre is a worthwhile – and important – addition to your checklist of Cape Town museums.

Castle of Good Hope

Buitenkant Street (021 787 1249/www.castleofgood hope.co.za/www.museums.org.za.wfc). **Open** 9am-4pm daily. **Admission** R18; R8-R15 concessions. Half price all Sun. **No credit cards. Map** p283 I4.
The Castle of Good Hope is the oldest building in South Africa. Built between 1666 and 1679, the pentagonal fortification has five bastions, named after the main titles of Willem, the Prince of Orange. You may wonder why there is a need for a castle in laid-back Cape Town? You'll be pleased to hear that the Castle has a 100 per cent defensive record. Only two shots have ever been shot at it: one by a drunken sailor from the top of Table Mountain (fortunately, he missed and lost his salary), and once by a passing ship giving the standard blank salute from its on-board cannon (somebody forgot to remove the cannonball). Both assailants avoided spells in the gloomy dungeons – but there's nothing preventing you from paying a visit to the Castle's dark and dingy bowels. A highlight of any tour of the Castle is spending 30 seconds alone in the dark in the notorious 'Dark Hole': a pitch-black, damp, windowless cell. Having been constantly restored over the years, the Castle is now maintained in the style of the British regency period. You can give the Military Museum a miss if you are pressed for time (unless, of course, you're a fan of colonial military power), but the famous William Fehr Collection is worth a look: a unique collection of priceless Africana, it includes historical paintings, furniture and ceramics dating back to the first settlers at the Cape.

District Six Museum

25A Buitenkant Street (021 461 8745/ www.districtsix.co.za). **Open** 9am-3pm Mon; 9am-4pm Tue-Sat. **Admission** R10; R5 concessions. **No credit cards. Map** p283 H4.
District Six was once a vibrant, cosmopolitan community. Now it's an ugly scar on the city's landscape. The apartheid government ordered the people of District Six to be relocated and the houses bulldozed to make room for new houses for whites only – a plan that never materialised. The area now stands open and unoccupied: the uneasy silence providing a discomforting reminder of this part of Cape Town's history. Refreshingly, though, the District Six Museum is a touching and uplifting tribute to District Six. It feels as if an entire community has been crammed into a single building: street signs, photographs, maps and trinkets flesh out the story of the community, while the unmistakable spirit of District Six lingers in the creaky floorboards and uneven stairs. An essential part of Cape history.

Gold of Africa Museum

Martin Melck House, 96 Strand Street (021 405 1540/www.goldofafrica.co.za). **Open** 9.30am-5pm Mon-Sat. **Admission** R20; R10-R16 concessions. **Credit** AmEx, DC, MC, V. **Map** p283 H3.
Set in the restored Martin Melck House (built in 1783), the Gold of Africa Museum is a dazzling addition to the city's places of interest: it's literally filled

Sightseeing

with gold. Ever since the discovery of gold near Johannesburg, the shiny yellow metal has come to be synonymous with South Africa (we produce about a third of the world's gold). The Gold of Africa Museum has the largest collection of African golden artefacts under one roof, and focuses on the exquisite artworks crafted by West African goldsmiths in the 19th and 20th centuries. The collection – acquired in 2001 from Geneva's Barbier-Müller Museum – features treasures from the Asante people of Ghana and Côte d'Ivoire, as well as artefacts from Mali, Senegal and Zimbabwe's lost cities of gold. There are hundreds of items on display, including precious masks, birds, crocodiles, elephants and human figures, as well as a crown and the striking golden lion from Ghana – the symbol of the museum.

Grand Parade & City Hall

Doorstep of Castle of Good Hope & flanked by Buitengracht & Darling Streets. **Map** p293 H4.
Over the years the Parade has been the scene of many a military and political gathering – including the infamous Party That Never Was, when Cape Town lost out in the 2004 Olympic Games bid. These days it's occupied by a flea market and a parking area. Overlooking the Grand Parade is the City Hall, which houses the Municipal Library.

Greenmarket Square

Burg Street (www.greenmarket.co.za). **Open** *Stalls* 9am-6pm Mon-Sat. **Admission** free. **Map** p283 H4.
Cape Town's thriving flea-market trade has its roots in Greenmarket Square, a cobbled square in the city centre. Originally a vegetable market (and then a parking lot), the square is now home to a charming, bustling market. Here you can buy anything from hand-carved artworks to antique cutlery. Most people, however, go to Greenmarket Square to enhance their wardrobe. The stalls offer a bizarre and Bohemian selection ranging from tie-dyed frocks and hand-stitched socks to printed scarves and edible sandals. Remember, though, that if you can't find the malachite chess set or African carving you're looking for here, there's always Pan African Market in Long Street and the Green Point flea market.

Jewish Museum

88 Hatfield Street (021 465 1546/www.sajewish museum.co.za). **Open** 10am-5pm Mon-Thur, Sun; 10am-2pm Fri. **Admission** R50; R15-R25 concessions. **Credit** MC, V. **Map** p282 G5.
The South African Jewish Museum, located next door to the Holocaust Centre, explores the history and influence of Cape Town's Jewish community. The museum's steep entrance fee is just about justified by the multi-media experience and trained guides who show visitors through the museum.

Koopmans-De Wet House

35 Strand Street (021 481 3935/appointment 021 464 3280/www.museums.org.za/koopmans). **Open** Mon by appointment. **Admission** R5; R2 concessions; free under-6s. **No credit cards.** **Map** p283 H3.

The Koopmans-De Wet House was opened to the public in 1914. The former residence of Maria Koopmans-De Wet, a 19th-century society gal, the museum has been furnished as a lived-in house from the turn of the 19th century, complete with a superb collection of Cape furniture, Dutch Delft, Chinese and Japanese ceramics, paintings, glass and silverware. The museum offers an intriguing and finely-detailed glimpse into the life of the rich and famous during Cape Town's colonial times.

Long Street

www.longstreet.co.za. **Map** p283 H3.
Stretching across more than 20 blocks of the city's centre, Long Street certainly is long – and in many ways it's also the spiritual heart of the city. Long Street is many things to many people: for backpackers, it is the South African equivalent of Bangkok's Khoa San Road or Sydney's King's Cross. For fashionistas it's Cape Town's Trend Centre. For motorists it's a nightmare of parking tickets and informal parking assistants (ranging from helpful and polite to drunk and threatening). And for thirsty late-night revellers, Long Street is one long stretch of bright lights and bars. By day upper Long Street is a Bohemian hive of bookshops, boutiques, backpacker lodges and quaint shops that haven't changed hands for the past five generations. By night it turns on the lights and livens up as the spot for clubbing, drinking, eating and meeting the city's daysleepers. Even since the opening of the V&A Waterfront, Long Street hasn't lost its vibrant atmosphere – if anything, it has developed an edge that makes it an essential stop (by day and night) for any visitor to the Mother City.

Long Street Baths

Corner of Long & Orange Streets (021 400 3302). **Open** 7am-7pm daily. *Women only* 10am-4pm daily. **Admission** R8; R3.50-R5 concessions. **No credit cards.** **Map** p282 G4.
It's foreign and steamy… and best of all, it's good for you. It's the Turkish baths, located at the top end of Long Street. The baths are housed in a complex that dates back to 1908, and have changing rooms, a massage parlour, a heated swimming pool and Turkish baths with steam and dry-heat rooms. Rather than being a steamy spot for exhibitionists (it's far too impersonal for that), the baths are all about health and cleansing. You'll leave feeling exhausted, sanitised and strangely satisfied – and with a grin on your steamed-up face.

Methodist Church

Greenmarket Square (021 422 2744/5). **Open** 9am-2pm Mon-Fri; 10am-noon Sat. *Services* 1.10pm Tue; 10am Sun. **Map** p283 H4.
The Metropolitan Methodist Church, decorated in Gothic Revivalist style, was once considered the finest place of worship in the country. These days, it's enough that the church provides some much-needed peace and quiet from the riot of noise on Greenmarket Square, situated right on its doorstep.

Michaelis Collection

The Old Town House, Greenmarket Square (021 481 3933/www.museums.org.za/michaelis/ index.html). **Open** 10am-5pm Mon-Sat. **Admission** free. **Map** p283 H4.

The Michealis Collection is kept in the Old Town House, which faces bustling Greenmarket Square and usually boasts a harmless, if untidy, sprawl of *bergies* (tramps) and loafers on its stairway. But that's not intended to put you off. It was built in 1755 in Cape rococo style, and the Michaelis Collection, a wealth of paintings by 17th-century Dutch and Flemish painters, donated to the city by Sir Max Michaelis in 1914, is well worth seeing. After the SA National Gallery (*see p54*) the collection is a must

for art lovers: boasting works by Frans Hals, Jan van Goyen, Jan Steen, Jacobs Ruijsdael, Rembrandt van Rijn, Anthony van Dyck and numerous others.

Pan African Market

76 Long Street (021 426 4478/www.panafrican. co.za). **Open** 9am-5pm Mon-Fri. **Admission** free. **Map** p282 G4.

As you step into the Euro-centric Art Nouveau entrance hall, you'll be struck by an African renaissance of wood-carved artworks and papier mâché creations. Continue into the building and you'll find more than 30 stalls, each selling a variety of antique and contemporary arts and artefacts. Pieces range from the finest beadwork to big and bold masks.

Roads to nowhere

So you're waiting at the traffic lights at the Coen Steytler/Buitengracht Street intersection in the centre of Cape Town, and you can't help feeling that something's not quite matching up. Then you spot them: the frayed flyovers of Cape Town's infamous unfinished 'highway to nowhere'.

International film-location scouts love them: countless foreign TV advertisements and action movies have featured car chases ending in spectacular plunges off the edge of the incomplete flyovers.

The flyovers have inspired urban legend ever since they were first (not quite) built. One theory speculates that an engineering miscalculation is to blame – geometrically, 'they' reckon, the two unfinished flyovers can't match up evenly. Another theory suggests that the owner of the café located below the last pillar of the onramp on

the Sea Point side refused to sell his land, forcing the builders to abandon the project.

The truth, sadly, is far less interesting: when the flyovers were first built in the 1960s, traffic patterns simply didn't warrant the completion of the outer viaducts, but the flyovers were still constructed in such a way that future link-ups would be a simple matter of join-the-dots… or join-the-flyovers, in this case.

You'd expect the locals to be embarrassed about the hacked-off highway. Well, they aren't. There's something tragically romantic about those flyovers that seem destined to be forever apart (not unlike a pair of star-crossed lovers). There's also a charming kitsch about them – they're like an unfinished music symphony of urban planning.

Architecture: beauty and the beast

Cape Town architecture, not surprisingly, represents the cosmopolitan heritage of the city – this bit borrowed from here, that piece nicked from there, all coming together to create a wonderfully eclectic mix. From shacks to castles, Art Deco to Bauhaus, we've got the lot. And what's more, we've got a lot of it. Since Cape Town ascended to its current status as one of the world's 'It' spots, fewer open spaces remain immune to the advances of opportunistic developers; and city officials have notoriously rubber arms when it comes to those with greasy palms. Fortunately, most of the new structures are fairly handsome beasts, and residents don't have much cause for complaint; our architecture generally complementing the city's reputation of being one of the most beautiful in the world. Local architects, such as the Stefan Antoni, Revel Fox, Derrick Hemstra and Louis Karol, might have set the pace, but there are a great many other Cape Town architects not far off their lap-time.

The City Centre itself has a strong Art Deco influence (*pictured*), though it is fair to say that all too few of the buildings are presented to their fullest advantage and would benefit from the odd lick of paint. Standing cheek-by-jowl with these older classic structures are office blocks bearing the rather distinctively function-before-form Bauhaus stamp and, which, in fairness, are no better or worse than their international counterparts, depending on your politics in that regard. Many of these establishments have recently received face-lifts as companies transfer base camp to more reasonably priced office parks and the more skywards-leaning of buildings get transformed into New York-style loft apartments. In addition to generally improving the city's face, these developments may yet prove the City Centre's salvation if they do encourage gentrification of the city like numerous developers are hoping.

If Cape Town stands somewhere between yesterday and tomorrow's games, the big explosion of the past decade has been the Atlantic Seaboard, an area running roughly from Hout Bay to the V&A Waterfront. As international money has moved into the area, so too has international styling, mostly what might be termed 'modernist Californian beach house chic'. While some locals mourn a certain loss of charm, claiming these new mega-residences tend to stamp themselves on the surroundings in a rather jack-booted fashion, there is no denying that some staggeringly impressive houses have appeared on the hill front in recent years. But then with some of the more opulent domiciles coming to the table at between 20 and 100 million Rand – hardly lunch money – one wouldn't exactly expect them to be lean-to shacks. Fans of the money-over-sense school of architecture would do well to pay a visit to Nettleton Road, situated between Camp's Bay and Sea Point along Upper Kloof Road, it is reportedly the most expensive single street in the country and the short spin down the cul-de-sac will show you why.

Rust en Vreugd

78 Buitenkant Street (021 465 3628/www.museums. org.za/rustvreugd). **Open** by appointment Mon. **Admission** free, but donations welcome. **Map** p283 H4.

With an imposing three-storey structure and a delicately carved rococo fanlight (ascribed to German sculptor Anton Anreith), Rust en Vreugd is considered the finest surviving example of an 18th-century Cape Dutch townhouse. The building houses part of the William Fehr Collection, including etchings and watercolours depicting the events, people and buildings of the early Cape. Declared a Heritage Site in 1940, Rust en Vreugd's period-styled garden was recreated from the original layout in 1986.

Sendinggestig Museum

40 Long Street (021 423 6755). **Open** 9am-4pm Mon-Fri; 9am-noon Sat. **Admission** free. **Map** p282 G4.

Cape Town's first slave church (established in 1804) boasts unique architecture and a restored pulpit, organ and furniture, and now houses displays detailing the story of missionary work in the Cape. Interesting, but not necessarily a must see.

Museum Mile

Museum Mile is the city's busiest walk. Running roughly between Wale and Orange Streets and parallel to Queen Victoria Street, it takes in the museums and churches around the Company Gardens, in the heart of the City Centre. It is generally accepted that Museum Mile runs the distance along Government Avenue between the South African Museum at the top end of the Company Gardens, past the Slave Lodge at the gardens' lower entrance to the Groote Kerk next door.

Things are a little more subdued out in the Southern Suburbs, traditionally the preserve of Old Money as opposed to the Atlantic Seaboard, which, let's call a spade a spade, is pretty much nouveau riche and therefore quite keen to provide less than subtle evidence of just how well it has done for itself. The Southern Suburbs, in particular areas like Constantia and Bishopscourt, tend to show their pedigree, and Victorian and Cape Dutch architecture rule the day here. Properties are larger and houses smaller; if Atlantic Seaboard architecture is trendy, Southern Suburbs architecture is gracious.

But this is not to say that we don't have some awe-inspiringly, must-be-seen-to-be-believed hideous architecture as well. We do. Indeed so bad are some of the buildings that the head of the Design Indaba, one of the world's premiere design events held in the city annually (*see p153*), threatened to go about issuing citations to some of the more aesthetically disenfranchised Cape Town structures. Many of the state buildings erected during the apartheid era were clearly designed by someone employing strategic use of a blindfold when at the drawing board. And, quite frankly, anything short of razing them to the ground would be pretty much akin to giving a legless man platform shoes.

To sum up local architecture, it's like a menu varied enough to suit every taste but increasingly few pockets. A bit like visiting an upmarket art gallery, one goes not to buy, but rather simply to appreciate.

While the name has a nice ring to it, Museum Mile is a complete misnomer. The **Company Gardens** (*see p53*) cover less than six hectares of the site originally laid out as a vegetable garden for the Dutch East India Company, and the so-called 'mile' is actually less than a kilometre (barely half a mile) long. And without any stops – for example, to feed the squirrels, to sit and contemplate, or to visit the South African National Gallery – this walk shouldn't take more than 15 minutes. It's a very pleasant 15 minutes, though: no cars are allowed in the Gardens, and the tall oak trees provide ample shade from the African sun. Museum Mile is also relatively safe: among the crowd of tourists, you're likely to encounter buskers, a handful of Cape Town's ubiquitous street people and more than a few lazy locals taking a leisurely break from the office.

Strolling from the mountain end of the lush Company Gardens, you'll pass the **South African Museum** (*see p54*) and **Planetarium** (*see p53*), the bold **South African National Gallery** (*see p54*), the **Houses of Parliament** (*see p53*), **St George's Cathedral** (*see p54*) and the **Cultural History Museum and Slave Lodge** (*see p53*) all within a kilometre or so.

The city's diversity – cultural, architectural and historical – can be dizzying: a few hundred metres separate Cape Town's first church (**Groote Kerk**, *see p53*), first mosque (the **Auwal**, *see p57*), first synagogue (Great Synagogue, 88 Hatfield Street/021 465 1405) and first cathedral (St George's Cathedral). This diversity makes for a cosmopolitan cultural mix: the air is filled with a sonic stew of languages from French to Swahili, German to Xhosa and English to Afrikaans.

What Londoners take when they go out.

Time Out London
EVERY WEEK

Bertram House

Corner Orange Street & Government Avenue (021 481 3940 /www.museums.org.za/bertram/index.html). **Open** by appointment Mon. **Admission** R5; R2 concessions; free under-6s. **No credit cards.** **Map** p282 G5.

This early 19th-century Georgian House is filled with treasures such as Georgian furniture, porcelain and silver, as well as a rare Clementi piano and a 200-year-old Grecian harp.

Centre for the Book

62 Queen Victoria Street (021 423 2669/ www.centreforthebook.org.za). **Open** 8.30am-4.30pm Mon-Fri. **Admission** free. **Map** p282 G4.

Located in Victoria Street next to the Company Gardens, the Centre for the Book aims to promote reading, and to make books more accessible to one and all. Visitors can browse though contemporary South African books in the central reading room, or surf the Web at the on-site Internet Café. It feels very much like a well-stocked book shop, where the books are free, browsing is encouraged and you can't take any of the volumes home with you. The building itself – a graceful, domed Edwardian edifice – was the focus of world attention a few years ago when it hosted the King Commission's enquiry into Hansie Cronjé's cricket match-fixing scandal.

Company Gardens

Upper Adderley Street/Government Avenue. **Open** daily. **Admission** free. **Map** p282 G4.

The Company Gardens are more of a thoroughfare than a sightseeing spot, but they form the green heart of Museum Mile. Bookended by St George's Cathedral and the Mount Nelson Hotel (*see p27*), the Gardens were established in 1652 by the Dutch East India Company. Government Avenue (which runs through the gardens and is closed to cars) offers the easiest – and prettiest – access to spots like the St George's Cathedral, Old Synagogue, the SA National Gallery, the SA Museum, the Planetarium and the Cultural History Museum. The gardens have been described as 'an oasis of calm in the city rush', and with the trees, the squirrels and lunch-hour love birds it's easy to forget that you're in the middle of one of South Africa's most important cities. Today, the gardens are a favourite spot for photographing newlyweds and for oxygen-starved office workers. Spots of interest include a sundial dating from 1787, a Saffren Pear Tree (believed to be South Africa's oldest cultivated tree) and a statue of mining magnate Cecil John Rhodes pointing north and proclaiming 'Your hinterland lies there'. Rhodes, by the way, is the man who, among other notable feats, imported the gardens' squirrels from North America.

Cultural History Museum & Slave Lodge

Corner of Wale & Adderley Streets (021 460 8240/ www.museums.org.za/slavelodge). **Open** 9.30am-4.30pm Mon-Sat. **Admission** R7; R2 concessions; free under-6s. **No credit cards.** **Map** p283 H4.

While this is the second-oldest colonial building in Cape Town, it is also the oldest-surviving slave lodge. Built in 1679 as a lodge for the Dutch East India Company's 600 slaves, the building (which also once served as the Supreme Court) now houses the South African Cultural History Museum. If you're a fan of fascinating facts and artefacts, you'll love this museum. Exhibitions examine aspects of Cape Town's history during the 17th and 18th centuries, as well as collections from far-flung cultures such as Ancient Greece and the Far East. And if ever you wanted to see what the world's only collection of postal stones looks like, the Cultural History Museum is the place for you.

Groote Kerk

Upper Adderley Street (021 461 7044). **Open** 10am-2pm Mon-Fri. *Services* 10am, 7pm Sun. **Admission** free. **Map** p283 H4.

The Groote Kerk (Great Church) is sadly not as 'great' as it once was: these days it's all but hidden away between corporate buildings on Adderley Street, a block down from the Cultural History Museum. The Groote Kerk (built in 1703) has had a stop-start history, as suggested by its mixed bag of architectural styles: Gothic at one end, Egyptian at the other, with a splash of Classical somewhere in between. While the Groote Kerk isn't really worth a special trip, if you're passing by you may as well pop your head through the doorway to catch a glimpse of the magnificent carved pulpit (the work of master sculptors Anton Anreith and Jan Graaff).

Houses of Parliament

Parliament Street (021 403 3683/2266/www. parliament.gov.za). **Open** *tours* 9am, 10am, 11am, noon Mon-Fri. Booking is essential. **Admission** free. Overseas visitors must show passport. **Map** p282 G4.

During the apartheid, the Houses of Parliament were divided into separate houses for whites, 'coloureds' and Indians – no house for blacks was allowed. These days, all South Africans are represented in parliament, and tourists of all colours and creeds are allowed to stroll through its halls.

Planetarium

25 Queen Victoria Street (021 481 3900/ www.museums.org.za/planetarium). **Open** 8.30am-4.30pm Mon-Fri; 10am-4pm Sat, Sun. **Admission** R20; R6-R8 concessions. **No credit cards.** **Map** p282 G4.

If your scheduled stay in the Cape doesn't set time aside for a journey into the deep, dark Karoo (*see p237*), your best chance of catching a glimpse of a clear South African night sky is at the Planetarium. Situated adjacent to the SA Museum (*see p54*), the 'theatre of stars' is one of only two planetaria in South Africa – and one of a precious few in Africa. Forty 35mm slide projectors (controlled by 12 microcomputers) are used to project an exact replica of the night sky – as seen from any location in the world – onto the Planetarium's imposing dome.

St George's Cathedral

*1 Wale Street (021 424 7360/www.stgeorges
cathedral.com).* **Open** *General* 8.30am-4.30pm Mon-
Fri. *Services* 7.15am, 1.15pm Mon, Tue, Thur, Fri;
7.15am, 10am, 1.15pm Wed; 8pm Sat; 7.15am, 10am,
1.15pm, 7pm Sun (addition of 11am last Sun of
mnth). **Admission** free. **Map** p282 G4.

The imposing structure of St George's Cathedral
(built in 1901) is located at the entrance to the
Company Gardens (across the way from the Cultural
History Museum and Slave Lodge, *see p53*).
Affectionately known as the People's Cathedral, this
was where Nobel Peace Prize winner Archbishop
Desmond Tutu was installed during the apartheid
era. The church's doors are open daily, but the 11am
Mass on the last Sunday of each month is particu-
larly well worth attending.

St George's Mall

St George's Street. **Map** p283 H3.

St George's Mall is a pedestrian walkway that runs
through the heart of the city, parallel to Long Street.
While it would only take you a few minutes to walk
from one end of the street to the other, there are loads
of distractions along the way. St George's Mall is
punctuated by performance artists – be it a Bible-
toting street preacher, a blind busker or a group of
traditional street dancers – and informal traders, ranging
from the Zambian with the woodcarving stall to the
dodgy geezer with the selection of Rolex watches
stashed in his trench coat. St George's Mall offers
easy access to spots like Greenmarket Square and
the Cape Town Tourism Centre (located one block
up on the corner of Burg and Castle streets, 021 426
4260), and security is good: mounted police clip-clop
up and down delighting the street children and shoo-
ing away dodgy characters selling fake Rolexes.
Keep an eye open for the far-out post-modernist public sculpture 'Africa' by local artist Brett Murray,
located at the Foreshore end of the mall. You can't
miss it: it's the traditional African statue with the
Bart Simpson heads sticking out of it.

South African Museum

*25 Queen Victoria Street (021 481 3800/
www.museums.org.za/sam/index.htm).* **Open** 10am-
5pm daily. **Admission** R8; free concessions. Free to
all Sun. **No credit cards**. **Map** p282 G4.

The South African Museum – which started out as
two crowded rooms above a bookseller's shop – is
the oldest museum in South Africa. And it's packed
with fascinating exhibitions. Dioramas featuring
hundreds of different birds and beasts let visitors
admire all creatures great and small: ranging from
dinosaurs to quaggas and rhinos to coelacanths. The
displays depicting the cultures of South Africa's
indigenous people are constantly either being taken
down or restored – but that inevitably comes with
the territory in politically-sensitive South Africa.
The famous Lydenburg Heads (ancient African artworks dating back to 500BC) are also on display.
The fossil gallery plots the evolution of life in the
Karoo, while the massive, 20m (65ft) long blue-whale

skeleton is the main attraction of the whale well. The
South African Museum could easily keep you occupied for a full day – and you'll probably still end up
missing more than a few exhibits.

South African National Gallery

*Government Avenue, Company Gardens (021 467
4660/www.museums.org.za/sang/index.html).*
Open 10am-5pm Tue-Sun. **Admission** R10; free
concessions. Free to all Sun. **No credit cards**.
Map p282 G4.

South Africa's premier art museum, the SA National
Gallery (SANG to its friends) is an art lover's dream
come true, housing works from all relevant schools
and periods, from both Europe and Africa, and featuring constantly changing exhibitions of paintings,
photography, sculpture, beadwork and textiles.
SANG is truly representative of South African history – with an important collection of apartheid-era
Resistance Art. It's not the sort of place you can rush
through, though: SANG should be enjoyed slowly,
and preferably on a weekday morning when you're
likely to have many of the gallery's vast spaces to
yourself.

Rest of the City Bowl

The City Centre itself has no residential area
(unless you count the backpackers' lodges or
the dozens of street people), which means that a
number of Capetonians find their homes in the
City Bowl, on the Centre's outskirts, and each
microsuburb has its own unique character.

The Bo-Kaap neighbourhood, at the foot of
Signal Hill, was previously known as the Malay
Quarter as it was populated by descendents of
17th- and 18th-century Muslim slaves. Under
the apartheid government's Group Areas Act
(which placed separate racial groups in their
own exclusive residential areas), the Bo-Kaap
was a 'coloured' area. Since the fall of apartheid,
though, the Bo-Kaap has kept its distinct
ethnicity. *See also p56* **Kaleidoscopes
and cobblestones.**

Moving anti-clockwise along the lower slopes
of the mountains, the City Bowl's crowded
central suburbs include trendy Tamboerskloof,
Gardens and Oranjezicht, which tickles the
slopes of Devil's Peak. Like the Bo-Kaap,
Tamboerskloof and Gardens are home to
several excellent restaurants (*see p97*), and the
higher you go up the slopes of the mountain
(especially in Oranjezicht), the better the views
are for sunsets over Lion's Head.

The Bo-Kaap, while the prettiest of the
residential areas, is the most dangerous to visit
at night. If you're going to a restaurant in the
outer reaches of the City Centre (or the Centre
itself, for that matter), be sure to park in a well-
lit area; alternatively, order a taxi to take you
there, and pick you up again (*see p248*).

Once a political hotspot, now a parking lot: **Grand Parade** overlooked by **City Hall**. *See p48.*

Kaleidoscopes and cobblestones

A burst of colour explodes from the lower slopes of Signal Hill (at the western end of Cape Town) in the charming neighbourhood of the **Bo-Kaap** (Upper-Cape). Too central (geographically) to be a suburb and too isolated (spiritually) to be swallowed up by the City Centre, the Bo-Kaap covers the small area from Strand Street to Dorp Street, and from Buitengracht to Signal Hill.

The historical neighbourhood is home to doctors' surgeries, bakeries, butcheries, schools and seven mosques… and, of course, the residential homes that dominate the streets. The buildings are painted in kaleidoscopic crayon colours – bright pink, purple and yellow walls stand side by side along steep, narrow, cobblestone roads, with freshly-washed laundry left out to dry on the *stoep* (front porch).

During the New Year celebrations the area is a riot of noise and colour. Most of the locals trace their history back to the slaves of the Cape Colony, and for them Tweede Nuwe Jaar (Second New Year) on 2 January is a holiday of almost sacred proportions. Historically, this was the only day the slaves were allowed off during the entire year. The banjo-playing Kaapse Klopse and Cape Minstrels dance a careful one-step-two-step

rhythm through the Bo-Kaap's cobblestone streets, while delighted onlookers look forward to another colourful year.

The shabby chic and enviable location have seen Bo-Kaap real estate attracting interest from yuppies and trendy businesses, and 'buy

Table Mountain

Cape Town's reputation as the most laid-back city in South Africa (locals adhere to 'Africa time' – the polar opposite to an amped-up 'New York Minute') could be because of Table Mountain, which is known to be one of the most spiritual places on Earth. You can't really call yourself a traveller until you've been to the top of Table Mountain. While a network of hiking trails leads to the summit, the **Table Mountain Aerial Cableway** (*see p57*) is the quickest way up. At the summit– 1,086 metres above sea level – you'll be treated to dramatic views over the whole Cape Peninsula.

Noon Gun

Military Road, Signal Hill (follow the signs from the corner of Bloem & Buitengracht Road) (021 787 1257). **Open** 8am-4pm Mon-Fri, 8am-1pm Sat. *Guns loaded* 11.30am Mon-Sat. Closed Sun. **Admission** free. **Map** p282 F3.

Don't be alarmed if you hear a loud boom echoing through the city at midday. It's not a bomb, despite the 'Don't go to Cape Town' warnings from sections

of the foreign press. It's the daily blast of the Noon Gun, one of two 18-pounder guns located at Lion Battery in the Bo-Kaap. The Noon Gun is one of Cape Town's oldest traditions, dating back to 1806, when the gun allowed passing ships to measure the accuracy of their chronometers. You can watch the gun being fired – visit the battery at about 11.30am and watch as the guns are loaded with 3.1kgs (8.3lbs) of gunpowder. Bring along a packed lunch (or visit the nearby Noon Gun restaurant), and be sure to pack a set of earplugs.

Signal Hill & Lion's Head

Follow the Signal Hill directions from the top of Kloofnek (the road that passes over the saddle between Lion's Head & Table Mountain). **Map** p281 D5.

Don't have the time to climb Table Mountain? Try its little sister, Lion's Head. A hike to the top of Lion's Head is relatively easy, and more than worth all the huffing and puffing. If you happen to be in Cape Town when there's a full moon, try walking up Lion's Head by moonlight. The contour path offers gorgeous views of Camps Bay, Clifton beach, Signal Hill and Cape Town harbour (time your climb now!' advertising agencies are creeping into the neighbourhood with surprising subtlety. But any fears of the Bo-Kaap's impending gentrification are blown away by a flip through the pages of local history. The Bo-Kaap is a tough nut to crack.

It's the birthplace of Islam in South Africa (the ancient Auwal Mosque has called the faithful to prayer since 1794; see p57) and when the Group Areas Act of 1950 named District Six a 'whites-only' area, Bo-Kaap was declared a residential zone for (exclusively, under the apartheid laws) 'Muslim Malays'. Fortunately, the area was named a National Monument before the bulldozers could swagger in, and the predominantly Muslim community has remained intact ever since.

As a result, the Bo-Kaap does have an insular feeling to it: the locals can spot an outsider from the other end of the street, and their friendliness seems tempered with a guarded sense of apprehension. Perhaps that's why it doesn't feel like the sort of area you'd want to visit on your own at night – you'd be the unwelcome intruder – but it does have an undeniable small town charm, despite being only a short stroll away from Long Street.

to coincide with one of Cape Town's irresistible Atlantic sunsets). You probably won't have the summit to yourself – some Capetonians make it a monthly ritual to climb Lion's Head and howl at the full moon. Situated next to Lion's Head is Signal Hill. Signal Hill Road, which winds its way along the eastern slopes of Lion's Head's eastern slope, past the Kramat, offers spectacular views of the city below. From the parking area at the top of the hill 350m (1,148ft) above sea level, you'll see the famous Camp's Bay and Clifton beaches, as well as Sea Point, Green Point and the V&A Waterfront.

Table Mountain Aerial Cableway

Lower cable station is situated on Tafelberg Road (021 424 5148/www.tablemountain.net). **Open** daily weather permitting; phone to check. *May-Sept* 1st cable car 8.30am; last car 5pm, returning 6pm. *Nov-Apr* 1st car 8am; last car 5.30pm, returning 10pm. **Admission** *Cable car* R55, R105 return; R28-R39 single, R55-R77 return concessions; R270 family (2 adults, 2 children); free under-4s. **Credit** AmEx, DC, MC, V.

Unless the Mother City is cloaked in an impenetrable fog, you can't help but notice Table Mountain looming over the city. And you can't call yourself a

traveller if you haven't been up the mountain. Table Mountain is believed to be the most-climbed massif in the world, and it's an absolute must for any visitor. If your time in the city is limited, take the cable car to the upper cable station. The cable car rotates as it goes up, providing a panoramic view of the city bowl and Table Bay. The upper cable station boasts a restaurant, abseiling facilities and scenic picnic spots – not that you'll notice. You'll probably be too busy admiring the view of the City Bowl, spotting the landmarks and staring out over the bay. If time and energy allow, take one of the many free hiking trails up the mountain. These vary from the relatively easy Constantia Nek and Platteklip Gorge to the tougher Kasteelspoort and Porcupine Ravine.

Bo-Kaap

Also known as the Malay Quarter, the Bo-Kaap ('Upper-Cape') is populated by the descendants of the Muslim slaves who were brought to the Cape Colony in the 17th and 18th centuries, and who have since developed a colourful dialect of Afrikaans. The streets are filled with 19th-century Dutch and Georgian terraces, which conceal a network of bad-news alleyways that are best avoided, particularly at night. The area is filled with mosques, narrow streets, cobbled lanes and picturesque houses. There's a deceptively quaint feel to the Bo-Kaap, but be warned: this really isn't the sort of area to explore on your own. A R55 two-and-a-half hour tour of the area is run by locals, part of an operation called Bo-Kaap Guided Tours (021 422 1554).

The Auwal Mosque

Dorp Street. **Map** p282 G4.
One block south of the Bo-Kaap Museum is South Africa's first official mosque, the Auwal Mosque. Founded in 1795 by Tuan Guru, legend has it that this is where Afrikaans was first taught. The Auwal is best admired from the outside; the goings on inside respected with privacy.

Bo-Kaap Museum

71 Wale Street (021 481 3939/www.museums. org.za/bokaap). **Open** 9am-4pm Mon-Sat. **Admission** R5; free-R2 concessions. **No credit cards.** **Map** p282 G3.
Fitted and furnished as a typical 19th-century Muslim home, the small Bo-Kaap Museum captures the spirit of this community within a few rooms (much like the District Six Museum does). The museum consists mainly of possessions of Abu Bakr Effendi, a 19th-century religious leader who was brought out from Turkey by the British in 1862 to act as a mediator between the city's feuding Muslim factions. The museum takes up only a few rooms in the house, but your visit – which will probably be very brief – is well worth the effort for insight into this colourful Capetonian community.

Atlantic Seaboard

Stunning views, great surfing and long afternoon sunshine.

The Cape Peninsula's Atlantic coast, that takes in Granger Bay, Green Point, Sea Point, Clifton, Camps Bay and Llandudno, has some of the most spectacular coastal scenery in the world, as well as Cape Town's trendiest beaches, where the emphasis is on strutting and sunbathing. The beaches are mostly popular because they are protected from the south-eastern wind, and soak up more hours of afternoon sunshine than the False Bay coast.

But, on the other hand, the water comes straight from icy Antarctica, and even on a sweltering summer's day, the waves are somewhere on the cold side of freezing.

Swimming, while possible, doesn't remain pleasant for too long – quick, bracing plunges are probably the best approach. Not everybody bothers with the water. You can work on your tan, admire the bronzed bodies, and when the heat gets too unbearable, head to one of the street-side, beach-side bistros for a refreshing drink, or just spend a few hours wandering around the shopping malls.

The **V&A Waterfront** (see below) – Cape Town's biggest seaside attraction, next to the beaches of course – nestles in the old Table Bay dockyards, just around the corner from the Atlantic beaches. From the Waterfront, Beach Road takes you south around the rocky coastline of Mouille Point and Sea Point, before reaching the expensive neighbourhoods of Bantry Bay and Clifton, and the gorgeous Clifton and Camps Bay beaches.

If the weather turns nasty or the water is too cold, pack away the beach towels and head for the shelter of the Waterfront's shops and restaurants. The Waterfront stays open until the late evening (generally 9pm), so it's easy to fit the shops and the beaches into a busy schedule. Spend your days – especially the sunny ones – baking on the beaches, and leave the power-shopping until after sunset.

From the V&A Waterfront, pass under the picture picture-perfect Mouille Point lighthouse, and you'll get to **Green Point** stadium (see p60), and its excellent flea market, held in the parking lot every Sunday – expect to see bargains, knock-offs, treasures and trash. The next stop south is **Sea Point** (see p61), which has only one or two small sandy coves, but several good restaurants and – for those who're looking – more than a few ladies of the night.

For another beach beauty, try Bantry Bay with its million-dollar real estate and exquisite sea views, before you get to the Atlantic Seaboard's busiest beach, **Clifton Fourth** (strangely, there are four beaches in a row alongside Camps Bay – and they're all named Clifton; see p61). Here beautiful, non-swimming people indulge in volleyball, Frisbee or simply sunbathing. Clifton has something of a Riviera flavour: yachts, speedboats and jet-skis play in the bay, while palm trees sway beside the long, white stretches of sand.

With Table Mountain's spectacular Twelve Apostles range providing the backdrop and with soft, white sand baking beneath your feet, **Camps Bay** (see p62) is one of the most beautiful beaches in the world. It also happens to be only 15 minutes away from Cape Town's City Centre, making it – and neighbouring Clifton – extremely popular.

There are more beaches further away from the City Centre, both south and north. Among the better ones are the exclusive **Llandudno** (see p62), nudist **Sandy Bay** (see p63), family-friendly **Hout Bay** (see p63) and the surfing spot **Noordhoek** (see p63) to the south; and **Bloubergstrand** (see p63) and **Milnerton** (see p63), with their stunning views, to the north. To the west is the historic **Robben Island** (see p59), situated only 11km (6.8 miles) from Cape Town in the middle of Table Bay's shark-infested waters.

V&A Waterfront

According to some estimates, the V&A Waterfront (021 408 7600/www.waterfront.co.za) attracts up to 12 million visitors every year. Yet somehow it has avoided becoming a tourist trap. Sure, it's fair to say that the V&A Waterfront complex is geared towards tourists (the main entrance is cluttered with bureaux de change), but the shops are also swarming with locals, dashing in after work to pick up groceries or a fast-food takeaway.

Commercially, the Waterfront couldn't be more diverse: shopping outlets range from international fashion boutiques (with international fashion price tags) and sparkling jewellery stores to small craft stalls and curiosity kiosks. The restaurants are just as varied: you could grab a bite at one of the dockside fast-food joints, enjoy a pint at one of the many bars (best to be avoided when there's a major – or minor for that matter – sports match on the TV) or indulge in a five-course meal at one of the Waterfront's five-star restaurants. For more on the area's eating options, *see p106*.

But despite all the pedestrian activity, the V&A Waterfront is still a fully functional harbour (it was named after the Victoria and Alfred basins). While you stroll along the quayside you can watch fishing boats departing for Table Bay and pleasure cruises floating away to nowhere in particular, or hop on board the Robben Island ferry as it departs for Table Bay's former penal colony. The Waterfront's Nelson Mandela Gateway, located at the old Clock Tower, is the point of departure for ferry trips to Robben Island, where the former President, Nelson Mandela, and other anti-apartheid activists were imprisoned (Mandela for some 18 years). It was used as a prison from the early settler days right up until the first years of majority rule in the mid 1990s. The island is now a museum and World Heritage Site, and regular tours on a super-fast catamaran depart from the V&A Waterfront. But if you're not in the mood for power shopping or political history, the Waterfront offers several other attractions, including the fascinating Two Oceans Aquarium and the kids' paradise of the Scratch Patch.

IMAX

BMW Pavilion, corner of Beach & Portswood Roads (021 419 7365/www.imax.co.za). **Open** daily; check website for show times. **Admission** R35; R25 concessions. **Credit** AmEx, DC, MC, V. **Map** p282 G1.

The IMAX has the magical ability to turn a 45-minute nature film into a full-throttle, ear-straining, eye-bulging audiovisual extravaganza. The cinema's five-storey-high screen, 15,000-watt speakers and six-channel wrap-around sound system create a larger-than-life movie-going experience: anybody with an hour to kill and/or a passing interest in television or the movies should give it a try, no matter what's showing.

Robben Island Museum

Ferries depart from Nelson Mandela Gateway (021 409 5100/021 413 4200/www.robben-island.org.za). **Departure** 9am, 10am, noon, 1pm, 2pm, 3pm; weather permitting. **Admission** R150; R75 concessions; free under-4s. **Credit** AmEx, DC, MC, V. **Map** p283 H1.

Since Nelson Mandela's release from jail and the subsequent birth of democracy in South Africa, a trip to Robben Island has become an essential pilgrimage for visitors to (and citizens of) South Africa. Mandela spent the bulk of his political imprisonment locked up in Robben Island's infamous Maximum

Two Oceans Aquarium. *See p60.*

Security Prison – Cape Town's Alcatraz, just with greater socio-political significance. Once the symbol of political oppression, the former penal colony has since been transformed into a symbol of reconciliation. Ferry tours to the island depart from the V&A Waterfront's Nelson Mandela Gateway. The three-and-a-half hour tour includes a return trip across Table Bay, a tour of the Maximum Security Prison, interaction with a former political prisoner and a guided bus tour of the island. If you can fit it into your schedule and budget, this is a trip you must do. *See also p14* **SA in an island**.

Promenade kings and queens: **V&A Waterfront**. *See p58*.

Scratch Patch

Dock Road (021 419 9429). **Open** 9am-6pm daily.
Admission free. **Map** p283 H2.

The Scratch Patch gives you an opportunity to discover South Africa's fascinating mineral wealth – and then take some of it home with you. You could either spend hours choosing your own semi-precious stones in the Scratch Patch, or pick one of the shiny rocks (ranging from unusual stones to expensive gems) off the shelf in Mineral World. Kids and teens can mess about on the Cave Golf putt-putt course, while ma and pa are left wondering how they're going to pay for the journey home. Note that you have to pay for the Cave Golf, and if you take stones from the Scratch Patch.

South African Maritime Museum

Dock Road (021 405 2880/ www.museums.org.za/ maritime/index.html). **Open** 10am-4.45pm daily.
Admission (incl visit to SAS Somerset) R10; free-R2 concessions; R20 family (2 adults with children).
No credit cards. **Map** p283 H2.

The South African Maritime Museum examines the role shipping has played in Cape Town's history and the effect of the ocean on the city's people. The museum houses the biggest collection of model ships in the country, a ship-modelling workshop and an interactive Kiddies Discovery Cove; it is also home to the retired Naval Boom Vessel, the SAS Somerset (which also happens to be the only boom defence vessel in the world).

Telkom Exploratorium

Union Castle House (021 419 5957/ www.exploratorium.co.za). **Open** 9am-5pm Mon-Sat.
Admission R10; R5 concessions. **No credit cards**.
Map p283 H1.

The Telkom Exploratorium is a bells-and-whistles collection of interactive exhibits, providing hours of fun and games. The hands-on displays include a simulated Grand Prix racing car; a stomach-churning gyroscope; virtual reality; a piano, which is played by jumping from note to note (think Tom Hanks in *Big*); and the hair-raising (literally) Van der Graaf's generator, which has tickles of static electricity to rearrange your hairdo.

Two Oceans Aquarium

Dock Road (021 418 3823/www.aquarium.co.za).
Open 9.30am-6pm daily. **Admission** R55; free-R45 concessions. **Credit** AmEx, DC, MC, V. **Map** p283 H2.

The Two Oceans Aquarium is home to more than 3,000 living creatures – from sharks and short-tailed stingrays to turtles and African penguins. Whether you're a marine biologist or just somebody who once watched *Jaws*, the Aquarium is a must-see. Music concerts, shark feeding and kids' sleepovers are just some of the diverse attractions of this spectacular underwater nature reserve.

Green Point

Green Point Market

Parking lot, Green Point Stadium. **Open** 8.30am-6pm Sun; weather permitting. **Map** p282 F1.

Green Point's Sunday-morning flea market is a bit of a mixed bag. Stalls selling valuable antiques and African artworks stand alongside traders trying to flog useless kitchen utensils or bootleg CDs. There are some excellent bargains to be found – just be prepared to search, and keep a discerning eye: many a foreign traveller has been horrified to learn that the 'unique and original African artwork' they bought at Green Point was actually mass-produced in a factory outside Durban. Larger in scale than the Milnerton market on the opposite side of Table Bay, and more of a sprawl than the bustling Greenmarket Square, Green Point Market is a useful spot for picking up last-minute souvenirs.

Sea Point

Sea Point Promenade

Beach Road, Sea Point. **Map** p281 C2.
Take a 6km (3.7-mile) round trip on Sea Point's beachfront promenade to the Sea Point Public Pool (021 434 3341, open 7am-6pm daily). This is the perfect sunset location for fleeting meetings of strollers, pram-pushers and dog-walkers; rollerbladers and ice-cream eaters.

Clifton First, Second, Third & Fourth

Map p281 B5.
Clifton's four beaches (named, unsurprisingly, First, Second, Third and Fourth) attract beautiful folk from all over the world. The fairly wind-sheltered beaches – separated by huge granite boulders – differ slightly in tone. First Beach is the most secluded – it's sheltered by the wind and is usually the least crowded. Second and Third Beaches are laid-back and friendly (all baggy shorts and scruffy surfers), while Fourth Beach is trendy and often a bit crowded. If you're even slightly self-conscious, give Fourth Beach a miss: this is where

Sightseeing

Township tourism

'Upon entering the informal settlement, I saw the shacks and poverty; I wondered what I, as a 20-something black South African, was doing here. How weird it was that along with my white companions, I was paying someone for the privilege of exploring townships in a minibus with a guide named Basil from **Grassroutes Tours** (021 706 1006/ 082 951 1016).

'I'd been indecisive for some time about the potential insensitivity of these townships tours. The idea of peeking at impoverished people's lives for leisure purposes didn't seem kosher. However, this dilemma was resolved as soon as I realised how much insight the tour was offering into these sidelined communities, as well as into their significant political history.

'The tour began in District Six, which is the cradle of Cape Town's coloured and African population before these dusty remote townships became their homes.

'It's impossible not to like these vibrant townships with their thriving pavement markets where you can get your hair cut, your shoes polished and shined, purchase fresh fruit and meat and even get custom-tailored traditional outfits while you wait.

'The warm communal ambience is known as ubuntu (meaning 'togetherness'), in which the residents heartily welcome visitors, introducing them to the Mzansi ('South African') township way of life. It's also here where you meet strong women like Rosie who pilot developmental initiatives such as soup kitchens and homes for HIV/AIDS victims. The result: a tenacious, at-ease and vibrant, unified, welcoming community.

'Whatever reservations you might have held about the tour before, they are swept away with a deeper insight into, and appreciation of, the people who live in these informal settlements. As a visitor to South Africa you need this eye-opener. You simply can't visit Cape Town and not experience the heart-warming, communal love and the cultural vibrancy that's abundant in our townships.' *Vuyokazi Matshikiza*. For more information go to www.grassroutetours.co.za.

Picture perfect

All self-respecting South Africa holiday albums need a snap of Table Mountain. **Milnerton** beach (*see p63*) is the ideal vantage point. Drive along Otto Du Plessis Road and at the traffic intersection, turn left and over the bridge that leads to the lighthouse. Take your shoes off, feel the sand and walk knee-high in the icy Atlantic waters towards the mountain.

swimsuit models peer through their designer sunglasses at the Speedo-wearing poseurs while they work on their already-perfect tan. The beaches themselves are undeniably beautiful (even more so than the beachgoers), but the waters are usually pretty empty. This side of the Cape Town coastline is tickled by notoriously chilly waters: it gets its water supply from Antarctica, express-delivered by the icy Benguela Current. Finding parking at Clifton is almost impossible in season – you'll have to find a spot somewhere in the residential roads, and wind your way down the hill to the steps that lead down to the beaches.

Camps Bay

Map p284 B8.

Camps Bay, set against the spectacular Twelve Apostles mountain range, is the heart of the 'Cape Riviera'. As trendy as (but friendlier than) Fourth beach, Camps Bay has a long, golden, palm-lined beach, with a promenade boasting some of the city's hottest restaurants. The beach is easily accessible – Victoria Road (the M6)

passes right alongside its golden sands – and the crowd are a friendly bunch. Camps Bay is popular among families: its tidal pool, beachfront restaurants, ice-cream stalls and *braai* ('barbecue') area are reason enough to hang around for a few sun-soaked hours.

Southern suburbs

Llandudno

A few kilometres south of Camps Bay down scenic Victoria Road, Llandudno beach is tucked away in an exclusive and expensive seaside suburb. Nestled between steep dunes and a shady forest, this secluded beach is known for its laid-back atmosphere. Parking at Llandudno can be a problem on busy weekends, and apart from the forest there's not much protection from the wind, but this is why it is also a popular spot for Hobie Cat sailors, which dart backwards and forwards in the waves. The beach is an ideal chill-out spot for sitting and watching the incredible sunsets over the Atlantic Ocean.

Sandy Bay

Sandy Bay is South Africa's only nudist beach – and it's also one of Cape Town's most scenic. A (predictably) sandy, 20-minute stroll from Llandudno, Sandy Bay has developed a reputation for having a seedy side. Naked beachgoers plus secluded beach plus inspiring sunsets equals... you do the maths. Sandy Bay is sadly not the hotspot it once was – most of the visitors these days are dog-walkers or surfers – but if you do want to take your clothes off while you dip your toes (and your other bits) in the cool Atlantic, this is the place to do it.

Hout Bay

With only three access roads into town (an occupational hazard if you're fortunate enough to be a resident), Hout Bay is considered to be separate from the rest of the peninsula. So much so that, according to local legend, one independent-spirited resident once travelled the world (successfully) with a fake 'Republic of Hout Bay' passport. Located on the western side of the Peninsula, Hout Bay is dominated by the imposing Sentinel on one side and by the scenic Chapman's Peak Drive on the other. In the early days Hout Bay was a natural paradise where animals roamed free – now the wildlife is limited to the bronze leopard that watches over the bay from Leopard Rock. Hout Bay has a safe, family-friendly bathing beach (unlike Sandy Bay, the nude beach around the corner in Llandudno) and the bustling Mariner's Wharf. Built around the hull of a 1940s trawler, Mariner's Wharf boasts bistros, fresh-fish markets and a harbour-front emporium. The marina harbours a fleet of private boats and yachts, while the harbour serves as the departure point for diving expeditions, trips to the huge seal colony at Duiker Island and sunset cruises around the Atlantic Seaboard to the V&A Waterfront. For more information contact Hout Bay Tourism (021 790 1264).

Mariner's Wharf

Hout Bay Harbour (021 790 1100/ www.marinerswharf.com). **Open** 9am-5pm daily. **Admission** free.
Mariner's Wharf is a lovely place to spend an afternoon. You can eat, drink, shop and even do some sightseeing. Not difficult with an array of little shops and eateries, including the museum-like Wharfside Grill Restaurant, a pearl factory and a fish market.

World of Birds

Valley Road (021 790 2730/www.world ofbirds.org.za). **Open** 9am-5pm daily. **Admission** R40; R28-R30 concessions. **Credit** AmEx, DC, MC, V.

One of Hout Bay's top attractions is the World of Birds. The largest bird park in Africa, its aviaries offer sanctuary to nearly 4,000 indigenous and exotic birds of 350 different species. Visitors stroll through tropically landscaped walk-through enclosures, getting up-close and personal with their feathered friends or dodging the flying squirrel monkeys. The World of Birds is interesting enough to justify the round-the-mountain trip to Hout Bay.

Noordhoek

This wild expanse of almost-deserted beach offers a stretch of 6km (3.7 miles) of pristine sand and dunes to walk and ride horses on. It's also a popular surf spot.

Northern suburbs

Bloubergstrand

Bloubergstrand is a must-see, especially in the evenings. The beaches that stretch along Blouberg offer superlative views of Table Mountain, with Cape Town and Table Bay visible in the foreground. The beach itself is family-oriented, with kite-flyers and – increasingly – kite-surfers taking advantage of the winds. The beach is also easily accessible from the R27 beach road, making it a perfect spot for off-loading your jet-ski.

Milnerton

Cape Town's northern Atlantic seafront starts with the deep industria of Paarden Eiland (reclaimed land from the Salt River delta), before hitting the pretty beach at Milnerton. About ten minutes north of Paarden Eiland along Marine Drive you'll find the Milnerton Flea Market (083 275 9872), a weekly car boot sale where 200 stallholders peddle household items and other suburban treasures.

Milnerton – the oldest of the suburbs along this northern part of Table Bay – is a solely residential area. Its 15-kilometre beach is extremely popular for surfing, sunbathing and quiet walks, and the view from the beach is famous for its picture-postcard views of Table Mountain, the city and Table Bay. The beach can be very windy (it's a popular kite-flying spot, with kite hire stalls often available), though, so you may want to head instead for the bird reserve at the protected Milnerton lagoon. Tucked in between the lagoon and the beach is the Milnerton lighthouse and the popular and fairly challenging (because of the high winds) 18-hole, par 72 Milnerton Golf course (Bridge Road, Milnerton, 021 522 1047/ www.milnertongolfclub.co.za).

Sightseeing

Southern Suburbs

Wines, gardens, forests... and beer.

Plain (flour) sailing: **Mostert's Mill** *See p67.*

With all the attractions of Table Mountain, the V&A Waterfront, the City Bowl and the sun-kissed Atlantic beaches, few visitors ever make it out into Cape Town's quieter Southern Suburbs, except perhaps to pop into the Kirstenbosch Botanical Gardens or to admire the view from Rhodes Memorial. However, there is plenty of entertainment in southern suburbia, from quaffing the fine wines of Groot Constantia to knocking back a free beer on the SAB's brewery tour.

But the big attraction is **Kirstenbosch Botanical Gardens** (*see p65*), which count among the most beautiful in the world. About 9,000 of southern Africa's 22,000 flora species grow here – particularly the low-lying, scratchy fynbos of the Cape Floral Kingdom. The 36-hectare (0.13-square mile) landscaped section merges seamlessly with the 492 hectares (1.9 square miles) of fynbos cloaking the mountain slopes. The forests in the surrounding area are beautiful, and Newlands and Cecilia forests and the Tokai arboretum all boast wonderful walks and quiet forest pools.

South of Kirstenbosch is **Constantia** (*see p65*), South Africa's oldest and most venerable wine-growing region. It is also one of Cape Town's most upmarket (rich and white) suburbs. **Groot Constantia** (*see p66*) is the grandest estate in the area, but if time – and

sobriety – allow, the Buitenverwachting, Klein Constantia and Steenberg estates are also worthwhile stops on the Constantia wine route.

But besides the obvious attractions of Constantia and the Kirstenbosch gardens, there are more than a few hidden treasures in these expensive residential suburbs, which cling to the eastern slopes of Table Mountain, south of the bulk of Devil's Peak.

The first main stop leading south from the city is the offbeat suburb of **Observatory** (*see p67*). Obs – as it's known affectionately to its inhabitants – buzzes with unpretentious bohemian hipness, and while it's a superb place to spend a rowdy evening, it doesn't offer much to the casual, camera-bearing tourist.

Studenty **Rondebosch** (*see p68*) boasts the Baxter Theatre, a '70s architectural gem, renowned for its refreshing programme of contemporary playwrights. Further south, Wynberg's Maynardville Park is home to the open-air theatre (*see p65*), most famous for its annual summer run of a famous Shakespeare play. Be warned, though: shows at Maynardville take place under the stars, and the artistic temperament of Cape Town's summertime means you could get a chilly *Midsummer Night's Dream* or a balmy *The Winter's Tale*.

On the southern slopes of Table Mountain, the leafy suburb of **Newlands** (*see p69*) is famous for its sports stadia: Newlands Cricket Ground and Newlands Rugby Stadium. In between them is South African Brewery, which is as much a part of local games as actually sampling the good stuff while you're watching the big game. Believe it or not, alcohol is served at live matches at both grounds.

One train stop south of Newlands is **Claremont** (*see p70*), but – obeying the global rule of sprawling suburbia – the boundaries of Cape Town's Southern Suburbs appear to segue seamlessly into one another. It's hard to tell where, say, Newlands ends and Claremont begins, especially with local residents staking claim to neighbouring suburbs in their quest for the most prestigious address. Newlands Cricket Ground, for example, is only a railway bridge away from Claremont's upmarket Cavendish Square shopping mall (*see p70*), where street traders crowd the pavements outside and ritzy boutiques glitter inside. Claremont's rather young population dominates the nightlife.

Further down Main Road, the Southern Suburbs dissolve into the 'deep south' and the Wynberg, Diep River and Plumstead suburbs, with fun junk shops lining the road. But there is a great opportunity for a nature-oriented day out – and the chance to see hippos – at the Rondevlei Nature Reserve, near **Zeekoevlei** (*see p70*), towards the coast of False Bay.

Constantia & surrounds

Kirstenbosch Botanical Gardens

Kirstenbosch, Rhodes Drive (021 799 8800/ www.nbi.ac.za). **Open** *Apr-Aug* 8am-6pm daily. *Oct-Mar* 8am-7pm daily. **Admission** R20; R5-R10 concessions. **Credit** AmEx, DC, MC, V.

Covering five square kilometres (two square miles) with more than 8,500 indigenous plant species, Kirstenbosch is one of the Seven Magnificent Botanical Gardens of the World. Established in 1913, it's most famous for its proteas (best in winter and spring) and Sunday summer sunset concerts and picnics. The theme gardens include a Braille Trail and Fragrance Garden, a Useful Plants Garden, a Restio Garden (textured reeds) and a Waterwise Garden. The grounds also house the Botanical Society Conservatory of desert plants, with a towering baobab presiding over the succulents. Most of the property is actually uncultivated and there are hiking trails through the fynbos and into Skeleton Gorge, which leads up the back of Table Mountain. It's an ornithologist's delight, with a wealth of bird species that regularly gate-crash picnics. If you're lucky you might even spot a little mongoose or a Cape fox. There are various walks and guided tours available, including twilight nature walks. There is also a restaurant, outdoor stone sculptures and a tea room. Events include orchid shows, rose shows, a regular craft market and indoor concerts in winter. To appreciate it in full glory, visit in early spring (Aug-Sept) when all the flowers are out.

Maynardville

Corner Church & Wolfe Streets, Wineberg (021 421 7695). **Open** *Dec-Feb* for Shakespeare; 4 days in Feb for Community Chest Carnival, phone for details. **Admission** prices vary. **Credit** AmEx, DC, MC, V.

Maynardville is best known for hosting Shakespeare under the stars, usually with a contemporary twist, whether it's gymnastic equipment for *Romeo and Juliet* or hot rods and rap for *The Two Gentlemen of Verona*. It's not for purists, but it's certainly popularised the Bard to the extent that it's now celebrating its 48th anniversary. It's a popular highlight of summer and people flock to the open-air theatre with picnic baskets and blankets in hand. The theatre is also used during the Cape Town festival for special events like the bizarrely wonderful performing contraptions of Odd Enjinears. Also in February, the Community Chest Carnival in the Maynardville grounds has food and drink stalls, music, climbing walls and carnival rides to raise money for charity.

Pollsmoor Correctional Services Restaurant & Driving Range

Steenberg Road, Tokai Restaurant, Tokai (021 700 1270/driving range 021 700 1128). **Open** *Restaurant* 9am-10am, noon-2pm Mon, Tue, Thur, Sat, Sun; 9am-10am, noon-2pm 6-9pm Wed, Fri. *Driving Range* summer 8am-6pm daily; winter 8am-5pm daily. **Rate** R13/50 balls. **No credit cards**.

The Pollsmoor prison inmates serving at the restaurant and running the driving range are all non-violent economic offenders (fraud, theft, burglary) almost at the end of their sentences, who are learning skills and business sense as part of the prison's rehabilitation programme. It's not a theme park, so don't expect a mess hall. Rather the restaurant is

Josephine's Mill.
See p69.

Sightseeing

unfussy à la carte, with a fully licensed bar, serving up steaks and burgers for very reasonable prices. The driving range is extremely popular with locals.

Tokai Arboretum & Manor House

Tokai Road, Tokai (Arboretum 021 712 7471/ Tea garden 021 715 4512). **Open** *Arboretum* 7am-5pm daily. *Tea garden* 9am-5pm Tue-Sun. **No credit cards**.

The arboretum was started as an experimental plantation by Joseph Lister in 1885, planting 43 exotic species from places such as Mexico and Australia to see which would flourish. While the National Park's Board is intent on uprooting exotics, the arboretum has been preserved as a National Heritage Site. There are walking and mountain-biking trails and it's worth taking the stiff hike up to the Elephant's Eye cave (two and a half hours uphill) for the view. The tea garden, in a rustic stone cottage, has a fireplace, Sunday roasts and cheap and simple eats. The historic manor house at the entrance to the arboretum is reputedly haunted by a boy on horseback, who clomps up the staircase at night. Ghoulish curiosities will be disappointed to learn that the manor is closed to visitors.

Wine estates

The Winelands of Constantia are the oldest in the Cape. Their fruits were held in high regard by such figures as Napoleon, Charles Dickens and even Jane Austen. They're conveniently close to Cape Town (less than 30 minutes' drive), so if you're pressed for time and aren't going to make it to the Winelands further afield, Constantia is a must. The estates are all gorgeously scenic with vineyards unfolding around them, lovely Cape Dutch architecture and Constantiaberg in the background. Buitenverwachting and Uitsig even have sea views. The estates all have gourmet restaurants and some offer excellent picnic facilities, too.

Buitenverwachting

Klein Constantia Road, Constantia (021 794 5190/ www.buitenverwachting.co.za). **Open** 9am-5pm Mon-Fri; 9am-1pm Sat. **Tastings** free.
Set on the Constantiaberg slopes, Buitenverwachting ('beyond expectation') is a beautiful and very laidback estate famous for picnics on the lawn beneath the oak trees (R85 per person, not including wine). At the end of a road that rambles past quiet paddocks with grazing horses and sheep is the manor house and the estate's acclaimed restaurant, with a glass wall that overlooks the vineyards up the mountainside. There is a seasonal café in the summer months, Café Petite (021 794 3522).

Constantia Uitsig

Spaanschemat River Road, Constantia (021 794 6500/www.uitsig.co.za). **Open** 9am-4.30pm Mon-Fri; 10am-3.30pm Sat, Sun. **Tastings** *Informal* free. *Formal* R40/8 wines. **Credit** AmEx, DC, MC, V.

'Uitsig' means 'view', in keeping with the vistas overlooking the valley and vineyards all the way to the ocean. The farm has been producing wine for only five years or so, but has already scooped awards both locally and internationally. Constantia Uitsig has three superb restaurants serving inventive fare and the Spaanschemat River Café (021 794 3010) is a favourite for brunches. Wine-tastings happen at the Wine Shop (021 794 1810) at the entrance to the estate. There is also a very exclusive country-style hotel in the grounds.

Groot Constantia

Groot Constantia Road, Constantia (021 794 5128/ www.grootconstantia.co.za). **Open** 10am-5pm daily. **Tastings** R20/5 wines. **Credit** AmEx, DC, MC, V.
Founded in 1685 by then Cape Governor Simon van der Stel, Groot Constantia is the oldest wine estate in South Africa. Famously, Napoleon Bonaparte asked for a glass of Constantia wine on his deathbed. The estate is now best known for its reds and busloads of visitors, who flock here from all over the globe to taste the wines and explore the historic grounds. Of particular interest is the Manor House Cultural History Museum (R8) and the wine museum in the original Cloete Cellar. The cosy Jonkershuis Restaurant (021 794 6125) serves classic upmarket Cape cuisine; its waiters are dressed in slightly preposterous historical garb. The Tavern has much simpler fare on offer. To have a meal in wonderful tranquillity, you can also order picnic baskets from the restaurant and meander up through the grounds to the various picturesque viewpoints that overlook the estate and the vineyards.

Klein Constantia Estate

Klein Constantia Road, Constantia (021 794 5188/ www.kleinconstantia.com). **Open** 9am-4.30pm Mon-Fri; 9am-1pm Sat. **Tastings** R20/6 wines; free for groups of 6 or less. **Credit** AmEx, DC, MC, V.
Once part of the original Constantia farm, Klein Constantia is now a family-owned farm, with historic Cape Dutch buildings tucked in between the trees. This estate is somewhat less commercial than its big sister, and is focused more on being a working winery than a tourist attraction. It's also very much ecologically committed (for example, the pest-control scheme includes encouraging Russian Steppe Buzzards to chase away smaller grape-devouring birds). Klein Constantia specialises in the off-dry Vin de Constance, which is a recreation of the legendary Constantia wine.

Steenberg Vineyards

Steenberg Estate, Steenberg Road, Tokai (021 713 2211/www.steenberg-vineyards.co.za). **Open** 9am-4.30pm Mon-Fri; 9am-1.30pm Sat. **Tastings** free/ 5-12 wines (big groups pay R5/person). *Tours* R20 by appointment only. **Credit** AmEx, DC, MC, V.
Founded in 1682, Steenberg is the oldest farm in Constantia, granted to Catharina Ras for whom the wine and the estate's restaurant is named. However, the farm only started producing wines in 1695. The

King of hearts

In early December 1967, medical history was made in Cape Town's Groote Schuur hospital. A 30-man surgical team led by Professor Christiaan Barnard transferred the heart of a 25-year-old motor-accident victim into the body of Louis Washansky, a South African grocer who would almost certainly have died without the transplant. It was the first human-to-human heart transplant, and although Washansky died of a lung infection within a month of the operation, the transplant was seen as a significant medical advance. But while the medical world hailed the operation as a major breakthrough, Barnard didn't see

any reason to fuss – to him, the operation was simply a natural step forward: 'I didn't even inform the hospital superintendent what we were doing,' he shrugged later. Barnard's medical accomplishment (combined with his natural good looks and charm) won the attention of the world's celebrities, and the 'film-star surgeon' soon became a global jet-setter, hanging out with movie stars, celebrity royals and even the Pope. Sadly, the king of hearts saw three marriages end in failure before his death in Cyprus in 2001. To visit, *see below* **Transplant Museum & Groote Schuur Hospital.**

farmstead, with its gorgeous gabled Cape Dutch manor house, is a National Monument. The style of the estate leans towards the sleekly upmarket with a gourmet restaurant, a country hotel and a golf estate adjoining the property.

Observatory

Mostert's Mill

Rhodes Avenue, Mowbray (Friends of Mostert's Mill 021 762 5127). **Open** by appointment. **Admission** R5. **No credit cards**.
A left-over relic from Cape Town's agricultural days, this fully restored Dutch windmill anomalously perched on the edge of the highway can be visited by appointment with the Friends of Mostert's Mill, who are qualified tour guides.

Transplant Museum & Groote Schuur Hospital

F Floor, Groote Schuur Hospital, Old Main Building, Main Road, Mowbray (021 404 5232/www.gsh. co.za). **Open** 9am-1.45pm Mon-Fri. **Admission** R5. **No credit cards**.
Commemorating the world's very first heart transplant operation by Dr Christiaan Barnard in 1967, the Transplant Museum recreates the scene with models in the very theatre where the pioneering surgery was performed. There are also recreations of the scrub room and of the patient, Mr Louis Washkansky, lying in ICU. Unfortunately, he died 18 days after the procedure, but his heart is still on display in the museum. Tours of the new hospital building (with its looming Arkhum Asylum-style façade) can be arranged by appointment.

Steps to knowledge at the **University of Cape Town.** *See p69.*

Rondebosch

Baxter Theatre Centre

Main Road (021 685 7880/www.baxter.co.za).
Admission prices vary. **Credit** AmEx, DC, MC, V.
The Baxter opened in 1977. At that time it was one of the country's few theatres open to all South Africans. It became known for its contemporary programme of local and international pieces and especially protest theatre. It wasn't afraid to court controversy, either, back in the apartheid days, featuring plays such as *Miss Julie,* which featured a contentious kiss between black actor John Kani and his white co-star, Sandra Prinsloo. Today the theatre's line-up includes interesting contemporary work by the likes of Brett Bailey as well as more audience-pleasing fare. It's also a great example of '70s architecture, designed by Jack Barnett to be an open space of brick and glass; retro-cool orange-and-yellow domes are scattered about on the ceiling.

Groote Schuur Estate

Groote Schuur Estate, Klipper Road (021 686 9100/083 302 5557). **Tours** by appointment. **Admission** R50. **No credit cards.**

By appointment, visitors can have a snoop at the Groote Schuur Estate's private collection of valuables. These include Cape Dutch and Batavian furniture, porcelains, silverware, books, paintings and tapestries among other items previously belonging to the notorious mining magnate Cecil John Rhodes. The house was due to re-open after closure for renovation purposes in March 2004.

Irma Stern Museum

Cecil Road, Rosebank (021 685 5686/www.irmastern.co.za). **Open** 10am-5pm Tue-Sat.
Admission R8; R4 concessions. **No credit cards.**
One of South Africa's great painters, Irma Stern (1894-1966) filled her house with not only her own works (in the German Expressionist style) but also a fine collection of artefacts from Africa, Asia, Greece, Columbia and Europe, which she gathered on her extensive travels. The painted cupboards, door panels and window panes are particularly eye-catching. Irma was known to be quite the entertainer and would no doubt have approved of her house being turned into a warm and intimate museum that regularly hosts contemporary exhibitions, poetry readings, concerts and book launches.

Rhodes Memorial

Groote Schuur Estate (restaurant 021 689 9151). **Open** 9am-6pm daily.

Cecil John Rhodes arrived in Cape Town in 1870 as a skinny, tubercular 17-year-old with barely a penny to his name. By the time of his death in 1902, he had made a fortune in diamond mining, helped set up De Beers Consolidated Mines, served as Prime Minister of the Cape, been involved in a botched coup attempt in the Transvaal Republic and brought almost a million square miles of African soil under British domination. And while he didn't see the realisation of his dream (building a railway line from Cape Town to Cairo), he did have a country – Rhodesia (now Zimbabwe) – named after him. Rhodes Memorial, the classical Doric temple with its bronze lions and equestrian 'Statue of Physical Energy' was built to commemorate Rhodes, who bequeathed this land to the city. The view of the city is spectacular. There are wonderful walks in the area and deer can be spotted wandering about. The restaurant is cosy and popular, with great views of the city, although the prices are inflated. On the grounds below the memorial, you can spot zebra, wildebeest, deer and the occasional model posing for a photo shoot against the convincingly bushveld-like background.

University of Cape Town

Slopes of Devil's Peak, Rondebosch (021 650 3748/ www.uct.ac.ca). **Tours** by appointment.

Once the seething heart of the struggle against apartheid, the university still has heated debates, but they are now likely to be more along the lines of whether Johannesburg or Cape Town is the cooler city. Hot topics in the cafeteria aside, the university is a distinguished and accomplished faculty. Founded in 1829, it was the first university in South Africa, although the campus under the Rhodes Memorial was built only 100 years later when Cecil John Rhodes bequeathed the sunniest spot under the mountain to the university. There are historic buildings aplenty built by the likes of British architect Sir Herbert Baker, such as Jameson Hall. The Woolsack building on lower campus was built for Rudyard Kipling and later donated to the university.

Newlands

Josephine's Mill

Boundary Road (021 686 4939). **Open** 9am-4pm Mon-Fri. **Admission** R8; R5 concessions. **No credit cards.**

Who knew that flour dust was explosive? You can learn this and more at this historic old mill that still produces stone-ground flour, rich in bran, pollard, semolina, gluten and wheatgerm for Cape Town bakeries and the Mill's own range of pasta and cookies for sale. The flour is also used to make the bread that makes the sandwiches served at the Miller's Plate (021 685 6233), a charming little restaurant situated in the bowels of the mill with a terrace on the

Obs observations

Hidden away in the crowded confusion of Cape Town's Southern Suburbs is the laid-back suburb of Observatory, so named because it was the site of South Africa's first observatory. Located between the gritty industria of Mowbray and Woodstock and the leafy academia of Rondebosch and Rosebank, Observatory (Obs to its friends) falls somewhere between bohemian and seedy on the social scale – as a result, it's one of Cape Town's happening suburbs and hottest student hangouts. Obs's edgy trendiness is illustrated by an organic fair and a beery festival, which complement each other through their contrasts. Obs hosts the monthly Holistic Lifestyle Fair (Observatory Recreation Centre, corner Station and Lower Main roads; 10am-4pm on the first Sunday of the month; entry R5; free for under-16s), where healthy living is celebrated through 130-odd stalls ranging from vegetarian snacks and 'life readings' to esoteric treatments and yoga demonstrations. Every October, revelling revellers roll out rowdily onto Obs's narrow Lower Main Road to celebrate the (in)famous

Obsfest, Cape Town's version of the Oktoberfest (just not exclusively catering for beer drinkers). Live music and herbal smoke fill the air, and drinkers at Obs's who's-who bars and restaurants spill onto the streets. Despite all the tranquil wholesomeness, visitors to Obs shouldn't expect a good night's sleep – the locals certainly don't.

Sightseeing

river. Built in 1822, the mill is now powered by electricity rather than the magnificent giant waterwheel outside. The minuscule museum is very charming and you can make off with a kilogram bag of your own stone-ground flour for R7.

Newlands Cricket Ground

146 Campground Road (021 657 2003/tours 021 686 2150/www.newlandstours.co.za). **Tours** Mon-Fri. **Tickets** R32. **No credit cards**.

Cricket lovers will already be familiar with Table Mountain looming above the Newlands Cricket Ground, from the TV coverage of the 2003 Cricket World Cup and the lavish opening ceremonies. Tours of the grounds take in the President's Suite, the exclusive South Club and the control rooms, including the scoreboard controller and the third umpire's room, which, the tour guide is quick to point out, is not bulletproof.

Newlands Rugby Stadium

11 Boundary Road (021 659 4600/www.wprugby.com/tours 021 686 2150/www.newlandstours.co.za). **Tours** Mon-Fri. **Tickets** R32. **No credit cards**.

The first rugby match kicked off here in 1890 when Newlands was still just a muddy field, making it the second-oldest test venue in the world. Between now and then it was built, renovated, demolished and rebuilt all over again, eventually becoming the modern 51,000-seater it is now. It plays host regularly to major provincial and international games and was the staging ground for the opening match of the 1995 World Cup. Tours take you backstage to check out the enviable view from the function room and the highest stands, through the player's entrance, into the hallowed ground of the changing room (not while the players are actually there, so don't get your hopes up too much) and out through the tunnel. There is also a very good rugby memorabilia shop just outside the stadium.

SARFU Rugby Museum

Sports Science Institute, Boundary Road (021 686 2151). **Open** 8.30am-5pm Mon-Fri or by appointment. **Admission** free.

SARFU Rugby Museum is housed in a rather forlorn little building (although apparently it's in the throes of being renovated) is dedicated to South Africa's national pastime. There are some good exhibits dating all the way back to 1891, including snippets of original radio commentary, loads of jerseys and trophies, a wall of rugby-club ties and pictures and a history of the game, including some information on black rugby.

South African Breweries

SAB Miller Boundary Road (021 658 7511). **Open** 10am-2pm Tue, Thur, Fri. **Tours** 10am, 2pm Tue, Thur, Fri. **Tickets** free.

When South African Breweries snapped up Miller for a cool US$5.6 billion in 2002, the company was catapulted into position as the second largest brewery in the world. So the US$10 million used to restore the historic Ohlsson & Mariendahl Breweries at the

Newlands premises was small change. Tours take in the historic malt house and the old brewery, both of which have been beautifully restored, with interesting exhibits on the history of brewing and malting as well as more traditional methods still used in rural areas today. Then it's on to the modern brewery, the fermentation tanks and the mesmerising tangle of conveyor belts at the bottling plant, which operates seven days a week, churning out hundreds of thousands of litres of beer. The tour ends with a 'tasting' – really two bottles of beer of your choice.

Sports Science Institute of South Africa

Boundary Road (021 659 5600/www.ssisa.com/ 021 686 2150/1/www.newlandstours.co.za). **Tours** Mon-Fri. **Tickets** R20. **No credit cards**.

Fitness freaks and professional sports people alike make use of the high-tech Institute's facilities and expert scientists, nutritionists and coaches to up their game and buff their bods. Sport Science includes a high-performance lab, a fitness centre and UCT's Exercise Sports and Medicine Faculty. Tours can be arranged and you might spot a sports star working up a sweat in the process.

Claremont

Claremont is home to the **Carmel Art Gallery** (66 Vineyard Road, Claremont, 021 671 6601), which offers a delightful variety of local artworks. Other southern suburban art galleries include the sister Carmel Gallery in Constantia (Constantia Village Shopping Centre, 021 794 6262) and the excellent Irma Stern Gallery (Cecil Road, Rosebank, 021 685 5686).

Claremont itself – due in part to the shopping mall, the sports stadiums, the university students and the surrounding boarding schools – has a bustling, young (very young – almost under-age) nightlife scene.

Zeekoevlei

Rondevlei Nature Reserve

Fisherman's Walk Road, Zeekoevlei, at the end of Perth Road (021 706 2404/tours 021 706 0842/ www.rondevlei.co.za). **Open** 8am-5pm daily. **Admission** R5. **No credit cards**.

The wetland nature reserve just off the M5 is home to a variety of bird species and five wild hippos, who are, unfortunately, secretive and shy. Hippos used to be as ubiquitous to the Cape as cellphones are now, but the population was shot out very early on. This is the only natural population in the province and they've been here for 25 years. You're probably more likely to see hippo tracks than the animals themselves, but the chances increase in summer when the water is low or if you stay overnight in the rustic cottage situated on an island in the middle of the vlei (lake). The reserve has excellent bird hides, boat rides, walks and an environmental centre.

False Bay

Caves, monkeys, fishermen and warm water from Mozambique.

There's no beach, but look out for the fishing boats at **Kalk Bay Harbour**. *See p74.*

While the Atlantic Seaboard sees beach-bronzed jetsetters strutting along Camps Bay and Clifton's gorgeous golden sands, not daring to dip their pedicured toes into the chilly Atlantic waters, False Bay's beaches (on the other side of the Cape Peninsula and in the Indian Ocean) paddle along at different pace.

False Bay boasts caves and monkeys, curious antique stores and Victorian-era beach huts, and a one o'clock date with the returning local fishermen. And – and there's no understating the importance of this – the water's warm. While the trendy Atlantic Seaboard gets its chilly water from Antarctica, False Bay enjoys the warmer touch of the Benguela Current, washing down from Mozambique.

If you're not hiring a car and you don't want to take a guided tour of the False Bay coast, your best, and most scenic, transport option is by rail. A working train line, which leads all the way to and from Cape Town station (punctuated by stops in the Southern Suburbs),

skirts the coastline south from the historic, and recently revamped Muizenberg station (177 Main Street/www.spoornet.co.za/0800 656463). An old joke went that Fish Hoek was at the end of the line: these days the train track ends at Simonstown station. This railway line is probably the best way to travel along the False Bay coast, offering excellent sea views while avoiding the traffic jams on the M4 road.

As you start following the seaside train tracks south from **Muizenberg** (*see p73*) along Main Road – past the surfer shops and shaggy-haired dudes – you'll notice **Muizenberg Beach** (*see p73*), stretching out towards the west, a beach that Rudyard Kipling considered his favourite in the world. Confusingly, this 35km (21.7mile) stretch of sand is unimaginatively known as both Muizenberg Beach and Long Beach (much like the Cape Peninsula's other Long Beaches at Kommetjie and Simonstown). The rhythmic waves and long wave break make it an excellent choice for

More than a mutt

As he would take up three seats on the train, the railway authorities were soon threatening to have him put down. But the sailors came up with a plan with their commanding officer and Just Nuisance 'volunteered' to join the Royal Navy. He was issued with a sailor's cap and given the rank of Able Seaman, at the same time becoming their mascot. His official trade was listed as 'bone crusher' and his religious denomination as 'scrounger'. No angel, his conduct sheet soon reflected a number of violations such as going AWOL, losing his collar and resisting eviction from pubs at closing time. However, as an enlisted officer he was entitled to a free train pass, which was attached to a collar made especially for him.

Just Nuisance died in 1944, just seven years old, due to complications from a motorcycle accident. He was buried with full military honours at Klaver Camp on Redhill. A statue of him by local artist Jean Doyle stands in Jubilee Square in Simonstown overlooking the docks (*pictured*).

Just Nuisance's owner ran a hostel for young Royal Navy sailors. The **Great Dane Just Nuisance** fancied himself as one of the lads and would follow the sailors everywhere, even catching the train to Cape Town with them.

surfing, bodyboarding or simply splashing around wildly in the waves. Sadly, though, Muizenberg is looking a bit run down these days, and its once grand Promenade (Atlantic Road) is one of many landmarks that looks in dire need of a good scrub.

In **Kalk Bay** (*see p74*) you'll want to stroll from door to door, admiring the old curiosities in the long line of antique shops. Time (and clichés) seems to have stood still in Kalk Bay, where antique stores and harbour-front fish sellers create an olde-worlde charm.

Boyes Drive leads along the mountainside between Muizenberg and Kalk Bay, providing excellent sea views and whale-watching spots. Boyes Drive is also the best place to park your car before donning a headlamp, packing a long rope and heading into the labyrinthine (and apparently haunted) Kalk Bay caves.

Travelling south past the brightly coloured beach huts at St James, you'll reach the quiet village of **Fish Hoek** (*see p74*), with its long, safe, sandy and – most importantly – wind-protected beach. During the late winter (July to October) whales come into Fish Hoek bay, frolicking around only metres from the shore (*see also p75* **Whale of a time**).

Simonstown (*see p75*) – a typical English seaside town – is home to the local naval base, so it's soaked in maritime lore and handsome

sailors. Jubilee Square is watched over by the statue of Able Seaman Just Nuisance, the navy's most famous World War II-era canine volunteer. Nuisance was the only dog ever to hold rank in the Royal Navy, and his statue – by local artist Jean Doyle – stands as the navy's tribute to this Great Dane (*see also above* **More than a mutt**).

Just south of Simonstown (almost at Cape Point, but not quite) is Boulders' Beach with its rare African jackass penguin colony, where these charming birds dodder along, minding their own business.

The final spot of interest on your False Bay excursion is Cape Point: the place – as the signposts won't tire of telling you – where two oceans meet. And just around the corner is the **Cape of Good Hope** (*see p78*).

Gordon's Bay (*see p78*) is located a good hour's drive from Muizenberg on the eastern (and less interesting) side of the bay – we suggest you take the coastal Baden-Powell Drive, as swimming across the bay is not recommended (only two people have ever swum across the bay – and False Bay's resident sharks are trying to keep the number low). Gordon's Bay's Bikini Beach is more than just a pretty name: it's an ideal spot for donning a pair of dark glasses and staring dumbstruck at the near-naked young beauties parading across the beach. On the way to Gordon's Bay, on the other side of the N2, is **Somerset West** (*see p78*) and its cluster of tourist attractions.

Muizenberg

Het Posthuys

Main Road (021 788 7972). **Open** 10am-4pm daily. **Admission** free, donations welcome.
To get the most out of the story of the Posthuys, it's best to settle in for a chat with one of the folk who man this museum. This building was built in 1670, so if early Cape history interests you, take your time as these three little rooms hold much of it.

Joan St Leger Lindbergh Arts Foundation

Lindbergh Arts Foundation & Conference Centre, 18 Beach Road (021 788 2795). **Open** *Coffee shop* 9am-3.30pm Mon-Fri. *Centre* 9am-4.30pm Mon-Fri. **Admission** free, but phone about concerts.
This is a find: a step directly back into the good old Muizenberg days, sans the stuffiness of the past. The foundation consists of four beautiful houses designed by renowned English architect Sir Herbert Baker (1862-1946). One of these buildings is the Lindbergh, which has an internet café, a wonderful, old-school browsing library with books on Africana, flora, wildlife and South African history, and a history room with old photos and newspaper clippings of Muizenberg. Concerts are held twice a month in the coffee shop, which must be the only place in Cape Town where you can buy a bottomless cup of coffee for R5 and a muffin for R3. Tucked away in the old and still quietly posh part of Muizenberg, Lindbergh is a great place to spend time in quiet contemplation, to do a little reading or gentle gossiping, discovering why they call them 'the good old days'.

Muizenberg Beach

Follow the M3 highway, turn left at Westlake & follow the signs to Muizenberg.
One of world's longest beaches, Muizenberg's beach follows a 40-km (25-mile) stretch of sand around False Bay to Gordon's Bay. Muizenberg also offers one of the longest wave breaks, making it a popular spot for young surfers and boogie boarders – and if you still need to buy the gear, the town itself features several street corner surf shops. Muizenberg is famous for its multi-coloured bathing boxes, but while it was once the playground of high society, the esplanade is a bit run down these days.

Natale Labia

192 Main Road, Muizenberg (021 788 4106). **Open** 10am-5pm Mon-Fri. **Admission** free.
Count Natale Labia, whose family lived in this beautiful home in Muizenberg, presented the museum in 1985, complete with its furniture and art collection. The reception rooms downstairs speak of the splendour of days when people knew how to entertain and live lavishly. It's a beautiful place, but ultimately you're left feeling rather unsatisfied. There is no information about the house displayed – although there is a loan copy of a booklet written by Count Natale Labia available at the front desk. The upstairs rooms accommodate exhibitions, lectures and art classes and the house is available for functions – Natale Labia would be the perfect venue for a wedding. Overall, it's a gorgeous place that begs to be brought back to life.

Rhodes Cottage

Main Road (021 788 1816). **Open** 9.45am-4.30pm daily. **Admission** donations welcome.
Even if you're not particularly interested in the life and times of mining magnate Cecil John Rhodes, a visit to Rhodes Cottage is worthwhile. This museum certainly doesn't ignore Rhodes' faults and is filled with satirical cartoons of the time, newspaper articles, some of Rhodes' belongings and numerous photographs. There's the opportunity to watch a ten-minute video of Rhodes' life if you want to brush up on your history and finally you can pause for a moment in the front room of the cottage where he died, aged 49. Perhaps the room's starkness is as telling as anything else in the museum.

Silvermine

Ou Kaapse Weg, Silvermine (021 701 8692/ www.cpnp.co.za). **Open** *May-Oct* 8am-5pm. *Sept-Apr* 7am-6pm. **Admission** R10; R5 concessions. **Credit** AmEx, DC, MC, V.
At the top of Ou Kaapse Weg, just inland from Muizenberg, is the turn-off to Silvermine. A beautiful National Park, its focal point is the reservoir where you can leave your car and pull on your hiking boots, or get on your mountain bike and set off to explore. You'll find awesome views around every corner – from out over False Bay to Noordhoek, Constantia and beyond. Aim to spend the day here – there are plenty of mountain-biking and hiking trails and in the summertime it's a popular picnicking spot. Pick up a brochure at the entrance for descriptions of the various trails.

St James Beach huts.
See p74.

Visit **Kalk Bay** in snoek season and buy the fish straight from the boat.

St James Beach

Park close to St James Station & access the beach via the tunnel from the station.

Apart from being photogenic, the beach huts at St James Beach are ideal for those who love the beach but hate sand getting into everything. You can hire a hut for the day (R20 during peak season, but at other times a donation will do) and live life like the Victorians; going for a genteel dip in the tidal pool, watching the kids play on the pretty white beach and eating your sand-free sandwiches in the shade of your private hut.

Kalk Bay

The Kalk Bay portion of Main Road (the tail-end of the M4 route) is flanked on the eastern side by the rocky Indian Ocean coastline, and on the western side by an apparently endless row of antiques shops. Here you'll want to park your car (or hop off the train) and stroll leisurely from door to door, admiring old curiosities and perhaps even accumulating an armful of lost treasures. Apart from the antiques, bric-a-brac and knickknacks, Kalk Bay's other claim to fame is its selection of excellent cafés and restaurants. Two of the most popular are the quirky Olympia Café and Deli (*see p117*), with its fabulous breads

and meat and fish dishes, and the breezy Brass Bell (Main Road, 021 788 5456), which is the closest you'll get to the breakers without actually taking the plunge.

While there's no beach at Kalk Bay, the shops and restaurants more than make up for the lack of sand and sunbathers. The fishing harbour is always busy, especially during snoek (a tasty species of fish) season (June and July), when daily catches of several thousand snoek are not unheard of. At midday the local fishermen offload their catch, and a favourite Kalk Bay experience is going down to the harbour to buy fresh fish straight off the boat. *See also p244* **Cape fish**.

Fish Hoek

Fish Hoek Beach

Park at the parking lot at the corner of Main and Clovelly roads, or try parking on the town end of the beach around the shops.

This is a lovely white curve of beach that's often sheltered even when the rest of the peninsula is buffeted by the wind. Park at the Clovelly end and you can take the dogs on a long walk in relative seclusion, or get onto it at the Fish Hoek end and enjoy beach culture with the throng. And yes, the water on the False Bay side really is warmer.

Fish Hoek Valley Museum
59 Central Circle, near the Civic Centre (021 782 1752). **Open** 9.30am-12.30pm Tue-Sat or by appointment. **Admission** R5. **No credit cards.**
This is a valiant effort to record Fish Hoek's history and character, but will probably appeal mostly to locals. If you're particularly interested in Peers Cave, where the 12,000-year-old Fish Hoek Man was found, stop in at the museum first. You'll find information about the cave and a map – handy, considering the trail to the cave isn't clearly marked (the easiest access to the cave is off Ou Kaapse Weg).

Heritage Museum (Amlay House)
59 Central Circle, Fish Hoek (021 782 1752). **Open** 11am-4pm Tue-Fri; by appointment Sat, Sun. **Admission** R3. **No credit cards.**
Step through Amlay House's wooden gate and you feel you're stepping into someone's home. Which you are. The museum is curated by Zainab 'Patty' Davidson, and it is the home she grew up in, which her family was forced to leave in 1975 and back into which they moved 20 years later. It's quite something to walk through the rooms that Patty grew up in – especially if she shows you around. They're filled with old photographs, newspaper clippings, embroidered wedding apparel, handwritten *Khitaabs* (prayer books) and lots of other artefacts of traditional Muslim culture. It's a fascinating visit, rather like listening to your gran reminisce while paging through old family photo albums. Except, of course, you can leave anytime you want.

Simonstown

Boulders' Beach
2km (1.2 miles) south of Simonstown on the M4, in the direction of Cape Point.
Even if the wind is howling at False Bay's other beaches, Boulders' will be perfectly still. The beach is protected by huge rocks that prevent the wind from shaking the tail feathers of the resident Cape penguin colony. The penguins are the biggest attraction at Boulders', and these peculiar birds make the beach a popular spot for tourists and kids. It will cost you R10 to stay at Boulders', and while the stillness of the air saves your beach hat from blowing off to Seal Island, it also prevents the penguin's pong from wafting away with the breeze.

Boulders Penguin Colony
Boulders' Beach, just out of Simonstown (021 786 2329/www.cpnp.co.za). **Open** 8am-6.30pm daily. **Admission** R15; R5 concessions. **Credit** AmEx, DC, MC, V.
When driving around Boulders keep a lookout for the locals – the tiny black-and-white ones, that is. In 1982 two breeding pairs of African penguins (once known as jackass penguins thanks to the braying sound they make) moved into prime beachfront estate at Boulders between Simonstown and Cape Point. Today there are well over 3,000 of the birds living here and the area is now a National Park. Still,

penguins tend not to stick to the rules so when driving outside the park keep your eyes open – you're more than likely to see penguin pairs waddling along the byroads. Boardwalks in the park take you within close range of the penguins, a new resource centre has information on display, and the beaches are great. All in all, a great place to meet the locals.

Whale of a time

From May to December, the whales visit False Bay. On any one of the coastal drives you may catch a quick glimpse of a spout – get ready to pull into a lookout point and make sure you've brought a pair of binoculars with you. There's nothing like seeing a whale. If you're really keen to see one, watch out for the following viewpoints:

● The walkway below Muizenberg Station near Bailey's Cottage. Boyes Drive also provides a lofty view.
● The Brass Bell in Kalk Bay where you can lunch while keeping an eye on the sea (*see p74*).
● The corner near the catwalk in Fish Hoek was once a whale-catching area, but today it's used for whale-watching.
● The Battery in Simonstown.
● Anywhere along Faure Marine Drive out of Gordon's Bay.

Bronze Age Art Foundry, Gallery & Sculpture Garden

King George Way (021 786 5090). **Open** 10am-5pm
Mon-Thur; 10am-4pm Fri; 10am-3pm Sat, Sun.
Admission free.

The Bronze Age Art Foundry is a working foundry
and the adjoining gallery displays works by artists
such as Beezy Bailey, Angus Taylor and Marina
Petropoulos in a large stone and timber structure.
After browsing between beautiful bronze pieces of
all shades and textures, you can go on a tour of the
foundry where everyone at work is keen to explain
what part of the process of creating art they're
responsible for. Be prepared that the experience is
noisy and hectic, but the enthusiasm is infectious.
Next door to it all is the artists' residency, which is
a listed National Monument, with a handsome sculpture garden that will definitely grab your attention
as you stroll by. Stop and have a closer look.

Jubilee Square

King George Street.

Jubilee Square is not so much of an attraction as a
perfect place to reach a lot of the Simonstown sights
(not to mention the excellent shops and restaurants).
Although it just looks like a shady parking lot,
Jubilee Square does have a few objects that are
worth seeking out – such as the statue of Great Dane
and Royal Navy mascot Just Nuisance (*see p72*
More than a mutt). From the square there is easy
access to the Stone Age Gallery, Amlay House, the
dock where you can board a sightseeing cruise, and
plenty more. The Simonstown publicity office is on
the corner of the square.

Just Nuisance's Grave

Off Redhill Drive. **Open** 9am-3.30pm daily.

From Simonstown, turn up Redhill Drive – it's a
scenic drive and an alternative route to the Cape
Point Nature Reserve. Towards the crest of the
mountain you'll see a sign to Just Nuisance's Grave.
Turn left and look out for the SAS Simonsberg sign.
Go through the boom at the Signal School and follow signs to visitors' parking. The school is housed
in the old sanatorium, and the grave of South
Africa's most famous Great Dane (Royal Navy Able
Seaman and mascot) is in front of it all, overlooking
False Bay. It's not like the Navy to get sentimental,
but this lonely, quiet spot and the
fact that it is open to the public in
an otherwise restricted-access
area, is an indication of just how
great this Dane was (*see p72* **More
than a mutt**).

Long Beach

*Off Main Road (which becomes
Station Road) in Simonstown.*

A similarly long beach to the
one near Kommetjie, you
won't need a wetsuit to swim
at this one. A pleasant
stretch of beach with a few

nearby wrecks you can snorkel around when the sea
is calm and flat. Try a kayaking trip from the dock
(make enquiries at the Simonstown Publicity Office)
– it's a pleasant paddle out to the beach and you'll
arrive just hot and sweaty enough to enjoy a dip
once you've beached your craft. Leave before the
wind comes up – or you'll find yourself paddling
against it all the way back.

Mineral World & Topstones

Dido Valley Road (021 786 2020). **Open** 8.30am-
4.45pm Mon-Fri; (Mineral World only) 9am-5.15pm
Sat, Sun. **Admission** free.

Mineral World offers you the chance to buy real
dinosaur eggs and balance your chakras. The eggs
will set you back about R5,000 (but are guaranteed
not to hatch in your living room), but chakra-bal-
ancing is substantially cheaper. So let the kids dive
into the Scratch Patch, while you get sucked into the
Fossil Shop where you can find out that the astro-
logical sign of trilobites (fossilised sea creatures) is
Capricorn. There's an unfussy blend of science and
other schools of thought here. Upstairs is Topstones,
the polishing factory where gemstones get their
gleam, along with a rather creaky mobile display of
gemstones that glow under ultraviolet light.
Downstairs is the factory shop where you can fill
your pockets with obsidian and leopard skin jasper
and rose quartz. Note that Topstones does not operate at the weekend. You can also find Mineral World
and Topstones at V&A Waterfront, Dock Road (021
419 9429) and Canal Walk (021 555 0111).

Simonstown Museum

*Court Road, Simonstown (021 786 3046/Tours
Audrey Read 021 786 1805; Bobby Wise 021 786
3189).* **Open** 9am-4pm Mon-Fri; 10am-1pm Sat;
11am-3pm Sun. **Admission** R5; R1-R2 concessions.
No credit cards.

Tucked away in one of the rooms of this museum is
a plaque listing the curator and staff of the
Simonstown Museum as 'Citizen of the Year' in 1990.
As old an accolade as it is, it's a small indication of
the amount of work and enthusiasm that has gone
into making this place a worthy record of
Simonstown past and present. There's something
here for everyone, whatever your particular interest.
If you're of the 'when I was a boy' ilk, the collection
of school memorabilia will fascinate. If you're a pre-
history addict, or are fascinated by the Boer Wars
or the role South Africa played in the World Wars
you'll find your fix here. Old Wedgewood stilton
containers? Got 'em. But the best is Project Phoenix;
a work in progress, aimed at illuminating the unique
mix of cultures and community life of Simonstown
before they were forcibly removed. A port town, a
naval base, with strong Malay and British influences, its blend of lifestyles is fascinating.

South African Naval Museum

*Off King George Street, Simonstown (021 787
4635/021 787 3850).* **Open** 10am-4pm daily.
Admission free.

Fish Hoek promenade. *See p74.*

Sightseeing

Main Road, **Simonstown**. *See p75.*

With models of famous South African vessels and naval artefacts, display cabinets (with dental-repair, snake-bite and manicure kits) and all sorts of interesting visual input you'll soon be able to tell your sextant from your diving submarine if you couldn't already. But boys of all ages will probably home in on the guns, rocket heads and other military paraphernalia in the downstairs exhibition rooms.

Warrior Toy Museum
St George's Street, Simonstown (021 786 1395). **Open** 10am-4pm daily. **Admission** R3. **No credit cards**.
If you have magpie instincts or if Meccano and Corgi classics make you nostalgic, then relive your childhood at the Warrior Toy museum. Better still, amaze the kids with how people kept themselves entertained in the days before Playstation. The displays at the museum consist of owner Percy van Zyl's private collection amassed over 43 years. There are Pickford furniture trucks, London buses, fantastically intricate doll's houses, model trains, planes, cars and ships, horse and carriage sets, toy soldiers and a 'carnival queen' from Rio. If you want to take a memory of the museum home with you, there's also some stuff for sale, and, if you're a collector, Percy will help you track down that longed-for little something. The museum is housed in the Warrior Room of the Town Hall – just down from the Sailors' and Soldiers' Rest Room.

Cape of Good Hope

Cape of Good Hope
Table Mountain National Park (formally Cape Point Nature Reserve). From the city take the M3 past Simonstown & follow the well-placed signs (021 780 9204/www.cpnp.co.za). **Open** Apr-Aug 7am-5pm (exit 6pm) daily. Sept-Oct 6am-6pm (exit 7pm) daily. *Restaurant* 9.30am-5pm daily. **Admission** R35; R10 concessions. **Credit** AmEx, DC, MC, V.
Cape Point is a magnificent sight (and the Flying Dutchman funicular a great way to cheat), but there is much more to be enjoyed here than simply making a beeline to the lookout point. Get here early and you could find yourself sharing pristine beaches with just the penguins and ostriches. Pack a snorkel, mask and permit and go crayfishing. Surfers love the generally uncrowded breaks here, and anglers think it's fab. In summertime the beaches at Buffels Bay and Bordjiesrif can get busy – with terraced lawns, places for a *braai* and baboons there's plenty to keep a family occupied – but when there's more than 77sqkms (30sqm) of land rich in birdlife and indigenous vegetation, you're sure to find a spot of your own. The Buffelsfontein Visitors Centre (021 780 9402) is friendly and inviting with signs that encourage you to open drawers and examine insects and shells and things from the reserve. There are also the commemorative crosses from Portuguese seafaring days, the lighthouse and the Two Oceans Restaurant and curio shop.

Gordon's Bay

Bikini Beach, Gordon's Bay
Take Beach Road through Gordon's Bay, past the Naval College & the harbour. In peak season you may need to park at Gordon's Bay Beach and walk.
Definitely a sightseeing stop if your tastes run to nubile university students playing volleyball and flaunting the latest in microkinis – it's not called Bikini Beach for nothing. It's a great swimming spot, too. Closer to town is Gordon's Bay Beach, near to plenty of fast-food joints and perfect for a family day out on the beach.

Somerset West

Lwandle Cultural Village
Off the N2 past Somerset West, follow signs to Lwandle (021 845 6119). **Open** 9am-4pm Mon-Fri; 9am-1pm Sat.
The first township-based, open-air museum in the Western Cape, the Lwandle Migrant Labour Museum serves to remind us of the hardships of migrant labourers under apartheid. Aerial photographs clearly demonstrate how the migrant labour hostels dominated the growth and development of Lwandle near Somerset West. Today, those hostels have been converted into family units, with the exception of number 33 which has been kept to document the past. Lwandle's museum is more than a collection of display boards (interesting reading though they are), it's the heart of the community. A visit will also include a tour of the township and community projects like the nearby Arts and Crafts Centre. A restaurant is due to open soon.

Monkey Town Primate Centre
Mondeor Road, Somerset West, just off the N2 (021 858 1060/www.monkeys.co.za). **Open** 9am-5pm daily. **Admission** R45; R26-R30 concessions. **Credit** AmEx, DC, MC, V.
Monkey Town houses more than 200 primates in a huge enclosure. Visitors are invited to walk through the monkeys' domain in a large wire tunnel – and there's no doubt as to who is the guest here. A tour is essential – they run on the hour (every half hour on busy days). While there are plenty of informative display boards, it's on a tour that you get to really meet the monkeys. You'll be sniffed at and checked out and your tour guide will tell you whether you meet the monkeys' approval or not. There are also three female chimps here, all of whom have excellent window-washing skills, exotic birds, duikers and even tiny suni antelopes to spot. Sometimes visitors can go into the spider monkeys' enclosure for an additional R20 where a new tour guide takes over, wrapping his prehensile tail around your wrist. Note that winter is a good time to visit as the cold and wet weather doesn't put the monkeys off. Alternatively, in the summer, this is a great place to bring a picnic, or you can top up your energy at the refreshment kiosk and spend the whole day here.

Winelands

Great architecture, fabulous mountains and pearly towns, and, of course, vat-loads of wine.

Only a leisurely hour's drive from the city, and culturally considered a part of it, the Winelands offer rolling vineyards, majestic mountains, relaxing drives, historic Cape Dutch architecture, farm fresh food… and wine. Good wine. And lots of it.

Cape wine has been gradually building an impressive reputation internationally, garnering jugfuls of awards and winning red-nosed admirers across the world. And the Winelands are home to most of the Cape's premier wine estates, practically all of which offer wine-tasting sessions. There are a ridiculous number of cellars and different regions to visit in the area, ranging from quiet and personal to commercial and touristy (as a yardstick, the number of flags outside an estate's gates is in direct proportion to the size of its crowds). We've listed the best of the bunch; if you want details of all the vineyards in the area, visit the tourist offices listed throughout the chapter.

While the larger estates offer slick sophistication, good wines and tourist-friendly service, it's well worth heading through the winefields and discovering a hidden wine farm, where you're more likely to be served by the owner or resident winemaker rather than by a PR rep or one of the ubiquitous fine young waiters. Wine-tasting costs are fairly arbitrary, and while one cellar could charge R25 per glass, the estate down the road might charge nothing at all, see the wine estates listed below.

The major stops on the Winelands route are Franschhoek, Stellenbosch, Paarl and Wellington. All are postcard-pretty towns peopled with friendly townsfolk, and all boast streets lined with historic buildings.

Exploring beyond the main wine route, you'll find many more wine- and fruit-growing regions that are well worth exploring. The Stellenbosch-Franschhoek-Paarl-Wellington quad also forms the start of the famous Route 62, which leads all the way beyond Oudtshoorn in the east. The world's longest wine route, Route 62 is one of the best – and most leisurely – drives in the Cape (see pp234-41).

Franschhoek (see p80) – originally settled by 17th-century French Huguenots who were fleeing religious persecution – fancies itself as the Cape's food and wine capital, and it boasts superb restaurants, French-style kerbside bistros and cafés… and more Tricolores than you can shake a baguette at. Franschhoek feels like Paris's distant cousin who ran away to the countryside a long time ago – and historically speaking, that's pretty much what happened.

Stellenbosch (see p81), on the other hand, is a thriving university town, and the local students are more than happy to study for their degrees in the Western Cape's most accessible wine-growing region. Stellenbosch is the second-oldest Cape settlement after Cape Town, with many historic buildings filling the old dorp (village) quarter.

Paarl (*see p87*) is hard to miss, located in a green valley at the base of a clump of granite rocks, which when wet – according to the early explorer Gobbema – looked like pearls, hence the town's name. Paarl is less touristy than Stellenbosch or Franschhoek, with historic buildings crowding the first stretch of the 12km (seven-mile) long main road before it turns into the town proper and then the industrial area.

Wellington (*see p90*) is the smallest of the four main towns, and while it's not quite sleepy, it certainly is a whole lot quieter and more conservative than its busier neighbours. Several Winelands tours are available for visitors – just pop in at the Cape Town Tourist Information Centre at the Pinnacle (Corner of Castle and Burg streets, 021 426 4260) or go to www.winelands.co.za.

If you're not hiring a car and would like to explore the Winelands, your options are limited to buses and trains, which will only take you to the major centres, such as Franschhoek and Stellenbosch, not to the estates themselves. The overwhelming majority of wine estates are located in the flowing fields around the towns, so you'll have to ask the local tourism offices for details of how to get to these if you are not driving. For details of train trips from Cape Town to Winelands' major towns, such Franschhoek and Stellenbosch, contact Spoornet/Shosoloza Meyl (*see p249*).

Guided tours are great if your time is limited, but you'll enjoy yourself more if you pack a map, hire a car and explore the Winelands with a couple of friends. If you do this, though, be sure to have a designated driver – especially if you intend tasting the fruits of the vines at every single estate. If you have a concentration of alcohol of 0.05 grams or more per 100ml (3.5oz) of blood, you're over the legal limit. And here's a sobering thought: that translates to only about three glasses of wine.

Franschhoek

Franschhoek is the self-appointed food and wine capital of South Africa. It's also undoubtedly one of the most beautiful areas in the Cape, with picturesque landscapes of vineyards set against craggy mountains. It's no wonder, then, that monied locals and foreigners alike have been snapping up their own little vineyards in the area, sending property prices through the stratosphere and thus turning the once sleepy little town into a vibrant cosmopolitan attraction. Franschhoek is very much geared towards visitors, but the sparkling atmosphere – not to mention the cap-classique sparkling wine – and the remarkable vistas, make up for it.

The Neo-Gothic **Moederkerk**. See p83.

Information and maps of the Franschhoek Winelands can be obtained from Franschhoek Tourism (*see p81*).

Franschhoek was originally known as Oliphantshoek for the elephants that used to calve here in the 1600s. It took on its current name only after the French Huguenots, fleeing religious persecution, settled here in 1688. You can catch up on the history at the **Huguenot Monument** and the museum at the end of the village, once you're done browsing the arts-and-crafts galleries and shops or whiling away the afternoon at one of the fine restaurants or street-side bistros. The Bastille Festival that happens in July and the Harvest Festival in March are the busiest times.

The gorgeous scenery makes for great opportunities for outdoors activities, especially in the Mont Rochelle reserve; whether you go hiking, mountain-biking, horse riding or fly-fishing, the latter of which is very popular.

Dewdale Trout Farm & Fly Fishery

Dewdale Farm, Robertsvlei (021 876 2755/ www.dewdale.com). **Open** *Winter* 7.30am-dusk daily. *Summer* 7.30am-9.30pm daily. **Admission** R100/day. *Rod rental* R50. *Mountain-bike rental* R70/half day. **No credit cards.**

Dewdale is set against the striking backdrop of Franschhoek mountains. It can provide you with rods, flies and tackle, along with friendly advice and professional lessons courtesy of the Bell's Fly Fishing Academy. The area is also perfect for outdoor pursuits, especially for those with a penchant for hiking and mountain-biking.

Huguenot Memorial Museum & Huguenot Monument

Lambrecht Street (021 876 2532/www.museum. co.za). **Open** 9am-5pm Mon-Sat; 2-5pm Sun. **No credit cards. Map** p275 Y3.

The Huguenot Museum, which celebrates the history of the French Huguenots who settled in Cape Town in 1688, is housed in an historic building that once stood in the city itself and was moved to its current location piece by piece. The museum's staff specialises in tracing Huguenot ancestry. The Huguenot Monument was built in 1938.

Wine estates

L'Ormarins

R43 to Franschhoek (021 874 1026/www.lormarins. co.za). **Open** 9am-4.30pm Mon-Fri; 10am-3pm Sat. **Tastings** R20/5 wines. **Credit** AmEx, DC, MC, V.

L'Ormarins is a sleekly sophisticated, relatively new wine estate that caters to the busloads. The entrance, with the stunning gabled manor house visible through an arch of trees, is postcard-perfect and L'Ormarins has fast become one of the top wine destinations in Franschhoek. But this is not the best place for a quiet visit, as it gets very busy.

La Motte

R45, just outside Franschhoek (021 876 3114/ www.la-motte.com). **Open** 9am-4.30pm Mon-Fri; 10am-3pm Sat. **Tastings** R10/5 wines. **Credit** AmEx, DC, MC, V.

Considering the owner of La Motte is mezzo soprano Hannelie Rupert, it's no wonder that the estate hosts classical recitals once a month as well as a popular Christmas concert. Pick up a brochure or check the website for upcoming events.

Môreson

Happy Valley Road, off the R43 (021 876 3055 /www.moreson.co.za). **Open** 11am-5pm daily. **Tastings** R10 for 10-15 wines. **Credit** AmEx, DC, MC, V.

Make your own wine at the Blessing of the Harvest festival on the second week in February. Pick grapes, stomp them yourself, extract the juice and design a label. Five months later you'll receive a free bottle of 'your' wine. The top-rated restaurant Bread and Wine (*see p117*) offers bread-making courses during the cooler months for R300 per person, which also includes lunch and wine.

Tourist information

Franschhoek Tourism

68 Huguenot Road (021 876 3603/ www.franschhoek.org.za). **Open** 9am-6pm Mon-Fri; 10am-5pm Sat; 10am-4pm Sun. **Map** p275 X2.

Stellenbosch

Stellenbosch is the second-oldest city after Cape Town. It's named for the Cape governor, Simon van der Stel, but it gets its 'City of Oaks' nickname from the venerable and exotic 200-year-old oak trees that line the streets, planted to provide wood for the wine industry.

It's a thriving student town with lively and youthful nightlife, and has also been described as the heart of Afrikaner liberalism. Most of the viti- and viniculturists are trained here.

Stellenbosch gave rise to the 'alternative Afrikaner' movement with its hosting of the anti-establishment Voëlvry ('Feel Free') concert tour in 1988. It would later be the launching pad for South Africa's best-loved rockers, the Springbok Nude Girls and cutting-edge comic-book artists Konrad Botes and Anton Kannemeyer of Bitterkomix notoriety. The town can still be quite conservative, though: for instance, the local ethics committee insisted that the pub 'The Drunken Springbok' drop the 'drunken' from its name.

Stellenbosch has some wonderfully preserved old buildings, especially round the grassy braak ('town square') and the university buildings, including a subterranean library. It also has one of the oldest pubs in the country, De Akker. The old town area is bristling with sidewalk cafés, interesting little shops and historic attractions, and it's best to wander through on foot. When driving around, beware of the mill-stream ditches lining the roads – more than one car has fallen into these – and look for street names on the kerb rather than on signposts.

There are easily more than 106 cellars within a 25-kilometre (15-mile) radius of Stellenbosch and those are just the ones that are listed on the

Sightseeing

LIVE FLAT OUT

Life takes on new meaning at the Spier Village Hotel, not least because here we have everything you need to lay back, relax and rejuvenate yourself. Enjoy a variety of restaurants, the Cape African experience at Moyo, a new deli, and a comprehensive range of superb wines from the wine centre. And you can also take advantage of our new boutique health spa, which offers a wide range of treatments. Now that's living.

The Village

WINELANDS HOTEL

To experience these and the many other pleasures call us on +27 21 809 1100.
email: info@spier.co.za website: www.spier.co.za

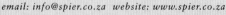

official wine route. **Spier** is probably the most popular destination in the Winelands, offering wine-tastings, picnics and several restaurants, as well as a cheetah centre, arts and culture at the amphitheatre, and a golf course. For maps and more information, contact the Stellenbosch Wine Route Office (021 886 4310/www.wine routes.co.za) or the Stellenbosch Tourist Centre (*see p87*).

Butterfly World

R44 Klapmuts (021 875 5628). **Open** 9am-5pm daily. **Admission** R25; R12.50-R20 concessions. **Credit** AmEx, DC, MC, V.
The location for the award-winning short film *Clowns*, Butterfly World has a sneaky way of delighting adults as well as their wide-eyed children. There are beautiful butterflies here, belonging to three continents, a variety of small birds flitting through the garden and some creepy-crawly spiders (behind glass) and stick insects too.

Heideveld Herbs

Blaauwklippen Road (021 880 1912). **Open** 8am-5pm Mon-Fri; 9am-5pm Sat; 10am-5pm Sun. **Credit** AmEx, DC, MC, V.
A superb little nursery of indigenous and exotic herbs and shrubs; also serves light lunches at the Crazy Kumquat restaurant.

Jonkershoek Nature Reserve

Jonkershoek Valley (021 866 1560). **Open** 8am-5pm daily, permits at the gate. **Map** p278 T2.
Jonkershoek Nature Reserve is a lushly green area of leafy countryside that rambles past mountain pools, forest and distinctive mountain peaks. There's loads to do for lovers of the outdoors: two waterfalls, as well as opportunities for fly-fishing, hiking, mountain biking and some beautiful picnic spots.

Moederkerk

2 Drostdy Street (021 883 3458/www.moederkerk. co.za). **Open** 9.30am-1pm, 2.30-4.40pm Mon-Thur; 9.30am-1pm Fri.
The second-oldest congregation in South Africa resides in the Moederkerk (which literally means 'Mother church'). Built in 1863, it was the vision of Rev Jan Neethling, whose statue is in the church garden, German master architect, Carl Otto Hager, and English builder James Jardine. This Dutch reformed church is well worth a visit, not only for its incredible Neo-Gothic architecture, awe-inspiring, and somewhat intimidating pulpit, and beautiful stained glass windows, but also to witness the string of back-to-back weddings hosted here (December and January is peak wedding season).

Oom Samie se Winkel

82-84 Dorp Street (021 887 0797). **Map** p278 P3.
This is an old-fashioned-style general dealer situated in an historic building. It is unashamedly touristy, with somewhat ratty shop assistants, but it still is a good place to pop into for old-fashioned sweets, crafts and bric-a-brac.

Stellenbosch Botanical Garden

Corner of Neethling & Van Riebeeck Streets (021 808 3054). **Open** 8am-5pm daily. **Map** p278 R3.
South Africa's oldest university garden features an impressive variety of exotic and indigenous plants. This is also a favourite garden getaway for university students and lecturers alike.

Stellenbosch Village Museum

18 Van Ryneveld Street, Stellenbosch Town Centre (021 887 2948). **Open** 9.30am-5pm Mon-Sat; 2-5pm Sun. **Admission** R15; R2 concessions. **Credit** AmEx, DC, MC, V. **Map** p278 Q3.
Comprising four historic residences that have been carefully restored and furnished, the Stellenbosch Village Museum embodies the major architectural styles of three centuries. Schreuderhuis was one of the first pioneer buildings; and then came the gabled Blettermanhuis, which was built in the late 1700s; Grosvenor House, a two-storey neoclassical edifice, dates back to around 1800; and Berghuis is a typical Victorian home. Historical walking tours go from tourist information centre (*see p87*) and take in the Rhenish church, the Kruithuis or powder house and the original Theological College or 'angel factory'. It's also worth checking out the Toy and Miniature Museum (021 887 2948).

University of Stellenbosch

Stellenbosch (021 808 9111/www.sun.ac.za). **Map** p278 R2.
The picturesque town of Stellenbosch is dominated by the university and its students. Established in 1866 as the Stellenbosch Gymnasium, it then became the Victoria College of Stellenbosch, and eventually the University of Stellenbosch. A mostly Afrikaans university, it boasts among its graduates and staff some of the great intellectual minds of South Africa. The university buildings and residences are all close to one another, an easy cycle ride; and in term time you will see that a bicycle is still the preferred mode of transport. It comprises ten faculties and three satellite campuses – the Health Science faculty in Tygerberg, a business school in Bellville and a Military Academy in Saldanha. *See also p84* **Stellenbosch Maties**.

Wine estates

Annandale

Take the N2 from Cape Town, turn onto the R310 towards Stellenbosch, turn right into Annandale Rd (021 881 3560/ www.annandale.co.za). **Open** 10am-5pm Mon-Fri; 10am-5pm Sat. **Tastings** R10/3 red wines. **Credit** AmEx, DC, MC, V.
Best known for its port, and set in an attractive converted stable, Annandale has an unpretentious, rustic atmosphere. The cellars are overseen by fifth-generation winemaker Hempies du Toit (formerly of Alto Estate and also an ex-Springbok rugby player). You can also go for walks or even carriage rides around the vineyards.

Sightseeing

Blaauwklippen

*R44 between Stellenbosch & Somerset West (021 880
0133/www.blaauwklippen.com).* **Open** 9am-5pm
Mon-Sat; 9am-4pm Sun. **Tastings** R18-R25/5 wines.
Credit AmEx, DC, MC, V.
Recently taken over by the Arabella Sheraton group,
Blaauwklippen has been relaunched as a chic venue
complete with a deli and an à la carte restaurant that
also puts together picnic baskets.

Delheim

*Down Knorhoek Road off the R44 Simonsberg
(021 888 4600/www.delheim.com).* **Open** 9am-
5pm Mon-Fri; 9am-3.30pm Sat; 11am-3.30pm Sun.
Tastings R15/5 wines; R20 groups. **Credit** AmEx,
DC, MC, V.
Delheim is infamous for its sweet Spatzendreck
('sparrow dung') wine, which was awarded 'worst
label' by the industry on its release in the '70s –
you'll have to go there and try it. The other ranges
are more prestigious than cheeky.

Morgenster

*Vergelegen Avenue, Somerset West (021 852 1738/
www.morgenster.co.za).* **Open** 10am-5pm Mon-Fri.
Tastings (and cellar tours) by appointment.
Credit AmEx, DC, MC, V.
Best known for its award-winning olive oil,
Morgenster also produces two excellent (and high-
priced) wines on an exclusive estate.

Muratie

*Down Knorhoek Rd, off the R44, Simonsberg (021
865 2330/www.muratie.co.za).* **Open** 9am-5pm Mon-
Fri; 10am-4pm Sat. **Tastings** R2/wine; R10 whole
range. **Credit** AmEx, DC, MC, V. **Map** p278 T1.
Muratie has been left untouched rather than being
pristinely restored, with ancient cobwebs draping
the windows of the gabled cellar, peeling walls and
rough floors. It's best known for its port.

Rust en Vrede

*Take the N2 from Cape Town, turn off onto
the R310 towards Stellenbosch, turn right into
Annandale Road (021 881 3881/www.rusten
vrede.co.za).* **Open** 9am-5pm Mon-Fri; 9am-4pm
Sat. **Tastings** free. **Credit** AmEx, DC, MC, V.
Rust en Vrede boasts gorgeous valley views and
beautifully restored buildings. That's not to mention
the very fine wines available here too.

Spier Estate

*Take the N2 from Cape Town, turn off onto
the R310 towards Stellenbosch (021 809 1100/
www.spier.co.za).* **Open** 9am-5pm daily. **Tastings**
Informal R8/5 wines. *Formal* R12/7 wines. **Credit**
AmEx, DC, MC, V.
Spier is probably the most popular tourist destination in the Winelands, offering a thoroughly comprehensive experience that includes wine-tasting,
dining, horse riding, golf, lakeside gourmet picnics,

Sightseeing

Stellenbosch Maties

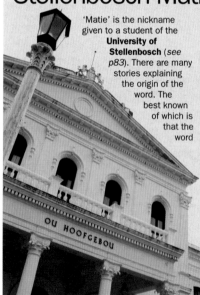

'Matie' is the nickname
given to a student of the
**University of
Stellenbosch** (*see
p83*). There are many
stories explaining
the origin of the
word. The
best known
of which is
that the
word is a shortening of the Afrikaans word *tamatie*,
meaning tomato, and referring to the
university colours.

But why would Maties be famous? Well,
because they can run very far, like Olympic
medalist Elana Meyer; or coach rugby, like
Springbok coach Rudolph Straueli. There are
other reasons, too, like being very wealthy,
in the case of Christo Wiese, South African
retail magnate and owner of the Lanzerac
Wine Estate. Or being very funny, like
Afrikaans comedian Casper de Vries and
comedian/singer/chef Nataniël. Maybe not
quite as funny, the first South African Pop
Idol, Heinz Winckler, is an ex-Matie. Being
beautiful sometimes happens when you
are a Matie, as in the case of two recent
Miss South Africa, Joanne Strauss and
Vanessa Carreira. Maties are also famous
for being deadly serious, like Edwin Cameron,
judge of the Supreme Court of Appeal
(whose president is an old Matie), when
he was one of the first public figures to
reveal his HIV-positive status in a bid
to raise AIDS awareness. Check out
www.sun.ac.za to find out more.

Franschhoek: the best place for food and wine, as well as leisurely street life. *See p80.*

a vintage train, a hotel (*see p39*), and musical and dramatic performances at the Spier amphitheatre (*see p184 and p213*). There are also raptor and cheetah outreach programmes here where you can see the magnificent birds and cheetahs (in different areas) up close. For a small donation you can even go in with the cheetahs (supervised) and pat them – and don't miss the raptor flying displays. Spier is also involved in agri-business and various social and arts development projects.

Vergelegen

Lourensford Road, Somerset West (021 847 1334/ www.vergelegen.co.za). **Open** 9.30am-4.30pm daily. **Admission** R10. **Tastings** from R2.50/wine. **Credit** AmEx, DC, MC, V.

Vergelegen is one of the most beautiful estates in the Cape Town area. It boast two good restaurants, a rose and herb garden and 360-degree stunning views from the cellar. Bill Clinton and the Queen Elizabeth have both stayed here.

Warwick

On the R44 between Stellenbosch & Klapmuts (021 884 4410/ www.warwickwine.co.za). **Open** 10am-4pm daily. *May-Sept* Closed Sat, Sun. **Tastings** *Informal* R5. *Formal* R20. **Credit** AmEx, DC, MC, V.
Warwick is a boutique estate with a warmly congenial atmosphere and award-winning wines. Make sure to ask the taster about the legend of the wedding cup that graces Warwick's labels.

Tourist information

Stellenbosch Tourism

36 Market Street (021 883 3584/www.istellenbosch. org.za). **Open** 8.30am-6pm Mon-Fri; 9am-5pm Sat; 10am-4pm Sun. **Map** p278 P3.

Paarl

Paarl is the third-oldest town in the country, and, at 12 kilometres (seven miles), also boasts the country's longest main street, its oldest church building still in use (Strooidak), its tallest steeple (Toringkerk) and its biggest wine cellar under one roof (KWV). It also has the second-largest granite rocks in the southern hemisphere. Looming above the town, the rocks were the inspiration for its name, when explorer Gabbema wandered through here in 1657 and decided that Paarl Rock, glistening in the rain, looked like a pearl.

It's a swell town (at least if you don't venture too deep into the industrial sector), with many historic buildings in Cape Dutch, Georgian and Victorian style, fine restaurants, great wine estates in the surrounding areas and the only museum and monument in the world dedicated to the Afrikaans language. And it's home to the Drakenstein Prison, formerly known as Victor Verster Jail, which is famous for being the site of Nelson Mandela's release in 1990 after 27 years of imprisonment.

Among Paarl's most famous estates and wineries are **Nederburg** and **KWV** winery, the latter of which produces brands like Roodeberg and Imoya, offers tours of its Wine Emporium. For a full list of wineries, contact the regional tourism bureaux. For maps and information on the Paarl Winelands, contact the Paarl Tourism Centre (*see p90*).

Afrikaans Language Museum

11 Pastorie Avenue (021 872 3441). **Open** 9am-5pm Mon-Fri. **Admission** R5. **No credit cards**.
While the ground floor of the Afrikaans Language Museum comes across as a fairly boring, run-of-the-mill place, dedicated to the eight men who decided to formalise and write down the Afrikaans language in 1875, upstairs you'll find interactive displays. Here, the language's evolution is visually mapped

out, showing that its roots are as much from African and Malay tongues as European languages. Indeed, the Malay slaves were the first to write down Afrikaans – in Arabic, in fact. There are also nifty games and displays, such as the oversized Afrikaans fridge magnet poetry board, and information about literature and works by 'alternative Afrikaners' including the controversial Bitterkomix, which were satirical comic strips that were so often offensive to the conservative Calvinists.

Le Bonheur Crocodile Farm

Babylonstoren Road, off the R44, South Paarl (021 863 1142). **Open** 9.30am-5pm daily. **Admission** R25; R5 concessions. **Credit** AmEx, DC, MC, V.
This really is a farm – the hatchling crocs are raised until they're just the right size to be harvested to make crocodile-leather goods. The skin is tanned, finished and sold on site. There is a conservation angle, however, and crocs up to 40 years old can be seen lying about in the sun.

Drakenstein Prison & Restaurant

Wemmershoek Road, between Paarl & Franschhoek (021 864 8095). **Open** 8am-2pm Tue-Thur; 8am-2pm, 5-10pm Fri; 5-10pm Sat. **Main courses** R25-R35. **Credit** AmEx, DC, MC, V.
Formerly Victor Verster Prison, this is where Nelson Mandela spent the last months of his imprisonment. Drakenstein Prison does not yet, however, have any kind of museum. What it does have, is a steakhouse-style restaurant where you can have dinner, by reservation only. The restaurant is situated just past the access gate within the prison, with inmates working as waiters and kitchen staff.

Het Gesticht Church

112 Main Street (021 872 3829). **Open** by appointment only.
This is the fourth oldest church in the country, more or less in its original state and built in 1720.

Paarl Mountain Nature Reserve

Follow the signs to the Taal Monument & then turn onto the dirt road on your right before you get to the gates.
The first colonists thought the hulking granite rocks above Paarl looked like 'pearls' thanks to recent rain, but the Khoisans' 'skilpadberg' ('tortoise-head mountain') nickname is probably more appropriate. You can take a slow drive to the top of the mountain for amazing views (although the road is pitted with nasty potholes) or join the droves of sunset mountain bikers and hikers. There have been muggings in the area, so don't go alone.

Paarl Museum

303 Main Street (021 872 2651). **Open** 9am-5pm Mon-Fri; 9am-1pm Sat. **Admission** R5. **No credit cards**.
The museum itself is a National Monument, housed in a Cape Dutch property that was built in 1787. It traces the history of the Paarl area, all the way back

Sightseeing

to the first settlers in 1687 through to the first forced removals of black people to emergency camps in 1951. Paarl Museum also holds the gravestone of the only South African slave to be sentenced to death for murdering another slave.

Strooidak Church
Main Road between Haarlem & Rose streets (021 872 4396). **Open** by appointment only.

Built in 1805, this is the oldest church still in use in the country. 'Strooidak' means 'straw roof'. It is possible to attend services (in Afrikaans) on Sundays.

Taal Monument
Follow the signs from town, up Gabbema Doordrift Street (021 863 2800). **Open** *Winter* 8.15am-5pm Mon-Fri. *Summer* 8.15am-9pm Mon-Fri. **Admission** R5; R2 concessions. **No credit cards**.

Strawberry-picking

The Western Cape is packed with fruit farms, but head to one of these three just outside Stellenbosch to sample the sweetest strawberries available. The season is November to February.

Mooiberge
R44 between Stellenbosch & Somerset West (021 881 3222). **Open** 2-5pm Sat; 10am-5pm Sun. **Rate** R14 per kilo. **Credit** AmEx, DC, MC, V.
With its original scarecrows (including a tableau of the Spice Girls), Mooiberge has become somewhat of a landmark in the area.

Mountain Breeze
R44 between Stellenbosch & Somerset West (021 880 1700). **Open** 9am-4.30pm daily. **Rate** R14 per kilo. **Credit** AmEx, DC, MC, V.

Here you can eat and pick your way through rows and rows of some of the freshest strawberries in the area.

Polkadraai
Polkadraai Road, Stellenbosch (021 881 3303). **Open** 9.30am-4.30pm daily. **Admission** R2; R1 under-10s. **Rate** R16 per kilo. **Credit** AmEx, DC, MC, V.
Entertaining strawberry-picking for kids.

Hillcrest Berry Orchards
Banhoek Valley, R310, Stellenbosch (021 885 1629/www.hillcrestberries.co.za). **Open** 9am-5.30pm daily. **Credit** AmEx, DC, MC, V.
You can't actually pick berries here, but sample the range of jams, vinegars, syrups, mustards and dried fruit, all made from raspberries, blackberries and gooseberries.

The soaring spires of the Taal Monument (a monument to the Afrikaans Language) are striking from afar, luring many a tourist into the region for a better look. Close-up, the monument is even stranger, like a leftover *Star Trek* set, especially with the mammoth granite boulders looming behind. The monument takes into account the contribution of African languages and Malay in shaping Afrikaans – the language that is spoken today by more coloured people than white. Picnics are available from the café for R40 per basket.

Toring Kerk
Corner of Main & Van der Lingen (021 872 6730). **Open** by appointment, groups only.
Toring Kerk, which means 'Tower Church', boasts the tallest steeple – towering up to 57m (187ft) high – in the whole of South Africa.

Wine estates

Boschendal
Pniel Road, Groot Drakenstein (021 870 4200). **Open** 8.30am-4.30pm Mon-Sat; 8.30am-4.30pm Sun. **Tastings** R12. *Vineyard tours* summer only R15. **Credit** AmEx, DC, MC, V.
Another venerable grande dame, Boschendal offers French-style country fare for picnics (R80), wine-tastings under hulking oaks, a historic manor house, an excellent restaurant (with a very good lunch buffet), a superior café and deli (*see p119*), and a crafts market that's located in the old coach house. The hour-long vineyard tour in summer ends at a viewpoint on the slopes of the Simonsberg mountain.

Fairview
Agter Paarl Road (021 863 2450/www.fairview. co.za). **Open** 8.30am-5pm Mon-Fri; 8.30am-1pm Sat. **Tastings** R10/8 wines & cheeses. **Credit** AmEx, DC, MC, V.
Best known for its 'goat's tower' that appears on many of the estate's labels. The family-owned Fairview estate is the largest producer of speciality goats' and cows' milk cheeses in the country. An essential stop for those that like smelly cheeses.

Glen Carlou
Simondium Road, Klapmuts (021 875 5528/ www.glencarlou.co.za). **Open** 8.45am-4.45pm Mon-Fri; 9am-12.45pm Sat. **Tastings** R10/6-8 wines & cheeses. *Group* R15/person. **Credit** AmEx, DC, MC, V.
Glen Carlou offers visitors superior Ayrsdale cheeses, along with a good selection of wines that can be tasted on this small and cheery farm.

KWV Cellars
Kohler Street (021 807 3007). **Open** 9am-4.30pm Mon-Sat. **Tastings** R15/5 wines. *Cellar tours* R20. **Credit** AmEx, DC, MC, V.
KWV is the biggest wine co-operative in the world, so it's only fitting that its cathedral-like wine cellar should be the largest under one roof in the country. It also makes some very good wines.

The futuristic **Taal Monument**. *See p88.*

Nederburg
R101 Sonstraal Road (021 862 3104/www.neder burg.co.za). **Open** 8.30am-5pm Mon-Fri; 10am-4pm Sat; 11am-4pm Sun. **Tastings** R17 Mon-Fri; R25 Sat. **Credit** AmEx, DC, MC, V.
One of the best-known giants of the Winelands with many awards under its belt, the Nederburg estate also offers picnics (R70 per person, by appointment) with a 250ml bottle of Nederburg wine. The harvest breakfast in February is R100 per person, which includes grape-picking and a farmhouse brekkie.

Nelson's Creek
R44 Paarl, Windmeul (021 869 8453/www.nelsons creek.co.za). **Open** 8am-5pm Mon-Fri; 9am-2pm Sat. **Tastings** R10/6 wines. *Cellar & vineyard tours* R20. **Credit** AmEx, DC, MC, V.
One of the oldest social-development programmes in the area. The New Beginnings label (which is served on South African Airways flights) was born seven years ago when land was granted to the farm's labourers to develop their own wines. The Pinotage is very good, but then so is that of the parent farm. Cellar tours include a tasting.

Old-style **Oom Samie se Winkel**. *See p83.*

Tourist information

Paarl Tourism
216 Main Street (021 872 3829/www.paarlonline. com). **Open** 9am-5pm Mon-Fri; 9am-1pm Sat; 10am-1pm Sun.

Wellington

Previously known as Wamakersvallei ('wagon-makers' valley'), Wellington assumed its current moniker in 1840 in honour of the hero of the battle of Waterloo. The little town is a mere 72 kilometres (45 miles) from Cape Town, but far enough off the main tourist track to provide a welcome respite from the city's crowds. It's not quite a sleepy town, but the pace here is definitely slower and the locals are friendly and chatty.

The town lies in a valley against the backdrop of the Groenberg mountains. Historic buildings are tucked between more modern shopfronts. The tourist information centre, for instance, is located in the Old Market Building, built in 1847; and the Dutch Reformed Church was raised in 1840. You can spend an hour or two on the attractions in town, including the **Wellington Museum** and **Ouma Granny's** house, with its odd collection of goodies of yesteryear; and the rest of the day cruising the outlying Winelands or indulging in outdoor activities like hiking the 150-year-old **Bains kloof Pass** or enjoying wine- and olive-tastings on horseback at **Diemersfontein**.

Wellington's wine route is small and intimate and it is home to many of the area's vine-cutting nurseries. The estates are generally more personal and much less commercial than their counterparts on busier wine routes; for example, there's no room for giant buses, and tastings are more likely to be presided over by the farm's owner or the winemaker rather than the ubiquitous svelte young things found elsewhere. Perfect for a quiet visit.

Bain's Kloof Pass
Take the R301 towards the pass.
Built in 1853, the road through the historic pass to Ceres recently celebrated its 150th anniversary. It's good for drives, mountain biking, hiking and horse riding (get permits and blurb from the tourist information centre). Stone-Age artefacts still turn up in the surrounding mountains.

Block House
Off the R44 towards Hermon.
Just outside the town is the Block House, built by the British in 1899 to protect the adjacent railway line during the Anglo-Boer war. It's only of minor interest as it's closed to the public and takes only 30 seconds to walk around.

Ouma Granny's
Fontein Street (021 873 4604). **Open** 9.30am-12.30pm Fri. **Admission** donations welcome.
Ouma Granny, aka Joyce Amelie Hoogenhout-Morse, was a pillar in the Wellington community and a keen writer until her death in her 80s a few years ago. A keen collector, her eclectic and sprawling collection of priceless antiques and bizarrely eccentric bric-a-brac is on display in a cute little Victorian house overlooking Victoria Park. Visiting this museum is a very unique experience.

Wellington Museum
Church Street (021 873 4710). **Open** 9am-5pm Mon-Fri. **Admission** donations welcome.
This quaint little museum traces the area's history back to its first Stone Age inhabitants through to the Khoi and the San, who left their mark on the area with rock paintings, and the French Huguenot settlers. Wellington Museum displays also cover the farming, wine and leather industries.

Wine estates

Diemersfontein

*On the eastern side of the R301 (021 873 2671/
www.diemersfontein.co.za).* **Open** 8.30am-5pm Mon-
Fri; 10am-5pm Sat, Sun. **Tastings** R15/6 wines.
Credit AmEx, DC, MC, V.

Diemersfontein's gardens have appeared in many
wedding photos and fashion shoots. The estate
offers wine-tasting on horseback, picnics in the garden (R120) and quality accommodation in cottages
or the historic manor house. A two-day wine course
is run here, together with the Cape Wine Association
(R2,300 per person including accommodation, visits
to other farms, all meals and wine-tastings).

Wamakersvallei

Distillery Road (021 873 1582). **Open** 8am-5pm
Mon-Fri; 8.30am-12.30pm Sat. **Tastings** free.

Don't visit Wamakersvallei for the scenery, but for
the estate's excellent flagship La Cave wines, which
have scooped several local and international awards.
Make sure to pick up a few bottles to take home with
you: you won't find anything like it anywhere else.

Tourist information

Wellington Tourism

*104 Main Road (021 873 4604/www.visit
wellington.com).* **Open** 8am-5pm Mon-Fri;
9am-2pm Sat.

Sightseeing

My kind of town Koos Kombuis

Cape Town is... the best place in the world.
Capetonians are... broke but beautiful.
Table Mountain is... the most important
object in the world.
Fabulous food is... found in the outlying
districts.
I buy take-aways at... my local chemist.
Sundowners are best spent... anywhere in
Hout Bay.
Lazy mornings are spent... in rush-hour
traffic.
The strange thing about this town is... the
fact that people are still living elsewhere in
South Africa.
Ever wondered why... so many Capetonians
have unroadworthy vehicles?
I soak up culture at... my local video-rental
company.
I'm frustrated by... Capetonians' habit of
double-parking in the centre of the city.
Spiritual nourishment is found... at my
local chemist.
The landmark I love is... Table Mountain.
The landmark I loathe is... the statue of
copulating Vienna sausages in front of the
Civic Centre (12 Hertzog Boulevard,
Foreshore, City Bowl).
My community is... laid-back.
Creativity flourishes in... the street flea
markets (Greenmarket Square, which has
creative clothing and adornments,
some art; Hout Bay, art and
crafts market; Green Point:
predominantly African curios).
I bare my body... in the mirror.
I go shopping in...the
Somerset Mall (Head out of
Cape Town towards
Somerset West on the

N2, then take the R44 Stellenbosch turn-off.
Somerset Mall is on your right-hand side).
I show off... my new PT Cruiser.
I take tourists to... the Winelands
(Winelands Tourism Office, 021 872 0686).
I listen to... my wife.
I find local politics... non-existent.
Koos A Kombuis is the original Alternative
Afrikaner.

This writer/poet/singer/songwriter
(www.kooskombuis.co.za) first crept into the
hearts of South Africans who were searching
for an anti-hero they could relate to. He and a
band of musicians, under the collective name
of Voëlvry ('feel free') toured campuses
across South Africa, singing political-protest
songs in Afrikaans. The ruling Nationalist
Party hated them, the Church denounced
them and the youth believed in them. Look
out for his latest book *The Secret Diary of
God* as well as his CDs,
particularly 'Madiba
Bay' in which he
sings in English and
Afrikaans.

CIRCA 1693
HE OLD MATURATIO
CELLAR
BELLINGHAM

BELLINGHAM

BELLINGHAM
EST. 1693

OUR FOUNDER'S
Shiraz

Made in honour of Bellingham's inspired and passionate
founding father, Bernard Podlashuk, this Shiraz
reflects his ingenuity, vision and love for fine wine

WINE OF SOUTH AFRICA

Classic, Modern, Exceptional

Eat, Drink, Shop

Restaurants

A city that likes to go out for its supper.

Unlike their up-country chums, Capetonians, in the main, tend not to entertain at home. This is to the extent that it is highly possible to be good friends with someone for years without having any more of an idea of where they live than the general area code. As such, Cape Town has something of a surplus of restaurants (at last count somewhere upwards of 7,500) to meet the rather prodigious entertainment needs. The upside of this is that there are many excellent restaurants, even more journeyman contenders but, alas, all too numerous are those that should be given a good spanking and sent to bed with no supper. Or, if justice were to be poetic, forced to eat their own issue.

So then, how to tell if your restaurant-of-choice is up to the job? Well, as a general rule of thumb: the longer it's been around, the better it probably is. Capetonians are notoriously fickle. So if the restaurant has survived a good long while, it must be good. Fast-food franchises are no worse than their international counterparts. The same cannot be said of their (slightly) more upmarket relatives that have somehow conned those who really should know better that indifferent service and food to match are somehow cool. These establishments, specialising in coffee (cold) and light meals (awful), and unable to attract clientele through any ploy other than proximity, are usually found in the more upmarket shopping malls.

Given the cosmopolitan nature of the city, it's not surprising that pretty much everything is on offer – heck, there's even restaurants that specialise in South African cuisine. Though, if that's what you're after, the best bet is to get a Capetonian to invite you to their house for a traditional *braaivleis*, which, unless the person in charge is an absolute butterfingers, should be the best barbequed food you've ever eaten.

If you're looking for something more exotic, you'll be hooked on Cape Malay cuisine, which is typified by the use of subtle spices such as turmeric, cinnamon and ginger. Fruit, whether canned or fresh, is also used with savoury dishes. The taste for mixing sweet, fresh fruitiness with heavy meat is an acquired one, but, once experienced, it is very easy to fall in love and search for it in your comfort food. Dishes such as bobotie, curries, masala fish, sosaties, yellow rice with raisins, and pickled fish are typical of the cuisine, and are often

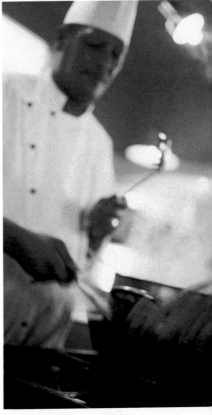

Pot luck: **Beluga.** *See p109.*

served with sambals such as coconut, cucumber relish and chutney. You are most likely to eat this kind of food at a specialist traditional restaurant. Sadly, there are few restaurants specializing only in Cape Malay food, but other establishments, promising traditional food, will inevitably include some of these dishes on their menu. (For more examples of South African food, *see p110* **Why local is *lekker*.**)

African food, with its heavy meat dishes and unique flavours can be found at restaurants such as the **Africa Café** (*see p99*) and

Eat, Drink, Shop

Marco's African Place (*see p99*). The food is excellent, vibe authentic and it will be a great introduction to the tastes of Africa, but be wary of the offal, if you're at all squeamish. Don't feel that adventurous? It's OK. Cape Town's restaurants tend to keep up with international trends and diners can expect contemporary cuisine that's cooked and presented with flair. Understanding the menus should pose no problem unless you are dining at a restaurant specialising in African or local cuisine, in which case, some friendly soul will probably be only too happy to help you out.

For an alternative to restaurants in Cape Town proper, why not get in the car and drive. While there isn't much going on in the Northern suburbs by way of sightseeing, it is home to a vast portion of Capetonians, which means that you'll find restaurants and a few bars that do not sway to the pretentions that sometimes are all too prevalent within the rest of the peninsula. What it does have is the West Coast (up to Melkbosstrand), which falls under the Northern suburbs geographical demarcation. Here you will find the pleasures of long beaches (cold water), promenades, kitesurfing and ice-cream vendors. The restaurants have great views and residents enjoy a laid-back lifestyle.

Unlike many other countries, local waiters are paid a pittance by establishments, and are, therefore, largely dependent on tip money. Restaurateurs claim this is because paying them a living wage would drive prices, which have already scampered up in recent years, to unacceptable levels. Besides which, if they have to 'sing for their supper' they're apt to provide better service. Sound in theory, much less so in practice: surly waiters are a bountiful local commodity, so don't be too surprised if they look at you like you've just pulled them out of their father's funeral when you ask for some black pepper. Still, in most establishments, a service charge is not included and, as such, a ten to 15 per cent tip is customary. Be warned: for dining parties of eight or more, numerous establishments do add a service charge and yes, my friend, a further gratuity is expected over and above that.

Smoking in restaurants is a big issue in South Africa at the moment, the Department of Health having decreed that restaurants must either create architecturally-segregated smoking sections or, like airplanes, be smoke-free zones. And anyone caught in breech will have electrodes attached to their more sensitive extremities, or something equally draconian. Indeed, it's only a matter of time before they start installing smoke detectors in the bathrooms. Many restaurants, due to space or financial considerations, have been unable to

comply. So if you fancy a bit of a puff between (or indeed during) courses, it's best to phone ahead and find out whether you'll have to skulk about outside every time Mr Nick O'Tine demands your attention. Smoking sections,

The best Restaurants

For gourmet food
Try **one.Waterfront** (*see p106*) for chef Bruce Robertson's incredible creations or **La Colombe** (*see p115*) for French sophistication. For subtle and spicy local flavours **Le Quartier Français** (*see p119*) is rarely surpassed. The **Savoy Cabbage** (*see p97*) has game and seafood for serious foodies.

For a trad African experience
Marco's African Place (*see p99*) is where the locals hang out in search of great music and authentic food. Or **Marimba** (*see p99*) has a more modern and international take on the whole African experience. For sheer African magic you should consider Moyo at **Spier** (*see p118*).

For the hippest scene
Tank (*see p109*) is where the chic hang out for sushi and good company. **Shoga** (*see p97*) offers unpretentious hipness and gourmet pizzas in an up-and-coming area.

For sea views
Wakame (*see p112*) has an incredible view of the Atlantic: ask for a seat on the balcony, feel the sun on your skin, and order the catch of the day. The welcoming **Tuscany Beach Café** (*see p110*) and **Blues** (*see p110*) offer great views of the Camps Bay Strip. While **On the Rocks** (*see p113*), the **Blue Peter** (*see p114*), and **Café Blouberg** (*see p114*) have the pick of the West Coast views.

For seafood
The food at **Harbour House** (*see p117*) and **Black Marlin** (*see p116*) is only surpassed by the sea views. **La Perla** (*see p110*) is legendary and the newer **Pigalle** (*see p112*) also offers good fishy fare.

For afternoon tea
Go **La Petite Tarte** (*see p113*) for elegant surroundings and tea that is better than chocolate; head to **Melissa's** (*see p105*) for a slice of polka-dot cake and **Cinn-full** (*see p105*) for hot cinnamon buns.

Eat, Drink, Shop

comprising only 25 per cent of floor space, are at a premium and tend to fill up more quickly than their clean-lunged cousins.

Booking, while not a bad idea, is not essential in most restaurants. Upper-enders traditionally require it, though, and in season, failure to buy tickets prior to the game might result in a significant heel-cooling (or kicking) period while you wait for a table. And while most major credit cards are accepted, be warned that if you try to pay by cheque, a goodly number of restaurants will issue you with a pair of rubber gloves and dispatch you straight to the kitchen to help with the washing-up.

City Bowl

Contemporary

Five Flies

14-16 Keerom Street, City Centre (021 424 4442/ www.fiveflies.co.za). **Open** noon-3pm, 7-11pm Mon-Fri; 7-11pm Sat, Sun. **Set meal** R135. **Credit** AmEx, DC, MC, V. **Map** p282 G4.

The revamped Dutch Club next to the High Court fills you with a sense of the dramatic. Well supported by the legal fraternity, this impressively spacious restaurant offers smaller dining rooms for private parties, fixed-price two-, three- and four-course menus and a wonderful bar. The food and service are at times erratic – sometimes you're lucky, and sometimes you're not. But still, Flies has a very loyal following, so give it a try.

Ginja

121 Castle Street, City Centre (021 426 2368). **Open** 7-11pm Mon-Sat. **Set meal** R135. **Credit** AmEx, DC, MC, V. **Map** p282 G3.

In a narrow, brick building that was once a small warehouse, this stylish restaurant offers eccentric glamour as well as impressive fusion food. Asian influences lend new tastes to once-familiar flavours. A fabulous night out for serious foodies.

Madame Zingara

192 Loop Street, City Centre (021 426 2458). **Open** 7-11pm Mon-Sat. **Main courses** R60. **Credit** AmEx, DC, MC, V. **Map** p282 G4.

This haven of good food, gypsy kitsch, fairy lights and strewn rose petals is a much-loved Cape Town restaurant. Owner Richard Griffin's signature dish of chilli-chocolate fillet medallions has graced more magazine pages than any other meal in town. All the food is beautifully presented and lives up to the hype. Tarot readers occasionally pitch up to predict futures and belly dancers appear later in the evening.

Manolo

30 Kloof Street, Gardens (021 422 4747/ www.manolo.co.za). **Open** noon-1am, Mon-Sat; 7pm-1am Sun. **Main courses** R82. **Credit** AmEx, DC, MC, V. **Map** p282 F5.

Chic. Chic. Chic. Manolo is well worth visiting for the decor and ambience alone. Fortunately the food is excellent too, which makes for a pretty good night out, if you can afford it. Manolo doesn't come cheap. The setting is an old Victorian house that now has soft white curtains billowing off the veranda and a fabulous bar area with vaulted pressed ceilings and blueish lighting. The restaurant consists of several rooms, all individually styled, which allows for a different room for each visit. And there will be more than one visit. The contemporary food is sublime – subtle flavours, interesting combinations and beautifully prepared. They also have an extensive wine list, and you will be tempted to linger long after you've finished your trio of crème brûlée.

Moja

98 Shortmarket Street, Heritage Square, City Centre (021 423 4989/www.fez.co.za). **Open** noon-11pm daily. **Main courses** R70. **Credit** AmEx, DC, MC, V. **Map** p282 G3.

This is the latest addition to the Fez group, whose other ventures include Strega, Po Na Na and the Fez. The look is best described as Afro-Bond chic, with retro-'70s decor, shockingly orange flooring and a piranha tank. The food and drink is great, but don't come if you're very hungry – you still have to cook most of it. Yes, in keeping with the theme, there is plenty of lava-stone cooking to be done, and lovely fondues to be melted. The boudoir-style lounge upstairs is a noteable crowd-puller.

Savoy Cabbage

101 Hout Street, City Centre (021 424 2626). **Open** noon-2.30pm, 7-10.30pm Mon-Fri; 7-10.30pm Sat. **Main courses** R100. **Credit** AmEx, DC, MC, V. **Map** p282 G3.

A dramatically beautiful interior (all brick, glass and concrete) and a high calibre, daily-changing menu make this a 'booking essential' sort of establishment. Food is served up from an open kitchen and uses local produce in abundance. The tomato tart is the stuff of legend and the game is superb, as is the seafood. Regularly bestowed with plaudits and awards, the Savoy Cabbage is one of Cape Town's unmissable gastronomic experiences.

Shoga

121 Castle Street, City Centre (021 426 2369). **Open** 7-11pm Mon-Sat. **Set meal** R165. **Credit** AmEx, DC, MC, V. **Map** p282 G3.

Slightly hidden in an up-and-coming area of town, Shoga is situated above its sister restaurant Ginja. Deliciously decadent martinis and cocktails help to wash down the gourmet pizzas and fusion food. The tandoor oven delivers some wonderful earthy flavours, and the superb selection of nibbles – garlic naan, chilli peanut sauce and rocket, pine nuts and fresh lemon – make for excellent starters. It's in a spacious environment overlooking the city, with fabulous art deco couches to relax in before or after your meal. And unexpectedly for such a trendy spot, the service is refreshingly friendly.

Eat, Drink, Shop

The chef's table

In the days of yore, if someone invited you to dinner and made you sit in the kitchen among 'the help', they'd receive no Yuletide greeting card from you the following year. If, however, someone invites you to a Chef's Table dinner in the Mount Nelson's kitchen, (*pictured*) you should offer to make their Christmas lunch. And provide the paper hats and crackers.

It's like being given a backstage pass and being treated like royalty all at once. You are lead through the kitchen and seated at a table where all are permitted to watch the culinary engagements of the staff while enjoying some of the finest food you'll ever experience. The menu is flexible and as such should you require that there be no dishes involving the presence of shellfish, tomato or the like, it shall be so.

The Chef's Table is limited to a minimum of six and a maximum of ten people and consists of a five-course meal, each course accompanied by a specially selected wine, each of which is explained by both chef and sommelier. Best of all, the preparation of one of the dishes will be demonstrated right next to the table. After the meal each guest is given a commemorative apron, but not, alas, a chance to have a go in what must be the cleanest and most well-appointed kitchen in all Christendom.

The whole shebang costs R500 per person, which ain't cheap but it does includes the aforementioned wines. Should the host prefer to choose bottles from the Mount Nelson's cellar wine list, the gourmet experience is priced at R380 per person excluding the cost of the selected wines.

The Mount Nelson Hotel
76 Orange Street, Gardens (021 483 1198/ www.mountnelsonhotel.orient-express.com). **Map** p282 G5.

African

The Africa Café
*108 Shortmarket Street, Heritage Square, City
Centre (021 422 0221).* **Open** 6.30am-11pm daily.
Set menu R125. **Credit** AmEx, DC, MC, V.
Map p282 G3.
If you're looking for the flavours of Africa, this is
where you'll find them. The food as well as the décor
takes its inspiration from the whole African continent, but focuses on the southern part. It requires
a slightly adventurous palate to appreciate the
offerings, but those who do find this an authentic
and pleasant local experience.

Marco's African Place
*15 Rose Lane, Corner Strand & Buitengracht
Streets, Bo-Kaap (021 423 5412/www.marcos
africanplace.co.za).* **Open** noon-11pm daily.
Main courses R55. **Credit** AmEx, DC, MC, V.
Map p282 G4.
While you could be forgiven for initially thinking
that this is a venue catering for tourists wanting to
try African specialities like tripe and crocodile, you
are soon proved wrong. As the night progresses,
Marco's is filled with locals and Africans ready to
party till the small hours. Always offering great live
music, this is an authentic African experience, where
local politicians, beautiful young things and the
partying classes let it all hang out.

Marimba
*Cape Town International Convention Centre,
Foreshore (021 418 3366/www.marimbaSA.com).*
Open noon-1am Mon-Fri; 6.30pm-1am Sat, Sun.
Main courses R120. **Credit** AmEx, DC, MC, V.
Map p282 G2.
Go for some lovely cocktails on the terrace, a cigar
in the lounge, or dinner and savour traditional dishes
or more global cuisine – with excellent service to
boot. You can try the authentic African experience
with springbok and even crocodile on the menu.
Other more international delicacies include duck
liver with cherry sauce and a great selection of
seafood. The décor is a glitzy African experience,
with wire wrapped around pillars, great mood lighting and beautiful wooden tables.

Gourmet

Aubergine
*39 Barnet Street, Gardens (021 465 4909/
www.aubergine.co.za).* **Open** 7-10.30pm Mon-Wed,
Fri, Sat; noon-2.30pm, 7-10.30pm Thur. **Main courses**
R98. **Credit** AmEx, DC, MC, V. **Map** p282 G5.
Aubergine offers fine dining in a relaxed, yet intimate environment, home in the 19th century to Sir
John Wylde, first Chief Justice of the Cape. Palm
fronds and the Cape Town night look down romantically on the alfresco terrace; the indoor tables are
smartly dressed. Immensely popular, the restaurant
specialises in a 'Degustation Menu', which offers the

Tank, ready for battle. *See p109.*

most winning dishes conjured up by the talented
chef, Harald Bresselschmidt. Think sirloin topped
with potato and red-wine onion crust and served
with creamy savoy cabbage and Merlot reduction;
and cottage-cheese omelette with mandarin ragout.

Blue Danube
*102 New Church Street, Tamboerskloof (021 423
3624).* **Open** noon-3pm, 7-11pm Tue-Fri; 7-11pm
Mon, Sat, Sun. **Main courses** R100. **Credit** AmEx,
DC, MC, V. **Map** p282 F4.
If you're keen to experience fine dining in an intimate environment, make your reservation at Blue
Danube, where the renowned chef Thomas Sinn will
produce inspired dishes using the freshest of South
African produce with his Austrian flair. There are
function rooms for private parties, which is good to
keep in mind.

Cape Colony
*Mount Nelson Hotel, 76 Orange Street, Gardens
(021 483 1198/www.mountnelsonhotel.orient-
express.com).* **Open** 6.30-10.30pm daily. **Main
courses** R100. **Credit** AmEx, DC, MC, V.
Map p282 G5.

Eat, Drink, Shop

Drinking up the atmosphere at **Vida e Caffè**. *See p105.*

Eat, Drink, Shop

Arguably one of the best restaurants in Cape Town. The Colony's reputation for excellence is such that living up to it is nigh-on impossible. And yet it does. The menu, sensibly, is fairly traditional Mediterranean, but does include some South African and Oriental influences. The setting is a grand colonial affair of dark wood, tall windows and heavy draped curtains, dotted with palm trees. Service is predictably superb and the wine list is fabulous. It is pricey, but not to the point of stupidity.

Leinster Hall

7 Weltevreden Street, Gardens (021 424 1836). **Open** 7-11pm Tue-Sat. **Main courses** R70. **Credit** AmEx, DC, MC, V. **Map** p282 F5.
An understated, yet highly-rated, dining experience is offered in these historical buildings. The exciting contemporary menu offers South African flavours in innovative ways. The terrace is gorgeous on summer evenings, while the crackling fire is inviting during the colder months. Highly recommended.

Asian

Bukhara

33 Church Street, City Centre (021 424 0000/ www.bukhara.com). **Open** 12.30-3pm, 6.30-11pm daily. **Main courses** R120. **Credit** AmEx, DC, MC, V. **Map** p282 G4.
Everybody's favourite Indian restaurant, this is not a local curry-in-a-hurry, but most definitely presents the best that North Indian cuisine has to offer. The heavy wooden tables, silk drapes and copper place settings make this a romantic venue as well as the sort of place to go with a large group of friends, order loads of different dishes and a continuous stream of Cobras. Its tandoori offerings are wonderful, it makes the best butter chicken, its vindaloo is dangerous, and the garlic naan formidable.
Branch: Grand West Casino, Goodwood, Northern Suburbs (021 535 444/www.bukhara.com).

Chef Pon's Asian Kitchen

12 Mill Street, Gardens (021 465 5846). **Open** 6.30-11.30pm Mon-Sat. **Main courses** R45. **Credit** AmEx, DC, MC, V. **Map** p282 G5.
Always buzzing, Chef Pon's can be bargained on for quick, satisfying Asian food. Whether you simply feel like a bowl of Thai noodles or want the deluxe Asian experience, this is the most unpretentious way to get it. There is a large smoking section and suitably Oriental decoration dotted about.

Saigon

Cape Swiss Hotel, corner of Kloof & Camp Streets, Gardens (021 424 7670). **Open** 2.30-10.30pm daily. **Main courses** R68. **Credit** AmEx, DC, MC, V. **Map** p282 F5.
This Vietnamese restaurant has recently been renovated and the contemporary new look will appeal to those wanting glamorous surroundings but the same excellent authentic Vietnamese food they've always ordered. The caramelised pork is still on offer, as are the sublime Vietnamese spring rolls (much to everyone's relief). The addition of a sushi bar will appeal to those wanting lighter fare.

Yindees

22 Camp Street, City Centre (021 422 1012). **Open** 6-11pm Mon-Sat. **Main courses** R45. **Credit** AmEx, DC, MC, V. **Map** p282 G5.
Here you will find great Thai food in a restaurant that has paid as much attention to the authentic décor as it has to the tastes of Asia. In this old City Bowl home diners can either sit at the heavy wooden tables and chairs, or for a more novel experience, you can eat Thai green curry and the like whilst seated on the floor. This is a popular place, so book.

Mediterranean

Bacini's

177 Kloof Street, Gardens (021 423 6668). **Open** 10am-10pm daily. **Main courses** R40. **Credit** AmEx, DC, MC, V. **Map** p282 F4.
This is the quintessential Italian trattoria, serving thin and crispy pizzas, hearty salads and mouthwatering osso bucco. Grab a spot on the sunny verandah on a Sunday afternoon and if you're a soccer or motorsport fan, you'll be in good company as all the big sporting events are shown on TV here. By no means a sports bar, but hell, the pizza's good, and the winning team's Italian.

Café Gainsbourg

64 Kloof Street, Gardens (021 422 1780). **Open** 8am-10.30pm Mon-Fri; 9am-10.30pm Sat; 9am-3.30pm Sun. **Main courses** R60. **Credit** AmEx, DC, MC, V. **Map** p282 F5.
This elegant café serves wonderful French-inspired meals. The coffee is excellent and the home-baked cakes are to die for. A perfect spot for breakfast (good croissants and sophisticated bacon and eggs), lunch (gourmet sandwiches and salads) and dinner (a blackboard full of tantalising specials).

Café Paradiso

110 Kloof Street, Gardens (021 423 8653/ www.cafeparadiso.co.za). **Open** 10am-11pm Tue-Fri; 9.30am-11pm Sat, Sun. **Main courses** R60. **Credit** AmEx, DC, MC, V. **Map** p282 F5.
Although not the buzzing Italian eaterie it used to be, it is still a great spot for quiet dining – perfect for alfresco breakfasts, quick lunches or lazy sundowners alongside one of the best views of Table Mountain. The menu is fairly limited, but offers some excellent Mediterranean options.

Carlyle's on Derry

17 Derry Street, Vredehoek (021 461 8787). **Open** 4-10.30pm Mon-Sat. **Main courses** R45. **Credit** AmEx, DC, MC, V.
Carlyle's is relaxed and casual and 'the place to be' if you are looking for great food and great vibes. They offer Italian-based options such as seared tuna salad, slow-cooked lamb shank and innovative

Eat, Drink, Shop

pizzas. This restaurant has never done any advertising – it hasn't really needed to, as the faithful locals have made it their best-kept secret.

Colcaccio

Seeff House, 42 Hans Strijdom Avenue, Foreshore (021 419 4848). **Open** noon-11.30pm Mon-Fri; 6.30-11.30pm Sat, Sun. **Main courses** R40. **Credit** AmEx, MC, V. **Map** p283 H3.

Colcaccio serves gourmet pizzas in a massive, airy space. Thin-based and crispy with toppings, these pizzas will bring you back again and again. There are large salads and pastas, too. There is even a Heart Foundation Approved pizza, which is a fine option if you're feeling virtuous. If the loud scene isn't for you, get take-aways.

Limoncello

8 Breda Street, Gardens (021 461 5100). **Open** noon-3pm, 6-11pm Mon-Fri; 6-11pm Sat. **Main courses** R55. **Credit** AmEx, DC, MC, V. **Map** p282 G5.

This tiny, understated Italian eaterie is perfect for gourmet, thin-based pizzas. The chairs are uncomfortable and the ambience unlike that of traditional Italian restaurants, but the clean lines, open kitchen and consistently good food attract many locals.

Maria's

Dunkley Square, Gardens (021 461 8887). **Open** 11am-11pm Mon-Fri; 5pm-1am Sat. **Main courses** R50. **Credit** DC, MC, V. **Map** p282 G5.

Situated in the lovely Dunkley Square, surrounded by fairy lights and other restaurants, Maria's serves hearty Greek food at outdoor tables when the evenings are warm; and when it gets colder diners crowd into the dark and cosy interior. It's vibey and relaxed – no wine glasses here, simply quaff from a tumbler. Start with a meze platter and go on to gorgeous seafood pilafi or the succulent lamb. Leave space for something sweet.

Strega

Heritage Square, 100 Shortmarket Street, City Centre (021 423 4889/www.strega.co.za). **Open** 7-11pm Mon-Sat. **Main courses** R50. **Credit** AmEx, DC, MC, V. **Map** p282 G3.

If you're lucky it will be someone's birthday when you visit Strega – it's more than likely that you'll hear the exuberant singing of the waiters. Fresh and innovative Italian fare is served in contemporary surroundings. As part of the Heritage Square complex, you can easily follow up your meal with drinks at the luxurious Po Na Na Souk Bar (*see p120*).

Moroccan

Cara Lazuli

11 Buiten Street, City Centre (021 426 2351). **Open** 7-11pm Mon-Sat. **Main courses** R65. **Credit** AmEx, DC, MC, V. **Map** p282 G4.

Chef Richard Griffin is the brains behind this extremely popular restaurant. Rose-scented hand bowls make a serene start to meals, which range

from piping hot chicken tagines and couscous to shanks of lamb and roast vegetables. The chocolate cigars served piping hot with pistachio ice-cream are a winner. Fresh-mint iced granitas are also delicious, served after dinner before you settle in with a hookah pipe and yet another strong coffee.

Seafood

Miller's Thumb

10b Kloof Nek Road, Tamboerskloof (021 424 3838). **Open** 12.30-2pm, 6.30-10.30pm Tue-Fri; 6.30-10.30pm Sat. **Main courses** R70. **Credit** AmEx, DC, MC, V. **Map** p282 F5.

This suburban institution deserves much praise. Fabulous fresh seafood is served to please your palate – everything from Cajun to Moroccan or good old piri-piri. It's great for meat-eaters too. With personalised service from the owners, you know you are in good hands. The place is always filled with regulars who know that they'll be hard-pressed to find better food in a more casual, laid-back environment. The prices are reasonable, with interesting wines available by the glass.

Belgium-worshipping **Zero932**. *See p109.*

My kind of food Bruce Robertson

Bruce Robertson is the Executive Chef at one.Waterfront, the Cape Grace Hotel (*see p106*). An ex-advertising type (art director to be precise) who believes that food and fashion are integrally linked, Bruce creates dishes at this award-winning restaurant that both look and taste sublime. He's a bundle of energy, an enthusiastic raconteur, a night owl, and generally all-round nice guy.

When he's not wearing his chef's hat, this is how he eats:

For breakfast I have... four cups of coffee and a Mars Bar.

My food philosophy is... don't chase food.

I drink... white-wine spritzers.

My favourite food is... chunky white-bread peanut butter and jam sandwiches.

I buy take-aways at... Call-a Pizza (57 Regent Road, Sea Point, Atlantic Seaboard, 021 434 0818) where Ricky makes the best pizza; Saul's Saloon & Grill (152 Main Road, Sea Point, Atlantic Seaboard, 021 434 5404) because they're open 24 hours a day and it's great after a rough night out. Nando's for chicken (128 Main Road, Sea Point, Atlantic Seaboard, 021 439 7999).

I go... clubbing.

I chill out at... The Polana (Kalk Bay Harbour, False Bay, 021 788 7162) because of fabulous couches and great sea views, you can lounge around there for hours with a bottle of wine. Bientang se Grot (below

Marine Drive, near the Old Harbour, Hermanus, 028 312 3454) because you get to chill out and eat in a cave while the waves are crashing all around you.

My kitchen... doesn't stop thinking.

I buy provisions at... The Real Cheese (*see p141*) for the best cheeses.

My favourite South African flavours are... Kalahari truffles and West Coast oysters.

Steakhouses

Nelson's Eye

9 Hof Street, Gardens (021 423 2601). **Open** noon-12.30pm, 6.30-10.30pm Mon-Fri; 6.30-10.30pm Sat, Sun. **Main courses** R160. **Credit** AmEx, DC, MC, V.
Despite the grim name and dark, orange-and-brown '70s interior (old, not intentional), the Nelson's is a secret kept well by City Bowl dwellers. The steaks are sublime and served with delicious sauces; the salads are old-fashioned; and the starters of the prawn cocktail variety. (More seafood comes in the form of oysters, chowders and langoustines.) Pull in for steak, excellent chips and a good bottle of red wine. Surprisingly pricey, though.

Robertson's

125 Buitengracht Street, City Centre (021 422 2465). **Open** 6.30am-11pm daily. **Main courses** R70. **Credit** AmEx, DC, MC, V. **Map** p282 G4.
Robertson's serves some of the best oxtail in town. It also has a café, which opens at 6.30am sharp for breakfast. The food tends to be wholesome and

meaty; the décor, by contrast, is slick. This is the sort of place where you could end up spending an awful lot of time – early breakfasts, casual long lunches, heavy dinners and even post-theatre nightcaps. The staff are friendly and as an added boon, valet parking is provided free of charge.

Cafés & casual eating

Arnold's

60 Kloof Street, Gardens (021 424 4344). **Open** 9am-11pm daily. **Main courses** R60. **Credit** AmEx, DC, MC, V. **Map** p282 F5.
This deli-restaurant is well frequented by the locals living in the City Bowl. Local residents use Arnold's for a quick cup of good coffee before heading off to work (or back to bed), as well as a late-night nightcap if they've run out of the stronger stuff at home. The numerous gourmet burger options are usually a sure bet for the hungry; less gung-ho appetites can choose from an expansive selection of lighter meals, the list of which is likely to cause much confusion for the indecisive among us.

Eat and drink your way around the world

some butternut and beef lasagna left over, although this is almost as popular as those buns. A good place to avoid the crowds of Greenmarket Square.

Frieda's
15 Bree Street, City Centre (021 421 2404).
Open 8am-5pm Mon-Fri. **Credit** MC, V.
Map p283 H3.
At the bottom end of town, just when you think there's nothing of interest left to see, you'll hit Frieda's. Offering breakfasts and lunch in a funky, '50s sort of way, it's a bit grungy with its faded brick walls and old kitchen cabinets but there is great cheesecake, excellent coffee and very good toasted cheese-and-tomato sandwiches on offer.

Melissa's
94 Kloof Street, Gardens (021 424 5540). **Open** 7.30am-8pm Mon-Fri; 8am-8pm Sat, Sun. **Credit** AmEx, DC, MC, V. **Map** p282 F5.
Here you will find very stylish deli-fare to enjoy in situ or take home. You can't pop in and browse without spending your cash on something that looks, and turns out to be, delectable. Try the chocolate pecan cake with coffee and take some meringues and lemon curd to munch at home.

Royale Eatery
279 Long Street, City Centre (021 422 4536).
Open noon-midnight Mon-Sat. **Main courses** R32. **Credit** AmEx, DC, MC, V. **Map** p282 G4.
Great retro décor and phenomenal gourmet burgers make this a Long Street favourite. The patrons are funky, jazz plays in the background and elegant white square plates serve reasonably priced choices such as brie on a burger and lamb burger patties. There are also thick milkshakes and a liquor licence.

Vida e Caffè
Shop 1, Mooikloof, 34 Kloof Street, Gardens (021 426 0627). **Open** 7am-5pm Mon-Sat; 8.30am-2pm Sun. **Credit** MC, V. **Map** p282 F5.
The slickest coffee café around, the Portuguese 'Vida', as it is known to its regulars, offers coffee, but no tea. There is also freshly-squeezed orange juice, two sorts of Portuguese pastries, some muffins and mineral water. This stylish café is everyone's first port of call when they need a caffeine fix.

Yum
2 Deer Park Drive, Vredehoek (021 461 7607).
Open 9am-4pm Mon, Sun; 9am-10pm Tue-Sat.
Main courses R45. **Credit** AmEx, DC, MC, V.
Map p282 F5.
This restaurant is appropriately named. You haven't had breakfast till you've had it here – think omelettes generously filled with bacon, potato, leeks, feta and sage; or coconut and lime pancakes with passion fruit, marscapone, and granola and honey. The pasta (available lunch and dinner) is fresh and the sauces inspiring – butternut ravioli with stir-fried baby gems in sweet Thai sauce with coriander, is just one good choice. This is stylish eating in a laid-back atmosphere. Yum yum.

Cara Lazuli. *See p102.*

Café Mozart
37 Church Street, City Centre (021 424 3774). **Open** 7am-3.15pm Mon-Fri; 8am-1pm Sat. **Credit** AmEx, DC, MC, V. **Map** p282 G4.
Café Mozart serves wonderful salads and sandwiches and cakes to accompany your pot of tea. It's also a good place to watch the area's many buskers.

Cinn-full
Bible House, 38 Shortmarket Street, Greenmarket Square, City Centre (021 424 5249). **Open** 7am-5pm Mon-Fri; 7am-2pm Sat. **No credit cards.** **Map** p282 G3.
The house speciality here is hot cinnamon buns drenched in creamy icing. Cinn-full also makes great sandwiches and if you're lucky there might even be

Sea and be seen at **Wakame**. *See p112.*

V&A Waterfront

Contemporary

The Atlantic
Table Bay Hotel, Quay 6 (021 406 5688). **Open**
6.30-11am, 7-10.30pm daily (lunch on request). **Main
courses** R85. **Credit** AmEx, DC, V. **Map** p283 H1.
Good hotel restaurants needn't be for residents
only. The Atlantic offers a view of the V&A
Waterfront, international cuisine and attentive service. Vegetarians have healthier options like potato
and Emmenthaler gnocchi with tomato and porcini
mushrooms, while carnivores will find an impressive, yet sophisticated, array of dishes.

German

Paulaner Brauhaus
*Shop 18/19, Clock Tower Square, V&A Waterfront
(021 418 9999/www.paulaner.co.za).* **Open** 11am-
midnight daily. **Main courses** R45. **Credit** AmEx,
DC, MC, V. **Map** p283 H1.

Beers and German food are the staples at this popular and vibey Waterfront spot. There's an oompah
band at weekends and the food is of the eisbein,
bratwurst and sauerkraut variety. A great place to
while away a few relaxed hours.

Gourmet

Emily's
202 Clock Tower, V&A Waterfront (021 421 1133).
Open *Restaurant* noon-11.30pm Mon-Sat; 6.30-10pm
Sun. *Coffee shop* 10am-11pm Mon-Sat. *Wine bar*
10pm-midnight Mon-Sat. **Main courses** R95.
Credit AmEx, DC, MC, V. **Map** p283 H1.
Emily's is a pricey establishment, but according to
some, well worth the money spent. Creative African
food is artfully served and the fusion of flavours
works, but at these prices few locals can afford it.

one.Waterfront
*Cape Grace Hotel, West Quay Road, Waterfront
(021 418 0520/www.onewaterfront.co.za/
www.capegrace.com).* **Open** 6.30-11am, 12.30-3pm,
7-10.30pm daily. **Main courses** R85. **Credit** AmEx,
DC, V. **Map** p283 H2.

Executive Chef Bruce Robertson is a genius – a former advertising type, he now lends his creativity to the food he prepares. His cuisine is infused with local flavours and includes West Coast oysters, springbok and ostrich, and his desserts are both decadently delicious and artistically presented. This is the sort of place you go to for a very special occasion, when you have the time to savour the intricate flavours of one of the Cape's finest restaurants and the inclination to linger over endless glasses of wine from an extensive winelist. La Bascule Whiskey Bar (also in the Cape Grace), overlooking the yacht basin, is the perfect place to start or end your meal.

Mediterranean

Balducci's

Shop 6162, Lower Level, Victoria Wharf (021 421 6002/www.balduccis.co.za). **Open** 9am-10.30pm daily. **Main courses** R90. **Credit** AmEx, DC, MC, V. **Map** p283 H1.
An eternal Waterfront favourite with great Italian/Californian food any time of the day or night. If you're not hungry, have one of the lovely long

cocktails. A nice addition is the sushi bar outside the restaurant in the V&A mall, if you can leave the comfy leather chairs of the main restaurant.

Greek Fisherman

Shop 157, Victoria Wharf (021 418 5111/ www.greekfisherman.co.za). **Open** 11am-11pm daily. **Main courses** R75. **Credit** AmEx, DC, MC, V. **Map** p283 H1.
With plenty of outdoor seating facing the working harbour, this is a popular venue for Mediterranean food and hearty Greek specialities. The seafood is good and the lamb is served traditionally.

Seafood & sushi

Baia Seafood Restaurant

12 Apostles Hotel, Camps Bay, Upper Level, Victoria Wharf (021 421 0935). **Open** noon-3pm, 7-11pm daily. **Main courses** R90. **Credit** AmEx, DC, V. **Map** p283 H1.
A restaurant where the chic and contemporary décor attracts as much attention as the food. If you're going to splurge on oysters, prawns and lobster,

Cape Town Fish Market chefs on a roll. *See p114.*

you'll want to do it here. The views of the waterfront are superb, the service attentive, but it's the food that steals the show. Seafood is the speciality, but there are excellent meat and vegetarian options as well.

Willoughby & Co

Shop 6132, Victoria Wharf (021 418 6115). **Open** 9am-10pm daily. **Main courses** R58. **Credit** AmEx, DC, MC, V. **Map** p283 H1.

For one of the best, and most personalised, sushi experiences in Cape Town, head to Willoughby's. Its seafood fare is also fantastic. If you don't know what you want to eat, Sam will whip up something to tickle your tastebuds. With sushi-heaven happening in your mouth, you'll forget for a little while that you are in a busy shopping mall.

Steakhouses

City Grill Steakhouse

Shop 155, Victoria Wharf (021 421 9820/ www.citygrill.co.za). **Open** 10.30am-10.30pm Mon-Fri; 9.30am-11pm Sat, Sun. **Main courses** R80. **Credit** AmEx, DC, MC, V. **Map** p283 H1.

The City Grill is an old-fashioned steakhouse in a modern setting. This restaurant has a distinctly South African flavour, offering such dishes as ostrich, springbok and kudu. Chicken and fish are also available and well prepared.

Atlantic Seaboard

Contemporary

Azure

12 Apostles Hotel, Camps Bay (021 437 9029). **Open** 7-10.30am, 12.30-3pm, 7-10.30pm Mon-Sat; 10.30am-12.30am Sun. **Main courses** R75. **Credit** AmEx, DC, V. **Map** p284 B8.

Azure refers to the colour of the Atlantic, which the restaurant overlooks. Fabulous views and an extensive wine list lend themselves to long lunches, while the food is of the South African/comfort food variety – think duck cottage pie served with orange marmalade and Cape Malay pickled fish with sweetcorn fritters. Attentive service (which you'd expect from a five-star hotel) make this good for a night out – be sure to be in time to watch the sun go down.

Beluga

The Foundry, Prestwich Street, Green Point (021 418 2948/www.beluga.co.za). **Open** 10am-11pm daily. **Main courses** R75. **Credit** AmEx, DC, MC, V. **Map** p282 G2.

Exquisite contemporary food in an understated, funky environment. It's popular with local media sorts, who are attracted by the great cocktails and good-looking waiters. The food on offer is as good as the vibe, with fish and meat being a popular choice; those in the know always order dessert. There is a more affordable lunch menu if your budget does not stretch as wide as your stomach.

Harveys at The Mansions

Winchester Mansions Hotel, 221 Beach Road, Sea Point (021 434 2351/www.winchester.co.za). **Open** 6.30am-10.30pm daily. **Main courses** R65. **Credit** AmEx, DC, MC, V. **Map** p281 D2.

Go to Harveys for a designer lunch and sit on the terrace where you can appreciate the cool sea breeze, or enjoy afternoon tea in the leafy courtyard. It's best for brunches – book for Sunday jazz.

Paranga

Shop 1, The Promenade, Victoria Road, Camps Bay (021 438 0404). **Open** 9am-11pm daily. **Main courses** R70. **Credit** AmEx, DC, MC, V. **Map** p284 B8.

One of the newer additions to the Camps Bay promenade, overlooking Camps Bay beach, this is well frequented by the so-called 'Beautiful Set'. It serves fusion food in a gorgeous restaurant. Not surprisingly, the owner is an interior designer, Christiaan Barnard. If you want to enjoy the view of the beach from the deck, be sure to book in advance.

Tank

Cape Quarter, De Waterkant Street, De Waterkant (021 419 0007). **Open** noon-3pm, 6-11pm daily. **Main courses** R65. **Credit** AmEx, DC, MC, V. **Map** p282 G3.

Tank is the very latest hotspot in Cape Town and the chosen place for the fashionistas and trendoids. The décor, rumoured to have cost millions – is awesome. A huge fish tank separating the restaurant from the bar and lounge is the main focus and the flattering blue lighting has been very well received by the hip patrons. The food is interesting, although some dishes are better than others – if you stick to the sushi and the crème brûlée, you'll be well satisfied. To be honest, a visit to Tank will probably not be the culinary highlight of your trip, but if décor and style are your thing, you won't miss out.

Zero932

79 Main Road, Green Point (021 439 6306/ www.zero932.com). **Open** 9.30am-11pm daily. **Main courses** R60. **Credit** AmEx, DC, MC, V. **Map** p282 E2.

Besides the great contemporary grills and seafood, the service here is awesome and puts most other Cape Town restaurants to shame. The interior is über-funky and there are 24 imported Belgian beers (Duvel, Chimay and so on) to sup your way through at the stylish bar, an ideal spot for chilling out.

French

Rive Gauche

Hotel Le Vendome, 20 London Road, Sea Point (021 430 1200/www.le-vendome.co.za). **Open** 7.30-10.30pm daily. **Main courses** R75. **Credit** AmEx, DC, MC, V. **Map** p281 D2.

This French-style hotel in the heart of Sea Point successfully creates an elegant dining experience. Crystal and silver and an impressive chandelier set the keynotes of the decor. Accordingly, the food is formal French. Recommended.

Gourmet

The Restaurant

51a Somerset Road, Green Point (021 419 2921). **Open** noon-3pm, 7-11pm Mon-Fri; 7-11pm Sat. **Main courses** R80. **Credit** AmEx, DC, MC, V. **Map** p282 G3.

The chef is well known for exotic culinary combinations, which rarely fail to thrill his fans at this highly-rated restaurant. Some diners have been known to moan about the prices, but if you've got money to burn, make your reservation.

Mediterranean

Anatoli's

24 Napier Street, Green Point (021 419 2501/ www.anatoli.co.za). **Open** 7-11pm Tue-Sun. **Main courses** R55. **Credit** AmEx, DC, MC, V. **Map** p282 G3.

Be transported into a corner of Turkey where you are cosseted next to extravagant wall carpets that would look 'oh so good' in your home. Stick to the mezze – the choice is astounding and makes for good conversation if yours dries up.

Chef

Corner De Waterkant & Rose Streets, De Waterkant (021 419 6767). **Open** 7-10.30pm Tue-Sat. **Set meal** R175. **Credit** AmEx, DC, MC, V. **Map** p282 G3.

This restaurant dishes up stunning food from a pedantic chef, who believes in the 'my way or no way' school of cooking. The pastas are creative and diligently prepared by hand, and the antipasto options tempting. The phrase 'new generation Italian' has been used to describe this restaurant, which basically means not the usual stodgy fare, and (gasp) not a pizza in sight.

Clifton Beach House

72 The Ridge, 4th Beach, Clifton (021 438 1955/ www.cliftonbeach.co.za). **Open** 8.30am-10pm daily. **Main courses** R55. **Credit** AmEx, DC, MC, V. **Map** p281 B6.

A casual, spacious eatery above one of the world's most famous beaches, this is perfect for a quick pizza or pasta after a sundowner on the beach. Or if you don't feel like getting sand between the toes, come here to sit back, enjoy a cocktail and enjoy the panoramic views of the Clifton shoreline.

Eat, Drink, Shop

Why local is *lekker*

To understand the South African mind and tastebuds, you have to understand the concept of 'lekker'. This Afrikaans word means 'nice' or 'tasty' in its most basic form. In its usage, however, it surpasses the bounds of expected meaning. Lekker can describe food, mood, clothing, your latest boyfriend, your holiday and just about anything else you enjoyed. Here is a list of some foods that South Africans find lekker...

Beskuit Rusk is not just eaten by babies, but by everyone. Copious dunking in coffee or tea with subsequent slurping is essential.

Biltong is cured, salted meat, eaten in strips. Best while drinking generous amounts of beer. Locals are known to consume vast quantities of it in a single snacking session.

Bobotie is spicy mince pie with a topping of savoury egg custard. Traditional comfort food and not as gross as it sounds.

Boerewors is spicy sausage that is lekker at a braai. Perfect to put in a long bread roll then you have... surprise, surprise... a boerewors-roll.

Braai Barbecue: if you say 'barbecue' people will laugh at you and never invite you to another braai. South Africans do not braai hamburgers or hotdogs. That is for losers.

Bredie stew can be made from a variety of ingredients. Spicy or not.

Bunnychow consists of half a white bread loaf, hollowed out and then filled with curry.

Chakalaka is a fiery, tomato-and-onion based vegetable dish that is used to accompany meat dishes.

Droëwors is spiced dried sausage (see eating tips for 'biltong').

Fruit preserves Whole preserved fruit in syrup eaten with fish or cheese.

Koeksisters Plaited deep-fried dough smothered in sweet syrup. Addictive and many claim to make the perfect

La Perla

Beach Road, Sea Point (021 434 2471). **Open** 11am-midnight daily. **Main courses** R90. **Credit** AmEx, DC, MC, V. **Map** p281 D2.

This has been a Cape Town favourite for as long as most Capetonians can remember. In a town where restaurants have a short lifespan, this one has graciously stood the test of time. The seafood platters are phenomenally good and the pasta is always up to scratch too. Sit inside where it's most intimate and, if you prick up your ears, you could catch up on some local gossip. Alternatively sit outside on one of the terrace tables overlooking the Sea Point Promenade and pool, and see if you can spot the celebrities dining behind dark glasses.

Tuscany Beach Café

41 Victoria Road, Camps Bay (021 438 1213/ www.tuscanybeach.co.za). **Open** 7.30-10.30pm daily. **Main courses** R60. **Credit** AmEx, DC, MC, V. **Map** p284 B8.

Tuscany Beach has a 'Locals Always Welcome' policy, which means that come high season and a mass of visitors, it still makes sure that the locals supporting it throughout the year get a table. This takes some doing at a very busy restaurant. This is not only an Italian restaurant, it also specialises in seafood. Order a cocktail at one of the pavement tables and watch the passing parade, before doing justice to the well-prepared and unstuffy food.

Seafood & sushi

Blues

The Promenade, Victoria Road, Camps Bay (021 438 2040/www.blues.co.za). **Open** noon-midnight daily. **Main courses** R75. **Credit** AmEx, DC, MC, V. **Map** p284 B8.

In past years, the popular Blues was better known and mostly frequented for its gorgeous sea view and bold use of negative space rather than for its menu,

Eat, Drink, Shop

Koeksister – you'll have to do your own research to determine that. It's much like a syrupy version of Spanish churros.
Koeksuster is a small cake of sweetened dough, usually dipped in syrup. The plaited sort is the Afrikaans speciality, while the round, coconut-covered one is typically Cape Malay.
Maas is soured milk, drunk on its own or used in dishes.
Malva pudding Rich and oozy pudding much like sticky toffee sponge, made with lashings of cream and butter. Perfect for balancing out all the activities you've been doing.
Melktert is baked custard tart with cinnamon. Grannies are famous for making this 'milk tart'.
Potjie Stew made in a little cast-iron pot (potjie) at a *braai*. Can contain any number of ingredients: Fish, veggie or meat. Cooks for around four hours which is more than enough time to get seriously mellow while giving the occasional stir.
Roosterkoek Small ball of bread baked on a *braai*.
Umngqusho is a granular maize staple with brown sugar beans.

Sosatie cubes of meat served on a skewer.
Umfino is a dish of mixed and boiled corn, spinach, cabbage or any handy vegetables.
Umphokoqo is crumbled corn with maas.
Upentse is a traditional African dish of tripe with vegetables.
Vetkoek Think of a savoury doughnut without the hole. Can be served with anything from cheese to mince to jam.
Waterblommetjiebredie is stew made from waterblommetjies (water plants found in the Cape) and lamb of mutton.

Cape Malay cuisine is typified by the use of subtle spices such as turmeric, cinnamon and ginger. Fruit, whether canned or fresh, is also used with savoury dishes. The taste for mixing sweet, fresh fruitiness with hearty, heavy meat, is an acquired one, but once experienced, it is very easy to fall in love and search for it in your comfort food. Dishes such as bobotie, curries, masala fish, sosaties, yellow rice with raisins, pickled fish are typical of the cuisine, and are often served with sambals such as coconut, cucumber relish and chutney.

which has been through its ups and downs. Fortunately, the increase in competition in the Camps Bay area has forced Blues to jack up its socks and it now boasts superb food and good service. Happily, the restaurant decided the view was fine as it was. The venue is upmarket, but relaxed and fairly casual. Seafood is the speciality, but its hoofier fare is nothing to be ashamed of, either. A legendary Cape Town restaurant and one that now lives up to its much-hyped reputation.

Chapman's Restaurant

Chapman's Peak Hotel, Chapman's Peak Drive, Hout Bay (021 790 1036). **Open** noon-10pm daily. **Main courses** R60. **Credit** AmEx, DC, MC, V.
Fantastic seafood is complemented at Chapman's by classic alternative options such as steak. But it's the delicious grilled calamari served in large frying pans that has given this place its legendary reputation. Chill in the hotel's pub on a Sunday afternoon or grab a table outside and watch as the colourful life of Hout Bay goes by. This is an informal, cold-beer, good-food type of place. A perfect retreat.

Codfather

41 The Drive, Camps Bay (021 438 0782). **Open** noon-10.30pm daily. **Main courses** R80. **Credit** AmEx, DC, MC, V. **Map** p281 B8.
If it's fish you're after, look no further. This trendy Camps Bay restaurant will satisfy cravings for crustaceans, as well as offering a wide variety of fresh fish and an impressive selection of sushi.

Mariner's Wharf

Hout Bay Harbour, Hout Bay (021 790 1100/ www.marinerswharf.com). **Open** 9am-10.30pm daily. **Main courses** R70. **Credit** AmEx, DC, MC, V.
Slightly old-school, Mariner's Wharf remains an enduring favourite among both locals and visitors. It is that rarest of things, a smart but unpretentious restaurant for all occasions. Private rooms are also

available for more clandestine dining. The house wine comes in quirky, fish-shaped souvenir bottles that make excellent mementos or gifts – if that's your kind of thing. Dependably good.

Pigalle

57 Somerset Road, Green Point, Atlantic Seaboard (021 421 4848). **Open** noon-2.30pm; 7pm-late Mon-Sat. **Main courses** R75. **Credit** AmEx, DC, MC, V. **Map** p282 G3.

Situated in the unofficial red light district of town (hence the name), this glamorous, 400-seater restaurant is a real crowd-pleaser. It offers live jazz and a dance floor, which appeals to those who remember the era of dinner-dance venues, as well as the younger hipper set who now realise what they've been missing out on. The décor is fabulous – think red carpets and huge chandeliers. The food is good, (none of the fussy stuff) with some outstanding seafood specialities (at sensible prices). The service is great, but be warned they do have a rather odd policy that forbids diners from asking for ordinary tap water. It's annoying, but if you can live with that, Pigalle promises a great night out.

Wakame

1st Floor, Corner Surrey Place & Beach Road, Mouille Point (021 433 2377). **Open** 12.30-3pm, 6.30-10.30pm daily. **Main courses** R72. **Credit** AmEx, DC, MC, V. **Map** p282 F1.

Offering zen minimalist chic, outstanding sea views and some lovely seafood, Wakame is a firm favourite among the fashionable set. It offers sushi as well as fish caught off local shores. The portions are small and the prices aren't, but the attentiveness of the waiters and the quality of the wine list will ensure a great lunch or a very promising date. Book, if you can, a table at the window.

South American

Buena Vista Social Café

81 Main Road, Green Point (021 433 0611). **Open** noon-midnight Mon-Fri; 5pm-midnight Sat, Sun. **Main courses** R60. **Credit** AmEx, DC, MC, V. **Map** p282 E2.

Perhaps even Fidel would feel at home in this place – puffing a cigar and slowly sipping a mojito. And it's not hard to see why: soulful Latin beats reverberate in the authentic setting, and a delicious array of traditional Cuban drinks and dishes are served to the lively crowd. Oh, and the nachos are probably the best in town. Booking is essential – after 8pm, you'll battle to wedge yourself in at the bar. Be warned, this is a noisy night out.

Steakhouses

Buz-Bey Grill

14 Three Anchor Bay Road, Three Anchor Bay (021 439 5900). **Open** 6-11.30pm Tue-Sat. **Main courses** R55. **Credit** AmEx, DC, MC, V. **Map** p282 G3.

The Buz-Bey Grill is one of Cape Town's oldest restaurants, and in a foodie city as fickle as Cape Town this has the equivalent of a three-star rating from those Michelin people. Everything on the menu is a speciality, and all dishes are overseen by the legendary chef-patron Jimmy Kyritsis. The choices include some truly incredible steaks and the best calamari in town – bar none. The décor is authentically retro – think Rat Pack era. Nearly all of the clientele are faithful regulars, which should tell you something. Consistently excellent.

Theo's

163 Beach Road, Mouille Point (021 439 3494). **Open** noon-3.30, 6-10.30pm Mon-Fri; 6-10.30pm Sat, noon-4.30pm, 6-10.30pm Sun. **Main courses** R65. **Credit** AmEx, DC, MC, V. **Map** p282 E1.

Wholesome steaks, well-prepared fish and an excellent wine list make this is safe and good bet for a meal. There is always an excellent supply of oysters. The Mouille Point branch is a good one to visit, because after a heavy meal you can walk off those calories on the Sea Point promenade.

Branch: Victoria Road, Camps Bay (021 438 0410).

Red, black and white hot: **Shoga**. *See p97.*

Cafes & casual eating

Café Manhattan

*74 Waterkant Street, De Waterkant (021 421 6666/
www.manhattan.co.za).* **Open** noon-midnight daily.
Main courses R40. **Credit** AmEx, DC, MC, V.
Map p282 G3.

Russel Shapiro's restaurant is a landmark in the gay
village that is De Waterkant. It has been a popular
haunt for ages, and once you've been you'll know
why – the vibe is chatty and relaxed, the food great,
and there is live entertainment and frequent art exhibitions. Straights are also welcome and the place
buzzes long after everyone else has gone to bed.

Dutch

34 Napier Street, De Waterkant (021 425 0157).
Open 8.30am-6pm Mon-Fri; 8.30am-3pm Sat, Sun.
Credit AmEx, MC, V. **Map** p282 G3.

This quaint sidewalk bistro has bright décor and a
very interesting menu that includes Dutch
favourites such as kroketten on rye and ham or
cheese uitsmijters. It's a perfect resting spot between
exploring the neighbourhood shops. It has a pet-
friendly policy, which is great for some, but those
with allergies had best sit outside.

Newport Deli

47 Beach Road, Mouille Point (021 439 1538). **Open**
7.30am-7pm Mon-Fri; 8am-7pm Sat, Sun. **Main
courses** R30. **Credit** DC, MC, V. **Map** p282 E1.

Everyone's favourite deli in the New York style. It
offers healthy, home-cooked meals that can be
enjoyed inside the deli, or can be packaged and taken
home. The fruit smoothies are superb and it's hard
to believe that they're fat-free. Good coffee and delicious goods make this a wonderful place whether
you're hankering after breakfast, lunch or an early
dinner. The view is spectacular and the management will treat you like old friends.

La Petite Tarte

*Shop A11, Cape Quarter, Dixon Street, De Waterkant
(021 425 9077).* **Open** 8am-5pm Mon-Fri; 8am-3pm
Sat. **Credit** MC, V. **Map** p282 G3.

This minute, very expensive café offers a limited
menu of superb French tarts. The elegant venue,
with its fine, crystal chandelier, is a wonderful place
to perch for an hour or two.

Northern Suburbs

Contemporary

Durbanville Hills Winery

*Tygerberg Valley Road, M13, Durbanville (021 558
1300/www.durbanvillehills.co.za).* **Open** 9am-4.30pm
Mon-Fri; 9.30am-2.30pm Sat; 11am-3pm Sun. **Main
courses** R60. **Credit** DC, MC, V.

We would like to call this a 'come for the wine, stay
for the food' kind of place, but alas, the wine far out-
shines the food. Not to say that the food isn't good,
it's great. The wine, however, is just superlative. The

fare is contemporary South African cuisine on a
small and stylish menu. And with the stunning
sweeping views of Table Bay and Table Mountain,
it makes for a perfect Sunday lunch.

De Oude Welgemoed

Pandoer Street, Welgemoed (021 913 4962). **Open**
noon-2pm, 7-10pm Mon-Fri; 7-10pm Sat. **Main
courses** R80. **Credit** AmEx, DC, MC, V.

One of the rare true gourmet experiences to be found
in the northern suburbs. The beautifully restored,
300-year-old farmhouse complements the refined
country cuisine, served à la carte or as a set menu.
Wine connoisseurs will be impressed by the walk-
in wine cellar, which houses an extensive and
award-winning selection of wines.

Poplars

*Terra D'aria, Springfield Farm on the M13
Tyger Valley Road, Durbanville (021 975 5736/
www.daria.co.za).* **Open** noon-3pm, 7-10.30pm daily.
Main courses R88. **Credit** AmEx, DC, MC, V.

Unfortunately, the northern suburbs are a jumble of
family and franchise restaurants. But a place like
Poplars gives hope to the yearning crowd of ex-city
slickers. It is smart and trendy, yet very relaxed. The
extensive menu is fresh and innovative, tending to
a wide variety of tastes. Favourites include the pot-
roasted lamb shank and flame-grilled ostrich and
kudu. Be sure to check out the dessert menu before
you order your other courses – they are devilishly
decadent and you need to save some space for them.

Mediterranean

On the Rocks

45 Stadler Road, Bloubergstrand (021 554 1988).
Open noon-10pm Mon-Fri; 9am-10pm Sat, Sun.
Main courses R70. **Credit** AmEx, DC, MC, V.

The name says it all. On the Rocks boasts one of the
best views of any Cape Town restaurant. Built on
the rocks in Blouberg, it has waves breaking outside
the windows and a picture-postcard view of the
magnificent Table Mountain. The food is good and
well presented, and while the feature is slightly too
contrived (paint effects for a Tuscan effect) it's quite
possible just to lose yourself in the view.

Primi Piatti

*14 Beach Boulevard, Tableview, West Coast (021 557
9770).* **Open** 9am-11pm daily. **Main courses** R45.
Credit AmEx, DC, MC, V.

Snappy, Italian food courtesy of this industrial-
style restaurant chain is served by hyped-up wait
staff. The extensive menu and good cocktails are
popular with a young crowd.

Seafood & sushi

The Blowfish

*1 Marine Drive, Dolphin Beach Hotel, Tableview,
West Coast (021 556 5464).* **Open** 6am-midnight
daily. **Main courses** R68. **Credit** AmEx, DC, MC, V.

Eat, Drink, Shop

The winning views of the beach and the breathtaking vista of Table Mountain, as well as fresh seafood, should entice you to the Blowfish. Choose from a selection of sushi, or from the fresh seafood on display. Your chosen item will be measured and served to you according to your specifications. There are often all-you-can-eat prawn specials – so beware, excess is inevitable.

Cape Town Fish Market
Shop 485 Canal Walk, Century City (021 555 1950). **Open** 11am-11pm daily. **Main courses** R50. **Credit** AmEx, DC, MC, V.
Those nifty sushi conveyor belts are an old trick these days, but this seafood restaurant is so popular there is no need to do away with the food carrousel just yet. The sushi itself has a good reputation.

Cafés & casual eating

Blue Peter
Blue Peter Hotel, 7 Popham Road, Bloubergstrand, West Coast (021 554 1956/ www.bluepeter.co.za). **Open** 11am-11pm daily. **Main courses** R60. **Credit** AmEx, DC, MC, V.
The lower deck is where you'll want to be, it's so much nicer than the slightly stuffy restaurant upstairs (and indoors). The Blue Peter is where you'll eat pizzas and fish and chips at wooden tables or on the grass patch overlooking the beach, with your shoes off and a bottle of beer in your hand. It's always crowded on hot days with friendly locals and rowdy small ones all having a good time.

Café Blouberg
20 Stadler Road, Bloubergstrand, West Coast (021 554 4462/www.cafeblouberg.co.za). **Open** 9am-10pm daily. **Main courses** R65. **Credit** AmEx, DC, MC, V.
This place proves once again that Capetonians will excuse mediocre service if there is an awesome view to be enjoyed. Looking out over Table Mountain, Blouberg Café is a perfect early-morning breakfast spot. The menu is quite extensive, but tapers down when lunch and dinner time arrives. The portions are big and use fresh and imaginative ingredients.

Café Orca
88 Beach Road, Melkbosstrand, West Coast (021 553 4120). **Open** 9am-9pm Mon, Wed-Sat; 9am-3.30pm Tue, Sun. **Main courses** R65. **Credit** AmEx, DC, MC, V.
It may be a little far out of town, but should you be in the relaxed vicinity of Melkbos and in need of sustenance this is where you'll find it. Café Orca offers informal dining and an outstanding seafood spread. You'll love this place and will need the long walk on the beach you've been staring at during lunch, before you drive back home.

Dale's Place
47 Blaauberg Road, Tableview, West Coast (021 557 4212). **Open** 11am-2.30pm, 5.30-10.30pm Mon-Sat. **Main courses** R68. **Credit** AmEx, DC, MC, V.

While Dale's Place doesn't offer the views that other West Coast restaurants do, it does offer attentive service, good wholesome food, and a generally friendly environment. It's always filled with locals chomping through 1kg steaks or generous portions of eisbein and sauerkraut, or the robust oxtail. And the selection of game (kudu, springbok and, for the brave, warthog) is extensive. The '70s throwback of avocado ritz and ice-cream served with chocolate sauce are welcome comfort foods.

Southern Suburbs

Contemporary

Catharina's
Steenberg Country Hotel, Spaanschemat River Road, Constantia (021 713 2222/www.steenberghotel.com). **Open** 7.30am-11pm daily. **Main courses** R120. **Credit** AmEx, DC, MC, V.
Dine on Cape-Continental cusine in the romantic setting of what was once the original Steenberg winery. Winters consist of log fires, red wine and robust fare, while summertime will have you yearning for Catharina's terrace, where, under the oak trees, you'll find the resident squirrels amusing and the lighter bistro-style lunches the perfect accompaniment to the estate's white wines.

African

Cape Malay Restaurant
The Cellars-Hohenort, 93 Brommersvlei Road, Constantia (021 794 2137/www.cellars-hohenort.com). **Open** 7-11pm daily. Closed June-Aug. **Main courses** R140. **Credit** AmEx, DC, MC, V.
Sadly, there aren't that many restaurants serving traditional Cape Malay cuisine, which is a real pity as its fruity, spicy flavours are delicious. This restaurant, at the rather fancy Cellars-Hohenhort hotel, does sophisticated versions of this local cuisine. The food is beautifully presented and the flavours are authentic. Short of being invited to someone's home, you'll be hard pressed to find anything more appealing.

Gourmet

Buitenverwachting
Klein Constantia Road, Constantia (021 794 3522/ www.buitenverwacting.co.za). **Open** *Restaurant* noon-9pm Mon-Sat. *Café* 11.30am-4.30pm Mon-Sat. **Main courses** R100. **Credit** AmEx, DC, MC, V.
Popular with the foie gras set (if the posh lot can be called that), this frighteningly polysyllabic restaurant offers haute cuisine. Located in a glorious wine farm, it is perfect for whiling away the afternoon over a leisurely meal, once you've explored the estate. And where better to drink the wines than overlooking the vineyards from where they stemmed? Reservations are advised.

Olympia Café & Deli. See p117.

La Colombe

Constantia Uitsig, Constantia (021 794 2390/
www.lacolombe.co.za). **Open** 12.30-2.30pm, 7.30-9.30pm
daily. Closed July. **Main courses** R102. **Credit**
AmEx, DC, MC, V.
Pretend you're in the Provençal countryside and
order everything in French at this exquisite spot.
The food is southern French and superb, while
the service is impeccable and knowledgeable.
Presentation is artful and delicate. This place also
has great winter lunch specials that are more affordable than the regular fare. During summer, pre-
dinner drinks can be taken in style around the calm
waters of the plush outdoor swimming pool.

Constantia Uitsig

Uitsig Farm, Spaanschemat River Road, Constantia.
(021 794 4480/www.uitsig.co.za). **Open** 12.30-2.30pm,
7-9.30pm daily. **Main courses** R250. **Credit** AmEx,
DC, MC, V.
This award-winning restaurant takes mainly Italian
culinary inspiration, with the odd Asian twist. It's
owned by the same people who run La Colombe
(*see above*), which is a marker of its quality. Situated
on a picturesque wine farm that also houses a wonderful boutique country hotel, it has a loyal following. The beautiful presentation of the food does
justice to its flavours and tastes. This is well worth
loosening your wallet for.

Asian

Wangthai

Corner Constantia & Groot Constantia roads,
Constantia (021 794 0022). **Open** 6-10.30pm Mon;
noon-2.30pm, 6-10.30pm Tue-Sun. **Main courses** R60.
Credit AmEx, DC, MC, V.
Wangthai serves authentic Thai food in a sophisticated setting, with elegant touches of Thai art and
craft. Hot, spicy curries and very good starters, as
well as charming service make for a most satisfying
dining experience. The set menus are generously
proportioned and interesting, and allow you to
sample a variety of specialities in one sitting.
Branch: Main Road, Green Point (021 439 6164).

Mediterranean

Bardelli's

51 Kenilworth Road, Kenilworth (021 683 1423).
Open 6-10pm daily. **Main courses** R58. **Credit**
AmEx, DC, MC, V.
A great neighbourhood trattoria, serving some
incredible pastas and delicious home-cooked Italian
specialities. This unpretentious local conjures up an
array of pizza toppings, such as butternut, camem-
bert and caramelised onion; or bacon, cherry toma-
toes, feta cheese and rosemary. A big favourite is
blue cheese and green-fig preserve topping. Budget-
conscious foodies love this venue.

Diva Caffè Ristorante

88 Lower Main Road, Observatory (021 448 0282).
Open 10.30am-11.30pm daily. **Main courses** R33.
Credit AmEx, DC, MC, V.
Diva arguably makes the best pizzas in town. They
overflow with lashings of cheese and toppings,
including inventive options such as pine nuts. The
pastas and desserts are also fantastic. It's terribly
popular, so try to book in advance. If not, have a
drink at one of the surrounding bars, and the waiters
will come and call you when your table is ready.

Magica Roma

8 Central Square Shopping Centre, Pinelands (021
531 1489). **Open** noon-2pm, 6-10pm Mon-Sat. **Main**
courses R58. **Credit** AmEx, DC, MC, V.
The Italian restaurant's Italian restaurant, Magica
Roma is one of the few eateries where you actually
have to make a booking well in advance. Everything
about the place is utterly superb. While all the food
is wonderful, the vegetables do deserve an hon-
ourable mention – they're the best in town. The
relaxed atmosphere complements the food wonderfully. We have never heard a single complaint about
this restaurant. Well, apart from the inability to
secure a table whenever the mood takes you. It's well
worth the trip to suburban Pinelands.

Mamma Roma

Dean Street Arcade, Newlands (021 685 2051).
Open noon-2.30pm, 6.30-10.30pm Mon-Sat. Closed
July. **Main courses** R60. **Credit** AmEx, DC, MC, V.

A very good Italian restaurant that serves outstanding calamari, excellent pastas and great Italian specialities. It also manages to source the best West Coast oysters. Don't be put off by the commercial shopping mall location – the food more than compensates for the lack of a view. The waiting staff are solicitous and old-fashioned.
Branch: Steenberg Village, Constantia (021 701 8585).

Seafood & Sushi

Wasabi
Shop 17, Old Village Centre, Constantia Shopping Centre, Constantia Main Road, Constantia (021 794 6546/www.wasabi.co.za). **Open** noon-3pm, 6-10pm daily. **Main courses** R80. **Credit** AmEx, DC, MC, V.
The older brother of the sexy Wakame, this place is just as popular. Sit at the counter and watch the chefs diligently preparing stir-fries, rolling sushi and sashimi, and grilling seafood or steaks.

Steakhouses

Barristers Grill Room & Café on Main
Corner Kildare & Main Streets, Newlands (021 674 1792). **Open** 8am-10.30pm Mon-Sat; 5-10pm Sun. **Main courses** R70. **Credit** AmEx, DC, MC, V.
Although it isn't a trendy venue, carnivores love this old-fashioned steakhouse, which seems to have been around forever. The fried onion rings, fat potato chips and a glass of red wine make the perfect match for the steaks. Service is efficient, which is great if you're in a rush, but you can also linger in the dark corners if you're so inclined.

The Famous Butchers Grill
Protea Place, cnr of Protea & Dreyer Streets, Claremont (021 683 5103). **Open** noon-11.30pm daily. **Main courses** R55. **Credit** AmEx, DC, MC, V.
Strictly for meat lovers: the set-up is for diners to choose a steak from the friendly resident butcher and the chef will then prepare it to your liking.

South American

Fat Cactus Café
47 Durban Road, Mowbray (021 685 1920/www.fatcactus.cjb.net). **Open** noon-10pm Mon, Sun; noon-midnight Tue-Sat. **Main courses** R55. **Credit** AmEx, DC, MC, V.
A lovely little Mexican joint where it is easy to drown yourself in a sea of frozen margaritas, the Fat Cactus serves Texan-style burgers and steaks, and all the tacos, nachos and fajitas your appetite can cope with. The place is noisy and smoky, and often filled with hordes of student types, yet it's not unusual to find the occasional suburban parents and kids on a family outing.

Cafés & casual eating

Peddlars on the Bend
Spaanschemat River Road, Constantia (021 794 7747). **Open** noon-11pm daily. **Main courses** R57. **Credit** AmEx, DC, MC, V.
This relaxed restaurant and popular pub is a favourite with locals, who know that the food is consistently good. The leafy courtyard is the ideal place to escape from the sun and enjoy great steaks with tasty sauces while the comfort food on offer will see you through the winters.

Spaanschemat River Café
Constantia Uitsig Farm, Spaanschemat River Road, Constantia (021 794 3010). **Open** 8.30am-5pm daily. **Main courses** R55. **Credit** AmEx, DC, MC, V.
Gorgeous food in a lovely setting. This café serves familiar food in innovative ways. Beautifully prepared and accompanied by a good bottle of one of Constantia's best wines, this food will have you begging for more. Or returning again and again.

False Bay

Contemporary

Railway House
177 Main Road (above the old railway station), Muizenberg (021 788 3251/www.railwayrestaurant.co.za). **Open** noon-10pm Wed-Sun. **Main courses** R60. **Credit** AmEx, DC, MC, V.
This National Heritage Building houses a restaurant that enables you to imagine the Golden Age of Muizenberg, when colonial representatives lived in grandeur and when this part of the False Bay coast was the height of fashion. Nowadays, the warm, earthy tones of the interior make for a pleasant contrast against the ocean outside the windows. The food (from game to oysters) is varied enough to suit most tastes, and the grilled fish is freshly caught.

Mediterranean

The Red Herring
Corner Pine & Beach Roads, Noordhoek (021 789 1783). **Open** noon-10pm daily. **Main courses** R60. **Credit** AmEx, DC, MC, V.
Head for the leafy restaurant downstairs or the vibey deck to watch the sun set. Order the pizza and eat it all up on your own – it'll be that good. Otherwise calamari is always a great option. Perfect for a post-beach stroll drink or two.

Seafood

Black Marlin
81 Main Road, Miller's Point (021 786 1621/www.blackmarlin.co.za). **Open** noon-3.30pm, 6-9pm Mon-Sat; 6-9pm Sun. **Main courses** R75. **Credit** AmEx, DC, MC, V.

It's not a bad idea to plan your trip to Cape Point around a lunch here. Make sure to book outside where you can see the magnificent bay (and perhaps even a whale or two). Seafood should be your main choice (lobster bisque, catches of the day grilled or on platters, kingklip wrapped in honey ham and grilled on the spit), but the restaurant also caters for those who prefer their food to have been land-based.

Harbour House

Kalk Bay Harbour, Kalk Bay (021 788 4133/ www.harbourhouse.co.za). **Open** 11.30am-midnight daily. **Main courses** R95. **Credit** AmEx, DC, MC, V.
Go here for the incredible views (if you're lucky you may catch sight of a whale) and the seafood (lots of calamari, plus prawns, crayfish and many other catches). Other options, such as meat and vegetarian-friendly fare, are good, but you'd be mad not to order something fresh from the local waters.

South American

Cape to Cuba

Main Road, Kalk Bay (021 788 1566/www.cape tocuba.com). **Open** noon-10pm daily. **Main courses** R55. **Credit** AmEx, DC, MC, V.
Step into old Havana and set to work on the hefty rum-based cocktails served at this busy restaurant. The décor is opulent and eclectic – and it's all for sale: from the ornate chandeliers to your chair and table. From the menu, the chicken and lime soup or the great calamari are both good choices. This is not a place to go if you are in a rush. Always friendly and funky, Cape to Cod leaves you feeling like you've been on a faraway island for the afternoon.

Cafés & casual eating

Bertha's

1 Wharf Road, Simonstown (021 786 2138). **Open** 6-11pm Mon-Sat. **Main courses** R60. **Credit** AmEx, DC, MC, V.
Seekers of a relaxed waterfront experience will be vindicated at this family-friendly restaurant. Well-prepared food and reliable Catch of the Day specials make this a great place to eat before you head off to explore the attractions of this naval town.

Empire Café

11 York Road, Muizenberg (021 788 1250). **Open** 7am-4pm, 6-9.30pm Tue-Sat; 7am-4pm Sun. **Main courses** R60. **Credit** AmEx, DC, MC, V.
A wonderful new place in what has for a while been a rather grim Muizenberg. Thanks to a renewal program this seaside town is rapidly being restored to its former glory and the Empire Café (named after the original art deco cinema down the road) is an important part of this process. Crowds flock to the stylishly simple place for creative cuisine. Breakfast may consist of fluffy omelettes with bacon, banana and honey. And dessert may be the chilli-chocolate cake. The daily specials are written on the black-

board and the waiters are all surfers who, while charming and laid-back, can't wait to get the hell out of there and hit the waves.

Olympia Café & Deli

134 Main Road, Kalk Bay (021 788 6396). **Open** 7am-10.30pm daily. **Main courses** R115. **Credit** AmEx, DC, MC, V.
A 'No Reservations' policy has avid fans of Olympia standing patiently at the door. There are no tantrums, only patient resignation – once you get in it will all be worth it. A phenomenal bakery churns out excellent breads, which you can dip into olive oil and balsamic vinegar while waiting for the food to arrive. Meat dishes such as chicken with cashews compete with the fish, which includes freshly harvested mussels and just-caught line fish. Breakfasts are good and lunches even better; dinners have a magical feel to them and are perhaps the best dining experience here, as you eat lovingly pre-pared food in this slightly scruffy, candlelit space.

Winelands

Contemporary

Bread & Wine

Môreson Wine Farm, Happy Valley Road, La Motte, Franschhoek, off R45 to Franschhoek (021 876 3692/ www.moreson.co.za). **Open** *Jan, Feb* noon-4pm Wed-Sun. *Mar-June, Oct-Dec* noon-10pm Wed-Sun. Closed July-Sept. **Main courses** R90. **Credit** AmEx, DC, MC, V.
Rated as one of the winelands' top restaurants, this colourful country venue serves colourful country food. It specialises in bread-making and meat-curing, so the breadbaskets and sausages and meats are exquisite. Added to that is an imaginative mix of Mediterranean and Asian dips, sauces and spices. Children are most welcome – the adjacent orchard is perfect for running around in.

Laborie Restaurant

Main Road, Suider-Paarl (021 807 3095). **Open** 11.30am-3.30pm daily. **Main courses** R55. **Credit** AmEx, DC, MC, V.
A new lease of creativity has been blown into the culinary approach of this wine farm. The à la carte menu now offers contemporary and imaginative takes on salads, vegetables, lamb, fish and more. The dessert menu changes daily.

Monneaux Restaurant

Franschhoek Country House, Main Road, Franschhoek (021 876 3386). **Open** noon-2pm, 7-9pm daily. **Main courses** R80. **Credit** AmEx, DC, MC, V.
Despite the name and location, this is not a French restaurant – Monneaux offers daring combinations of African and Asian tastes in dukkas, marinades and chermoula, plus game, quail, trout and other dishes. The small garden is beautiful so try and get a table looking out over the water feature.

96 Winery Road

Off the R44 between Somerset West & Stellenbosch (021 842 2020). **Open** noon-2pm, 7-10pm Mon-Sat. **Main courses** R78. **Credit** AmEx, DC, MC, V.

This restaurant is in a lovely country setting, frequented by the wine-making community and with flavoursome food and an impressive selection of wines. The menu changes regularly, but nearly always includes some Asian, European and traditional South African dishes.

Olivello

Mont Destin Estate, R44, Stellenbosch (021 875 5443/ www.olivello.co.za). **Open** 7am-10.30pm daily. **Main courses** R65. **Credit** AmEx, DC, MC, V.

The former team from Café Paradiso has found a new home on a working wine farm in the winelands. And what a great move it was. The cooking here is uncomplicated and delicious, using distinct Mediterranean and Asian flavours.

The Restaurant at Pontac

Pontac Manor, 16 Zion Street, Paarl (021 872 0445/ www.pontac.com). **Open** noon-3pm, 6.30-10pm daily. **Main courses** R78. **Credit** AmEx, DC, MC, V.

This intimate restaurant in a Paarl guesthouse is a popular choice for diners who favour elegant food. The restaurant is in the Cape vernacular style, but the culinary style is French. The menu changes according to the seasons (a good reason to go more than once) and special emphasis is placed on pairing wine and food. The dishes are beautifully presented and inspiring. And the Cape wines are a perfect complement to the European flavours.

Wijnhuis

Corner Church & Andringa Streets, Stellenbosch (021 887 5844). **Open** 11am-11pm daily. **Main courses** R85. **Credit** AmEx, DC, MC, V. **Map** p278 Q3.

The name, and the fact that the wine list is much longer than the menu, makes it clear what reigns supreme in this part of eatery. Luckily, a strong cosmopolitan menu backs up the variety of alcoholic delights. Popular choices include calamari, baby chicken, steaks, pastas and schnitzels.

African

Moyo at Spier

Baden-Powell Drive, outside Stellenbosch (021 809 1100/www.spier.co.za). Take N2 from Cape Town, turn onto R310 towards Stellenbosch. **Open** noon-4.30pm; 6pm-10pm daily. **Main courses** *Buffet* R150/person. **Credit** AmEx, DC, MC, V.

Moyo is spectacular. It celebrates all that is magical and beautiful about the African continent. Set in the large lawns of the Spier Estate, Moyo is an African fantasy where diners lounge in tents, swathed in rich fabrics, or chill out under the trees on carpets and cushions by the light of lanterns and flaming torches. Some of them dine on platforms set up in the trees from where they have a bird's-eye view of the inter-active entertainment of gumboot dancers who perform opera, African face painting, fortune-telling and live music from almost forgotten parts of Africa. The food is served as a buffet, and offers an astonishing array of freshly prepared dishes from all over the continent. Meals here are a long, leisurely affair, and diners are encouraged to stay and party on under the African sky.

Le Pommier Restaurant

Banhoek Valley, Helshoogte Pass, Stellenbosch (021 885 1269/www.lepommier.co.za). **Open** 7.30am-11pm daily. **Main courses** R55. **Credit** AmEx, DC, MC, V. **Map** p278 T1.

As the name suggests, this restaurant stands on the part of the 300-year-old Zorgvliet farm that used to be a thriving apple orchard fed by the rich soil of the area. Today it is used as a tranquil country restaurant, focusing on traditional South African cuisine but infused with French flavours in its basic but essentially tasty menu.

Restaurant 1802

30 Church Street, Stellenbosch (021 886 5671/ www.ouwewerf.com). **Open** 7am-10.30pm daily. **Main courses** R78. **Credit** AmEx, DC, MC, V. **Map** p278 Q3.

D'Ouwe Werf hotel was founded in 1802 and this restaurant pays tribute to this date as well as the culinary heritage of the Cape. Recently renovated, the restaurant now boasts clean modern lines which should appeal to those wanting traditional food in unstuffy surroundings. A leafy courtyard with modern water features and artistic walkway will welcome you to a restaurant which serves the familiar Cape Malay flavours, along with Afrikaans specialities such as wild game pie. A wonderful wine list offers ample examples of the best bottles the Cape winelands have to offer.

Spier

Baden-Powell Drive, outside Stellenbosch (021 809 1100/www.spier.co.za). Take the N2 from Cape Town, turn onto R310 towards Stellenbosch. **Open** 12.30-3.30pm, 6-11pm Mon-Sat. **Main courses** R30-R90. **Credit** AmEx, DC, MC, V.

A popular destination for tourists and family outings, Spier offers several decent dining options. Jonkershuis offers an extensive Cape Malay buffet, the Taphuis lighter pub lunches, Figaro's alfresco breakfasts, and the Spier Café tea and light meals in a coffee shop setting. And if you want to do it yourself, assemble your own picnic at the Spier Deli.

De Volkskombuis

Aan de Wagenweg, off Dorp Street, Stellenbosch (021 887 2121). **Open** noon-3pm, 6.30-9.30pm daily. **Main courses** R65. **Credit** AmEx, DC, MC, V. **Map** p278 P3.

If traditional South African cooking is what you want, this is the place to go. De Volkskombuis offers fun and fresh takes on age-old favourites such as springbok and ostrich. It also has smoked snoek (a type of fish), oxtail and chicken pie.

Gourmet

Boschendal

*Pniel Road, off the R310, Groot Drakenstein
(021 870 4274/www.boschendal.com).* **Open** 10am-
5pm daily. **Main courses** R58. **Credit** AmEx, DC,
MC, V.

The historic wine estate offers various dining
options. The main restaurant is set in the original
wine cellar of the Boschendal Manor House homestead, and offers an extensive lunch buffet of pâtés,
salads, roast beef and ham and cheeses. Le Café
serves lighter à la carte options, including quiches
and baguettes with unusual toppings. From May to
October, French-style country fare in picnic baskets
is available from Le Pique Nique.

Bosman's

*The Grande Roche, Plantasie Street, Paarl (021 863
2727/www.grandroche.com).* **Open** 7am-9pm daily.
Closed June, July. **Main courses** R140. **Credit**
AmEx, DC, MC, V.

An award-winning restaurant that has foodies
raving, the Bosman's may not make the same
impression on mere mortals. The portions are modestly sized and the prices put high. It's set in the
swish Grande Roche Hotel, which may go some
way to explain the expense. But if you're serious
about food, you won't want to miss the extensive
wine list and sophisticated cuisine.

La Couronne

*Robertsvlei Road, Franschhoek (021 876 2770/
www.lacouronnehotel.co.za).* **Open** 7-11am, noon-3pm,
7-11pm daily. **Main courses** R78. **Credit** AmEx,
DC, MC, V. **Map** p275 W3.

This stylish, hilltop restaurant offers fancy dining
and spectacular views. The cooking is full of local
flavour and textures and dining here is a sumptuous affair. The freshest ingredients are used and
executive chef Roger Clement has planted a staggering selection of 860 herbs to ensure elegant
flavours. We'd recommend the 'Menu Degustation'
which changes daily and is a five-course gourmet
feast. Wines are matched to every course which
ensures that you taste the very best this excellent
restaurant has to offer. Lunches are great in that you
can appreciate the view, but evenings offer a pianist
and candlelight. The choice is yours.

Haute Cabrière Cellar Restaurant

*Cabrière Estate, halfway up Franschhoek Pass,
Franschhoek (021 876 3688).* **Open** noon-3pm, 6.30-
10pm daily. **Main courses** R85. **Credit** AmEx, DC,
MC, V. **Map** p275 W3.

Chef Matthew Gordon and vintner Achim von
Arnim join forces in one of South Africa's most
respected restaurants. In fact, it has several times
been voted as one of the top-ten restaurants by *Eat
Out*, South Africa's leading native restaurant guide.
Served in full or half portions, the food caters for a
variety of tastes. Favourites include porcini-
flavoured risotto topped with linefish.

Klein Olifants Hoek

*14 Akademie Street, Franschhoek (021 876 2566/
www.kleinoliphantshoek.com).* **Open** 9am-noon, 2-9pm
Mon, Tue; 2-10pm Thur-Sat. **Main courses** R85.
Credit AmEx, DC, MC, V. **Map** p275 W1.

A cooking spectacular where the husband-and-wife
team cooks an entertaining five-course meal in a
walk-through kitchen. Local produce and wines are
cleverly used to create simple, but enjoyable flavours
such as pan-fried sweetbreads with porcini mushrooms or lobster with fresh herbs, baby cob and
saffron potatoes. Booking is essential.

Le Quartier Français

*16 Huguenot Road, Franschhoek (021 876 2151/
www.lequartier.co.za).* **Open** 7.30-10.30am, 12.30-3pm,
7-11.30pm daily. **Main courses** R80. **Credit** AmEx,
DC, MC, V. **Map** p275 W1.

Often picked out for praise by foodie magazines, Le
Quartier Français consistently delivers innovative
cooking, courtesy of outstanding chef Margot Janse.
The quality of the service matches the food. The
style is Cape Provençal with subtle and spicy local
flavours complementing each other marvellously.
The wine list is also award bait.

Tokara

*At the crest of the Helshoogte Pass, Stellenbosch
(021 808 5959).* **Open** 12.30-2.30pm, 7.30pm-
midnight Tue-Sat; phone to check in winter.
Main courses R105. **Credit** AmEx, DC, MC, V.
Map p278 R1.

Chef Etienne Bonthuys is known to be tempera-
mental… and a genius. Overlooking vineyards and
olive groves, this minimalist modern restaurant, on
the Helshoogte Pass, is where he works and offers
some of the finest food in the region – and that takes
some doing. It's pricey, but well worth it.

Mediterranean

Decameron

50 Plein Street, Stellenbosch (021 883 3331). **Open**
noon-10pm Mon-Sat; noon-2.30pm Sun. **Main courses**
R56. **Credit** AmEx, DC, MC, V. **Map** p278 Q2.

Locals love this place for its easygoing atmosphere
and great Italian cooking. The selection of wood-
fired pizza, pasta, steaks, fish and veal caters for all
tastes. Children under six are not allowed.

Cafés & casual eating

Blaauwklippen

*Blaauwklippen Estate, R44 between Stellenbosch and
Somerset West (021 880 0134/www.blaauwklippen.
com).* **Open** 9am-5pm daily. **Main courses** R55.
Credit AmEx, DC, MC, V.

Tourists and locals, mostly with a few kids in tow,
flock to this zippy wine farm. Before or after wine
tasting, casual cooking (salads, pizzas, burgers,
risottos, steaks and so on) is enjoyed on the sunny
terrace or lawns. Great big family buffets served on
Sundays are another attraction.

Eat, Drink, Shop

Pubs & Bars

From beach views to cigar bars, Capetonians have discerning taste.

Luridly good views at **Baraza**. See p122.

Most Capetonians would rather live in a broom cupboard in the right area than venture into the suburbs. As a result, the younger set largely socialises in the more cosmopolitan areas, where the bars vary from acceptable to excellent. And because this city believes in image above all else, lesser establishments are mostly ignored – no Capetonian worth their salt would be caught venturing into some dreadful hole-in-the-wall.

The majority of bars serve until 2am but there are plenty who either flout their licences or have permission to keep leading you astray well past the witching hour. Capetonians, however, regard a night out as part of the daily landscape. As they say: 'Tomorrow's another night!'

GETTING AROUND
Capetonians in general have always been notoriously lax when it comes to obeying drinking-and-driving laws, the result of underpolicing, a woeful lack of affordable public transport, especially after hours, and the LA-like geographic sprawl of the city. Metered cabs are your best option, but be warned: they're not cheap. The best policy is to go with a group, appoint a designated driver, or confine your revelling to establishments fairly near your lodgings.

City Bowl

Asoka Son of Dharma
68 Kloof Street, Gardens (021 422 0909/ www.asokasonofdharma.com). **Open** *Nov-Apr* 11am-2am Mon-Fri; 7pm-2am Sat. *May-Oct* 5.30pm-2am Mon-Sat. **Credit** AmEx, DC, MC, V. **Map** p282 F5.
Very chilled, very feng shui'd bar in the City Bowl, with Eastern, slick decor to die for, be reincarnated for and die for again. The clientele is ultra-chic.

Café Bardeli
68 Kloof Street, Gardens (021 423 4444).
Open 8.30am-midnight Mon-Sat. **Credit** AmEx, DC, MC, V. **Map** p282 F5.
This stylish lounge with great couches is just the place to grab a post-work tipple during the 5-7pm cocktail hour. Popular with the media crowd (it's right next door to e.tv), it has a contemporary urban feel, especially in the in-house cigar bar, the Cohibar. Summer evenings here lift off with smooth house beats, and the pizzas are among the best in town.

Castro's
10 Dixon Street, Green Point (021 425 3857).
Open 7pm-4am Mon-Sun. **Credit** MC, V.
Map p282 G3.
A hugely welcome addition to the Cape Town pool scene, which of late has been largely dominated by the lower-rent Stones. Castro's is a perfectly fine place to get the evening started – the brew is bone-marrowingly chilled and the place is generally in good nick. It's just a shame there's no food.

Cool Runnings
227 Long Street, City Centre (021 426 0584).
Open 4pm-3am Mon-Thur; 11am-3am Fri-Sat; 5pm-3am Sun. **Credit** V. **Map** p282 G4.
This chain of Jamaican-themed bars, based on the Disney movie, manages to pull off a laid-back and young-at-heart vibe. The Rasta wall murals and roughly hewn tables set the mood. Drink flows freely and the natives are friendly – just the thing for re-living student or backpacking days. Expect a laid-back sundowner on the balcony to turn into a late night. Popular with locals and tourists alike. The menu complements the venue.
Branch: 96 Station Road, Observatory (021 448 7656).

Fireman's Arms

Lower Buitengracht Street, City Centre (021 419 1513). **Open** 11am-11pm Mon-Sat. **Credit** AmEx, DC, MC, V. **Map** p283 H3.

This central Cape Town institution is named after the firemen who used to be its major customers. Flame-fighting memorabilia decorates the entire place. A bit rough around the edges, but still with sufficient character to really enjoy a decent pint.

Jo'burg

218 Long Street, City Centre (021 422 0142/www.lb-lounge.co.za). **Open** 5pm-4am Mon-Fri, Sun; 2pm-4am Sat. **Credit** AmEx, DC, MC, V. **Map** p282 G4.

Probably the most popular meeting spot in Cape Town. Everybody from trendy fashionistas to struggling artists can be spotted at Jo'burg's. The fab decor includes a mirror ball shaped like the Johannesburg skyline, and there is an ironic charm missing in other parts of the nightscape. Its nextdoor dancefloor – jokingly referred to as 'Pretoria' – features some great DJs. The newly opened upstairs 'art installation' lounge (Lb's) is so retro-porn that it would probably turn Hugh Hefner green.

Marvel

236 Long Street, City Centre (021 426 5880). **Open** 8pm-4am Mon-Sat. **No credit cards**. **Map** p282 G4.

This funky little bar plays all kinds of eclectic beats every night. The art students that frequent it are clever enough not to clog up the tiny space by dancing. A full range of board games is provided.

Mavericks

68 Barrack Street, City Centre (021 461 9988/www.mavericks.co.za). **Open** 7pm-4am Mon-Thur; 1pm-4am Fri; 7pm-4am Sat. **Credit** AmEx, MC, V. **Map** p283 H4.

An upmarket strip club situated in an old bank and done up to the nines, Mavericks is an impressive venue with a good kitchen and fine selection of drinks – think Rick's Café in Casablanca spliced with a gentleman's club. At last visit the dancers were not, however, equal to their surroundings.

Po Na Na Souk Bar

Heritage Square, 100 Shortmarket Street, City Centre (021 423 4889/www.fez.co.za). **Open** 11am-1am Mon-Sat. **Credit** AmEx, DC, MC, V. **Map** p282 G3.

A little oasis in the concrete wilderness, the Arabian-themed Po Na Na comes complete with Bedouin-style rooms and terraces. Situated in the historic Heritage Square, it will soon make you forget you are right in the heart of the city.

Raffiki's

13b Kloofnek Road, Tamboerskloof (021 426 4731). **Open** 11am-2am daily. **Credit** AmEx, DC, MC, V. **Map** p282 F5.

This laid-back bamboo bar has of late become very popular. Locals, students and backpackers all love the bar with the longest balcony in town. Hang out in a hammock, play table soccer, shoot some pool or just the breeze in this unassuming spot.

Roberts

13C Kloofnek Road, Tamboerskloof (021 422 4738). **Open** 6pm-1am Tue-Sat. **Credit** AmEx, DC, MC, V. **Map** p282 E5.

This snug little lounge bar has comfy couches and the relaxed feel of a friend's living room. Perfect for an intimate rendezvous.

The Shack

43 De Villiers Road, Zonnebloem (021 461 5892). **Open** 1pm-1am daily. **No credit cards**. **Map** p283 H5.

Multi-roomed, student-friendly bar that is busy until the wee hours. It boasts an upstairs pool hall, a lounge with a fireplace and two (extra-small) bar areas. There's also an on-site Mexican cantina.

Teazers

179 Loop Street, City Centre (021 422 4000/www.teazers.co.za). **Open** 7pm-3am Mon-Thur; noon-3pm Fri; 7pm-3am Sat. **Credit** MC, V. **Map** p282 G4.

Known euphemistically as a cabaret and revue bar, Teazers is essentially the Cape Town equivalent of Stringfellows, Pure Platinum and the like. The venue is lavishly appointed and features dancers of the highest calibre as well as remarkably good food at surprisingly reasonable prices. Bring your wallet, though – it's certainly not a case of ten cents a dance. This is as clean as dirty fun gets.

The best Pubs & Bars

For cocktails

Baraza (*see p122*) is one of Cape Town's most perfect spots to watch the sun set over the Atlantic Ocean, while **Tank** (*see p124*) is great for a chic, big-city feel.

For local beers

There's no competition here – **Ferryman's Tavern** (*see p123*) is where you want to be: during good weather the beer garden is wonderfully relaxing; during foul weather the interior is agreeably cosy.

For people-watching

Café Caprice (*see p123*) is a superb location for watching the beautiful set, passers-by and beach folk.

For watching sport

Match (*see p126*) has all the major sporting events, as well as slick designer decor, good food and a hip crowd.

For sundowners

La Med (*see p123*) is a perfect meeting place, and **Radisson** (*see p124*) near the Waterfront is a tad more sophisticated.

Eat, Drink, Shop

Zanzibar

255 Long Street (inside Carnival Court), City Centre
(021 423 9003). **Open** 5pm-2am Mon-Sat; 5-11pm
Sun. **No credit cards. Map** p282 G4.
Attracting the usual band of travelling misfits and
lost Aussies, Zanzibar has a location (in the hub of
Cape Town nightlife) and an eclectic DJ (Zero) that
make it a cut above the 'dormitory' brigade.

Atlantic Seaboard & Waterfront

Baraza

The Promenade, Victoria Road, Camps Bay
(021 438 1758/www.baraza.co.za). **Open** noon-late
daily. **Credit** AmEx, DC, MC, V. **Map** p284 B8.
This slick, comfortable lounge bar overlooks Camps
Bay beach. Huge open windows and an extensive
cocktail list make this one of the perfect spots to
watch the sun set over the Atlantic Ocean. It's very
popular in summer, as you would expect, so arrive
early if you want a window seat. DJs kick in at sunset until the wee hours with cool, down-tempo tunes.

La Bascule

Cape Grace Hotel, West Quay, V&A Waterfront
(021 410 7100/www.capegrace.co.za). **Open** 11am-
1am daily. **Credit** AmEx, DC, MC, V. **Map** p283 H2.

One of Cape Town's gems, this is a cosy and understated bar, nestled by the side of the quay with
superb views of Table Mountain. An excellent wine
cellar and a choice of cigars is bolstered by over 420
whiskies. To add to its already overflowing cup, the
bar has Africa's only all-girl string quartet, Muse,
performing here, every Wednesday. Lovely.

Buddhabar

39 Main Road, Green Point (021 434 4010/
www.buddhabar.co.za). **Open** 5pm-midnight Mon-
Fri; 7pm-midnight Sat. **Credit** AmEx, DC, MC, V.
Map p282 F2.
No relation to the world-famous Parisian bar of the
same name, but the inspiration is there nonetheless.
An upmarket, luxurious, Eastern lounge theme
extends through the decor and music; the multi-
room layout, with terrace, makes for a relaxed feel.

Buena Vista Social Café

81 Main Road, Green Point (021 433 0611). **Open**
noon-2.30am daily. **Credit** AmEx, DC. **Map** p282 F2.
The Little Cuba-in-Cape-Town feel of the decor
here is matched handsomely by laid-back ambience,
friendly service and really wonderful food. Its range
of cigars is pretty impressive too – there can be few
better venues in which to sit back, fire up and relax
in true Cape Town style. Monday night's live jazz
sessions are alone worth a visit.

Local brews

A wise man once observed that water is vitally
important to human survival, in that it is an
essential component of beer. This is clearly
something South Africans believe – according
to South African wine fundi Dave Hughegs we
put away 25 billion litres of the stuff every
year. In fact beer makes up 80 per cent of
our total liquor sales, which is to say South
Africans take their beer very seriously. Throw
insults at a fellow's choice of brew and he
may well consider them fighting words.

The market has always been overwhelmingly
dominated by South African Breweries (SAB),
which has recently merged with US giant
Miller to create the second largest beer
manufacturer in the world. Brand is just as
important to local drinkers as to labels are to
fashionistas. Indeed it's not too much of a
stretch to say: 'And by his beer shall ye know
him.' Black Label tends to cater to students
and those desperate for that extra 0.5 per
cent of alcohol and as such does not carry
a huge amount of cache value. A step up on
the ladder is Castle Lager, a no-nonsense
beer and enduring favorite, essentially SA's
Budweiser. Its lack of sexy image and heavy

connection with sport has, however, made it
less desirable to yuppie drinkers, who lean
more towards the more upmarket image of
beers such as the internationally linked
Amstel Lager and the newly launched Miller
Genuine Draft. Castle Milk Stout remains
largely the preserve of the black market.

Namibian Breweries, the second largest
manufacturer in the region, makes Windhoek
Lager and Windhoek Lite. Status-wise these
fall somewhere between Castle and Amstel.
South Africans, being no less attracted by
cosmopolitanism than any other nation, still
place a premium on imported beers, Heineken
and Corona being particular favourites.

While SAB accounts for over 95 per cent
of local beer sales, there are some very good
products coming out of microbreweries such
as Mitchells, which was founded in Knysna
back in 1983 and has been doing itself proud
producing a range of quality beers that come
satisfyingly close to the taste of British real
ales. Mitchell's flagships, Bosuns Bitters
and the more creamy Forrester's Lager, are
available either on tap or bottled, and go
down very nicely indeed. Cheers!

Jo'burg meets Cape Town. *See p121.*

Café Caprice
Victoria Road, Camps Bay (021 438 8315).
Open 9am-1am daily. **Credit** AmEx, DC, MC, V.
Map p284 B8.
This beach-side café and bar is currently one of the hippest in town. Owned by SA rugby 'bad boy' James Small, Caprice has become the place to show off your sleek, tanned body to the admiring masses. There are also stunning views and chilled beats.

Club House
The Meadway, Camps Bay Sports Club, Camps Bay (021 438 1412). **Open** 4pm-midnight Mon-Fri; noon-2am Sat, Sun. **Credit** AmEx, DC, MC, V.
Map p284 B8.
This lovely bar has a superb terrace looking out across sports fields to the palm trees on the coastline. It's the perfect place to enjoy the views away from the 'beautiful people' who clog up the Camps Bay strip. Prices are far more reasonable here too.

Dizzy's Jazz Café
41 The Drive, Camps Bay (021 438 2686).
Open 1pm-2am daily. **Credit** AmEx, DC, MC, V.
Map p284 B8.
Quaint, diminuitive and almost Parisian, this pavement café bustles with a complete lack of purpose during the summer months.

Dunes
1 Beach Road, Hout Bay (021 790 1876).
Open 9am-1am daily. **Credit** AmEx, DC, MC, V.
Hout Bay is one of the nicest areas of the Cape Province and Dunes is not only its best sundowner venue, but also embodies the spirit of the place – it's

accessible, child-friendly (with its jungle gym and sand-pits) and good fun. Indoor and outdoor seating is available, and service and menu are both good. Parking is abundant and the locals don't bite.

Eclipse Promenade Complex
Victoria Road, Camps Bay (021 438 0882/ www.eclipse-ventures.com). **Open** 5.30pm-2am Tue-Sat; 5.30pm-midnight Sun. **Credit** AmEx, DC, MC, V.
Map p284 B8.
Linked to the stylish London chain of funky cocktail bars, SA's own branch is the latest addition to the Camps Bay strip. With stunning views, an extensive cocktail range and light and funky comfortable surroundings, it is already attracting more than its share of the young-and-happening sundowner set.

Ferryman's Tavern
East Pier Road, V&A Waterfront (021 419 7748).
Open 11am-11pm daily. **Credit** AmEx, MC, V.
Map p283 H1.
Ferryman's is where to go for good local brews. In addition to the wonderful Mitchell's range, they serve all the usual suspects as well as some decidedly unusual ones. The beer garden is wonderfully relaxing and the interior agreeably cosy. The upstairs restaurant and pub grub are decent.

La Med
Victoria Road, Clifton (021 438 5600). **Open** 11.30am-midnight daily. **Credit** AmEx, DC, MC, V.
Map p281 B5.
This Cape Town institution claims that this is 'where the world meets Cape Town'. It is certainly true that almost every Capetonian has been here at

some time. The views are gorgeous, the drinks plentiful and the food isn't bad, either. In season, Friday and Sunday nights are the biggies, when dancing joins drinking as the order of the evening. But they really do need to retire some of their CDs.

Mitchell's Waterfront Brewery & Scottish Ale House
East Pier Road, Quay 4, V&A Waterfront (021 419 5074). **Open** 11am-2am daily. **Credit** AmEx, DC, MC, V. **Map** p283 H2.
Mitchell's has its own micro-brewery on site, and daily guided tours are rounded off by sampling the fine lagers, bitters and stouts. The Ale House itself has a great atmosphere with a wooden bar and an upstairs attic that always pumps when the footie's on. It's a shame that a change of ownership has meant an end to Scottish beers on tap, but they do still offer a handful of good, traditional English ales.

Nose Wine Bar
Cape Quarter, Dixon Street, De Waterkant (021 425 2200/www.thenose.co.za). **Open** 11.30am-midnight Mon-Sat. **Main courses** R65. **Credit** AmEx, DC, MC, V. **Map** p282 G3.
Wine bars where you can drink by the glass seem to be a novel concept in Cape Town, so we're happy to have this one. The wine menu changes every month and to keep you horizontal the bar serves delicious snacks (in peckish or hungry-sized portions) plus a few more substantial dishes.

On the Rocks
Ambassador Hotel, 34 Victoria Road, Bantry Bay (021 439 6170). **Open** 10am-midnight daily. **Credit** AmEx, DC, MC, V. **Map** p281 B5.
Swanky and old-school, this cocktail bar is literally built on the rocks overlooking the ocean. Not cheap and a little stuffy, but with that view, who cares?

Opium
6 Dixon Street, De Waterkant (021 421 4501). **Open** 8.30pm-late. **No credit cards. Map** p282 G3.
Dreadfully trendy, stocked to capacity with model-watchers, would-be models and occasionally the genuine article. This is essentially the new 'in' spot for ex-Rhodes Housers. Not bad if you can see past the pretensions; rather better if you turn up in a flashy ride. Clothing: gents, black; women, minimal.

Paulaner Brauhaus
V&A Waterfront (021 418 9999/ www.paulaner.co.za). **Open** 11am-2am daily. **Credit** AmEx, DC, MC, V. **Map** p283 H1.
An authentic, German, micro-brewery with some pretty fine and reasonably-priced beers on tap. The huge outdoor patio boasts views of the harbour and Signal Hill, which, when combined with great bar snacks and big-screen sport, make this the perfect pitstop after hitting the shops at the V&A.

Radisson
Beach Road, Granger Bay (021 418 5729). **Open** noon-1.30am daily. **Credit** AmEx, DC, MC, V.
Not only does it feature one of the best views in Cape Town, Radisson is also the perfect place to have a chilled tall one and pretend you're an LA film mogul. The menu unfortunately does not live up to the venue, and the entrance through the underground car-park is regrettably grotty. There is no indoor smoking section, but it's the outside deck where you'll want to be seen anyway.

Sandbar
31 Victoria Road, Camps Bay (021 438 8336). **Open** 9.30am-10pm daily. **Credit** AmEx, DC, MC, V. **Map** p284 B8.
This small sidewalk café is a somewhat inexplicably popular locale with the Models 'n' Mustangs crowd, but not as pretentious as some of its neighbours on the Camps Bay strip. It's worth stopping off here for an afternoon cocktail or two.

Tank
72 Waterkant Street, Cape Quarter, Green Point (021 419 0007/www.the-tank.co.za). **Open** noon-3am Tue-Sun. **Credit** AmEx, MC, V. **Map** p282 G2.
Situated in the just-plain-wonderful Cape Quarter, Tank has become the closest thing Cape Town has to a New York 'in' spot. Superbly designed and amply stocked with pretty (slightly older) things, it is, surprisingly, not nearly as stand-offish as many Cape Town bars. If things go well, the excellent restaurant (*see p109*) is just a jump to the left. Dress like you're going out for the night.

Southern suburbs

Billy the B.U.M.'s
Letterstead House, Fedsure-on-Main Corner Main & Campground Roads, Newlands (021 683 5541/ mwbums@mweb.co.za). **Open** noon-4am Tue-Sat. **Credit** AmEx, DC, MC, V.
The home of the southern suburbs' sporty crowd. This is where good-looking and healthy people go to be unhealthy in slick, comfortable surrounds. Co-owned by Springbok rugby player Bobby Skinstad, it's always good for sport celeb-spotting. It can get rowdy, especially after big sporting internationals.

Café Carte Blanche
42 Trill Road, Observatory (021 447 8717). **Open** 6pm-2am. **Credit** AmEx, DC, MC, V.
A weird, idiosyncratic little bar that has become an institution in Observation. The upstairs lounge, made out like a Dada-esque living room straight out of *Moulin Rouge*, is in itself worth a visit.

The Curve
Lower Main Road, Observatory (021 448 0183). **Open** 8.30pm-4am Mon, Tue, Thur-Sun; 8.30pm-1am Wed. **No credit cards.**
Situated in the foyer of a dilapidated cinema, the Curve has become a bit of a haven for the arty bohemian set that has settled in Woodstock and Observatory. A venue that's well known for its world-music parties and occasional art installations.

Bars for cigar buffs

In these (some might say) regrettably politically-correct times, when smokers practically have to retreat to the garden shed when they fancy a cigarette, it's nice to know that there are still some establishments where the convivial enjoyment of rolled-up leaves is not just sanctioned, but heartily endorsed. As cigar smoking continues to increase the world over, cigar bars have become something of a fixture on the Cape Town leisure scene. Given that there are now almost as many different groups of cigar smokers as there are cigars, it is quite fitting that Cape Town has establishments to suit most tastes.

Kennedy's Restaurant & Cigar Lounge

251 Long Street, City Centre (021 424 1212). **Open** noon-1am Mon-Fri; 6pm-2am Sat. **Credit** AmEx, DC, MC, V. **Map** p282 G4. When Kennedy's first opened, the more charitable among us gave it six months – 'An up-market cigar bar in Cape Town?' we chortled. 'It'll never last' (Capetonians being notoriously fickle when it comes to 'in' spots). It didn't just last, it thrived and became a local institution. It has the biggest and best range of cigars in town, some 400 at any given time, a selection of wines and spirits to complement the variety and trained staff on hand to help you make the perfect match. The decor is equally phenomenal: think old-world Cuba meets Rick's Café in Casablanca. And the menu is more than up to the job. The valet-parking service is an added bonus. The original and still the best. If you're a cigar aficionado you owe yourself a visit.

The Leopard Lounge

The 12 Apostles Hotel, Victoria Drive, Oudekraal Bay, Atlantic Seaboard (021 437 9000). **Open** 11am-midnight daily. **Credit** AmEx, DC, MC, V. **Map** p284 A10. It's not the cigars that'll leave you short of breath at the Leopard Lounge, it's the views, which are some of the most spectacular in the country. In all fairness the decor could be described as a tad touristy: squishy leather sofas, Big Five murals... but this is more than made up for by the fine service (if you could find a way to replicate the staff you'd be in the money), excellent selection of drinks and

competent choice of cigars. The complimentary snacks and superb live entertainment are wonderful bonuses.

Planet

Mount Nelson Hotel, 76 Orange Street, Gardens, City Bowl (021 483 1000). **Open** 4pm-1am daily. **Credit** AmEx, DC, MC, V. **Map** p282 G5. Planet is part of 'the Nelly's' ongoing effort to divest itself of its somewhat fogeyish image. The venue is divided into three areas, one of which is a smoking section. The first is decorated with a mobile of the planet system; the second room features fibre-optic lights depicting the Milky Way; and the terrace boasts the genuine African night sky. From the onyx bar to the leather carpet, the massive banquette, nothing is done by halves. Expect the choice of stogies to be formidable.

Raleigh's

Arabella Sheraton, Cape Town Convention Square, Lower Long Street, City Centre (021 412 9999). **Open** 9pm-3am daily. **Credit** AmEx, DC, MC, V. **Map** p282 G4. The Arabella Sheraton is reminiscent of a set from a science fiction movie, and its cigar bar, Raleigh's, is no exception – it's all chrome, glass and designer goodies. The cigar selection is very good, most of the major brands finding accommodation in the humidors. However, Raleigh's, unfortunately, lacks a certain soul and the outlook onto the Cape Town International Convention Centre leaves much to be desired. To make the most of it, come here during the day or the wee hours when the view doesn't matter.

Foresters Arms

52 Newlands Avenue, Newlands (021 689 5949).
Open 11am-11.30pm Mon-Thur; 11am-midnight Fri;
10.30am-11.30pm Sat; 10.30am-6pm Sun. **Credit**
AmEx, DC, MC, V.

An English pub situated in the leafy environs of
Newlands. It feels sometimes as if the whole building has been uprooted from Kent and shipped over
intact. Affectionately known as 'Forries', this is the
perfect place for the fortysomethings to hang out in
if it is too wet for the golf course.

Match

*Stadium-on-Main, Main Road, Claremont (021 674
1152).* **Open** 8.30am-12.30am Mon-Sat 11am-7pm
Sun. **Credit** AmEx, DC, MC, V.

Without a doubt, Match is as sexy as a sports bar
can get. Designer decor that has featured in more
than a few fashion shoots and tasty food make this
a great spot to watch the Big Event. The crowd is
youngish at night and mixed during the day.

Peddlars on the Bend

*Spaanschemaat River Road, Constantia (021 794
7747).* **Open** 11am-11pm daily. **Credit** AmEx, DC,
MC, V.

The Peddlars is drinking trough of choice for Cape
Town's own mink-and-manure set. In summer the
outdoor patio, and in winter the roaring fireplace,
make it very well worth a visit if you are out hob-
nobbing with the local gentry.

False Bay

Brass Bell

Seafront, Kalk Bay (021 788 5456). **Open** noon-
11.30pm daily. **Credit** AmEx, DC, MC, V.

Characterful and cheerful pub below the railway line
right next door to the picturesque Kalk Bay harbour.
In summer, sit outside and feel the swell as it rips
almost over the bar. In winter sit inside in the tiny,
glassed-in, sea-facing, side section and watch the
waves wash against the windows.

Polana

Main Road, Kalk Bay (021 788 7162). **Open** 4pm-
midnight daily. **Credit** AmEx, DC, MC, V.

A cute, comfy and cosy bar, right on the sea in Kalk
Bay. Read a book or chill with the locals and do nothing in a suburb known for it laid-back attitude. The
restaurant makes way for a DJ late on a Friday
night, when Polana becomes the only cool dance
spot this side of the mountain.

Skebanga's

*Above the Red Herring Restaurant, Beach Road,
Noordhoek (021 789 1783).* **Open** noon-midnight
Tue-Sun. **Credit** AmEx, DC, MC, V.

A friendly pub with a great deck that gives stunning
views over the ocean. Well worth a sundowner
detour on the way back from a visit to Cape Point.
There is live music on a Sunday night that has the
place packed and pumping.

Northern suburbs

Blue Peter

Beachfront, Bloubergstrand (021 554 1956).
Open 10am-11pm daily. **Credit** AmEx, DC, MC, V.

If you have one 'tourist beer' in Cape Town, then it
should be at the old Blue Peter. Sitting on its slop-
ing grassy lawn with a cold beer looking out on what
must be the most photographed view in the world
is pure nirvana. More than a few locals make an
annual pilgrimage here, just to remind themselves
of how lucky they are to live in Cape Town.

Cubana

Edward Road, Tygervalley (021 910 4963).
Open 8am-1am daily. **Credit** AmEx, DC, MC, V. .

A sophisticated, Cuban-themed bar that has established itself as the crème of the 'Edward Road' strip.
A smart-casual, but easygoing, social lounge which
incorporates a cigar lounge and cocktail lounge,
perfect for the pre-club drink.

Stones

72 Main Road, Claremont (021 674 4233).
Open noon-2am daily. **No credit cards**.

A perennial favourite among student types and
those generally giving their youth a long goodbye,
the Stones has been frequented by almost everyone
in Cape Town at some time or another. The convivial
atmosphere assures that partners (pool and otherwise) are not hard to find, and the music is generally
there to remind you of the youth you spent misbe-
having. Most patrons are get-along folk, but there
are a few sharks out there too, so common sense is
in order. Parking in Observatory also tends to be a
case of blind trust and bravery.

Branches: 166A Long Street, City Centre (021 424
0418); Lower Main Road, Observatory (021 448 9461);
2nd Floor, Blouberg Mall, Tableview (021 556 2756);
Regent Road, Sea Point (021 439 9498).

Winelands

Bohemia

*Corner Victoria & Andringa Street, Stellenbosch
(021 882 8375).* **Open** 8am-late Mon-Fri; 9am-2am
Sat; 11am-2am Sun. **Credit** MC, V. **Map** p278 Q3.

This artsy student bar would not look out of place
in any student town from Austin to Edinburgh.
Expect lots of arty types discussing eternal questions with budding intellectuals over bottles of red
plonk. Homely and warm, its bohemian decor and
roaring fireplace make it great for winter.

De Akker

90 Dorp Street, Stellenbosch (021 883 3512). **Open**
10.30am-late Mon-Sat. **Credit** MC, V. **Map** p278 P3.

This place is legendary. It's been around for ages
(being the third oldest pub in the country) and will
probably outlive most of us. Dark and smoky with
comfortable seats and a lovely terrace, it's never
empty and almost never closed. The crowd tends to
consist of students and tourists.

Shops & Services

Malls may dominate the scene, but there's still a lot of local lustre.

Join the crowds at **Victoria Wharf**, V&A Waterfront. See p128.

While not quite up to the heady levels of London, New York and Paris, the cosmopolitan nature of the city and the recent influx of foreign tourists made Cape Town an exciting place to shop. International designers are shoulder to shoulder with their equally worthy local counterparts and, while locals still find the prices of many items somewhat north of the ceiling, they are comparatively reasonable for international visitors. In addition to clothing, local artwork is also plentiful (see pp168-174), as well as reasonably priced. The only thing limiting what you buy during your stay, is what you can comfortably carry home with you.

The face of Cape Town shopping has changed dramatically over the past decade or so. There was a time when the City Centre was The Place To Be. Nowadays, however, it has become something of a white elephant, with most locals favouring the malls. The reasons for this shift are manifold – the rise of the mega-mall is probably the key one, but petty crime, lack of parking and the increasing inaccessibility of the inner city have also played a major part. Due to vandalism, parking meters have been changed to a parking-card system. However, cards are a

hassle to get hold of and most Capetonians use parking garages, which charge a handsome rate.

Most shops in the City Centre close at 5pm or earlier and, despite the beefing up of security cameras ,it's not a great idea to be in the area after dark. During daylight hours, Church Street and Long Street, Greenmarket Square and the accompanying St George's Mall make for good browsing for artwork, clothes and jewellery, though the once-vibrant Grand Parade is a shadow of its former self. Likewise, the open-air shopping area outside the station looks buzzing from a distance but it is mostly just cheap knock-offs and is best avoided.

When it comes to game, South Africa has the Big Five; when it comes to malls, Cape Town has the Big Three. There is no doubt that Victoria Wharf is, and probably always will be, king, but you'll find that fact reflected in its prices. The newer Canal Walk, situated a 15-minute drive from the city, is a more reasonable affair. You may find Cavendish Square a tad confusing, but it has some very fine shops, including one of the best CD stores in the country and some particularly good boutiques.

Finds for the beady-eyed at **Heartworks**. *See p145.*

Malls

Canal Walk

Century Boulevard, Century City, Milnerton, Northern Suburbs (0860 101 165/www.canalwalk.co.za). **Open** 10am-9pm Mon-Fri; 9am-9pm Sat; 10am-9pm Sun. **Credit** varies.

This is 'the big one', the one that elevated the status of malls in the Western Cape. It boasts 400 shops, 18 cinemas, a huge food court and many restaurants. There's no chance of getting bored here. Put on comfortable shoes and get ready to work that credit card.

Cavendish Square

1 Dreyer Street, Claremont, Southern Suburbs (021 671 8042/www.cavendish.co.za). **Open** 9am-6pm Mon-Thur; 9am-9pm Fri, Sat; 10am-4pm Sun. **Credit** varies.

This sleek mall is a label shrine. Top-end fashion creativity from local and international fashion labels can be found inside as well as outside in Cavendish Street. It also boasts a great assortment of restaurants (the usual shopping-mall chains and some other exotic eateries) and cinemas.

Gardens Centre

Mill Street, Gardens, City Bowl (021 465 1842). **Open** 9am-6pm Mon-Fri; 9am-3pm Sat; 10am-2pm Sun. **Credit** varies. **Map** p282 G5.

Gardens Centre is the best place for a pit stop after work to stock up on the essentials. Whether it's food (ready-made or ingredients for home-cooking), wine, a video or a new dress, you'll get it at this smallish, local shopping mall.

Palms Décor & Lifestyle Centre

145 Sir Lowry Road, City Centre (021 462 0394). **Open** 8am-5pm Mon-Fri; 8am-1.30pm Sat; varies Sun. **Credit** varies. **Map** p283 I4.

Feel like decorating? In need of inspiration? The Palms should be your first port of call. A lifestyle centre dedicated to decor, you'll find furniture, bath fittings, tiles, paints and accessories here.

Somerset Mall

Intersection of N2 & R44, Somerset West, False Bay (021 852 7114/www.somerset-mall.co.za). **Open** 9am-6pm Mon-Sat; 10am-2pm Sun. **Credit** varies.

You won't leave empty-handed from this huge shopping mall on the wine route, offering the usual array of shops, cinemas and large grocery stores as well as gift shops, book stores and clothing boutiques.

Tygervalley Shopping Centre

Willie van Schoor Avenue, Durbanville, Northern Suburbs (021 914 7891). **Open** 9am-7pm Mon- Fri; 9am-5pm Sat; 9am-2pm Sun. **Credit** varies.

On weekends you might well feel the urge to run someone over with your shopping trolley as Tygervalley is filled with fussy families and teenagers, but it offers a great variety of shops and goods and it's well worth fighting back the crowds. The mall is family-orientated and strong in areas such as home appliances and electronics. It also offers a bowling alley and cinema.

Victoria Wharf

V&A Waterfront, Atlantic Seaboard (021 408 7600/ www.waterfront.co.za). **Open** 9am-9pm daily. **Credit** varies. **Map** p283 H1.

This centre forms the bulk of the retail space at the V&A Waterfront, and presents the shopper with a selection of national retailers, boutiques and services, along with a spread of restaurants, coffee shops and fast-food outlets. There are also two cinema complexes, with one focusing on art-house movies. Even though shops officially close at 9pm, many only pull the shutters down at 11pm. Security is superb but unobtrusive. That said, it is an expensive venue.

Antiques

Bruce Tait Antiques & Kitsch Collectibles

Buitenkloof Centre, 8 Kloof Street, City Centre (021 422 1567). **Open** 10am-6pm Mon-Fri; 9.30am-2pm Sat; 10am-2pm Sun. **Credit** AmEx, DC, MC, V. **Map** p282 F5.

This fabulous haven of kitsch is the perfect place to shop for authentic lava lamps, old record covers and religious memorabilia, and other must-have items such as cocktail sticks, hatboxes and whacky newspaper posters. Perfect gift material.

Burr & Muir

82 Church Street, City Centre (021 422 1319). **Open** 9.30am-4.15pm Mon-Fri; 9.30am-1pm Sat. **Credit** AmEx, DC, MC, V. **Map** p282 G4.

This shop specialises in art-nouveau and art deco collectibles. It has a beautiful selection, which changes regularly as the sought-after pieces change hands. The eminent art deco potter Clarice Cliff is well represented, among other big names.

Delos

140 Buitengracht Street, City Centre (021 422 0334). **Open** 10am-6pm Mon-Fri; 10am-2pm Sat. **No credit cards**. **Map** p282 G4.

A fabulous shop that borders the Bo-Kaap, Delos looks sublime at night, illuminated from within by a huge number of antique light fittings and chandeliers. You'll want to go back during opening hours where you'll be mesmerised by the crystals.

Gilles de Moyencourt

54 Church Street, City Centre (021 424 0344). **Open** 9.30am-4pm Mon-Fri; 9.30am-1pm Sat. **No credit cards**. **Map** p282 G4.

In the heart of pedestrian Church Street, this shop has a wide variety of antiques, some more valuable than others, but always interesting. Here you will find European antiques as well as Africana.

Private Collections

Corner of Hudsin & Waterkant Streets, City Bowl (021 421 0298). **Open** 8.30am-5pm Mon-Fri; 8.30am-4pm Sat. **Credit** AmEx, DC, MC, V. **Map** p282 G3.

Some wonderfully impressive pieces make their way from India to this beautiful shop. Old doors, large dining room tables, chairs and the like will transform your home into something palatial.

Books

Clarke's

211 Long Street, City Centre (021 423 5739/www.clarkesbooks.co.za). **Open** 9am-5pm Mon-Fri; 9am-1pm Sat. **Credit** AmEx, DC, MC, V. **Map** p282 G4.

Young Designers' Emporium. *See p134.*

This is a shop for true book lovers only. Wooden floors, winding staircase and crowded bookshelves make this the bookshop you've always longed for. You'll find rare and valuable books, as well as the latest offerings of the literary kind.

Exclusive Books

Victoria Wharf, V&A Waterfront, Atlantic Seaboard (021 419 0905). **Open** 9am-10.30pm daily. **Credit** AmEx, DC, MC, V. **Map** p283 H1.

You will find a branch in most major shopping malls dotted about the city and suburbs. It's big and bold with a massive range of titles. Staff are well informed and helpful and it's a browsing-friendly type of place. In addition to the big names and the best-sellers, there is a very good selection of books on South Africa and works by local authors.

Branches: For details, phone head office (011 803 3773).

Wordsworth

Gardens Centre, Gardens, City Bowl (021 461 8464). **Open** 9am-7pm Mon-Thur; 9am-8pm Fri; 9am-6pm Sat; 9am-4pm Sun. **Credit** AmEx, DC, MC, V. **Map** p282 G5.

Come here for a more personalised reading experience. The staff have read widely and are keen to share their love of books. Strong on fiction.

Branches: For details, phone head office (021 424 8582).

Electronics

Audio Vision

Tygervalley Centre, Dubanville, Northern Suburbs (021 914 2117). **Open** 9am-7pm Mon-Fri; 9am-5pm Sat; 10am-2pm Sun. **Credit** AmEx, DC, MC, V.

People who know what they want from their home entertainment know they will find it all at this store. Those who are new to the audio- and video-equipment market will be happy to know that the staff are patient and will also deliver and install.

Cinema Espresso

Steenberg Village Centre, Steenberg Road, Tokai, Southern Suburbs (021 701 2809). **Open** 8am-7pm Mon-Fri; 9am-7pm Sat; 10am-6pm Sun. **Credit** AmEx, DC, MC, V.

The in-house coffee bar offers the perfect escape for parents or grumpy girlfriends while their kids and boyfriends browse the more-than 1,600 titles of DVD movies, music videos and Playstation games.

Hi-Fi Corporation

N1 Value Centre, Solly Smit Street, Goodwood, Northern Suburbs (021 595 1480). **Open** 9am-6pm Mon-Fri; 8am-5pm Sat; 10am-2pm Sun. **Credit** AmEx, DC, MC, V.

These stores offer electronics at competitive prices. TVs, video machines, DVDs, toasters, cameras, kettles and heaters, this is where you'll come to shop around for the best prices.

Branches: For details, phone head office (011 372 7300).

Signals Audio & Video

Canal Walk, Milnerton, Northern Suburbs (021 552 0014/www.signals.co.za). **Open** 10am-9pm daily. **Credit** AmEx, DC, MC, V.

Turn your TV room into a home theatre with the help of the experts who staff this store. Signals Audio & Video also specialises in acoustic analysis and the soundproofing of homes. Spoilt for choice? The two demonstration rooms will ensure that the decision is less daunting.

Fashion

Budget

Truworths

Cavendish Square, Claremont, Southern Suburbs (021 683 1310). **Open** 9am-6pm Mon-Thur; 9am-9pm Fri; 9am-6pm Sat; 10am-4pm Sun. **Credit** AmEx, DC, MC, V.

One of the more trendy chain stores around, Truworths stocks a wide range of clothing for almost everyone, from petit teens to budget trendoids. Truworths Man looks after the boys.

Branch: For details, phone head office (021 460 7911).

Woolworths

Cavendish Square, Claremont, Southern Suburbs (021 674 3050/www.woolworths.co.za). **Open** 9am-6pm Mon-Thur; 9am-9pm Fri; 9am-6pm Sat; 10am-5pm Sun. **Credit** AmEx, DC, MC, V.

Woollies, as everyone affectionately calls it, is South Africa's version of Marks & Spencer. It stocks quality homeware, foodstuffs and clothing for the whole family. Good for essentials.

Branch: For details, phone head office (021 407 9111).

Mid-range

Alternative Design

81 Long Street, City Centre (021 424 2883). **Open** 8.30am-5pm Mon-Fri; 8.30am-3.30pm Sat. **Credit** AmEx, DC, MC, V. **Map** p282 G4.

This is a treasure trove of funky, feminine clothes and jewellery conceived by imaginative designers who push the creative envelope to its limits. But never beyond what is wearable. Trying on outfits in this shop is like playing fancy dress, with the added difference that you can take your fantasies home with you. At very reasonable prices, too.

Branch: West Coast Shopping Village, Tableview, West Coast (021 544 0195).

Cigar

Shop B14, Cape Quarter, Dixon Street, De Waterkant, Atlantic Seaboard (021 418 4846). **Open** 10am-5pm Mon-Fri; 10am-3pm Sat. **Credit** AmEx, DC, MC, V. **Map** p282 G3.

The variety of well-sourced clothing from Europe forms the perfect base to build the working girl's wardrobe around. There are lovely tailored pants and jackets, with shirts and knits to go with them.

Eat, Drink, Shop

Most wanted

Brace yourself ❶

Whether buying for yourself or for your home, your itinerary must include a stop at **East of Eden** (*see p145*). It comes from the creators of the highly successful clothing brand Icuba (sold in store as well as at a range of other equally hip outlets) and is a jumble of weird and wacky clothing, shoes, accessories, crockery, lamps and other home furnishings. It is impossible to choose one signifying item, but we quite like their jewellery.

Shaking that ass ❷

Young Designers' Emporium (*see p134*) is one of the leaders of the fashion pack in Cape Town. Showcasing the bright and bold produce of young, up-and-coming designers, you're sure to find inspiring stuff here. They stock a great spread of women's and men's clothing, as well as shoes and accessories.

No Suffer-ring ❸

If you've got it, why not flaunt it in an ironic fashion? And if you can afford it, why not be understated? Desirable jewellery by Carine Terreblanche can be found at **Bread & Butter** (*see p144*), where art and design mix.

Flower power ❹

It was not enough to please Cape Town's girls. The creators of India Jane had to try their luck with the boys as well. So along came **A Suitable Boy** (*see p136*), a charming and edgy collection of menswear. Definitely aimed at the eternally hip, with funky T-shirts a strong feature.

Light up your life ❺

Brett Murray's lights make perfect gifts for those who are afraid of the dark. Red hot chillis, sacred hearts, penguins, steaming cups of coffee and rockets are great for those who just don't want to grow up. Find them at **Bruce Tait Antiques & Kitsch Collectibles** (*see p129*), where you'll be tempted by the divine kitsch, the '50s memorabilia and anything else that appeals to a slightly twisted sense of humour.

Dolled up ❻

The Monkeybiz Beading Project creates employment for women (and some men) in poverty-stricken areas. Using a craft technique passed down through generations, the beaders create dolls with a modern creative edge. Find them at the **Cape Town Visitors' Centre** (Pinnacle Building, corner of Castle and Burg streets, City Centre, 021 426 4260/www.monkeybiz.co.za) where you'll love the assortment of uniquely South African crafts.

Skirting the issue ❼

Frequented by stylists and fashion editors, and much loved by numerous well-dressed Capetonians, **India Jane** (*see p134*) is a home-grown gem. Garments from local trendsetters such as Maya Prass fill up the colourful store – where

clothing
is conveniently
organised
according to colour.
Gorgeous jewellery and
accessories are also to be found.

If the shoe fits... ⑧

Expert shoppers, by definition, have a thing
about shoes. A sure favourite is **Fredric &
Olivia**, brainchild of Beth Alpert, and maker of
some of the most delectable local footwear.
Her very trendy pointy mules and single-strap
sandals are available in every imaginable
colour, some with exquisite beading that has
been carried out through a community
empowerment project. The shoes
are sold at selected boutiques
countrywide, and can also be
ordered in your specific size
and material preference. For
more information visit
www.fredricandolivia.com

Eat, Drink, Shop

Hip Hop

*12 Cavendish Street, Claremont, Southern Suburbs
(021 674 4605).* **Open** 9am-5.50pm Mon-Fri; 9am-
4pm Sat; 10am-2pm Sun. **Credit** AmEx, DC, MC, V.
Whatever the occasion (a black-tie event, a job inter-
view, a night on the town), Hip Hop will glam up
your outfit. It stocks ballgowns, stunning suits and
a gazillion tops to mix and match with.

India Jane

*125 Agter Waterkant Street, Cape Quarter, Atlantic
Seaboard (021 421 3517).* **Open** 9.30am-5.30pm
Mon-Sat. **Credit** AmEx, DC, MC, V. **Map** p282 G3.
Arguably the best thing that has ever happened to
Cape Town fashion. India Jane stocks a delectable
variety of local designers and fresh-from-London
creations. Come here to find beaded bags and shoes,
ballgowns, sexy little tops, long flowing skirts,
embroidered cardigans and fun, funky underwear,
all organised according to colour. The range of jew-
ellery is also particularly fantastic.
Branches: 14 Cavendish Street, Claremont,
Southern Suburbs (021 683 7607); Station Building,
Main Road, Kalk Bay, False Bay (021 788 3020).

Jenni Button

*Cavendish Square, Claremont, Southern Suburbs
(021 683 9504).* **Open** 9am-6pm Mon-Sat; 10am-
4pm Sun. **Credit** AmEx, DC, MC, V.
Consistently trendy and glamorous, Jenni Button
(incidentally, no longer owned by Ms Button) is
much loved by the stylish creatures of South Africa.
The store stocks everything from underwear and
shoes to suits and eveningwear.
Branch: Victoria Wharf, V&A Waterfront, Atlantic
Seaboard (021 421 1346).

Juanita Pacheco

*Canal Walk, Century City, Milnerton, Northern
Suburbs (551 4555).* **Open** 10am-9pm Mon-Fri, Sun;
9am-9pm Sat. **Credit** AmEx, DC, MC, V.
Frequent trips to Paris by the owners and the use of
gorgeous material is what make this shop a must-
see-and-try-on. The evening wear often sticks to just
one basic look, with lots of colour and material
options for the same pattern.
Branches: 2B Dean Street Arcade, corner Main &
Dean Streets, Newlands, Southern Suburbs (021 689
9891); Victoria Wharf, V&A Waterfront, Atlantic
Seaboard (021 424 9663).

Mememe

279 Long Street, City Centre (021 424 0001). **Open**
10am-6pm Mon-Fri, 10am-2pm Sat. **Credit** AmEx,
DC, MC, V. **Map** p282 G4.
Mememe stocks an impressive array of cutting-edge
young designers. Many of the designers are actually
artists in their own right, like the award-winning
Doreen Southwood, co-owner of the store. The place
is an effortless blend of art and fashion.

Pure Solid

*Victoria Wharf, V&A Waterfront, Atlantic Seaboard
(021 421 9556).* **Open** 9am-9pm Mon-Sat; 10am-
9pm Sun. **Credit** AmEx, DC, MC, V. **Map** p282 G4.

Be transported into the wacky East with this
mish-mash of eastern influences – silk slippers, jade
jewellery, Power Puff paraphernalia and much,
much more. Yet, it is perhaps the small selection
of exclusively designed clothes that keep people
coming back for more.

Scar

183 Long Street, City Centre (021 424 8521). **Open**
10am-6pm Mon-Fri; 10am-4pm Sat. **Credit** AmEx,
DC, MC, V. **Map** p282 G4.
Fashion stylists adore Scar. Its broad selection of
male and female clothing lines includes designs by
local talent such as Miss Money Penny, Amanda
Laird Cherry and Coppelia. A must for designer chic.

Slate

*Tygervalley Centre, Durbanville, Northern Suburbs
(021 914 1424).* **Open** 9am-7pm Mon-Fri; 9am-5pm
Sat; 10am-2pm Sun. **Credit** AmEx, DC, MC, V.
Slate is a refreshing find in an overcrowded suburban shopping mall. The range of signature and
designer clothing and accessories is a feast of
colours and textures. Be sure to find the season's latest styles in whimsical permutations.

Young Designers' Emporium

*Cavendish Square, Claremont, Southern Suburbs
(021 683 6177).* **Open** 9am-6pm Mon-Thur; 9am-
9pm Fri; 9am-6pm Sat; 10am-4pm Sun. **Credit** AmEx,
DC, MC, V.
As the name implies, new designers strut their stuff
here. The result is a jumble of progressive fashion –
all very inspiring . The style is fun and fashionable,
and will last you the whole season.
Branch: Victoria Wharf, V&A Waterfront, Atlantic
Seaboard (021 425 6216/ www.yde.co.za).

Upmarket

Errol Arendz

*Corner Hout & Loop Streets, City Centre (021 423
7973).* **Open** 9am-4.45pm Mon-Thur; 9am-4.30pm
Fri. **Credit** AmEx, MC, V. **Map** p282 G3.
Errol and his sister Gloria are a bit like the Versace's
of South Africa. They have been in business for
ages, creating dress after awesome dress, all glamourous, and always setting the pace.

Gert van de Merwe Couturier

110 Long Street, City Centre (021 424 3413). **Open**
8am-5pm Mon-Thur; 8am-4pm Fri. **Credit** AmEx,
DC, MC, V. **Map** p282 G4.
Throw together numerous local fashion awards, a
simple design ethic, superbly designed garments
and pure professionalism, and you get Gert van de
Merwe. He is famous for his outrageous ostrich-
feather creations and dreamy wedding gowns.

Maya Prass

Glynn Street, City Centre (021 465 5499). Clothes
stocked at The Space, India Jane, Purr. **Open** by
appointment only. **Credit** AmEx, DC, MC, V.
Map p283 H5.

Eat, Drink, Shop

Say it with a T-shirt

Want to wear your anti-globalisation feelings on your sleeve? Try wearing them on a T-shirt instead. The Cape Town-based cultural commentators **Laugh It Off** (LIO) produce a popular clothing line that uses the power of big brands to make powerful social statements.

The trouble is, corporates seldom see the funny side: in 2003, LIO used Carling Beer's Black Label brand to comment on South Africa's social inequalities (the Black Label logo was changed to read 'Black Labour: White Guilt' and 'Black Neighbour: White Fence'). Carling's parent company, SABMiller (the world's second-biggest beer corporation), sued LIO, claiming the shirts infringed on its trademark and were offensive to beer-drinkers. LIO maintained they had a right to free speech. What followed was the courtroom equivalent of a bar-room brawl, with a crowd of LIO supporters demonstrating outside the courthouse with posters reading: 'We've drunk with you, now laugh with us'.

LIO founder Justin Nurse started selling novelty T-shirts while he was a student at Rhodes University. By subverting recognisable big-brand icons, Justin found his message was more effective with the young crowd. Quite simply, people – and the youth

especially – recognise logos. LIO's cultural revolution grew from there.

'Laugh It Off is not just about witty slogans on T-shirts,' says Justin. 'We tackle issues pertaining to the role of governments or corporates in society.'

No social stone is left unturned, whether it be health ('MTN: Hello the Future' becomes 'HIV: Hello the Future'); rampant consumerism ('Coca-Cola: You Can't Beat the Feeling' becomes 'Corruption: You Can't Beat the Stealing') or government-charity mismanagement (the National Lottery logo is twisted into both 'National Robbery' and 'National Poverty'). Of course, there's also plenty of schoolboy humour: Lego becomes 'Legover', and so on.

'When a brand becomes a cultural icon, it should be open to cultural comment,' Justin points out.

Ultimately, the Cape High Court ruled in favour of SABMiller (although LIO was granted leave to appeal), and Laugh It Off was barred from using the Black Label trademark. You sense, though, that it might only a matter of time before shirts hit the shelves claiming 'Black Libel'.

Laugh It Off T-shirts are available at Space Station stores across Cape Town (*see p139*). *For more information go to www.lio.co.za.*

Eat, Drink, Shop

So young, yet so damn good. With her quirky wedding dresses and magnificent made-to-measure outfits Maya Prass has made a good name for herself on the local fashion scene.

Paul van Zyl Couture

74 Loop Street, City Centre (021 422 4796/ www.paulvanzylcouture.co.za). **Open** 9am-5pm Mon-Fri; 9am-1pm Sat. **Credit** DC, MC, V. **Map** p282 G4.
Paul is a wedding-gown institution. He is famous for creating luscious works of tulle and taffeta.

Menswear

A Suitable Boy

125 Upper Waterkant Street, Green Point, Atlantic Seaboard (021 671 5879). **Open** 9.30am-5pm Mon-Fri; 9am-4pm Sat. **Credit** AmEx, DC, MC, V. **Map** p282 G3.
Innovative menswear can be hard to find. Here the creators of India Jane have rustled up a great selection of cutting-edge clothing for hip boys (sorry, men). Look out for the fun T-shirts by Craig Fraser.

Diesel

Victoria Wharf, V&A Waterfront, Atlantic Seaboard (021 425 5777). **Open** 9am-9pm Mon-Sat; 10am-9pm Sun. **Credit** AmEx, DC, MC, V. **Map** p283 H1.

It's not really necessary to elaborate here. Suffice to say that SA's Diesel is well on a par with the rest of the world, and that we do love the deconstructive, minimalist things they're doing here.

Dockers

Cavendish Square, Claremont, Southern Suburbs (021 671 0866). **Open** 9am-6pm Mon-Thur; 9am-9pm Fri; 9am-6pm Sat; 10am-4pm Sun. **Credit** AmEx, DC, MC, V.
This will be the same stuff you will be used to all over the world – casual, urban street wear supported by its signature khaki pants. Other favourites include stonewashed cargo pants, checked shirts, cotton twills and corduroys.

Fabiani

6 St George's Mall, City Centre (021 425 2500). **Open** 8.30am-5.30pm Mon-Fri; 8.30am-1pm Sat; 10am-9pm Sun. **Credit** AmEx, DC, MC, V. **Map** p283 H4.
Oh, so very trendy! This menswear shop is always at the forefront of international fashion. It stocks all the big names (Giorgio Armani, G Star and the rest) as well as its own exclusive Fabiani label.
Branch: Victoria Wharf, V&A Waterfront, Atlantic Seaboard (021 425 2500).

Gifts that glitter

Whether you want a truly African keepsake or a potential family heirloom, you'll find it in one of the many exquisite jewellery shops speckled in and around Cape Town. Push your nose against the window or pull up a chair and try on everything they have. South Africa is known for its diamonds, gold and all other things sparkly. You can buy loose certified gems at most jewellery shops – just ask.

Charles Greig & Sons

Victoria Wharf, V&A Waterfront, Atlantic Seaboard (021 418 4515). **Open** 9am-9pm Mon-Sat; 10am-9pm Sun. **Credit** AmEx, DC, MC, V. **Map** p283 H1.
This is where brides-to-be come to drool. The Greig family has been in the jewellery business for years and anything you acquire here, your grandchildren will one day fight over. The studio also does remodelling and sells well-known watch brands.

Olga Jewellery Design Studio

Victoria Wharf, V&A Waterfront, Atlantic Seaboard (021 419 8016). **Open** 9am-9pm daily. **Credit** AmEx, DC, MC, V. **Map** p283 H1.
All designs are done by Olga Goodman, and her mantra of customer service, individual designing and quality craftsmanship clearly

shows in these gorgeous shops. They polish and cut their own diamonds and whatever you want, they can exquisitely deliver.

Uwe Koetter

Shop 14, Alfred Mall, V&A Waterfront, Atlantic Seaboard (021 421 1039). **Open** 9am-9pm daily. **Credit** AmEx, DC, MC, V. **Map** p283 H1.
This award-winning store offers fresh, creative and contemporary designs with more than three decades of experience. The staff can assist you in German, Italian and French while you choose from the glamorous designs, or pick out your certified diamond.

Wolf Bros

Canal Walk, Century City, Milnerton (021 555 4418). **Open** 10am-8.45pm Mon-Fri, Sun; 9am-9pm Sat. **Credit** AmEx, DC, MC, V.
Something for everyone, from your dream engagement ring to the perfect gift for any celebration, Wolf Bros' in-house designer will assist you in bringing your fantasies to life. If you don't know the four Cs of a diamond, the helpful shop assistants will take you through them and ensure that you get high-quality, certified gems at wholesale prices. It also houses the likes of Tag Heuer, DKNY and Hugo Boss watches.

Bride and glory: **Paul van Zyl Couture.** *See p136.*

Hugo Boss

Victoria Wharf, V&A Waterfront, Atlantic Seaboard (021 421 3052). **Open** 9am-9pm Mon-Sat; 10am-9pm Sun. **Credit** AmEx, DC, MC, V. **Map** p283 H1.
It is entirely possible to fall in love with the slick, minimalist décor of this shop before you fall for the white suit. Sexy, luxurious materials that make up unbelievably glamorous, yet understated, clothing.

Icuba

11 Rawbone Lane, Green Point, Atlantic Seaboard (021 419 5763/www.icuba.co.za). **Open** 9am-6pm Mon-Fri; 9am-4pm Sat. **Credit** AmEx, DC, MC, V. **Map** p282 G2.
For clothes with a whack of irreverence and attitude, look no further than Icuba. A wide range of men's and women's clothing is on offer, but it is the Cape Town boys who especially love it. Sometimes tight and tiny, but always bright and bold.

Levi's

Victoria Wharf, V&A Waterfront, Atlantic Seaboard (021 418 8479). **Open** 9am-9pm Mon-Sat; 10am-9pm Sun. **Credit** AmEx, DC, MC, V. **Map** p283 H1.
A whole store dedicated to everyone's favourite jeans wear. But as we've realised over the past few years, Levi's also offers interesting takes on shirts, T-shirts, jackets, skirts, shoes and other accessories. **Branches:** For details, phone head office (021 403 9400).

Quiksilver Boardriders Club

Canal Walk, Century City, Milnerton, Northern Suburbs (021 555 4930). **Open** 10am-9pm Mon-Fri; 9am-9pm Sat; 10am-9pm Sun. **Credit** AmEx, DC, MC, V.

Surf's up! The full range of Quiksilver and Roxy gear is carried here, as well as other surf and skate favourites like DC, Globe, Oakley and Island Style.

Uzzi Clothing

Cavendish Square, Claremont, Southern Suburbs (021 683 0350). **Open** 9am-6pm Mon-Thur; 9am-9pm Fri; 9am-6pm Sat; 10am-4pm Sun. **Credit** AmEx, DC, MC, V.
Uzzi Clothing stocks a very fashionable range of off-beat office wear and casual club gear. The colours are vivid and the materials appealing. It also stocks an interesting range of leather jackets. **Branch:** Victoria Wharf (021 418 0334).

Wylde Oscar

Gardens Centre, Gardens, City Bowl (021 461 5909). **Open** 9am-5pm Mon-Fri; 10am-1pm Sat. **Credit** AmEx, DC, MC, V. **Map** p282 G5.
Oscar Wilde, himself, would definitely have loved this shop. On offer are funky variations on the classic shirt, pants and pullover theme. Colours and materials are daring and fun.

Children

The Fairy Shop

311 Main Road, Kenilworth, Southern Suburbs (021 762 1546). **Open** 9am-5.30pm Mon-Fri; 9am-1pm Sat. **Credit** AmEx, DC, MC, V.
Make your little princess even more glamorous with this shop's dazzling range of tiaras, feather boas, make-up, perfumes and crystals. It also has a great selection of fancy dress clothes and fairies.

The Victoria & Alfred Waterfront
is located within the breathtaking
setting of a dynamic working harbour and includes
over 400 specialist stores, more than 70 restaurants,
coffee shops, pubs and takeaways, an aquarium, boat and
helicopter charters, art and craft markets, a variety of leisure
attractions as well as a choice of world-class
conference and hotel facilities.

The V&A Waterfront offers a range of cultural
landmarks including museums, historic buildings and
exclusive access to one of South Africa's essential heritage
sites; Robben Island. All of this, coupled with
ongoing events and entertainment within a vibrant
cosmopolitan atmosphere, ensures that
the V&A Waterfront is the heart of your visit.

The Warm Heart of Africa

VICTORIA & ALFRED WATERFRONT CAPE TOWN SOUTH AFRICA
For further details please contact Waterfront Information on +27(0)21 408 7600,
email info@waterfront.co.za or visit www.waterfront.co.za

TEQUILA\CAPE MP20960

Mad Dogs
Cavendish Square, Claremont, Southern Suburbs (021 671 8477). **Open** 9am-6pm Mon-Thur; 9am-9pm Fri; 9am-6pm Sat; 10am-4pm Sun. **Credit** AmEx, DC, MC, V.

Mad Dogs is a truly South African gem. There is a wide range of play-friendly clothes for everyone – from newborns to grannies. Clothing is made from colourful cotton or cuddly fleece, adorned with delightful line drawings of dogs, puppies, bones and paw prints. A treat for everyone.
Branches: Tygervalley, Nothern Suburbs (021 914 1571).

Naartjie
Victoria Wharf, V&A Waterfront, Atlantic Seaboard (021 421 5819). **Open** 9am-6pm Mon-Thur; 9am-9pm Fri, Sat; 10am-4pm Sun. **Credit** AmEx, DC, MC, V. **Map** p283 H1.

What started out as a small stall on Greenmarket Square has grown into a famous brand with a chain of successful stores, not to mention a booming export business. Naartjie caters for the whole family, but it's mums in particular who love dressing up their little beloveds in the gorgeous cottonwear.
Branches: Cavendish Square, Claremont, Southern Suburbs (021 683 7184); Canal Walk, Milnerton (021 551 6317).

Seven Ounces
Canal Walk, Milnerton, Northern Suburbs (021 551 3003). **Open** 10am-9pm Mon-Fri; 9am-9pm Sat; 10am-9pm Sun. **Credit** DC, MC, V.

Seven Ounces may be small, but it's bursting with chic and trendy clothing for boys and girls. Watch out for the sheepskin-lined caps, denim jackets and rugged boots; the more domestically inclined will find matching chef's hat and apron sets.

Second-hand

Déjà Vu
278 Main Road, Kenilworth, Southern Suburbs (021 797 7373). **Open** 9am-5pm Mon-Fri; 9am-1pm Sat. **No credit cards.**

Familiar big-hitting labels to be found here include Armani, DKNY, Fendi and the occasional piece by Ralph Lauren. A great place to shop for evening wear for end-of-year functions.

Glam
083 383 7535. **Open** by appointment only. **Credit** AmEx, DC, MC, V.

This popular shop has now closed, but you can still get your hands on the vintage shoes and flaring frocks. The owner now trades from her home, but any collector or browser will be interested to know that she might occasionally stock original Audrey Hepburn gloves.

Glitterati Vintage
127 Long Street, City Centre (021 422 0843). **Open** 9.30am-4.30pm Mon-Fri; 9.30am-1.30pm Sat. **Credit** AmEx, DC, MC, V. **Map** p282 G4.

Whether it's for a fashion shoot, TV commercial or costume party, you can rent or buy vintage clothes from this store. All clothes, hat bins and shoes date back to the '70s and earlier.

Never on a Sunday
4A Buiten Street, City Centre (073 250 1042). **Open** 10am-5.30pm Mon-Fri; 10am-4pm Sat. **No credit cards. Map** p282 G4.

Consignées include fashion stylists who travel the world and bring home retro garments. The shop focuses on '70s and '80s items, but also has evening dresses from as early as the '20s.

Second Time Around
126 Long Street, City Centre (021 423 1674). **Open** 9am-5pm Mon-Fri; 9am-1pm Sat. **No credit cards. Map** p282 G4.

Find antique and vintage clothes, jewellery, handbags, shoes and leathers in this gem of a shop. The shop assistant, Nuraan, has been working here for ten years and knows on which cluttered rail to find the perfect number for every occasion.

Stock Exchange
116 Kloof Street, Gardens, City Bowl (021 424 5971). **Open** 10am-5pm Mon-Fri; 10am-1pm Sat. **No credit cards. Map** p282 F5.

Stock Exchange will fulfill your desire for designer labels at a fraction of the price. It is celebrating its 18th year of selling unique garments to a number of well-established clients. The focus is more on modern clothes and international labels.

Fashion accessories

Amber
Canal Walk, Milnerton, Northern Suburbs (021 555 4747). **Open** 10am-9pm Mon-Fri; 9am-9pm Sat; 10am-9pm Sun. **Credit** AmEx, DC, MC, V.

Round off your outfit with a wonderful leather handbag (whether it is a bulky shopper or a tiny cocktail accessory), belt, some jewellery or a hat.

Icing
Canal Walk, Milnerton, Northern Suburbs (021 555 0256). **Open** 10am-9pm Mon-Fri, Sun; 9am-9pm Sat. **Credit** AmEx, DC, MC, V.

Icing is just as delicious as its name suggests. There are shoes, handbags and purses aplenty, plus costume jewellery and scarves. The shop also stocks the occasional bit of clothing.
Branch: Somerset Mall, Somerset West, False Bay (021 851 2471).

Space Station
Cavendish Square, Claremont, Southern Suburbs (021 683 6135). **Open** 9am-6.30pm Mon, Wed, Thur; 9am-8pm Tue; 9am-9pm Fri, Sat; 10am-5pm Sun. **Credit** AmEx, DC, MC, V.

Come here for seriously cutting-edge stuff. Be sure to find the season's must-have accessories (bags, belts, scarves, earrings, watches and more).
Branch: Victoria Wharf (021 419 3666).

Eat, Drink, Shop

Say 'cheese'

While trotting between wine farms in the winelands, it's well worth stopping at one of the many, and award-winning, cheese farms and shops – even if it is just to line your stomach.

Cottage Fromage

Vrede en Lust Farm, near the Klapmuts-Simondium Road crossing with the R45, Winelands (021 874 3991). **Open** 9am-6pm daily. **Credit** AmEx, DC, MC, V.
Sample more than 30 cheeses and ten olive oils in this charming thatched cottage. The producers are all local, and mostly unknown.

Fairview

Suid Agter-Paarl Road, exit 47 from the N1, Paarl (021 863 2450/www.fairview.co.za). **Open** 8am-5pm Mon-Fri; 8.30am-1pm Sat. **Credit** AmEx, DC, MC, V.
The herd of white Saanen goats is a familiar sight to visitors. Fairview uses both goats' and Jersey milk to make its speciality cheeses.

La Masseria Cheese

Delvera Farm, R44 outside Stellenbosch, Winelands (021 884 4940). **Open** 8am-5pm Mon-Fri; 10am-5pm Sat, Sun. **Credit** AmEx, DC, MC, V.
A cheese factory and shop stocking, among other things, delectable fresh and mature pecorino, mozzarella, creamy duetto blue and dolce.

Simonsberg Cheese Shop

9-13 Stoffel Smit Street, Stellenbosch, Winelands (021 809 1017). **Open** 9am-5pm Mon-Fri; 9am-1pm Sat. **Credit** AmEx, DC, MC, V. **Map** p278 P1.
This is a factory outlet for the well-known Simonsberg brand. Apart from the shop-ready cheeses, they also sell a variety of off-cuts, underweight and catering-sized cheeses.

Truckles Traditional Cheese

La Fromagerie at La Grange, 13 Daniel Hugo Street, Franschhoek. Winelands (021 876 2155). **Open** 9am-5pm Mon-Fri; 10am-5pm Sat, Sun. **Credit** AmEx, DC, MC, V. **Map** p275 W3.

Truckles offers local and international-styled cheeses. Its selection includes the award-winning Boerenkaas, a herb-flavoured Dutch-style Gouda.

Zevenwacht Wine Estate

Langverwacht Road, Kuilsriver, Winelands (021 903 5123/www.zevenwacht.co.za). **Open** 8am-5pm daily. **Credit** DC, MC, V.
This wine estate is kept very busy: it is used variously as a conference venue, country inn and picnic spot. But its biggest claim to fame is undoubtedly its Farmhouse Cheddar. Delicious flavoured cheeses to look out for include mustard seed, bell pepper and Madagascar green pepper.

Shoes

Camper

Victoria Wharf, V&A Waterfront, Atlantic Seaboard (021 452 3937). **Open** 9am-9pm Mon-Fri; 9am-9pm Sat; 10am-9pm Sun. **Credit** AmEx, DC, MC, V. **Map** p283 H1.

This famous shoe heaven has revolutionised the world of shoes by making use of graphic-design elements to distinctive effect. Here you will find fantastic leather loafers, sandals, boots and more.

Fairheads

Victoria Wharf, V&A Waterfront, Atlantic Seaboard (021 421 4066). **Open** 9am-9pm Mon-Fri; 9am-9pm Sat; 10am-9pm Sun. **Credit** AmEx, DC, MC, V. **Map** p283 H1.

This much-loved Cape Town store sells a lovely and reliable range of leather shoes, sandals and boots, as well as backpacks and briefcases. A favourite is the Spanish 'Practica' line, which caters for both adults and children. An accessories staple.

Nina Roche

Cavendish Square, Claremont, Southern Suburbs (021 671 3533). **Open** 9am-5pm Mon-Fri; 9am-4.30pm Sat. **Credit** AmEx, DC, MC, V.

This woman knows her shoes and they are all very beautiful, well crafted and desirable. The best of international brands find their way here.

Planisphere

Cavendish Square, Claremont, Southern Suburbs (021 683 0677). **Open** 9am-6pm Mon-Thur; 9am-9pm Fri; 9am-6pm Sat; 10am-4pm Sun. **Credit** AmEx, DC, MC, V.

Here lives high-fashion footwear at extremely affordable prices. The Planisphere range is sold through some of the bigger chain stores, but it's best to go to the home shops, where you'll find all the colour and style variations you need.
Branch: Victoria Wharf (021 418 8719).

Yuka Shoes

Gardens Centre, Gardens, City Bowl (021 465 8288). **Open** 9am-5.45pm Mon-Fri; 9am-3pm Sat. **Credit** AmEx, DC, MC, V. **Map** p282 G5.

Yuka Shoes stocks a fantastic variety of shoes, sandals and boots. Surprisingly, it's very affordable and always slightly ahead of season.

Flowers

Arum Flowers

2 Brunswick Street, Unit 5, Tamboerskloof, City Bowl (021 422 3373). **Open** 8am-5pm Mon-Fri. **Credit** AmEx, DC, MC, V. **Map** p282 F4.

A truly lovely little place where the mood changes according to the seasons. Sometimes it's the fragility of peonies, other days exotic orchids will steal the show, while roses lend an air of romance. Glorious bunches are made up while you wait, or you can leave it to the creative flair of the florists.

Aspen Flowers

113 Long Street, City Centre (021 424 6511). **Open** 8am-4.30pm Mon-Fri. **Credit** AmEx, DC, MC, V. **Map** p282 G4.

Gorgeous flower arrangements are made here with quirky artistic touches and natural creativity. This small flower shop is delightful and you will be as happy and satisfied walking out with a bunch of blooms as you will be with placing an order and having it delivered to a friend.

Okasie

Blackhorse Centre, Dorp Street, Stellenbosch, Winelands (021 887 9904). **Open** 7am-3pm Mon; 8am-5pm Tue-Fri; 8am-1pm Sat. **Credit** AmEx, DC, MC, V. **Map** p278 P3.

They remove the petals of flowers, bend Arum lilies into perfect arcs and deconstruct proteas here. Enthusiasm and creativity is the mark of the floral designers who work in this shop.

Trafalgar Place

Trafalgar Street, City Centre. **Open** 6am-6pm daily. **Map** p283 H4.

Florists who encourage romantically challenged Romeos to 'say it with flowers' have obviously never heard Cape Town 'say it' with flowers: '*Tyen renner bunts! Tyen renner bunts!*' That's Cape Town-speak for 'Ten rand a bunch', and R10 is the going rate for a beautiful bouquet of blooms from the city's famous flower sellers. As much a part of the local landscape as the docklands' fishermen, the flower sellers offer a variety of blooms in a spectacular variety of colours – and at spectacularly reasonable and negotiable prices. A must for any occassion.

Food & drink

Cheese

The Real Cheese

79 Durban Road, Mowbray, Southern Suburbs (021 689 5256). **Open** 9am-5pm Mon-Fri; 9am-noon Sat. **Credit** AmEx, DC, MC, V.

Even though this superb little cheese emporium supplies all the hotels and restaurants, it also allows locals to buy from it, at very sensible prices. The Real Cheese stocks a great assortment of the best cheeses made in South Africa, from blues and bries to gouda and mozzarella. The best part? You get to taste (and smell) it all before you buy.

Confectioners

Charly's Bakery

20 Roeland Street, City Bowl (021 461 5181). **Open** 7.30am-4pm Mon-Fri. **Credit** AmEx, DC, MC, V. **Map** p283 H5.

Arguably the makers of the biggest and best special-event cakes in town. The delightful coffee shop and confectionery also offers interesting sweet and savoury pies, muffins and cakes.

Eat, Drink, Shop

Delicatessens

Carlucci's

Corner Upper Orange Street & Montrose Avenue, Oranjezicht, City Bowl (021 465 0795). **Open** 8am-8pm daily. **Credit** AmEx, DC, MC, V.

Somewhat hidden from the general flow of traffic, but by no means forgotten, this place is buzzing with hungry city slickers, tourists and ladies of leisure, and stocks everything (and more) you'd expect from an Italian food store.

Branch: 29 Victoria Road, Bantry Bay, Atlantic Seaboard (021 439 6476).

Giovanni's Deliworld

103 Main Road, Green Point, Atlantic Seaboard (021 434 6893). **Open** 8am-8.30pm daily. **Credit** AmEx, DC, MC, V. **Map** p282 F2.

Giovannis carries meats, cheeses, spices, oils, pasta and much more. The great variety of ingredients is mirrored by the fantastic spread of ready-made food. It includes chicken and pesto salads, sandwiches, bagels, trays with carpaccio, spaghetti bolognaise, penne arabiata and gnocchi.

Melissa's The Food Shop

94 Kloof Street, Gardens, City Bowl (021 424 5540/ www.melissas.co.za). **Open** 7.30am-8pm Mon-Fri; 8am-8pm Sat, Sun. **Credit** AmEx, DC, MC, V. **Map** p282 F5.

Go for a bite, go to get a gift, go to get dinner provisions, but just go and indulge yourself in this lovely food shop. Melissa's has an abundance of yummy food (ingredients or ready-made) beautifully presented and packaged.

Newport Market & Deli

47 Beach Road, Mouille Point, Atlantic Seaboard (021 439 0366). **Open** 7.30am-7.30pm Mon-Fri; 8am-8pm Sat, Sun. **Credit** AmEx, DC, MC, V. **Map** p282 E1.

A friendly, contemporary-styled food store with a big sit-down deli section, take-away meals and fresh fruit, vegetables, pastries and baked goods.

Wines & spirits

Harley's Liquors

Corner Wale & Buitengracht Street, City Centre (021 424 1128). **Open** 10am-10pm Mon-Fri; 10am-7pm Sat; 10am-5pm Sun. **Credit** AmEx, DC, MC, V. **Map** p282 G4.

Harley's is best known for the fact that it's open till late in the evenings and that it's one of the few places where you can buy booze on a Sunday. Flower sellers also sell their wares outside the shop.

Vaughan Johnson's Wine & Cigar Shop

Dock Road, V&A Waterfront, Atlantic Seaboard (021 419 2121). **Open** 9am-6pm Mon-Fri; 9am-5pm Sat; 10am-5pm Sun. **Credit** AmEx, DC, MC, V. **Map** p283 H2.

A specialist wine store where you'll find the very best that wine-producing South Africa has to offer. This shop has an unstuffy, no-nonsense attitude and you'll find obscenely priced bottles next to good, everyday drinking wine at sensible prices.

Waterfront World of Wine

Clock Tower Centre, V&A Waterfront, Atlantic Seaboard (021 418 0001/www.waterfrontworldofwine. com). **Open** 9am-8pm Mon-Fri; 10am-5pm Sat, Sun. **Credit** AmEx, DC, MC, V. **Map** p283 H1.

Here you can enjoy wine tastings at the water's edge. Waterfront World of Wine offers a selection of wine tasting packages, and all the sales staff are knowledgeable and passionate about the wine.

Health & beauty

Camelot Spa

Table Bay Hotel, Quay 6, V&A Waterfront, Atlantic Seaboard (021 406 5904). **Open** 8am-9pm daily. **Credit** AmEx, DC, MC, V. **Map** p283 H1.

Camelot Spa is a warm and friendly salon in a five-star hotel. The facilities are first class and each treatment is designed to relax you, whether you're going for a massage or a manicure.

Environ Skincare Clinic

9 Primrose Avenue, Bishops Court, Southern Suburbs (021 761 5141). **Open** 8.30am-5pm Mon-Fri. **Credit** AmEx, DC, MC, V.

This locally-developed skincare range has gained international recognition. It's a superb product, but needs to be used correctly. This clinic offers intensive treatments and assessments.

Evolve

Canal Walk, Milnerton, Northern Suburbs (021 555 0852). **Open** 10am-9pm Mon-Fri; 9am-9pm Sat; 10am-9pm Sun. **Credit** AmEx, DC, MC, V.

A beauty salon for men, offering music, satellite TV, a bar facility as well as facials, manicures, shaves and haircuts. You'll feel quite at home here in the masculine environment dedicated to male grooming.

Kashush

43 Prestwich Street, Green Point, Atlantic Seabord (021 425 5655). **Open** 9am-5pm Mon-Fri; 8.30-5pm Sat. **Credit** AmEx, DC, MC, V. **Map** p282 G3.

An orange building welcomes you into a haven that will transform you. At this City Spa you'll be able to get your hair done, have a massage and have all undesired hair waxed into oblivion.

Serenite Wellness Centre

16 Debaren Close, Constantia, Southern Suburbs (021 713 1760/www.serenite.co.za). **Open** 7am-8pm Mon-Fri. **Credit** AmEx, DC, MC, V.

A quiet restful place in the lush Constantia valley, this wellness centre is open to casual visitors as well as those who've checked into the spa for longer stays. It offers all the usual spa and beauty treatments as well as some pleasurable Vinetherapy treatments that consist of healing grape seed oil.

The best Cape tipple

Vaughan Johnson, wine fundi and purveyor of the Cape's finest tipple gives us his choice of the ten best white wines and ten best red wines. For **Vaughan Johnson's Wine & Cigar Shop** *see p142.*

White wines

Boschendal Blanc de Noir: a rose-coloured wine, ideal for our warm climate and outdoor dining.

Bouchard Finlayson Chardonnay: the cool sea breezes of Hermanus contribute a delicacy and gentleness that is refreshing in a Chardonnay.

Buitenverwachting Sauvignon Blanc: an exceptional wine – the taste of zesty gooseberries abound with great finesse.

Kanu Chenin Blanc: the best qualities of the Cape's most-planted variety (redolent of melon and guavas) at an affordable price.

Klein Constantia Vin de Constance: good enough for the likes of Jane Austen, Napoleon and former President Nelson Mandela. A sought-after pudding wine, in a delicate, refined style.

Meerlust Chardonnay: this wine has achieved worldwide recognition as a Burgundy-styled classic: ripe and fruity with rich mouth feel.

Mulderbosch Sauvignon Blanc: an extrovert wine. It is bursting with exotic summer fruits and has achieved cult status.

Simonsig Kaapse Vonkel: the Cape's original and still one of the best Champagne-method bubblies – made from Pinot Noir and Chardonnay. Bracingly-crisp.

Steenberg Sauvignon Blanc: crisp and elegant with delicious tropical flavours.

Vergelegen White: a finely crafted blend of Sauvignon Blanc and Sémillon, aged in French oak barrels.

Red wines

Beyerskloof Pinotage: good quality at a bargain price, this grape is unique to South Africa and reflects our warm summers in its broad style.

Bredells Port: the equal of some of the best Portuguese ports.

Bouchard Finlayson Pinot Noir: the most seductive and also difficult of red grapes, this extraordinary wine has a vibrant and stylish texture.

De Toren Fusion V: a blend of Cabernet Sauvignon, Franc, Merlot, Malbec and Petit Verdot – as used in Bordeaux – to realise a seamless wine of extremely elegant and charming character.

Kevin Arnold Shiraz: exotic spices and herbs, with violet and leather aromas evident in this full-flavoured red, ideal with African game and meat.

Luddite Shiraz: produced in minuscule quantities by very traditional techniques. As the name implies, it is a deep, ruby red, with ample violets and plum flavours. Keep it for two to eight years.

Meerlust Merlot: the Cape's best stylish Merlot, produced at the iconic Stellenbosch estate – rich, fleshy layers of fruit and subtle aromas of oak.

Rietvallei Muscadel: probably the Cape's most underrated category of sweet Muscat-flavoured, world-class wines. Best for the traditional after-dinner spot.

Rust and Vrede Estate: arguably the Cape's best red, this blend of Cabernet and Shiraz has a robust and well rounded character, and offers some intense cherry and blackcurrant flavours.

Thelema Merlot: always in short supply, this Merlot is highly prized for its rich, lush flavours. It deserves a few years ageing in bottle to reach its full potential.

Shelf life at **Clarke's**. *See p129.*

A few hours in the gardens bordering the Tokai forest and a couple of treatments later you'll forget all about that nagging urban stress.

s.k.i.n The Wellness Spa

Dock Road, V&A Waterfront, Atlantic Seaboard (021 425 3551). **Open** 9am-9pm Mon-Fri; 9am-6pm Sat, Sun. **Credit** AmEx, DC, MC, V. **Map** p283 H2.
This is a stylish hide-out for stressed-out urbanites. Chandeliers and zen-inspired fountains set the scene for a relaxed few hours of pampering. The whole range of treatments is available.

Home decor

African Fusion

Palms Décor & Lifestyle Centre, City Centre (021 462 2878). **Open** 9am-5pm Mon-Fri; 9am-1pm Sat, 1st Sun of mth. **Credit** AmEx, DC, MC, V. **Map** p283 I4.
In a profusion of colour, creating what can only be described as a Modern African look, this is a wonderful home decor shop with some gorgeous fabrics. But be warned: this is not for the fainthearted.

African Image

52 Burg Street, City Centre (021 423 8385). **Open** 9am-5pm Mon-Fri; 9am-1.30pm Sat. **Credit** AmEx, DC, MC, V. **Map** p283 H4.
Here you will find a wonderful assortment of modern African artefacts and colourful crafts. A huge array of recycled materials are used in innovative fun ways, and brightly coloured African fabrics vie for your attention. This great shop appeals to locals and foreigners alike.

Block & Chisel Interiors

Main Road, Diep River, Southern Suburbs (021 712 5193). **Open** 9am-5pm Mon-Fri; 9am-2pm Sat; 10am-1pm 1st Sun of mth. **Credit** AmEx, DC, MC, V.
A lovely collection of furniture, fabrics, lamps and ornaments. Best yet, they employ their own cabinetmakers, who produce most of their furniture.

Bread & Butter

Cavendish Square, Claremont, Southern Suburbs (021 671 4204). **Open** 9am-6pm Mon-Thur, Sat; 9am-9pm Fri; 10am-4pm Sun. **Credit** AmEx, DC, MC, V.
Bread & Butter is where home-starters pick up their first furnishing and accessory staples. All goods in the store are designed by well-known and up-and-coming young artists. A real favourite.

Bright House

Corner Bree & Shortmarket Street, City Centre (021 424 9024). **Open** 9am-5pm Mon-Fri; 9am-1pm Sat. **Credit** AmEx, DC, MC, V. **Map** p282 G3.
With simple, clean-lined furniture and accessories for the home and office, Bright House stocks everything from cutlery, crockery and candles, to desks, dining room tables and doorknobs.

Cape to Cairo

100 Main Road, Kalk Bay, False Bay (021 788 4571). **Open** 9.30am-5.30pm daily. **Credit** AmEx, DC, MC, V.
Even without the spectacular Kalk Bay scenery, the drive here would still be worth it. Cape to Cairo is an incredible find, sporting an eclectic mix of contemporary African and Cuban collectibles.

Carrol Boyes Shop

Victoria Wharf, V&A Waterfront, Atlantic Seaboard (021 424 8263/www.carolboyes.co.za). **Open** 9am-9pm daily. **Credit** AmEx, DC, MC, V. **Map** p283 H1.
The place we've all been waiting for. Finally, Carrol Boyes has an entire shop dedicated to her pewter functional art. From table settings to vases; tables to clocks; magazine racks to pens and business-card holders; she's made them all. Come here and you're sure to fall in love with everything.

Dash

20 Vrede Street, Durbanville, Northern Suburbs (021 975 1821). **Open** 9am-7pm Mon-Fri; 9am-4pm Sat. **Credit** AmEx, DC, MC, V.
Another hidden suburban gem. Dash is a fun collection of accessories for the home and body – vases, picture frames, shimmering shoes, handbags and Christmas angels. A great place for gifts.

East of Eden

A17 Cape Quarter, 72 Waterkant Street, De Waterkant, Green Point, Atlantic Seaboard (021 425 9147/www.icuba.co.za). **Open** 9am-3pm Mon-Fri; 9am-4pm Sat. **Credit** AmEx, DC, MC, V. **Map** p282 G3.
East of Eden is what happens when a highly successful clothing range (Icuba) decides to branch out to lifestyle. The result is a mish-mash of kitsch and cool accessories for your home and office, as well as some rather funky clothing. The theme is very much Asian, and includes lampshades, fairy lights and vases to brighten the home, plus some slick silk kimonos and wooden shoes.

Heartworks

98 Kloof Street, City Centre (021 424 8419). **Open** 9.30-5.30 Mon-Fri; 10am-2pm Sat. **Credit** AmEx, DC, MC, V. **Map** p282 F5.
Heartworks offers gorgeous gifts and home accessories with a uniquely South African flavour. Bright papier mâché bowls, beautiful ceramics and beaded ware all celebrate local creativity.

LIM

86A Kloof Street, Gardens, City Bowl (021 423 1200). **Open** 9am-5.30pm Mon-Fri; 9am-5.30pm Sat. **Credit** AmEx, DC, MC, V. **Map** p282 F5.
LIM stands for Less Is More. And this stylish shop shows you just how well that approach can be done. The simple, sleekly designed furniture is over-whelmingly chic. There are fabulous leather couches in the softest, richest chocolate brown, plush white suede chairs and slick black tables.

Loft Living

122 Kloof Street, Gardens, City Bowl (021 422 0088). **Open** 9.30am-5.30pm Mon-Fri; 9.30am-1.30pm Sat. **Credit** AmEx, DC, MC, V. **Map** p282 F5.
This store is aimed at all those living in spaces where clutter is a maddening nuisance and high style is all important. Contemporary homeware and furniture are all designed to keep your place in slick, ship-shape order. A must for the messy.

Mr Price

Canal Walk, Milnerton, Northern Suburbs (021 551 4416). **Open** 10am-9pm Mon-Fri, Sun; 9am-9pm Sat. **Credit** AmEx, DC, MC, V.
Although it is aimed at the mass market, Mr Price has lots of funk. The stores stock clothing for the whole family, and there is an excellent separate Homeware store, aptly called Mr Price Home. **Branches**: for details, phone head office (021 670 2910).

Nocturnal Affair

Gardens Centre, Gardens, City Bowl (021 461 7412). **Open** 9am-6pm Mon-Fri; 9am-3pm Sat; 10am-2pm Sun. **Credit** AmEx, DC, MC, V. **Map** p282 G5.
From bed linen and pyjamas to candles, mirrors and linen spray, here you will find all the ingredients for a bedroom filled with sweet dreams.
Branch: Victoria Wharf (021 419 2291).

Plush Bazaar

30 Somerset Road, Green Point, Atlantic Seaboard (021 419 8328). **Open** 8.30am-4.30pm Mon-Fri; 8.30am-2pm Sat; 9am-2pm Sun. **Credit** AmEx, DC, MC, V. **Map** p282 G3.
This is a lovely place to go browsing for all sorts of collectibles – enamel crockery, sofas, cushions, wrought iron chairs, antiques and lots of posh junk. It offers a full decorating service too.

Street treats

A wealth of creative talent can be found on the streets of Cape Town. At most intersections and traffic lights there's someone selling colourfully-beaded insects; or outrageous chickens made from recycled plastic; impressive wire sculptures; and star-shaped lanterns made from discarded cold-drink tins. Try and support these informal traders, as, while their wares are not traditional African curios, their creativity, combined with entrepreneurial skills, is indicative of the spirit of the new South Africa.

Eat, Drink, Shop

Spirit

Gardens Centre, Gardens, City Bowl (021 462 4959).
Open 9am-6pm Mon-Fri; 9am-3pm Sat; 10.30am-2pm
Sun. **Credit** AmEx, DC, MC, V. **Map** p282 G5.
The shelves at Spirit are overflowing with chic
trends in homeware, with most aspects of domes-
ticity covered: there's everything from cooking utensils, tablecloths and clocks, to sweet baby bottles,
dustbins and stationery. Very cute.

Still Life

229C Long Street, City Centre (021 426 0143).
Open 10am-5pm Mon-Fri; 10am-1pm Sat. **Credit**
AmEx, DC, MC, V. **Map** p282 G4.
Lovely , girlish things like cushions and throws to
bring comfort to your home. Some quirky gifts, like
photo light-boxes and love-inspired paintings. If
you're feeling romantic, pop in for a look-see.

Thin Ice

*Mooikloof Centre, 34 Kloof Street, Tamboerskloof,
City Bowl (021 424 4648).* **Open** 9.30am-5.30pm
Mon-Fri; 10am-2pm Sat. **Credit** AmEx, DC, MC, V.
Map p282 F5.
Thin Ice stocks haute furniture with a hint of '70s
style. The designs are sleek and simple, with mini-
malist lines in leather, wood and chrome.

Trade Roots

*13 Hudson Street, Green Point, Atlantic Seaboard
(021 421 0401).* **Open** 10am-5pm Mon-Fri; 10am-
1pm Sat. **Credit** AmEx, DC, MC, V. **Map** p282 G3.
A paradise for collectors of rare and exotic oriental
goods, this place specialises in Chinese antiques.
With the stockists making frequent forays to the
mainland, the items on sale change at a refreshing
rate and are invariably interesting.

Tree House Children's Home Store

Canal Walk, Century City, Milnerton (021 555 4050).
Open 10am-9pm Mon-Fri; 9am-9pm Sat; 10am-9pm
Sun. **Credit** AmEx, DC, MC, V.
This is the way a kid's bedroom should look. Lots
of fun and fresh checks and candy colours are used
to create range of beds, cots, beanbags, linen and
toys. And with plenty of material to choose from,
parents who have DIY leanings will easily be able
to rustle up something fun.
Branch: Cavendish Square, Claremont, Southern
Suburbs (021 671 1611).

Weylandts

*Corner Alfred & Hospital Street, Green Point, Atlantic
Seaboard (021 425 5282/www.weylandts.com).*
Open 9am-5.30pm Mon-Fri; 9am-2pm Sat. **Credit**
AmEx, DC, MC, V. **Map** p283 H3.
It's impossible not to fall in love with something
here. A multi-storey garden-and-home warehouse,
it stocks an incredible selection of furniture and
trimmings for the modern-day home.

Zwilling JA Henckels

*Victoria Wharf, V&A Waterfront, Atlantic Seaboard
(021 418 7941).* **Open** 9am-9pm daily. **Credit**
AmEx, DC, MC, V. **Map** p283 H1.

Decent knives and useful, stylish things for the
domestic gods and goddesses can be found here. For
serious chefs and foodies only, the prices aren't
cheap but the products will last a lifetime.

Markets

The Blue Shed

*Dock Road, V&A Waterfront, Atlantic Seaboard
(021 408 7600).* **Open** 9.30am-6pm daily. **No credit
cards.** **Map** p283 H2.
This micro-business development initiative is
conveniently situated on the V&A Waterfront.
Brush up on your drumming techniques or visit the
in-house clairvoyant for a tarot reading. If that's not
enough, you can have a massage or some reflexolo-
gy at one of the many wellness stands.

Greenmarket Square Flea Market

*Corner of Shortmarket & Berg Streets, City Centre
(083 692 2864/083 247 4190).* **Open** 9am-4pm
Mon-Sat. **No credit cards.** **Map** p283 H4.
This cosmopolitan market is only a walk away from
the Houses of Parliament, the Company Gardens
and South African Museum (*see pp53-4*). It provides
a vibrant atmosphere for shopping with varied stalls
selling everything from clothes to second-hand
books and African art. Various street performers,
are also drawn to this vibrant venue.

Green Point Flea Market

*Green Point Stadium Main Parking Area, Green
Point, Atlantic Seaboard (083 321 2072).* **Open**
8.30am-6pm Sun. **No credit cards.** **Map** p282 F1.
Check out rows upon row of stalls, which pile up
everything from African art and fabrics to clothes.
It's a fairly classic flea market set-up, but special to
Green Point is the big selection of sidewalk food,
enabling shoppers to stop for a bite when all that
rummaging gets too much.

Holistic Lifestyle Fair

*Observatory Recreation Centre, Corner of Station &
Lower Main Roads, Observatory, Southern Suburbs
(021 782 8882).* **Open** 10am-4pm 1st Sun of mth.
No credit cards.
Come here to balance your chakras, replenish your
energy fields, stock up on crystals, have a psychic
reading and an aura massage. The bohemian spirit
of the Observatory lives on with this much-loved
holistic lifestyle monthly fair.

The Red Shed Craft Workshop

*Victoria Wharf, V&A Waterfront, Atlantic Seaboard
(021 408 7600).* **Open** 9am-9pm daily. **No credit
cards.** **Map** p283 H1.
Adjoining the Victoria Wharf centre, this indoor
craft market is the place to find and have unique
home-decor items made – design your own cushions
or have lampshades covered in the material of your
choice. And no visit to the Mother City is complete
without a unique metal memento from a stall called
Tintown (083 458 9863) that captures the essence of
South African life in its tongue-in-cheek way.

Music

African Music Store

134 Long Street, City Centre (021 426 0857). **Open** 9am-5pm Mon-Fri; 9am-2pm Sat. **Credit** AmEx, DC, MC, V. **Map** p282 G4.

Music-wise, the rich diversity of the African continent is comprehensively covered in this store. Traditional, folk, reggae, pop, gospel, dance – it has it all. And if it doesn't have it in the shop, it will try and find it and order it for you.

CD Warehouse

Dock Road Complex, V&A Waterfront, Atlantic Seaboard (021 425 6300). **Open** 9am-9pm Mon-Thur, Sun; 9am-10pm Fri, Sat. **Credit** AmEx, DC, MC, V. **Map** p283 H2.

This is, apparently, one of the biggest CD shops in the southern hemisphere. That's quite a boast, but to back it up there are regular gigs and appearances by local (and if you're lucky, international) stars, with several competitions and other activities completing a year-long events calendar.

Look & Listen

Cavendish Square, Claremont, Southern Suburbs (021 683 1810). **Open** 9am-10.30pm daily. **Credit** AmEx, DC, MC, V.

This music mega-store should satisfy almost any entertainment taste. It stocks an overwhelming variety of CDs, DVDs, business-oriented and children's movies, computer games and all the accessories that go with it. There are also great listening facilities available, for the mass-market albums as well as the slightly more obscure releases.

Musica

Victoria Wharf, V&A Waterfront, Atlantic Seaboard (021 418 4722). **Open** 9am-11pm daily. **Credit** AmEx, DC, MC, V. **Map** p283 H1.

Another of SA's big music chains, Musica is a safe choice for your mainstream music: pop, rock, reggae, world music, dance and gospel. Basic listening facilities are available in store.

Branches: For details, phone 0860 687 422.

Outlaw Records

55 Castle Street, City Centre (021 423 8145). **Open** 9am-4.30pm Mon-Fri; 9am-1pm Sat. **Credit** AmEx, DC, MC, V. **Map** p282 G3.

It's hard to find quality second-hand music stores, but Outlaw Records is one of them. It has an excellent return policy, so you can rest assured that you won't be buying duds. Its range mainly consists of CDs, but also throws its net wider to include quality vinyl, DVDs and computer games.

Sports

Bowmans Cycles

153 Bree Street, City Centre (021 423 2527). **Open** Open 8.30am-5.30pm Mon-Fri; 9am-1pm Sat. **Credit** MC, V. **Map** p283 H3.

New mountain bikes and racer bikes can be picked out with the help of the knowledgeable staff, who, crucially, are all keen cyclists themselves. Bowmans also stocks a small selection of second-hand bicycles. Another added bonus is the workshop in the back that hosts its very own wheel-builder.

Cape Union Mart

Victoria Wharf, V&A Waterfront, Atlantic Seaboard (021 419 0019/www.capeunionmart.co.za). **Open** 9am-9pm Mon-Thur, Sun; 9am-11pm Fri, Sat. **Credit** AmEx, DC, MC, V. **Map** p283 H1.

Starting out in 1933 as an Army and Navy store where you could find anything from an anchor to a toothpick, it's now a national chain. These are still Cape Town's favourite outdoor shops.

Branch: for details, phone 0800 034 000.

Chandlery Shop

The Royal Cape Yacht Club, Cape Town Harbour, Foreshore, City Bowl (021 419 4835). **Open** 8am-5.30pm daily. **Credit** AmEx, DC, MC, V. **Map** p283 H2.

An all-in-one DIY hardware shop for yacht owners and enthusiasts. Other essentials, such as yachting shoes, clothes and equipment such as Maglites and Leathermans are also available.

The Kite Shop

Victoria Wharf, V&A Waterfront, Atlantic Seaboard (021 421 6231/www.kiteshop.co.za). **Open** 9am-9pm Mon-Sat; 10am-9pm Sun. **Credit** AmEx, DC, MC, V. **Map** p283 H1.

Cape Town's weather is perfect for flying kites. So before you go down to Blouberg or Muizenberg, pop in the Kite Shop and get a kite to suit your mood or ability – single-string kites, two-string stunt kites, power kites or surf kites. The Balinese single-string animal kites are awesome.

Branch: Canal Walk, Century City, Milnerton (021 555 1855).

Surf Zone

45 On Castle Building, Castle Street, City Centre (021 423 7853). **Open** 9am-6pm Mon-Fri; 9am-2.30pm Sat. **Credit** AmEx, DC, MC, V. **Map** p282 G3.

Dedicated to the ladies, who will find the brands and beach gear they need. For round-the-clock surf babes, there are even Billabong pyjamas. It also stocks a big selection of guy's clothes and wetsuits and surfboards are available to rent. The shop is staffed by champion surfers, kneeboarders and skateboarders, and lessons are available.

Toys & games

Avatar

Riverside Mall, Rondebosch, Southern Suburbs (021 686 2947). **Open** 9.30am-5.30pm Mon-Fri; 9am-2pm Sat. **Credit** AmEx, DC, MC, V.

This is just what our generation of computer game-crazed kids really needs: a place to buy new and used PC and Gameboy games.

Eat, Drink, Shop

Hi-Ho Cherryo

90 Tokai Road, Tokai, Southern Suburbs (021 715 9033). **Open** 8.30am-5pm Mon-Fri; 9am-1pm Sat. **Credit** AmEx, DC, MC, V.

Between all the face paint, DIY jewellery, fantasy toys and games your kids will have lots to keep their minds and fingers busy. A big variety of activities for newborns to pre-teens.

Peggity's Toy Store

Victoria Wharf, V&A Waterfront, Atlantic Seaboard (021 419 6873). **Open** 9am-9pm daily. **Credit** AmEx, DC, MC, V. **Map** p283 H1.

At Peggity's Toy Store, you'll find great gadgets and games to entertain and educate your little ones.

Reggies

Cavendish Square, Claremont, Southern Suburbs (021 683 2312). **Open** 9am-6pm Mon-Thur; 9am-9pm Fri; 9am-6pm Sat; 10am-4pm Sun. **Credit** AmEx, DC, MC, V.

Reggies is one of those reliable toyshops where you are bound to find something to stop the tears. There is an excellent variety of toys, games and goodies coupled with friendly service.

Speed Models

Canal Walk, Century City, Milnerton (021 555 4955). **Open** 10am-9pm Mon-Fri; 9am-9pm Sat, 10am-9pm Sun. **Credit** AmEx, DC, MC, V.

Speed Models has radio-controlled aeroplanes and cars, Scalextric and plastic modelling kits for kids from eight to 80. No other entertainment needed.

Toys-R-Us

Raglan Road, Bellville, Northern Suburbs (021 949 6030). **Open** 9am-5.30pm Mon-Fri; 8.30am-5.30pm Sat; 9.30am-1.30pm Sun. **Credit** AmEx, DC, MC, V.

Kiddie heaven: a huge toy warehouse filled with every toy, game, party costume and kid accessory imaginable. Tantrums can occur if you resist buying.

Traveller's needs

Formal dress rental

Top Hat Suit Hire & Sales

63 Buitengracht Street, City Centre (021 424 3579). **Open** 9am-5pm Mon-Fri; 9am-1pm Sat. **Credit** DC, MC, V. **Map** p282 G4.

This is where you'll go to find all manner of suits, tuxes and tails. Better still, you can view the wares at www.tophat.co.za and book in advance through the website. Ample parking is available at the close-by Heritage Square parking lot.

Laundry

Econ-O-Wash

Adelphi Centre, Main Road, Sea Point, Atlantic Seaboard (021 434 9728). **Open** 7.30am-7pm Mon-Fri; 8am-5pm Sat, Sun. **Rate** *5kg laundry* R35. **No credit cards. Map** p281 D2.

This is one of the many self-service and drop-off-and-collect laundrettes around the Peninsula. As a useful additional service Econ-O-Wash also does dry-cleaning, and collection and delivery can be organised through management.

Nannucci

Head office: 20 Newmarket Street, City Centre (021 462 7000). **Open** 7.30am-5.30pm Mon-Fri; 8am-noon Sat. **Rate** *5kg laundry* R27. **Credit** AmEx, DC, MC, V. **Map** p283 J4.

This well-established company takes care of your domestic laundry and ironing as well as dry-cleaning. Unfortunatley, though, they don't collect or deliver. Phone the head office telephone number above to find the branch closest to you.

Branches: throughout Cape Town.

Luggage

Barksole

7 Riebeeck Street, City Centre (021 421 7803). **Open** 7.30am-5.15pm Mon-Thur; 7.30am-5pm Fri; 8am-noon Sat. **No credit cards. Map** p283 H3.

If your luggage has suffered from being thrown onto one too many airport carrousel, Barksole is the place to get it repaired. With more than 20 branches in and around Cape Town it should be easy to find one that's convenient for your location.

Branches: throughout Cape Town.

Frasers

Shop 6136, V&A Waterfront, Atlantic Seaboard (021 418 0718). **Open** 9am-9pm Mon-Sat; 10am-9pm Sun. **Credit** AmEx, DC, MC, V.**Map** p283 H1.

A good range of quality luggage, from handbags to wallets, travel bags to briefcases, fill this shop. Frasers also does repairs, but be warned that the turn-around time is about seven days. If the Waterfront is too far from you, call and find out where the other five branches are.

Photographic services

Orms

Unit 5, Roeland Square, Roeland Street, City Bowl (021 465 3573). **Open** 8am-6pm Mon-Fri; 8am-1pm Sat. **Credit** AmEx, DC, MC, V. **Map** p283 H5.

While it's all but impossible to walk through a mall without bumping into a one-hour or same-day photographic developer, for truly superb printing – digital or film – Orms is the place to go. This company is generally excellent for all your photograph-ic needs, no matter how esoteric.

Photographic Repairs Central

1 Park Road, Gardens, City Centre (021 424 7881). **Open** 8.30am-5pm Mon-Fri; 9am-1pm Sat. **Credit** AmEx, DC, MC, V. **Map** p282 F4.

Most places send cameras away, causing added delay and middle-man costs. Offering a far better service, this repairs centre does the work on-site and maintains good standards.

Arts & Entertainment

Festivals & Events

Every week there's a new excuse to party in Cape Town.

Capetonians love a good party, and any minor event soon turns into an excuse for a good time. It's the day after New Year's Day? Let's throw a party (New Year Karnaval). There's a horse race on the go? Let's throw a party (J&B Met). The gay community likes visiting Cape Town? Let's throw a party (Mother City Queer Project).

And the locals, traditionalists that they are, do have their favourites: these tend to be long-standing, annual community events such as **Tweede Nuwe Jaar** (Second New Year, see *p151* **Sunny Christmas cheer**), the **Twilight Run** and the **Big Walk** (for both *see p151*), which always draw big crowds.

With the local populace covering so many communities, everybody's interests are taken care of, from fine dining connoisseurs (**Cape à la Carte**, *see p151*, and the **Cape Gourmet Festival**, *see p154*) to ultra-fit sports enthusiasts (**Cape Argus Pick 'n' Pay Cycle Tour** *see p153*) and rowdy students (**UCT Rag Float Procession**, *see p153*). But be prepared that some of the events listed are a bit of a drive out of Cape Town; check out the **Trips Out of Town** section, *see p218-46* if you want to take a longer excursion.

Go to www.capetownevents.com for a detailed calendar, or pop into the Cape Town Tourist Information Centre (Corner of Burg and Castle Streets, City Centre, 021 426 4260/ www.cape-town.org) to make bookings.

Spring

V&A Waterfront Spring Flower Show

V&A Waterfront, Atlantic Seaboard (082 872 7901/www.waterfront.co.za). **Map** p283 H1.
Date mid Sept.
If the distant Namaqualand is too far to travel, head to the V&A Waterfront for its annual Spring Flower Show. The show marks the dawn of spring, and comes directly after a similar event in the flowery Cedarberg town Clanwilliam.

Cape Argus/Woolworths Gun Run

Beach Road, Mouille Point, Atlantic Seaboard (021 426 5775/www.gunrun.co.za). **Map** p282 E1.
Date late Sept.
A flat scenic route takes runners along the edge of the Atlantic. For many running this popular half-marathon the challenge is to finish the race before the Noon Gun is fired from Signal Hill (*see p56*).

Hermanus Whale Festival

Hermanus, Whale Route (028 313 0928/ www.whalefestival.co.za). **Date** late Sept.
Ah, spring. The birds are chirping, the flowers are blooming… and the whales are humping. Peeping Toms from far and wide head to the South Coast seaside town of Hermanus (about 90 minutes from Cape Town) to watch the visiting Southern Right Whales as they splash, blow, breach and – ahem! – play the whale equivalent of Barry White's Greatest Hits in the romantic waters of Walker Bay. The Whale Festival is held at the peak of whale-watching season, and it offers arts, crafts and thousands of whale-themed souvenirs. The Hermanus Whale Crier (he's the guy with the traditional horn, cellphone and corporate sponsorship) roams the harbour, calling out whenever the Big Fish are getting frisky. While the harbour area gets pretty crowded (avoid driving through town and don't even think of trying to find parking), there are a couple of fairly secluded whale-watching spots on the lagoon side of town. To make a trip out of going to Hermanus, *see p221* for accommodation and restaurants in the area.

Smirnoff International Comedy Festival

Baxter Theatre Complex, Rondebosch, Southern Suburbs (021 685 7880/www.baxter.co.za). **Date** late Sept-mid Oct.
There'll be good jokes, bad jokes and tasteless jokes… courtesy of side-splitting stand-ups. This popular laugh-fest includes local and international japesters and jokers, providing cosmopolitan colour to some seriously off-colour comedy routines (when one of the auditoriums is designated the Danger Zone, you know they're not telling the family-rated brand of knock-knock joke).

Whiskey Festival

Clock Tower Square, V&A Waterfront, Atlantic Seaboard (021 408 7632/083 288 1202/www.water front.co.za). **Map** p283 H1. **Date** early Oct.
Experts and amateur drinkers flock to the Whiskey Festival for three days of whiskey admiration. Fans will be pleased to know that there are more than 120 of the world's finest whiskies available for tasting.

Big Walk

Simonstown to Hartleyvale Stadium, Observatory, Southern Suburbs (083 910 6551/www.bigwalk. co.za). **Date** mid Oct.
One of the oldest and most popular events in Cape Town, the Big Walk attracts more than 20,000 participants from all corners of the city. With seven distances to choose from (ranging from the 5-km/3-mile

stroll to the 80-km/50-mile slog, the emphasis at the Big Walk is on taking part, getting lost in the crowd and enjoying the spring sunshine.

Cape à la Carte

Cape Town International Convention Centre & various other venues in Cape Town (021 426 0800/ www.rai.co.za). Map p283 I3. **Date** mid Oct.
During October, foodies can indulge in a festival that is dedicated to purely eating and entertaining. Cape à la Carte will entice food lovers to celebrate the best food that is coming out of some of the finest Cape restaurant's kitchens at various venues in and around Cape Town, phone for details.

Summer

For music festivals, *see p187.*

Community Chest Twilight Run

City Centre (021 424 3344/www.comchest.org.za). **Date** late Nov.
Saddam Hussein, Nelson Mandela and Darth Vader are just a couple of the famous faces you'll see on the annual Twilight Run (along with generic butlers,

fairies, devils and angels). A fun 4.5-km (2.8-mile) run (or walk or crawl, which ever you prefer) through the streets of Cape Town, the Twilight Run kicks off the city's season of summer silliness. Teams and individuals are encouraged to dress up for the occasion – and many do – the real winner of this race isn't the one who finishes first, it's the one whose outlandish get-up gets him or her onto the front page of the next morning's newspaper.

International Dragon Boat Festival

V&A Waterfront (021 551 8333/www.dragon boat.org.za). Map p283 H1. **Date** late Nov.
The International Dragon Boat Festival is a spectacular and exciting team event that originated in China over 2,300 years ago. It came to South Africa in 1992 when two beautiful wooden ceremonial dragon boats were presented to Cape Town by Taiwan. The mixture of Chinese, South African and international cultures – together with the explosive colours of the dragon boats themselves – makes this one of the most colourful events on the summer calendar. An event that is not to be missed.

Sunny Christmas cheer

A summery festive season may be something of a culture shock for northern visitors accustomed to a White Christmas and a freezing cold New Year, but Cape Town's warm weather lets you enjoy night markets, carol singing and raucous New Year's Eve events under a clear night sky.

The week before Christmas is packed with Carols By Candlelight events, the most popular being the annual four-day charity event at **Kirstenbosch Botanical Gardens** (021 799 8783/www.nbi.co.za), where a thousand swaying candles light up the lower slopes of Table Mountain. A similar gathering is held at the **Spier Amphitheatre** (Spier Wine Estate, Stellenbosch/021 809 1158/ www.spier.co.za), and there's also a free carol-singing show in the City Centre's **Company Gardens** (in front of the South Africa National Gallery/021 480 0603/ www.capetowncid.co.za).

Although the city's shopping malls are always packed to the rafters with last-minute Christmas shoppers, the **Adderley Street Night Market** (Adderley Street, 021 480 0603/www.capetowncid.co.za) has some creative Christmas gifts and treats that have been crafted by local artists.

New Year's Eve parties are held all over town (watch the local press and lampposts

for details), and the traditional fireworks at the V&A Waterfront light up the night sky (get there early or head up Signal Hill for a good, if crowded, view). You'll notice that Cape Town celebrates two New Year's Days (on 1 and 2 January): this is not an alcohol-soaked flashback, nor is it your party-addled mind playing tricks on you. **Tweede Nuwe Jaar** (Second New Year) is celebrated on 2 January by descendants of the Cape Malay slaves, whose only day off in the entire year was the day after New Year's Day. The day is marked by the **New Year Karnaval**, which sees the ever-colourful Cape Minstrels dancing their way from District Six into the Bo-Kaap and beyond. The constant sounds of banjos, choirs and trumpets fill the air, and masses of people hit the streets festooned in colourful outfits and sporting ornate (and completely superfluous) parasols. These Cape Minstrels are a joy to watch – for the best views, pack a camera and find a spot in among the crowds on Wale Street. After all the partying, nurse (or intensify) your hangover in the baking sun while watching South Africa's finest partake in a relaxing game of international cricket in the traditional **New Year's Cricket Test** (Newlands Cricket Stadium, Rondebosch/021 657 2043/ www.wpcricket.co.za).

Arts & Entertainment

J&B Met. *See p154.*

MCQP Festival

Cape Town International Convention Centre, City Centre (021 426 5709/www.mcqp.co.za).
Map p283 I3. **Date** early Dec.
Summer kicks off in gay old style with the annual Mother City Queer Project. This flamboyantly fun festival includes a string of magical and musical events, culminating in the big night out: a themed costume party. It's Cape Town's most decadent party of the year (hugely popular among both gay and straight people), with celebrities flying in incognito for a night of partying and painting the town pink. All are welcome. *See also p176.*

Ysterplaat Open Day & Air Show

Air Force Base, Ysterplaat, Brooklyn (021 508 6576/www.saafmuseum.org.za). **Date** early Dec.
Block your ears and watch in wonder as a fleet of Mirages, Pumas and Dakotas zoom past, tickling the sound barrier and blasting a series of sonic booms at Cape Town's top air show.

Good Hope FM/Vodacom Clifton Beach Challenge

Clifton 4th Beach, Atlantic Seaboard (021 426 5775/021 439 9020). **Map** p284 A6. **Date** mid Dec.
Mr and Ms Clifton provide the underdressed eye candy as Clifton's übertrendy Fourth Beach hosts a fitness challenge between celebrity Springbok national rugby team players and the Clifton Beach lifesavers. Chiselled abs, bronzed bodies and sandy games of touch rugby are the order of the day.

Shakespeare Festival at Maynardville

Maynardville Amphitheatre, Wynberg, Southern Suburbs (Artscape, 021 421 7695/www.artscape. co.za). **Date** mid Jan-end Feb.
Every summer the Maynardville open-air theatre presents a season of one of William Shakespeare's plays, performed under the stars. Knowing Cape Town's weather, this means that it's worthwhile dressing in a T-shirt but taking a jumper, blanket

becomes all too addictive. You can either go for a day trip or enjoy a break from Cape Town and go for all three days of the festival. For accommodation and restaurants in the area *see p124.*

Community Chest Carnival

Maynardville Park, Wynberg, Southern Suburbs (021 424 3344/www.comchest.org.za). **Date** last wkd in Feb.

Popular family fare abounds at this well-attended Community Chest Carnival. Local clubs and charity organisations host internationally themed food and drink stalls (pizza at the Italian tent, cheese at the Dutch tent, beer at the extremely popular German and Irish tents… you get the picture), providing hours of candyflossed fun.

Autumn

UCT Rag Float Procession

Streets of Cape Town, City Centre (021 650 3525/ www.uctrag.co.za). **Date** 1st Sat in Mar.

Students of the University of Cape Town invade the streets of the city, plundering charity money from unsuspecting passers-by. It's a colourful and fun event, with the students wearing bizarre outfits and riding a procession of outrageous floats.

Cape Argus Pick 'n Pay Cycle Tour

Cape Town (083 910 6551/021 685 6551/ www.cycletour.co.za). **Date** mid Mar.

A gruelling 109-km (68-mile) race across the Cape Peninsula, this top-class event is the highlight of the local cycling calendar. The course covers some of the most scenic parts of the Cape – not that the hot, bothered and exhausted competitors have much time to admire it, or even notice it for that matter.

Navy Festival

Simonstown Navy Dockyard, False Bay (021 787 3725). **Date** late Mar.

Simonstown's naval base opens to the public for a series of family-themed festivities. Boat rides and performances by the Navy Band culminate in the (in)famous Dry Dock Concert.

Out in Africa South African Gay & Lesbian Film Festival

Cinema Nouveau, V&A Waterfront, Atlantic Seaboard (082 167 89/www.oia.co.za). **Map** p283 H1. **Date** late Mar.

South Africa's biggest and most popular film festival sees 15,000 people passing through the doors, with about 50 locally and internationally produced films being screened. *See also p167.*

Klein-Karoo National Arts Festival

Oudtshoorn, Route 62 (044 203 8600/ www.kknk.co.za). **Date** Apr.

'*Afrikaners is plesierig*' (Afrikaners are jolly) goes the old *volkslied* (folk song). And while the Afrikaner community is indeed pleasant and fun-loving, in

and umbrella, as you never know. No matter the weather or the ropey accents, though, the productions are always excellent and the setting superb.

International Design Indaba

Cape Town International Convention Centre, City Centre (021 418 6666/www.designindaba.com). **Map** p283 I3. **Date** end Feb.

The Indaba is when the world's top designers gather to share (and steal) each other's ideas, innovations and inspirations. Designed to impress.

Savanna Up The Creek Festival

Breede River Valley, Swellendam, Route 62 (021 671 4360/ww.upthecreek.mweb.co.za/ www.overberginfo.com). **Date** Feb.

This three-day music and comedy festival takes place up a lazy river, on the chilled-out banks of Swellendam's Breede River, about two hours from Cape Town. Expect languid guitar playing, serene surroundings and the laid-back lifestyle that

Arts & Entertainment

many ways it's still trying to recover from the PR disaster that was the apartheid government. The KKNK (Klein-Karoo Nasionale Kunstefees) is an Afrikaans cultural festival that invites Afrikaans-speaking South Africans from all walks of life to enjoy, express and entertain themselves in the distant, rustic (and oh-so-Afrikaans) Karoo town of Oudtshoorn (about 450km/279 miles from Cape Town). You might not understand everything that's being said, done or eaten (trust us: go directly to *koeksusters*, *boerewors* or *braaivleis* on any menu you're given), but the KKNK is well worth the trip.

J&B Met

Kenilworth Race Course, Kenilworth, Southern Suburbs (021 426 5775/www.jbmet.co.za).
Date early Apr.
Cape Town's biggest race day, where you don't really have to watch the horse. Snooty punters go to drink whiskey and be seen, and loud hats, extravagant outfits, minor celebs and photo ops are the order of the day. The horses, jockeys and photo finishes are merely a mild distraction.

Nederburg Wine Auction

Nederburg Wine Farm, Paarl, Winelands (021 439 5063/www.nederburg.co.za). **Date** early Apr.
Held in the heart of the Winelands, this internationally acclaimed event sees local and overseas buyers bidding for a selection of the finest Cape wines. The highlight of the event is a charity auction where a range of very unusual wines are auctioned off in aid of the Hospice Association of South Africa.

North Sea Jazz Festival

Cape Town International Convention Centre, City Centre (021 422 5651/www.nsjfcapetown.com). **Map** p283 I3. **Date** mid Apr.
Dubbed 'Africa's Grandest Gathering', the ever-popular North Sea Jazz Festival is a world-class event boasting local and international musicians. Although the North Sea isn't anywhere in sight (you'll have to go the Den Haag in the Netherlands for that), the NSJF boasts enough smooth grooves and jazzy jams to keep your mind off the geographical misnomer. *See also p187.*

SA Cheese Festival

Bien Donné, Paarl, Winelands (021 975 4440/www.cheesefestival.co.za). **Date** late Apr.
Enjoy a taste of some of the country's best cheeses, complemented by the only thing more popular than cheese (namely, a bottle or two of Cape wine).

Cape Gourmet Festival

Cape Town International Convention Centre, City Centre (021 465 0069/www.gourmetsa.com). **Map** p283 I3. **Date** May.
South Africa's premier culinary event (and the African member of the World Gourmet Club) celebrates food and wine in abundance. With local and international chefs brewing up a melting pot of international cuisine, this festival sees dozens of events taking place around the city's finest tables.

Waterfront Wine Festival

V&A Waterfront, Atlantic Seaboard (021 851 1563/ 021 408 7632/www.waterfront.co.za).
Map p283 H1. **Date** early May.
The Waterfront Wine Festival is a dream come true for lovers of fine wines, with more than 350 wines – coming from many of the Cape's most celebrated wine estates – available to taste.

Pink Loerie Carnival

Knysna, Garden Route (072 322 2795/ www.pinkloerie.com). **Date** last wkd in May.
This is the Mardi Gras answer to the Knysna Oyster Festival (*see below*). Pink Loerie Carnival is a gay festival that attracts queens, queers and party animals from all over the Cape (and the country) for a weekend of fabulously flamboyant fun and games in South Africa's award-winning Town of the Year.

Winter

For Christmas festivals and events *see p151* **Sunny Christmas cheer**.

Red Bull Big Wave Africa

Dungeons, The Sentinel, Hout Bay, Atlantic Seaboard (082 423 1964/www.redbullbwa.com).
Date early-late June.
Dungeons in Hout Bay is one of the best big-wave surfing spots in the world – and one of the only spots in Africa that produces surfable big waves. In winter's blustery June, an international field of big-wave surfers descends on Hout Bay for the 20-day Big Wave Africa surfing spectacle. Under the watchful eye of the Sentinel, they wait – and eventually ride – massive waves in excess of 5m (15ft). Take a half-hour walk to the vantage point up on the Sentinel to watch them ride these monster waves.

Graça Knysna Oyster Festival

Knysna, Garden Route (044 382 5510/www.visit knysna.co.za). **Date** early July.
The Cape's biggest winter festival, this fortnight of fun in the glorious Garden Route offers a massive range of activities. The 470-km (292-mile) journey from Cape Town (and the terrible traffic) is well worth the effort, especially if you fancy a taste of the titular molluscs. For more on Knysna *see p231.*

V&A Waterfront Winter Food Fair

Market Square, V&A Waterfront, Atlantic Seaboard (021 556 8200/www.waterfront.co.za). **Map** p283 H1. **Date** mid Aug.
Just when the winter cold really starts to bite, the V&A Waterfront hosts this tantalising, tummy-warming feast of local food and wine.

Cape Town Fashion Week

Cape Town International Convention Centre, City Centre (021 422 0391/www.capetownfashion week.com). **Map** p283 I3. **Date** late Aug.
A glitzy, glam, high-profile fashion week that sees about 50 top designers from around South Africa and the rest of Africa showcasing their glad rags.

Children

Welcome to the world's biggest playground.

There's so much fun to be had in Cape Town… for children as well as adults. And this is what's so wonderful about the city: wherever there is something you would like to see or do, we can guarantee that there will be something nearby to keep your kids amused, too. If you need a break, there are a number of activities where you can leave the children in the capable hands of trained adults for a couple of hours. The relaxed attitude of Cape Town lends itself well to catering for the little ones and you'll find that Capetonians love well-behaved youngsters, and babies are much admired and fussed upon. The beaches and surrounding countryside as well as the various animal-petting zoos will delight even the most urban children. Most restaurants are child-friendly although some of the finer dining establishments would balk at having an unruly child offending the other patrons. All tourist attractions will hold some fascination for the kids, so refer to the Sightseeing chapter for more of those attractions. Here follows a list of things that are of particular interest to children.

To buy tickets for most events contact that ticket agency, **Computicket** (083 915 8000/ 8100/www.computicket.co.za; box office open 9am-5pm daily).

Activities

Cape Town Explorer Topless Bus
(021 426 4260). **Tour** 2hrs. **Tickets** R90; R40 children. **No credit cards**.
A perfect way to discover and explore the Mother City with your children. Kids will love the novelty of driving around Cape Town without a roof.

Hannah's Radical Kids' Cooking School
The Drive Camps Bay Bowling Club, Camps Bay, Atlantic Seaboard (021 438 4400). **Workshops** by appointment only. **Rate** R70. **Credit** AmEx, DC, MC, V. **Map** p284 B8.
These creative and interactive workshops allow kids to muck in and get sticky. Aprons are supplied and, if it is a birthday party, chef's hats are de rigueur. This is a popular birthday-party venue; the young chefs get to make both a sweet and a savoury dish. A maximum of ten 'chefs' are allowed.

Ratanga Junction
Canal Walk, Century City, Milnerton, Northern Suburbs (086 120 0300/www.ratanga.co.za). **Open** Nov-May 10am-5pm Wed-Fri; 10am-6pm Sat; 10am-5pm Sun. **Rates** Above 1.3m (4.2ft) tall R90; under 1.3m (4.2ft) tall R45. **Credit** AmEx, DC, MC, V.

Spill, spin and roll around this fantasy fairground. Kids yell with delight as they head off for rides such as the Cobra and Monkey Falls. Get them there early and fill yourself up with the snacks and food on offer. This is a really fun day's outing.

Thundercity

Tower Road, Cape Town International Airport, Southern Suburbs (021 934 8007/www.thundercity. com). **Open** 10am-5pm daily. **Admission** R30; *flights* prices vary. **Credit** AmEx, DC, V.

Both big and small boys will love Thundercity, the world's largest privately-owned collection of ex-military aircraft. Highly-trained pilots assess your threshold of endurance and take you on a ride of a lifetime. You have a choice of three ex-RAF planes: the English Electric Lightning, the Buccaneer low-level strike attacker and the Hawker Hunter (a combat trainer plane). And, just so you can take the experience home with you, there is a photographer to record you and your little one in the cockpit. But, if flying is a bit too much, you can always fake it by sitting yourself and your kids in the cockpit and making *vroom-vroom* noises for no extra charge.

Two Oceans Aquarium

Dock Road, V&A Waterfront, Atlantic Seaboard (021 418 3823/www.aquarium.co.za). **Open** 9.30am-6pm daily. **Admission** R55; R25 children. **Credit** AmEx, DC, MC, V. **Map** p283 H2.

'Come and see how the other two-thirds live'. At Two Oceans Aquarium children can smell, see and feel many of the sea's creatures. The sunfish in particular is spectacular. Go when the fish are feeding, especially the sharks, which is an awesome experience for absolutely anyone. You might even see some turtles here, or African penguins. The displays change regularly and are really beautiful, as well as wonderfully educational. There's also the facility for children's sleepovers – if they're brave enough to sleep among the marine life, that is.

Film & theatre

Baxter Theatre Centre

Main Road, Rondebosch, Southern Suburbs (box office 021 680 3989/021 685 7880/www.baxter. co.za). **Open** *Box office* 9am-start of performance Mon-Sat. **Tickets** prices vary. **Credit** AmEx, DC, MC, V.

The Baxter rocks for kids on a Saturday. Sithi at Baxter is a funky drama club for teenagers and runs from 5.30pm to 7.30pm on Wednesdays and Thursdays. Membership is R225 and is renewable. The courses are under the directorship of Mandla Mbothwe. There are also the Pulpit Baxter workshops (R50 per month), in which specialists teach children traditional dances and songs, theatre sports and modern dancing every Saturday from 10am to 3pm. Kidz Take Over (R375 for a four-month programme) is a project for kids who want to learn valuable acting skills, mime and projection as well as acting skills for camera.

Happy faces in child-friendly Cape Town.

IMAX

BMW Pavilion, corner of Beach & Portswood Roads, Atlantic Seaboard (021 419 7365/www.imax.co.za). **Open** daily; film times vary. **Tickets** R35; R25 concessions. **Credit** AmEx, DC, MC, V. **Map** p283 G1.

All kids will be gob-smacked by this larger-than-life cinema. From the nature films *Everest* and *Serengeti* to Disney's *The Lion King*, IMAX offers a range of giant entertainment for any ages. Coffee and snacks are available at the fairly decent restaurant.

Rainbow Puppet Theatre

Constantia Waldorf School, Spaanschemat River Road, Constantia, Southern Suburbs (021 794 2103). **Shows** 10-11.15am Sat. **Tickets** R15. **No credit cards**.

This traditional and very special puppet show enthralls children and adults alike. Kids are riveted by the lifelike puppets and love to interact with them. The theatre is pint-sized perfect down to the last detail, as are the puppets.

Planetarium

25 Queen Victoria Street, City Centre, City Bowl (021 481 3900/www.museums.org.za/planetarium). **Open** 10am-5pm daily. **Admission** R20; R6-R8 concessions. **No credit cards**. **Map** p283 H4.

A wonderful way to introduce your young would-be stargazer to the vast starscape. Fun and informative workshops are run regularly and the Planetarium will arrange parties for children, too.

South African Museum

25 Queen Victoria Street, City Centre (021 481 3800/www.museums.org.za/sam/index.htm). **Open** 10am-5pm daily. **Admission** R10. Free Sun. **No credit cards**. **Map** p283 H4.

Our favourite room for kids is the one that's tucked away upstairs displaying some of the marvels of the natural world. Sombre and darkly lit, it introduces children to the sheer magnificence and scale of nature. Then it's off to the Discovery Room where they can feel and touch and make all sorts of interesting natural objects. For the older children there is an e-centre to keep them distracted as well.

Warrior Toy Museum

St George's Street, Simonstown, Southern Suburbs
(021 786 1395). **Open** 10am-4pm daily.
Admission R3. **No credit cards.**
It's a delight to watch the faces of the youngsters
who go into instant 'I want everything' mode. And
there's something for adults as well, who are sure to
feel a substantial amount of nostalgia for the
Meccano, Dinky toys and other memorabilia.

Music

Living Music Workshops

Four venues: the Guga S'Thebe Centre in Langa,
Paul Bothner Music outlets, Ikwezi Centre in
Gugulethu, Cape Flats (021 790 8825/072 242
2685). **Workshops** 4 workshops/mth, times &
dates vary. **Rate** free. **No credit cards.**
This group offers ongoing monthly workshops in all
aspects of music. The Living Music Workshop
series has three objectives it is determined to meet:
to impart instrument skills, to nurture musical
appreciation, and to inspire, educate and inform
musicians and aspiring musicians. The introducto-
ry workshops are interactive and serious fun.

Soundhouse – Music Technology

Baxter Theatre Centre, Main Road, Rondebosch,
Southern Suburbs (021 686 2825/www.baxter.co.za).
Workshops by appointment only. **Rate** R16,50/
session 6-18s. **No credit cards.**
Soundhouse offers ongoing courses in making music
with computer technology. There is a variety of fun-
packed multimedia experiences for children, youths
and adults alike. The instruments are synthesised
and on the computer. The whole idea is that after
one hour, kids can mix their own music, cut their
very own CD and take it home with them.

Science

Cyberworld

Dock Road, V&A Waterfront, Atlantic Seaboard
(021 419 0156). **Open** 9am-9pm daily. **Admission**
R20. **No credit cards. Map** p283 H2.
Travel by cybercar on three-dimensional rides that
take you 'into' the shows. They are only six minutes
long and range in choice from the informative *Curse*
of Tutankhamen, to the scary *Doom Castle* and
thrilling *Escape from Nemo*.

MTN Science Centre

407 Canal Walk, Century City, Milnerton, Northern
Suburbs (021 529 8100/www.mtnsciencentre.
org.za). **Open** 9.30am-6.30pm Mon-Thur; 9.30am-
8pm Fri, Sat; 10am-6pm Sun. **Admission** R24; R20
under-18s. **Credit** AmEx, DC, MC, V.
There's so much to do at the Science Centre that it
is best to put a whole morning aside to see everything. There is an awesome array of interactive displays such as a 'building centre' where kids can
build their own house, as well as a camera obscura,
computer rooms and laboratories.

Telkom Exploratorium

Union Castle House, Dock Road, V&A Waterfront,
Atlantic Seaboard (021 419 5957/www.explora
torium.co.za). **Open** 9am-6pm Tue-Sun. **Admission**
R10; R5 children. **Credit** AmEx, DC, MC, V.
Map p283 H2.
Static electricity, lightning machines, as well as simulated cockpits – all make for a heady mix of science
and experiment. Children can whirl around on a
gyroscope, or 'drive' a Grand Prix racing car, all the
while discovering how much fun science can be.

Sport & leisure

Action Cricket

Stadium on Main, Main Road, Claremont, Southern
Suburbs (021 671 3665). **Open** *kids' parties* 3-5pm
Mon-Fri; 10am-noon, 12.30-2.30pm, 3-5pm Sat, Sun.
Rate R450/party. **Credit** AmEx, DC, MC, V.
Action Cricket offers birthday parties for kids who
love to play cricket, soccer, netball or beach volleyball. Parties go on for two hours and allow a maximum of 16 children per birthday party. Action
Cricket caters for children from ages six to 12 years.
If your child is under age, they do offer the use of
the volleyball sand court. A jumping castle is also
set up and the staff keep the young children occupied with ball skills and other activities.

Action Paint Ball

Tokai Forest, Tokai, Southern Suburbs (021 790
7603/www.actionpursuit.co.za). **Open** 9.15am-
1.15pm, 1-5pm daily. **Rate** R95; R85 children, incl
paintball gun, 100 paintballs, facemask, throat
protector & bush jacket. Additional paintballs
R35/100. **Credit** AmEx, DC, MC, V.
Get away from the television and don a face mask,
throat protector and bush jacket out in the forest.
For the young GI Joes or Janes (over 11s) this is the
definitive party. It's a real, fun rough and tumble.
The minimum number of players is 14; max. 60.

Boogaloos

Boogaloos Skate Shop, Stadium on Main, Main
Road, Claremont, Southern Suburbs (021 683
2495/www.boogaloos.com). **Open** 10am-5pm daily.
Admission *non-members* R20/day. **Credit** AmEx,
DC, MC, V.
This is skateboarding at its most rough and ready,
so we advise you to stay and watch the kids, especially if they are under 12. We're talking pipes, rails,
ramps graffiti and a very 'dude' atmosphere. All participants have to wear a helmet and a parent must
be on hand to sign in under-21s.
Branch: Canal Walk, Upper level, Milnerton,
Northern Suburbs (021 555 2895/www.boogaloos.com).

City Rock

Corner of Collingwood &Anson Street,
Observatory, Southern Suburbs (021 447 1326/
www.cityrock.co.za). **Open** noon-10pm Mon-
Thur; noon-9pm Fri; 10am-6pm Sat, Sun.
Admission R45; R29 concessions. **Credit**
AmEx, DC, MC, V.

City Rock has a climbing wall that kids can safely attempt to climb under supervision. Experienced staff take care of the kids and make sure they are attached to the ropes when they climb the wall. The high-jump mat absorbs all the falls. There is a junior training programme run specially for 10- to 14-year-olds for R15 (book in advance) for two hours at a time. City Rock also hosts birthday parties.

E-centre
46 Hof Street, Gardens, City Bowl (021 481 8301). **Open** 8.30am-5pm Mon-Fri. **Rates** R30/hr; R20/hr students. **Credit** AmEx, DC, MC, V. **Map** p282 F5.
Regular internet-based courses are on offer at this E-centre. Kids can join the e-club and have access to fun events and courses that are run through the Internet Café where they can play games, send e-mails and research school projects. An administrator is on hand at all times to monitor the café and kids. On Fridays, high-school kids play internet games right through the night. Holiday programmes offer a variety of exciting courses for children such as 'How to Make an Animation Cartoon' and 'How to Design Your Own Newspaper'.

Ice Station
Grand West Casino, Goodwood, Northern Suburbs (021 535 2260/ www.icerink.co.za). **Open** daily; times vary. **Admission** *half rink* R18; *full rink* R23; R28 Sat, for evening. **Credit** AmEx, DC, MC, V.
The weekends, when Radio DJs play, are the 'in' times to go. You could also take the kids to watch the ice-hockey league games. Prepare for December and book now for the rink's end-of-term party.

Indoor Grand Prix
Canal Walk, Century City, Milnerton, Northern Suburbs (021 551 8570/www.indoorkarting.co.za). **Open** 1.30pm-midnight Mon-Thur; 9.30am-midnight Fri-Sun. **Admission** R40/15 laps. **Credit** AmEx, DC, MC, V.
All drivers must wear helmets and be taller than 1.3m (4.2ft). The noise and the track are hard to beat for those who thrive on the hype and can't wait till they are old enough for their very own set of wheels.

Laserquest
Lower Level, Stadium on Main, Main Road Claremont, Southern Suburbs (021 683 7296). **Open** 10.30am-11pm Mon-Thur; 10.15am-midnight Fri, Sat; 10.30am-8pm Sun. **Admission** R30/1hr Mon-Thur, Sun; R25/30min Fri, Sat after 6pm; R25/45min Mon-Thur after 6pm. **No credit cards.**
This one's for would-be warriors. This action game, which involves laser guns and protective covering, will make Laserquest an essential venue for kids. Whether it's the dark lights, the pulsing red laser lights, the huge competition of it all – or just the monikers given to the kids.

Quad Bikes
Melkbos, off the R27 (084 454 7112/www.melkbos 4x4.co.za). **Open** Tue-Sun; times vary. **Rate** R150/hr. **No credit cards.**

Move over Schumacher, this is where kids can hit the trail, twisting through bush and dunes. The trails are graded; make sure to call before arriving. Parties and overnight camping are catered for. This is a dangerous sport, though, so obviously everyone gets crash helmets – but wear padding.

Stadium Bowling Alley
Stadium on Main, Main Road Claremont, Southern Suburbs (021 671 1893/www.letsgobowling.co.za). **Open** 9am-midnight Mon-Sat; 9am-10pm Sun. **Admission** R33; R25 concessions. **Credit** AmEx, DC, MC, V.
A particularly good place to visit in the winter months. Guardrails can be set up for smaller children. There are arcade games and pool areas. Kids' parties are very popular here.

Out & about

Mountain-biking
Day Trippers, 414 Voortrekker Road, Maitland, Northern Suburbs (021 511 4766/www.daytrippers. co.za). **Tours** by arrangement. **Rate** half-day R314; R195 concessions. **Credit** AmEx, DC, MC, V.
For children over ten years old. Tours include cycling the Constantiaberg mountains where the views over False Bay and beyond to the Hottentots Holland Mountains are worth the sweat. There are a lot of ups and downs, but that all contributes to the 'we did it' glow. The fee includes transport, guiding, helmets, bicycles, entry permits and snacks.

Surfing
Gary's Surf School, Beachfront, Muizenberg, False Bay (021 788 9839). **Open** 8.30am-5pm daily. **Rate** R240/child/day (incl lesson, board & wetsuit rental). **Credit** AmEx, DC, MC, V.
Each surfing lesson, which places great emphasis on safety, lasts an hour and a half. After that you are free to just practise and play. Surf camps are available over school holidays for a week at Kommetjie, offering a great mix of sandboarding, surfing and sailing to all taking part.

World of Birds
Valley Road, Hout Bay (021 790 2730/ www.worldofbirds.org.za). **Open** 9am-5pm daily. **Admission** R35; R25-R28 concessions. **Credit** AmEx, DC, MC, V.
With more than 4,000 birds in landscaped, walk-through aviaries, the World of Birds will hold most children spellbound. Budding veterinary students will be impressed with the rescue efforts of the centre – their achievements are remarkable. There is a small playground and you can choose to picnic or make use of the café.

Babysitting & childcare

Childminders
083 254 4683. **Open** daily by arrangement.
No credit cards.

Childminders supplies experienced nannies to take kids on outings, au pairs to come away with your family on holiday, qualified night nurses and babysitters for day- and night time.

Mary Poppins

021 762 6689. **Open** 8.30am-4.30pm Mon-Fri. **No credit cards**.

For the last seven years this training college has produced qualified au pairs for local residents, or visiting families. Stay-at-home mums who would like a break once or twice a week can register as a 'prac' family and have a student come to help out. It also offers placement of graduated Mary Poppins au pairs. No babysitters are provided.

Super Sitters

021 439 4985. **Open** 9.30am-5pm Mon-Fri. **Rates** R25-R35/hr; tutoring & help with homework R100. **No credit cards**.

Vicky Weinberg and Lisa Weinberg co-ordinate more than 100 non-smoking, highly experienced babysitters for local families as well as visitors. All babysitters have their own transportation, so there's no worry about getting them home. But make sure to book a sitter at least a day in advance.

Eating & drinking

The Barnyard Farmstall

Steenberg Road, Tokai, Southern Suburbs (021 712 6934). **Open** 9am-5pm Mon-Fri; 9am-6pm Sat, Sun. **Credit** AmEx, DC, MC, V.

A great place for everyone, the Barnyard Farmstall has a pet goat and pig to keep the kids occupied. The ducks and chickens have the run of the yard.

Fat Cactus Café

47 Durban Road, Mowbray, Southern Suburbs (021 685 1920). **Open** noon-2am daily. **Credit** AmEx, DC, MC, V.

Kids can go Mexican with a great kids menu covering everything from nachos to chicken and hamburgers. A lot of fun for grown-ups, too.

Spur

Santa Ana Spur Shop 280 Victoria Wharf, V&A Waterfront, Atlantic Seaboard (021 418 3620). **Open** 9am-midnight Mon-Thur; 9am-1am Fri, Sat; 9am-11pm Sun. **Credit** AmEx, DC, MC, V. **Map** p283 H1.

Mean Old-West look, slide-in booths-type seating with crayons and games to keep kids busy. There are sparklers and ice-cream and a song from the friendly staff for children.

Wimpy

Lower Level, Cavendish Shopping Centre, Claremont, Southerb Suburbs (021 683 9518). **Open** 8am-6pm Mon-Thur; 8am-9pm Fri; 8am-6pm Sat; 8.30am-5pm Sun. **Credit** AmEx, DC, MC, V.

It's certainly not high cuisine – we're talking bright red plastic chairs with a Playworld that makes this a hit with young children. And there's no surprise in telling you that the selection of hamburgers and milkshakes is will make any child happy.

Surfing in Muizenberg. *See p158.*

Comedy

Welcome to Caper Town.

There's a wonderful line in the film *Texasville*: 'Either you laugh about nothing or you cry about everything'. South Africans seem to have adopted the former position. They used to laugh at punchlines, now, increasingly, they find more to laugh about themselves.

But that's not to say that there aren't a lot of comedy opportunities in Cape Town: not long ago it was hard to find a decent comedian in the city; now Capetonians can't step out of their front door without tripping over one.

This in itself can be taken as a hopeful sign, even in the bigger scheme of things: in restrictive draconian societies, which South Africa once was, comedians, along with intellectuals, are among the first people to be put to the knife. The fact that the comedy business is now flourishing so well in the new South Africa is a promising sign for the young democracy.

That said, the comedy scene has taken a bit of a dip of late. Two well respected events have been given the chop: the Cape Comedy Collective's legendary Sunday night performances at the Independent Armchair Theatre; and the much less loved Comedy Warehouse is currently being changed into a furniture store, or worse.

But after a while, comedy fans realised that these developments have had positive consequences: both establishments gave up-and-coming stand-ups a venue to peddle their wares, some of which were incredibly good, most of which were not. The law of averages. Fortunately, the best survived and they're the ones who are still on the circuit. And what's more, now that the performers no longer have the option of propping up a multi-bill, they've had to dig deeper and come up with more original, individual one-man shows. As such, any local comedian you hear about is probably worth checking out.

For information and tickets, contact **Computicket** (083 915 8000/083 915 8100/ www.computicket.co.za; 9am-5pm daily).

My kind of town Marc Lottering

Cape Town is... like totally only the most beautiful city in the world.
Capetonians are... easygoing and friendly. Some of us might get OVERfriendly when it comes to your wallet and your expensive camera, but we generally mean you no harm.
Table Mountain is... flat.
Fabulous food is found at... Bukhara (*see* p101), if you like curry and all.
I buy take-aways at... Aneesa's (Victoria Building, Victoria Road, Grassy Park, 021 705 5279) or Cosy Corner (119A Ottery Road, Wynberg, 021 797 2498).
Sundowners are best spent at... Llandudno Beach, drinking from your cooler bag.
Lazy mornings are spent... wearing sexy shades, at coffee shops on Long Street or Kloof Street, where you are guaranteed to be spotted.
The strange thing about this town is... Plumstead.
Ever wondered why... most car guards don't have a driver's licence but insist on showing you how to reverse-park?

Venues

Artscape Theatre Centre

DF Malan Street, Foreshore, City Bowl (021 410 9800/bookings 021 421 7695). **Tickets** prices vary. **Credit** AmEx, DC, MC, V. **Map** p283 I3.

The re named Nico Malan Theatre still sports some of the most hideous architecture this side of Detroit and generally lends itself to more highbrow fare than low-key chuckle-fests. But the smaller venue, named On the Side, does occasionally host stand-up performances and theatre sports, which continue to be highly popular. There are other bonuses too: secure underground parking is available, and the restaurant is better than you'd expect. Try not to look at the ceiling and you should be alright.

Baxter Theatre

Main Road, Rondebosch, Southern Suburbs (021 685 7880/www.baxter.co.za). **Tickets** prices vary. **Credit** AmEx, DC, MC, V.

The Baxter is host to the Smirnoff International Comedy Festival, Cape Town's premier comedy event, held in September. Bigger-name comedians such as Marc Lottering, Mark Banks et al often perform in the main theatres, though they are perhaps a little larger than is ideal (the theatres, not the comedians). Newcomers have a better show of it at the smaller Baxter Studio venue upstairs. There is a restaurant, but looks rather like a hospital cafeteria. Go somewhere else to eat.

Evita se Perron

Darling Station, Arcadia Road, Darling, West Coast (50mins north of Cape Town on R27) (022 492 2851/022 492 2831/www.evita.co.za). **Open** 9am-5pm Tue-Fri, Sun; 9am-5pm, 6-11pm Sat. **Tickets** R50-R80. **Credit** AmEx, DC, MC, V.

Widely considered to be Pieter-Dirk Uys's folly at the time of its establishment, this venue has turned into an enduring success. Shows are held Saturday lunch and evening, and Sunday lunch. The quality of the show is matched by that of the excellent à la carte menu. Stick around afterwards to chat to Pieter-Dirk (aka Evita Bezuidenhout). The first week of September sees the launch of the Hello Darling Arts Festival featuring the Voorkamer Fest, a revolutionary in-home theatre experience staged with local and international acts.

On Broadway

On Broadway Green Point, 21 Somerset Road, Atlantic Seaboard; On Broadway Tableview, 1 Marine Circle, Atlantic Seaboard (both venues 021 418 8338/www.onbroadway.co.za). **Shows** 9pm Wed-Sat; special performances Sun. **Tickets** R45-R60. **Credit** AmEx, DC, MC, V. **Map** p282 G3.

Not strictly a stand-up venue, but On Broadway does host comedy evenings on Monday and Tuesday nights, and assorted light entertainment throughout the year. A small, intimate venue, it is one of Cape Town's best, known for its innovative programming. Shows are generally of good quality and tend to be geared towards an adult audience.

I soak up culture at... the bar at La Perla (*see p110*).

I'm frustrated by... waiters who don't give you loose change – they know you're too embarrassed to ask for it, thereby ensuring a fat tip comprising notes.

Spiritual nourishment is found... by calling your mum while nursing a hangover.

The landmark I love... Greenmarket Square.

The landmark I loathe... Greenmarket Square (when you don't have your mobile phone with you, and the people you've arranged to meet on the Square, are somewhere on the Square – somewhere).

My community is... always asking me for complimentary tickets to my shows.

Creativity flourishes... when cashiers at the supermarket ask me how many plastic carrier bags I think I will be needing? (By law South Africans need to pay for shopping bags).

I bare my body on... warm Sunday afternoons, in my garden, in full view of my two Daschunds.

I go shopping... with my credit card, to further annoy my nervous bank manager.

I show off... when I bump into old school friends who no longer look great.

I take tourists to... see my live shows.

I listen to... anyone who's foaming at the mouth, brandishing a loaded gun.

I find local politics... extremely riveting, particularly in my line of work.

Marc Lottering is a big mouth. A glorious big mouth, who, when he smiles, lights up a room, and when he laughs, causes heads to turn. He is one of the most popular actor/ comedians on the Cape Town stage and his characterisations of the so-called coloured community are spot-on. He laughs at himself, as well as at everyone else. And everyone loves him for it. He plays to sell-out audiences who can't get enough of his sharp wit, musical talents and slick performance style. A brilliant actor and a perceptive mind, Marc tells it like it is – the funny, heart-warming bits as well as the stuff that we'd prefer to keep hidden. For more, go to www.marclottering.com.

Comedians to watch

Keep an eye out for these new and old favourites. Competitions and festivals, particularly the **Smirnoff International Comedy Festival** in September (*see p161*), are reliable sources of new talent. Go to the **Computicket** website (*see p160*) for up-to-date booking details.

Cokey Falkow

Incredibly intelligent and likeably arrogant, Falkow is probably the most international of local talents. Blessed with a fantastic stage presence and a face designed for comedy, his adult-oriented material sets him apart from the crowd. He recently blew the international acts into the wings at the Smirnoff Comedy Festival and we fully expect him to go super-nova. Not for the youngsters, though. Like Chris McEvoy (*see below*), Falkow is the most likely to come up with a mind-blowing one-man show.

Melanie Jones

The diva from the Cape Flats, Jones burst onto the scene some two years ago with a wonderful American impression. Handicapped by the prejudice that a woman can't be both beautiful and funny, she has succeeded in what really is a man's, man's, man's world. It still remains to be seen whether she has the legs to go the distance.

Marc Lottering

The poster-child of Cape Town's emerging stand-up scene, young Lottering's star has waned a bit of late on account of some regrettable exploits into TV Land. He is, however, a mercurial talent that could re-surface at any time. We hope he does. The quintessential Cape Town comedian, his influence is clearly evident in a lot of the up-and-comers.

Chris McEvoy

Unjustly overlooked, McEvoy has a depth similar to international acts such as George Carlin and Denis Leary. His refusal to go for the easy laughs has proved to be somewhat of a problem for local audiences used to the 'love me, love me, love me' ingratiating school of stand-up. That said, along with Cokey Falkow (*see above*), he is a dark horse from whom great things are expected. Not for children.

Riaad Moosa

If Moosa weren't such a very nice chap he'd be universally disliked. As it is, he's probably hideously envied. Undoubtedly comedy's great hope, Dr Moosa is the complete package – he has the material, the delivery and, like Pieter-Dirk Uys (*see below*), he almost never gives a bad performance. Moosa's appearances are not as plentiful as we'd like.

Colin Moss

The country's sexiest man, according to *Cosmo*... and he's funny. Moss's extensive acting and presenting background (*Idols* and *Fear Factor*) stands him in good stead. Incorrectly dismissed as a vacu-

Mark Sampson gets cooking.

ous pretty-boy, Moss is, in fact, a consummate professional. Witty, urbane, charming and successful, and yet you still want to like him.

Mark Sampson

A British expat, Sampson has become one of the country's head cheerleaders, having founded the Cape Comedy Collective, the organisation that largely established the local comedy scene. He recently cut back on MC-ing to focus on his own material – with excellent results. Upbeat without being twee.

Kurt Schoonraad

Possibly the heir to Marc Lottering's throne, Schoonraad's motor-mouth material crosses over extremely well and his desire to please is evident. A Cape Comedy Collective alumnus, he's put in the work, and it shows. Rated in both belly-laughs and laughs-per-minute, he's in the heavyweight division.

Pieter-Dirk Uys

He's still SA's top funny man, and seemingly incapable of having an off night. His Evita Bezuidenhout remains 'the most famous white woman in South Africa,' and with good reason. Despite having been around forever he's managed to remain both funny and relevant – his work on AIDS awareness has been invaluable. A world-class talent.

Arts & Entertainment

Film

Locals may like big and brash, but the art-house scene is steadily growing.

South Africans love the cinema. The notable proliferation of cinemas over the past decade – the number of screens has more than trebled – is testament to this celluloid affair. Even steep ticket increases and hikes in concession-stand prices have not kept the crowds away. That said, these cinema-goers are not exactly the most discerning bunch, if a glance at any given week's 'Top Ten' box office takers is anything to go by. Generally the smash hits are like WWE wrestlers – big and loud. Schwarzenegger and Jackie Chan are still firm favourites and some people even started dribbling openly when they heard Sly was making *Rocky 9*.

More rarified tastes are not ignored – the number of screens showing art movies has also increased greatly and the perception that all art films are about homosexual Czechoslovakian violinists who have mother issues is gradually changing. The facilities are generally first-rate. Tuesday night is discount night, so either reserve in advance or expect to be standing in queues from here to Jericho.

MULTIPLEX CINEMAS

Most shopping malls of any significant size now boast American-style multiplex cinemas (*see p128*). Before the screen explosion of recent years the two major exhibitors, **Nu Metro** (V&A Waterfront, Atlantic Seaboard, 021 419 9700/1) and **Ster-Kinekor** (Cavendish Square, Dreyer Street, Claremont, Southern Suburbs, 0860 300 222) used to be a little precious about their titles, but these days it's location and not status that calls the shots.

Furthermore, there is no real discrepancy in prices (concessions for seniors are available on presentation of a card) and most of the cinemas now have wheelchair access. Show times are, however, not universal so you should check the listings in your local paper. Be warned that it's a good idea to call ahead to enquire about parking facilities – many malls only offer paid parking which can drive prices up considerably.

As yet, it is, unfortunately, illegal to block cellular phone signals in cinemas and the danger of being subjected to the latest Idols hit in all its polyphonic glory is one that is all too prevalent and can certainly start to test your nerves. Fortunately, ushers are beginning to take viewer complaints more seriously.

Cinemas

Cavendish Nouveau

Cavendish Square, Claremont, Southern Suburbs (021 167 89). **Tickets** R33. **Credit** AmEx, DC, V.
The biggest non-mainstream cinema complex in Cape Town, Cavendish Nouveau has for years provided patrons with otherwise unavailable films. It has a proud history of screening films by Jim Jarmusch, David Lynch and the like – films criminally hard to track down elsewhere. Cavendish Nouveau shows art films with all the technology usually reserved for mainstream multiplexes.

Cinema Nouveau Waterfront

V&A Waterfront, Atlantic Seaboard (082 167 89). **Tickets** R33. **Credit** AmEx, DC, V. **Map** p283 H1.
The mainstream face of arthouse cinema. If you're looking for a Resnais retrospective you're going to be disappointed, but you will find more foreign accents on display than usual. Members can visit the VIP Lounge and pretend they're about to fly somewhere. It has, however, displayed a rather vexing tendency to favour European independent movies over their equally worthy Yankee counterparts.

Cinema Privé

Canal Walk, Century City, Milnerton, Northern Suburbs (021 555 2510). **Tickets** R25-R40. **Credit** AmEx, DC, V.

Cinema Privé is located at Canal Walk, the city's most useful shopping mall. While it does have a more rarified air than the cinemas across the hall, it shows pretty much the same stuff, which is a shame. Given Canal Walk's 18 screens you'd think they'd be able to show something a hair more exciting.

IMAX

The BMW Pavilion at the V&A Waterfront, Atlantic Seaboard (021 419 7365/083 915 8000). **Tickets** prices vary. **Credit** AmEx, DC, V. **Map** p283 H1.

It's a cinema screen. And it's big. It was known for shortish documentaries about beasts and locations with musical titles like *Africa: The Serengeti!*, but happily it has now expanded to showing features such as *The Lion King* and the most recent *Matrix*. An outstanding cinematic experience, but only as good as the film it's showing.

The Labia

Orange Street, Gardens – next to the Mount Nelson Hotel, City Bowl (021 424 5927/www.labia.co.za). **Tickets** R25 (concessions available). **No credit cards**. **Map** p283 G5.

Despite its name, the Labia was named after a whole lady, not just part of one, and is not the preserve of questionable gentlemen in stained raincoats, but rather Cape Town's original art cinema and still an enduring favourite. It shows the most interesting films in town and plays host to a number of festivals. The coffee shop is perfect for pre- or post-screening discussions. Not the most technically advanced of cinemas and the seats have seen better days, but this all adds to the charm.

Stargazing

It's difficult to say whether the movies are losing a sense of romance. Cinemas, on the other hand, most certainly are. Ever since the advent of the multiplex with its garish neon lighting and stratospherically-priced concession stands, some of the mystery and romance of a trip to the pictures has been destroyed. Gone are the days of matinées and cartoons, of stern ushers waving flashlights like batons trying to police any hanky panky going on. Gone are the days when people would actually put on their Sunday Best when attending a film. And it's a shame.

Fortunately, there are still people like Trevor and Derek Daly who believe there is much more to the cinematic experience than just what's going on on-screen. Their **Stargazer** theatre in Worcester (*see p167*) really is a Cape treasure. Constructed in an old warehouse that had previously been used to produce Rugby World Cup 1995 merchandise, the brothers have turned what should have been an absolute disaster (Worcester hadn't had a cinema in more than ten years) into a complete delight.

For a start, they've brought in the seats and projector from the old Golden Acre Ster-Kinekor, one of Cape Town's grand old cinemas, now sadly closed. In keeping with the industrial feel of the warehouse, the entrance was made of an old shipping container, which has since been enclosed to create a food courtyard, and the projection booth stands atop an old diesel drum. Oh, right, and the authentic '50s diner is housed

in a vault that was the set from a popular toothpaste commercial. The rest of the theatre is decorated with props from various local and international shoots. Returning to their roots, the Dalys have recently added an outdoor screen, giving new meaning to the theatre's name.

In addition to the regular movies, the Stargazer also shows classics, wildlife documentaries and themed festivals. The in-house restaurant, Trevi's Fire Oven Factory, offers some of the best wood-fired pizzas and fresh oven bread around.

The townspeople regard Derek and Trevor as folk heroes. Quite rightly so.

My kind of town Bankole Omotoso

Cape Town is... a tapestry of different lights at night spread below De Waal Drive.

Capetonians are... different in types, in language, in places where they live, but they all know that Table Mountain belongs to them.

Table Mountain is... a tourist attraction; symbol of Cape Town; impediment in looking towards Cape Point; a hill to walk up and down.

Fabulous food is found at... The Maharajah (230 Long Street, 021 424 6607) and Bukhara (*see p101*) are just two of my favourites.

I buy take-aways... from the above restaurants as well as from Chai-Yo Thai Restaurant (Durban Road, Mowbray, 021 689 6156).

Sundowners are best spent... on the beach in Clifton.

Lazy mornings are spent... by the pool rescuing your morning paper from the south-easter or north-easter wind.

The strange thing about this town is... that it has the greatest number of cul-de-sacs of any city in the world.

Ever wondered why... all the roads in Cape Town, either in the rich areas or poor areas, are straight?

I soak up culture... from the Centre for the Book (62 Queen Victoria Street, Cape Town, 021 423 2669); Robben Island (*see p14*); Moroka Café (120 Adderley Street, 021 422 1129) and at Manenberg's Jazz Café (*see p187*).

I'm frustrated by... the impatience of this city's drivers when I indicate a left or right turn into traffic.

Spiritual nourishment is found... in the old churches and the new mosques and the places and spaces of the ancestors.

The landmark I love is... the now former British Embassy directly in front of the Houses of Parliament (Parliament Avenue, Cape Town, 021 403 2911).

The landmark I loathe is... Table Mountain, which is forever in your face whichever way you turn.

My community is... all of Cape Town, although some might not know this.

Creativity flourishes... thanks to the wine farms and the fruit orchards.

I bare my body on... the beaches, by the pools and in bed.

I go shopping at... the malls: modern marketplaces of no haggling, of sales pitches and e-foods!

I show off... the financial infrastructures – very often!

I take tourists to... Cape Point.

I listen to... Cape Talk Radio (AM 567) in the mornings, and Fine Music Radio (101.3 MHz FM) when there is no news.

I find local politics... absolutely absorbing what with the ANC in alliance with the National Party, which holds the premiership position, although the ANC has a majority in the provincial assembly.

Open a magazine, turn on the TV or drive past a billboard and one of the faces you're most likely to see will be that of cellphone-wielding Bankole Omotoso. Bankole gained a cult following almost ten years ago when he uttered what would become SA's most-affirmative catchphrase 'Yebo Gogo' ('Yes Grandma' in Zulu). But far more than just a household face, Bankole Omotoso is also a professor of drama at Stellenbosch University and an author of continental acclaim, having written novels, short stories and plays. Originally hailing from Nigeria, he emigrated to South Africa in 1991 to take up the life of an academic at the University of the Western Cape before moving across to Stellenbosch. Bankole Omotoso has become one of Cape Town's best-known imports.

On location

Some five years ago the film industry went to Cape Town, and residents were hugely enthusiastic about it... for about five minutes. Breathless telephone calls were made to friends and family when such luminaries as Dolph Lundgren and Alyssa Milano were spotted on the streets or hanging out at trendy nightspots. Much was made of the R2-billion or so the film industry was taking to the fair city, as well as the fact that Cape Town had more shooting days than any US city outside New York or LA. And then residents got cross. They wanted to have their cake and not have to shut the roads down, too.

Capetonian's first complaint was that the international film people had come trooping along to make movies in their town, but they hadn't come to tell their stories. Cape Town was being used as stand-in for LA or the South of France or wherever – the city had become... gasp... a set. Well never mind. The film industry is an industry and show business is, yes, a business, and not some altruistic nanny who makes sure we're all tucked-up nice 'n' cosy at bedtime. But no matter, because by then Capetonians had decided to be cross about the fact that the film crew occasionally close down a road or two. And also Natasha Henstridge kept turning down their dinner invitations.

Now why, you are wondering, are Capetonians such a bunch of whiners?

Well, living in Cape Town is a bit like living with a supermodel. You spend half the time bragging about her virtues, and the rest of the time being grumpy that other people want a piece of the action. But honestly, who can blame them? It's often said that the city's weather means you can experience all four seasons in a day, but in reality you can experience the whole world in an hour. Literally. Gorgeous beaches: check. Mountainous terrain: check. Countryside: check. Cityscapes: check. Industry: check. Luxury suburbs: check.

Cape Town is still primarily an advertising location – mostly for international shoots, but it is increasingly used for features as well, thus affording many Capetonians a 'Hang-on, I know that place' sensation when at the cinema or watching television. The beaches, particularly Camps Bay, Clifton and Llandudno, are popular, though the waves tend to be a bit loud and make the sound chap's job a little harder than usual. The city streets, however, are far more accommodating, even if the occasional Capetonian delayed by a closure isn't. But then the majority of residents have calmed down a bit and realised that they're always late for everything anyway, so what difference does it make? And besides which, maybe Alyssa Milano or Juliette Binoche will be more receptive to dinner invitations.

Labia on Kloof

Lifestyles Centre, Kloof Street, Gardens, City Bowl (021 424 5727). **Tickets** R25 (concessions available). **No credit cards. Map** p282 F5.
The Labia's younger sister shows slightly more mainstream fare, but still skews towards the artsy side. The theatre boasts the best seats in town and, in keeping with its European pretensions, patrons can even take a beer or glass of wine in with them.

The outer provinces

Cinema Starz

Grandwest Casino, Goodwood, Northern Suburbs (021 534 0250). **Tickets** R25 (concessions available). **Credit** MC, V.
Owned by South African mega-producer Anant Singh, Cinema Starz is situated at the Grandwest Casino. It's a good venue showing mostly main-

Arts & Entertainment

stream movies, but has a more unusual boast in its selection of Bollywood productions. Perfect for parents wanting 90 sprog-free minutes.

Drive-In Theatre

Sanlam Centre, Parow, Northern Suburbs (021 919 4971/www.stardrive.co.za). **Showtimes** 8.15pm daily. **Tickets** *per car* R40 Mon-Sat; R25 Sun; R20 concessions Mon. **No credit cards.**
There are two showings a night at the Drive-In. All films are new releases, and the programme changes weekly. There is a small shop, which sells the usual movie eats, as well as two fast-food restaurants for those in the mood for something a bit more substantial. Sound is supplied through either your car radio or a portable one – if you don't have one you can hire one for the evening at a nominal rate of R10. Furthermore, it doesn't matter how big your car or how many people you pack into it.

Minimax

Arcade Building, New Street, Paarl, opposite Virgin Active Gym, Winelands (021 872 0714/5). **Tickets** R20-R25 (concessions available). **Credit** MC, V.
The Minimax is true to its name. Boasting two screens seating 100 people each, it has both air-con and surround-sound. It traffics mainly in commercial films and has a rather nice little kiosk.

Neelsie

13 de Beer Street, Langenhofenen Student Centre, Stellenbosch, Winelands (021 887 2702). **Tickets** R20-R22. **Credit** MC, V. **Map** p278 Q2.
Students! Students! Students! Stellenbosch is Cape Town's premier university town and for almost a decade the Neelsie has provided appropriate fare for its charges. The cinema specialises in art movies and even, hold onto your hats, discusses them afterwards. The Film Forum, hosted by university academics and open to everyone, happens on Thursdays at 1pm, depending, of course, on what has been shown that week. *Charlie's Angels*: A Critical Analysis, we think not.

Rialto

Beach Road, Strand, False Bay (021 853 6240). **Tickets** R13-R18. **Credit** MC, V.
The Rialto opened its doors back in 1918 and has kept them open ever since. Probably the largest of the city's independent cinemas, it has around 800 seats including – nostalgia, nostalgia – 250 on the balcony. Rather bizzarely given the massive profit margins, drinks and snacks are not sold on the premises, so you'll have to take a picnic basket/bucket of popcorn with you.

Stargazer

Value Centre, Stökenstroom Street, Worcester, Breede River Valley (023 347 6757). **Tickets** R20. **Credit** MC, V.
It's a gem of a cinema, but the Stargazer is inconveniently situated a little more than an hour's drive from the city. Essentially a second-run cinema, but lag time is not great. Definitely worth a visit if you're

in the area. An authentic '50s-style diner completes the picture and a new outdoor screen has given new meaning to the name. Cinema owners Derek and Trevor Daly are generally on hand to have a chat. *See also p164* **Stargazing**.

Festivals

SA International Gay & Lesbian Film Festival

Cinema Nouveau, V&A Waterfront, Atlantic Seaboard (021 422 2485/6/www.oia.co.za). **Date** Mar. **Map** p283 H1.
Also known as Out in Africa, this ten-year-old festival is an annual event featuring films with a gay or lesbian theme. While some of the films are subsequently released on the art circuit, in many cases, this is the only chance to see them. As it's a very popular event, booking is a sage move.

Encounters – SA Documentary Festival

Cinema Nouveau, V&A Waterfront, Atlantic Seaboard (021 426 0405). **Date** July. **Map** p283 H1.
This is a forum for international and local documentaries and co-production. The range and selection of documentaries is good and filmmakers are often on hand for Q&A sessions afterwards.

Molweni Township Film Festival

Molweni (021 933 1514/www.rainbowcirclefilms. co.za). **Date** Sept.
The Molweni Township festival was started in 1999 and focuses on locally made films from the African continent. The festival has maintained strong community ties, and takes a pro-active approach to holding screenings and workshops in townships and outlying suburbs as well as in the city. The festival shows a wide mix of documentaries, short films and feature films and aims to create a bridge between emerging and established filmmakers.

South African International Film & TV Market (Sithengi)

Artscape Theatre, Foreshore, City Bowl (021 430 8160). **Date** Nov. **Map** p283 I3.
While there are daily film screenings, Sithengi, as it's popularly known, is more of an opportunity for buyers and sellers to meet and make deals. It attracts delegates from around the globe, but is really of restricted interest to those outside the industry.

RESFest Cape Town Digital Film Festival

021 418 6666/www.restfest.com. **Date** Nov.
The world's premiere digital film festival, RESFest showcases cutting-edge films involving a range of new and traditional media. The audience tends to be mostly young creatives, and programmes have a tendency to emphasise style over substance. Still, it's a great opportunity to see work from some of the most exciting up-and-coming filmmakers. Phone in advance to find out the venue.

Arts & Entertainment

Galleries

A Cape of creativity.

Cape Town slashed any divide between high and low art even before it was politically correct. Here, intrepid art-seekers are sure to find whatever they wish for in airy galleries – professional and established – as well as in odd little makeshift places tucked away in shopping malls, suburban hangouts and township hubs.

The city is a buzzing, crazy colony of creative people who will happily invite you (even into their houses) to see their works of art. From crafty neo-conceptual pieces, to caringly-conceived masterpieces, the generous and productive Cape provides it all.

The city's art scene ranges from high-art museums, such as the **South African National Gallery** (*see p54*) to cultural hang outs like the **Association for Visual Arts** (*see below*) to little corners of creativity.

What's hot at the **Bell-Roberts Gallery**?

City Bowl

Association for Visual Arts
35 Church Street, City Centre (021 424 7436).
Open 10am-5pm Mon-Fri; 10am-1pm Sat.
Credit AmEx, DC, MC, V. **Map** p282 G4.
One of the city's most important venues for promoting top talent – established as well as groundbreaking. Director Estelle Jacobs and her committee drive a large, influential, wide-ranging cultural outfit. This is one of the places where some of the best-known South African names hang out. You will find the works of established artists such as Francine Scialom Greenblatt (whose sensual, and at times voyeuristic, paintings captivate the onlooker), the striking sculptures of Kevin Brand and the witty observations of Sanelle Aggenbach. The AVA can hold up to three different exhibitions in one go in three areas, including an Artstrip reserved for the young, new and unknown. This non-profit organisation will give you unbiased, good advice regarding the South African art scene.

Atlantic Art Gallery
41 Church Street, City Centre (021 423 5775).
Open 9am-4.30pm Mon-Fri; 10am-1pm Sat. **No credit cards. Map** p282 G4.
Among Cape Town's most beloved art dealers, Riva Cohen knows them all: the old artists and the young ones, and she can offer good, clear-eyed advice. There's something Parisian about the set-up here, the climbing of the stairs and the paintings stacked against the walls. Riva's collection includes most of the better-known names in art, such as Willie Bester whose poignant mixed-media township scenes are much sought after by international collectors (*see p169* **Passionate painting**). Hannetjie de Clercq makes magic-realism a visual experience and Riva has a large selection of these whimsical works. The sort of place where you can spend edifying hours.

Bell-Roberts Gallery
199 Loop Street, City Centre (021 422 1100).
Open 8.30am-5.30pm Mon-Fri; 10am-1pm Sat.
Credit AmEx, DC, MC, V. **Map** p282 G4.
Brendan and Suzette are the co-owners of this spacious gallery. These entrepreneurs are determined to get hotshot new art into the local public domain. Expect the rooms to host the unexpected – and frequently the challenging. They exhibit the work of Brett Murray, an award-winning artist with flawless political credentials, who is known as the lovable 'bad boy' of the South African art scene. Pieces from White Like Me, his most recent exhibition, are for sale, and even if you're not in the buying market,

Passionate painting

If all great art carries an imprint of its creator's soul, then the marking of the Cape's most passionate artist – increasingly acclaimed in international circles – bears a resolute message, that art is a social matter.

Inspired by the belief that art can make a social and moral difference, Willie Bester creates works with compelling personal honesty. As a result, just about everything he puts on show – whether paintings or sculpture – creates the impression that the artist's hands forged those markings only a moment ago. It pricks our conscience, and the image of his work stays in our minds.

Bester arrived on the scene in the early 1990s with a series of art povera-style township collages, bringing his mostly self-taught, but skilled, painterly instinct to assemblies of discarded urban trash. Much of his work has a political intonation, arguing a point about the method of art in times of exigency. Even though his reputation is growing steadily around the world, Bester remains an essentially Cape artist, a man who works from and is inspired by his roots.

His delicate, smartly-painted images of the throwaway materials of township life are iconic celebrations of a very real life, while his large, clanking junk metal sculptures reinvent monumentality through their awkwardness. Ultimately, Bester's works are consistently marked by his passion. You can see Bester's work at **Atlantic Art Gallery** (*see p168*) and **Rose Korber Art Consultancy** (*see p173*).

you'll be challenged by the very easily-recognisable pop icons that have been altered to convey the tragicomedy of the South African psyche. It's always fun there – the work is great and the café is a good place to while away a few hours perusing a couple of the funky art books they publish.

Bell-Roberts Photographic Gallery
Roeland Square, Roeland Street, City Bowl (021 461 4190). **Open** 8am-5pm Mon-Fri. **Credit** AmEx, DC, MC, V. **Map** p283 H5.
A devoted camera-art room that more often than not hosts the real gripping stuff in a steady, professional manner. The convenient, light spaces register another plus for the Bell-Roberts couple's patronage. The works range from nudes and travel photography that imbues the onlooker with a sense of yearning to harrowing and poignant depictions by acclaimed war photographers such as Guy Tillim.

Cape Gallery
60 Church Street, City Centre (021 423 5309). **Open** 9.30am-5pm Mon-Fri; 9am-1pm Sat. **Credit** AmEx, DC, MC, V. **Map** p282 G4.
Cape Gallery is a gentle inviting space that shows pretty pictures and is situated in a buzzing 'gallery street' in the heart of the city. Gail Dorje has a very

well-established and deserved reputation in the art world. Visitors to the Cape often find themselves popping in just to have a look…. and more often than not, they walk out with a picture. The gallery represents many artists, sculptors and ceramicists and this is a good place to while away some time and learn more about the local art scene.

The Centre for Photography
Rosedale Building, Orange Street Campus, University of Cape Town, City Bowl (021 422 2625). **Open** 8am-5pm Mon-Fri; 10am-1pm Sat. **Credit** AmEx, DC, MC, V. **Map** p282 G4.
Under Geoffrey Grundlingh, this venue has brought a new focus to the art of photography. From time to time there are exhibitions that truly showcase very high talent. Both famous and upcoming photographers' work appears here.

João Ferreira Fine Art
80 Hout Street, City Centre (021 423 5403). **Open** 10am-5pm Tue-Fri; 10am-2pm Sat. **Credit** AmEx, DC, MC, V. **Map** p282 G3.
Talent-spotting skills and professional suss have turned João Ferreira into a key presenter in the vibey, current art scene. This increasingly influential gallery often has the best showing in town. The

Arts & Entertainment

Artist: SOLOMON SIKO

SNDEX 04042

THE CAPE GALLERY, 60 CHURCH STREET
deals in fine art reflecting the rich cultural diversity of South Africa.

Gallery Hours: **Mon to Fri:** 9h30 to 17h00 I **Sat:** 9h00 to 13h00
tel: 27 21 423 5309 **fax:** 27 21 424 9063
e-mail: cgallery@mweb.co.za **web:**www.capegallery.co.za

American express, Mastercard, Visa and Diner cards are accepted.
Reliable arrangements can be made to freight purchases to foreign destinations.

THE CAPE
GALLERY

various two-storey spaces, reminiscent of downtown New York, are light, unassuming and let the often quite cutting art speak vigorously and boldly.

Johans Borman Fine Art Gallery

In-Fin-Art, Buitengracht Street, City Centre (021 423 6075/www.johansborman.co.za). **Open** 10am-5pm Mon-Fri; 9am-1pm Sat. **Credit** AmEx, DC, MC, V. **Map** p282 G4.

Johans Borman offers art that is fine and classy, often executed with that kind of solid, technical self-assurance for which masters of oil and canvas are renowned. He talks of 'South African old masters and top contemporaries' and you can be sure that what you purchase will be valuable. On the contemporary side the gallery represents Walter Meyer, and Jacobus Kloppers, both artists who capture the South African landscape in a realistic fashion. The old masters are well represented by the likes of JH Pierneef, Maggie Laubscher, Gerard Sekoto and George Pemba. This gallery is a favourite among Capetonians who take their art seriously.

Pan African Market

76 Long Street, City Centre (021 424 2957). **Open** 10am-5pm Mon-Fri; 10am-2pm Sat. **Credit** AmEx, DC, MC, V. **Map** p282 G4.

If you're looking for African arts and crafts, you'll be spoilt for choice in this lovely old building just off Greenmarket Square. There are more than 35 stalls offering a wide variety of wirework, recycled items, ceramics, woodcarvings, stone sculptures, traditional masks and beautiful African jewellery.

Peter Visser Gallery

117 Long Street, City Centre (021 423 7870). **Open** 9.30am-4pm Mon-Fri; 10am-1pm Sat. **Credit** AmEx, DC, MC, V. **Map** p282 G4.

The man with the finest eye for ceramics has much to offer in his charming establishment. In this shop-cum-gallery, collectibles by some of South Africa's finest potters are to be found. The boldness of Barbara Jackson's vases is displayed alongside the quirky animal figurines of Shirley Fintz. While Yvette Weyers's serene mermaids contrast with the more robust African artefacts.

The Photographer's Gallery

87 Kloof Street, City Bowl (021 422 2762). **Open** 10am-5pm Mon-Fri; 10am-1pm Sat. **Credit** AmEx, MC, V. **Map** p282 F5.

Heidi Erdmann loves photographs. She plays an important role in bringing the best to the public. The gallery houses wonderfully quirky stuff.

Atlantic Seaboard

3rd I Gallery

95 Waterkant Street, De Waterkant (021 425 2266). **Open** 9am-5pm Mon-Fri; 9.30am-1pm Sat. **Credit** MC, V. **Map** p282 G3.

This is where to come if you would like to see pictures, paintings and photographs that tap into the alternative. If you thought that looking at pictures

was a simple matter for two eyes, this amiable place tries – as the name indicates – to show visitors a little more than colour and shape. Look out for intriging photographic exhibitions of far-flung destinations and other interesting subjects.

Alfred Mall Gallery

V&A Hotel, V&A Waterfront (021 419 9507). **Open** 9am-9pm daily. **Credit** AmEx, DC, MC, V. **Map** p283 H1.

Orali Alcock brings to visitors and locals some elegant visual fare. Given the gallery's prime situation on the V&A Waterfront, the well-selected work and small exhibitions are guaranteed to catch the eye – of tourists and locals alike. Here you will find a wide variety of African artists and sculptors as well as a small, yet impressive, display of jewellery, should your baggage allowance not cover the massive wall-hanging, which would look so stunning in the dining room back home. Perfect for gifts.

Everard Read Gallery

3 Portswood Road, V&A Waterfront (021 418 4527). **Open** 9am-6pm Mon-Fri; 9am-4pm Sat. **Credit** AmEx, DC, MC, V. **Map** p282 G2.

The local branch of the top-end art dealership offers not only the beautiful, the valuable and the collectably precious, but also the confidence that comes with reputation. Displayed here are the colourful works of acclaimed artist Speelman Mahlangu, whose uniquely African imagery reflects icons of traditional southern African life.

The Framery

67A Regent Road, Sea Point (021 434 5022). **Open** 9.30am-5.30pm Mon-Fri; 9.30am-1pm Sat. **Credit** AmEx, DC, MC, V. **Map** p281 C3.

Debbie Grewe's small but lively gallery in the heart of cosmopolitan Sea Point is where many cheerful and urbane pictures frequently excite buyers and where artists gather new fans.

Hout Bay Gallery

112 Main Road, Hout Bay (021 790 3618). **Open** 9am-5pm Mon-Fri; 11am-3pm Sat; noon-5pm Sun. **Credit** AmEx, DC, MC, V.

A solid, well-liked gallery with some good artworks, particularly for those wanting bold modern pieces. Hout Bay Gallery showcases artist Paul du Toit whose instantly recognisable colourful abstract faces are much sought after by collectors worldwide; as well as such talented newcomers as sculptor James Butler, whose enormous, beautiful copper-and-wood creations seem vibrantly alive.

Joshua Rossouw Gallery

Portswood Road, V&A Waterfront (021 425 9806). **Open** 10am-6pm Mon-Fri; 10am-3pm Sat. **Credit** V. **Map** p282 G3.

You will find young and vibey art at Joshua Rossouw Gallery. Designed for casual but comfortable viewing, the work of mostly unknown, yet upcoming artists is on show. An easy viewing experience with a strong emphasis on naive art.

Die Kunskamer

3 Portswood Road, V&A Waterfront (021 419 3226). **Open** 9am-5pm Mon-Fri; 10am-1pm Sat. **No credit cards.** **Map** p283 G2.

The city boasts no more distinguished a dealer of South African art than Louis Schachat. His 'art room' has always been home to the very best. A long-standing promoter and purveyor of fine local art, his eye, consideration and straight art advice are what the high-end collectors come out to seek. The entrance to the building (which it shares with the Everard Read Gallery) is striking. Sculptor David Brown was commissioned to create the bronze heads and hands of this functional work of art.

Michael Stevenson Contemporary

Hill House, De Smidt Street, Green Point (021 421 2575). **Open** 9am-5pm Mon-Fri; 10am-1pm Sat. **Credit** AmEx, DC, MC, V. **Map** p282 G3.

You could be in a smart New York art space, except that the carefully installed, often breathtaking pieces at Michael Stevenson Contemporary are as South

Art with an African aura

At home in Cape Town, **Jane Alexander**'s *The Butcher Boys* usually sits in one of the great rooms of the SA National Gallery (*see p54*). Their overwhelming presence fills the space and hushes conversation. They often travel to faraway places, where their shamanic African aura counters the ennui of grand first-world art halls, leaving first-time viewers enchanted.

While *The Butcher Boys* was the first work of art to catch the limelight, Alexander kept her characters coming: *The Bom Boys* and *The Lucky Girls* followed, along with fellows like the *Monkey With Rattling Maracas* and – more recently – *Pangaman* and his entourage. Over the years, all of these works have held us in their spell, demanded our inquisition of what they are and what they tell us. Alexander's is a silent world, a place

hooked on Africa, where the artist's imagination roams through her own metaphors and narratives.

She has international recognition (she received the prestigious Daimler Chrysler Award in 2002) but, as the title of her latest tableau indicates, her art can only be from here and now. The centrepiece of her prize-winning project, this dramatic and engrossing installation carries the enigmatic title of an *African Adventure*.

Fascinated by the theatrics, the ride to Alexander's alternative world is not an easy one. Yet you cannot help being enthralled, and once you're hooked, there's no escape. Her art hypnotises as it conjures up questions, with a realism that isn't real and a creativity that provokes powerful engagement.

Arts & Entertainment

Church Street: 'Gallery Street' and home to **Association of Visual Arts**. *See p168.*

African as can be. Relatively new in the city, it's already a home to high art. Stevenson's entrepreneurial skills as dealer are a large plus to his collector clients, as well as to visitors who are now regularly exposed to brilliant art from elsewhere in the country. It often hosts walkabouts when exhibiting artists give informal lectures on their work.

Rose Korber Art Consultancy

48 Sedgemoor Road, Camps Bay (021 438 626). **Open** by appointment only. **Credit** AmEx, DC, MC, V. **Map** p281 C7.

Many top South African artists and high-powered buyers of their work trust this well-known dealer implicitly. Rose Korber has access to top South African artists such as John Kramer, whose works perfectly capture the essence of the old-fashioned trading stores still to be found in rural South Africa. Louis Jansen van Vuuren's trademark blue irises can be found here as well as Willie Bester's mixed-media protest art. Rose knows her stuff and those in the art-buying market will find her knowledge and contact with reputable artists invaluable when it comes to taking home that very special painting that will forever remind them of the Cape.

Sembach Art Gallery

17 The Passage Way, Hout Bay (021 790 7324). **Open** 10am-5pm Tue-Sun. **Credit** AmEx, DC, MC, V.

The Sembach Art Gallery stocks a number of solid, well-known names. It has some interesting contemporary wildlife acrylics and sculptures as well as the popular Zimbabwean stone sculptures that are so evocative of that beautiful country.

VEO Gallery

8 Jarvis Street, De Waterkant (021 421 3278). **Open** 9am-5pm Mon-Thurs; 9am-4pm Fri; 10am-1pm Sat. **Credit** AmEx, DC, MC, V. **Map** p282 G3.

VEO is a vibrant gallery where fabulous and noteworthy paintings grace the walls and where modern sculptures beg to be taken home. They represent some established artists as well as some younger artists who are causing a sensation. Look out for the red hues of Heike Davies' work.

Southern Suburbs

Carmel Art Gallery

66 Vineyard Road, Claremont (021 671 6601). **Open** 9am-5pm Mon-Fri; 9am-1pm Sat. **Credit** AmEx, DC, MC, V.

For years these galleries in the southern suburbs have presented delightful pictures that can be found hanging in many houses. You sense that these professionals know what their customers want and which artists appeal to them. They exhibit the art of Gail Caitlin whose works of liquid crystal on glass create large striking, luminescent images.
Branch: Constantia Village Shopping Centre, Constantia (021 794 6262).

Irma Stern Museum

Cecil Road, Rosebank (021 685 5686). **Open** 10am-4.45pm Tue-Sat. **No credit cards.**

From time to time, this glorious museum puts on commercial shows, usually of smart art. Curator Christopher Peter, an expert on the museum's Stern collection, also has a fine eye for selecting and displaying smart shows by important artists from around the country. An interesting place to browse.

Jean Doyle Sculpture Garden & Gallery

6 Mountain View Road, Wynberg (021 761 5081/ www.doylebronzes.co.za). **Open** by appointment only. **Credit** AmEx, DC, MC, V.

Jean Doyle is one of South Africa's leading bronze sculptors and her work can be seen in her garden gallery where it is on permanent display. Her

Arts & Entertainment

Parisian-style **Atlantic Art Gallery**. See p168.

larger-than-life sculptures of joyous, voluptuous women are remarkable and her miniature sensual sculptures will have you reaching for your wallet. An added attraction is that you can visit the foundry and see how bronze is cast.

False Bay

A.R.T.Gallery
20 Main Road, Kalk Bay, False Bay (021 788 8718/ www.clementina/co.za). **Open** 10am-5pm Tue-Sun. **Credit** AmEx, DC, MC, V.
Albie Bailey and ceramic artist Clementina van der Walt offer a fresh and lively art experience in their seafront Kalk Bay gallery. Clementina's own famous tableware is on display, as well as exquisite pieces by other top potters that complement fine graphics.

Northern Suburbs

Art.b Gallery
Library Centre, Bellville (021 918 2301). **Open** 9am-5.30pm Mon-Fri; 9am-2pm Sat. **Credit** AmEx, DC, MC, V.
A vibrant space, supported by an active membership, this gallery has been showing increasingly exciting and new work. Powered by the owners hard-headed enthusiasm for finding budding talent, this place is building a reputation for the unusual and often quite daring. A favourite among art buyers looking for new cutting edge artists.

Lindy van Niekerk Art Gallery
33 Chantecler Avenue, Eversdal (021 975 1744). **Open** 9am-5.30pm Mon-Fri; 9am-2pm Sat. **Credit** AmEx, DC, MC, V.
A genial art place in tranquil suburban Eversdal. Lindy van Niekerk Art Gallery is a friendly place that has an efficient attitude, and you're guaranteed to find something you like.

Rust-en-Vrede Gallery
Wellington Road, Durbanville (021 976 4691). **Open** 9am-4.30pm Mon-Fri; 9am-12.30pm Sat. **No credit cards**.
The work of both established and emerging artists is shown at this well-regarded gallery. A number of top South African names turn up, among them Theo Kleynhans and Sandra Hanekom, and the gallery is known for often hosting unusual exhibitions.

Winelands

Bordeaux Street Gallery
Main Road, Franschhoek (021 876 4648). **Open** 9am-5pm Mon-Sat; 10.30-5pm Sun. **Credit** AmEx, DC, MC, V. **Map** p275 X2.
This neighbourly, friendly venue provides a special aesthetic service to the many tourists in search of something to take home, as well as to local art lovers.

Chelsea on 34
Mount Pleasant Street, Paarl (022 492 3745). **Open** by appointment only. **Credit** AmEx, DC, MC, V.
Owner Lieschen Heinze is a popular and enthusiastic supporter of well-known artists. Don't be surprised when visiting this charming village to find some fine work by famous artists.

Dorp Street Gallery
176 Dorp Street, Stellenbosch (021 887 2256). **Open** 9am-5pm Mon-Sat. **Credit** AmEx, DC, MC, V. **Map** p278 P4.
A good mix of the new, exciting and acceptably cheerful art changes in frequent shows at the Dorp. Ilse Griesel's enthusiasm is compelling and the atmospheric old building often buzzes with very exciting work by bright artists.

De Kraal Gallery & Studio
123 Main Street, Paarl (021 863 2207). **Open** 9am-5.30pm Mon-Fri; 9am-1pm Sat. **Credit** DC, MC, V.
Local artists and those from elsewhere brighten this cheery central venue. For those interested in local art, there is a good selection to be found here.

Johan Coetzee Gallery
71 Plein Street, Stellenbosch (021 886 5656). **Open** 9am-5.30pm Mon-Fri; 9am-1pm Sat. **Credit** AmEx, DC, MC, V. **Map** p278 Q2.
At Johan Coetzee Gallery you will find engaging paintings, prints and the like from top recognisable names. The owner will gladly discuss his art passions and give advice to tourists.

Stellenbosch Art Gallery
34 Ryneveld Street, Stellenbosch (021 887 8343). **Open** 9am-5.30pm Mon-Fri; 9am-1pm Sat. **Credit** AmEx, DC, MC, V. **Map** p278 Q2.
Many established, older South African artists show some fine work here and gems are to be found. Hester Borgelt is a most knowledgeable and professional consultant and you will find her recommendations honest and interesting.

Gay & Lesbian

The Mother City raises its arms to the gay scene.

Mother City Queer Project.
See p176.

Although Cape Town's gay and lesbian scene is small compared to that of cities like New York and Sydney, it remains the most visible and largest in Africa. A constant stream of overseas visitors from around the globe adds to this by giving the Mother City a quirky, cosmopolitan edge, which appeals to people from all backgrounds and persuasions.

And gays and lesbians are welcome almost everywhere: most straight-owned venues are gay- and lesbian-friendly (and vice versa). In addition, the gay quarter (De Waterkant and Somerset Road areas) has shed its raw 'ghetto' mentality and has emerged as a more relaxed and inclusive, less aggressive, district.

There is a wealth of activities on offer in Cape Town, even for the most world-weary queens and jaded dykes. The city has more to offer than its nightlife, when the bars and clubs create a neon-lit nirvana. During the day people spill onto the beaches and mountains, or chill out at one of the many chichi cafés.

Alternatively, you should try the underground comedy and cabaret circuit (*see p160*), or one of the many home decor shops with their fine collections of Africana (*see p144*), or take a walk in one of the historical neighbourhoods such as De Waterkant – the area known as the gay village – with its fine architecture, eateries and design warehouses.

The best way to get to know the city is to befriend a local – which will be easy, as Capetonians adore foreigners.

Accommodation

4 Glencoe Avenue
4 Glencoe Avenue, Oranjezicht, Gardens, City Bowl (021 461 4110/4287). **Rates** *R600/day.* **Credit** AmEx, DC, MC, V. **Map** p282 F7.
An Italian-style '30s luxurious private villa with two bathrooms, four bedrooms, pool and garage. It is situated on the slopes of Table Mountain and minutes from the city centre, waterfront and beaches.

Amsterdam Guesthouse

19 Forest Road, Oranjezicht, City Centre (021 461 5575/www.amsterdam.co.za). **Rates** R245-R595. **Credit** MC, V. **Map** p282 G7.

This guesthouse boasts an entertainment area in which clothing is optional, with a large sundeck.

Amsterdam Guesthouse Sea Point

5 Highworth Road, Sea Point Atlantic Seaboard (021 434 6550). **Rates** R395-R595. **Credit** MC, V. **Map** p281 D2.

This four-bedroom Victorian house near the Sea Point promenade is also close to the gay strip, shopping districts, City Bowl and V&A Waterfront. The decor can be described as South African Victorian, with contemporary touches. There are spanking new bathrooms in each room.

David's

12 Croxteth Road, Green Point, Atlantic Seaboard (021 439 4649/www.davids.co.za). **Rates** R420-R690. **Credit** AmEx, DC, MC, V. **Map** p282 F2.

In trendy Green Point, this classic building is decorated in a modern style, with eccentric touches such as every bedroom being named after a perfume.

The Glen

3 The Glen Road, Sea Point, Atlantic Seaboard (021 439 0086/www.glenhotel.co.za). **Rates** R375-R1,000. **Credit** AmEx, DC, MC, V. **Map** p281 D3.

A boutique hotel with comfortable, cosmopolitan surroundings. Well situated.

Guesthouse One Belvedere

1 Belvedere Avenue, Oranjezicht, City Bowl (021 461 2442/www.1belvedere.co.za.co.za). **Rates** R295-R750. **Credit** AmEx, DC, MC, V. **Map** p282 F6.

A Victorian manor with an wrap-around balcony and wide-angle views. Restored for the 21st century.

Metropole Hotel

38 Long Street, City Centre (021 424 7247). **Rates** R900-R1,300. **Credit** AmEx, DC, MC, V. **Map** p282 G4.

Dancing queens

Arts & Entertainment

When the **Mother City Queer Project (MCQP)** (021 426 5709/083 309 1553/www.mcqp.co.za) kicked off around a decade ago, it was shortly after the first democratic elections in South Africa. One of the world's most respected statesmen, Nelson Mandela, was the country's new President and the mood was gay and merry. What a perfect opportunity to have a celebration.

At the time, the city of Cape Town was bidding for the Olympics and the theme for the party was, therefore, a sports theme: the Locker Room Project. The event changed the annual party landscape of the city.

With its huge posters of Mandela dressed in party gear, and revellers adorned in sports attire, MCQP became a lighthouse of gay and

lesbian aspirations. Straights were welcome, too, and so was everybody who subscribed to democracy in all its forms.

The next party was called the Secret Garden Project and it grew wildly in numbers, dancefloors, DJs and stature. And so did the Twinkly Sea Project, the one after that. Soon the events became a full stop to the end of each year and many people started planning their holidays in the city around them.

So what's made them so popular? André Vorster is the man behind these projects, and as an architect, he's created parties with a powerful visual gravitas. They've become a melting pot for the city's creative talents, from fine artists, to photographers, to decorators. Hard-working squads of artists

A four-star venue in the heart of Bohemian downtown. Marvel at the funky modern interior and fab décor. There's a gay bar and a restaurant.

The Village Lodge
49 Napier Street, De Waterkant Village, Waterkant, Atlantic Seaboard (021 421 1106/www.thevillage lodge.com). **Rates** R300-R750. **Credit** MC, V. **Map** p282 G3.
The Village Lodge has an elegant mix of old-world charm and modern living. Chill and use this as a base to explore the cultural diversity of Cape Town.

Beaches

Clifton Third Beach
Below Victoria Drive, Clifton, Atlantic Seaboard. **Map** p284 B6.
This postcard-pretty beach is a gay Mecca every summer, spring and autumn, with gym-toned bodies, soft, white sand and endless vistas.

Sandy Bay
Drive down Victoria Road, turn off right just before Hout Bay, continue down towards Llandudno & Sunset Rocks, Atlantic Seaboard.
This is an untamed and unspoilt nudist beach. Pack a picnic, leave your costume at home and make a day of it. Cruising galore – not in the water, though.

Sea Point Promenade
Opposite Graaff's Pool & SABC. **Map** p281 C2.
Feeling lonesome? You can cruise (day and night) along the promenade and bump into strangers, who might turn into friends. Use your discretion though, as it sometimes attracts seedy characters.

Bars & clubs

What makes Cape Town's gay bars so appealing? A mixture of attitude, décor, cocktails and sex appeal. Some venues double up as clubs, with resident DJs spinning cool

focus on individual dance spaces and decorate them according to a theme. The results are always fresh, never mainstream.

You attend the party as part of a team and often months are spent planning and designing outfits. These parties have become a visual celebration of democracy, often in buildings loaded with political baggage, such as The Castle (with its military history) and the Artscape (formerly Nico Malan) theatre (with its apartheid-style architecture, and former whites-only admission policies).

Themes from past years include the Shopping Trolley Project, Safari Camp, Heavenly Bodies, Farm Fresh, the Wedding and Kitsch Kitchen – no doubt a real kitchen-sink drama with ample food for thought.

Arts & Entertainment

sounds on certain days of the week, or weekends. The crowds are pretty mixed, with lesbians preferring the bar scene to the club scene. Ditto for the leather crowds. Gay bars are cruisy (and rightly so) and most people dress up for the night out. The gay club scene is more intimate and small, yet diverse enough to please all the different tribes found in the local dance culture. It has loosened up (a bit) and lost some of its Calvinist hang-ups, but still suffers from pockets of inhibitions. But most straight venues are gay- and lesbian-friendly, *see pp192-6.*

Bar Code

18 Cobern Street, Green Point, Atlantic Seaboard (021 421 5305/www.leatherbar.co.za). **Open** 9pm-1am Mon-Thur, Sun; 10pm-3am Fri, Sat. **Admission** R20 (with free drink) Mon-Thur, Sun; R30 (with free drink) Fri, Sat; members free. **No credit cards**. **Map** p282 G3.
Themes for parties here range from Underwear and Leather, to Uniform, Rubber, Fetish or BDSM. But make sure you dress to the theme, or you won't be allowed in. It's lots of fun as long as you join in.

Bronx Action Bar

35 Somerset Road, De Waterkant, Atlantic Seaboard (021 419 9216/www.bronx.co.za). **Open** 8pm-4am daily. **Admission** free. **No credit cards**. **Map** p282 G3.
The oldest gay and lesbian bar in the city, where every visitor should pop in for a night on the razz. There's a hip dancefloor, groovy drinking area and smart sounds. You might even get lucky with a local.

Confessions

27 Somerset Road, Green Point, Atlantic Seaboard (021 421 4798). **Open** 11pm-4am Mon, Wed-Sun. **Admission** R40. **No credit cards**. **Map** p282 G3.
After a long break this new club is back in action. Its chic, swanky interior looks like a decadent church. Hard-core throbbing music, fabulously sexy, cocky crowds and fine and funky cocktails.

The Habit @ The Cohibar

Café Bardeli, Longstreet Studios, Kloof Street, Gardens, City Bowl (083 710 3130). **Open** 8pm-2am daily. **Admission** R20. **Credit** AmEx, DC, MC, V. **Map** p282 F5.
Good DJs for the post baby-dyke generation. It attracts a gorgeous professional crowd. The music is loungy. The bar area is dominated by an underlit marble counter, so that you can see the grain. There are dark corners, nooks and crannies for lovers, and sexy, slinky, modern extraction fans above each table which make it ideal for smokers. There's a women's night on the last Saturday of every month.

Leopard Room Bar & Cigar Lounge

The Twelve Apostles Hotel, Victoria Drive, Oudekraal Bay, Atlantic Seaboard (021 437 9000/ www.12apostleshotel.com). **Open** 11am-midnight daily. **Admission** free. **Credit** AmEx, DC, MC, V. **Map** p284 A10.

A melting pot of live music, African décor, exotic cocktails and great views across Oudekraal Bay boasts one of the Mother City's finest and largest cigar bar menus, the largest selection of vodkas in South Africa and has no fewer than 54 different martini varieties. The cocktail menu changes monthly.

M-Bar & Lounge @ the Metropole

38 Long Street, City Centre (021 424 7247/ www.metropolehotel.co.za). **Open** 9am-late daily. **No credit cards**. **Map** p282 G4.
If you're tired of tatty venues with tired queens, come here. It's fresh, suave and provocative. You can lounge around, sip cocktails or coffee, or stand in the corner and cruise your heart out. Ideal for after the movies, or a pre-party warm-up.

Sliver

27 Somerset Road, Green Point, Atlantic Seaboard (021 421 4798). **Open** 9pm-4am daily. **Admission** free. **Credit** AmEx, DC, MC, V. **Map** p282 G3.
New York-style, swanky cocktail lounge with low lighting and lots of cruising. There's a nice racial mix, the interior is sleek, with a plethora of good-looking crowds and come-to-bed attitude.

Velvet Lounge Chill Bar

136 Bree Street (Entrance in Dorp Street), City Centre (083 709 0419). **Open** 7pm-2am Mon-Sat. **Admission** free. **Credit** AmEx, DC, MC, V. **Map** p283 H3.
A relaxed atmosphere, loungy feel and games room, ideal for chilling out before and after the club. The pool area is butch and wild, the sofas are so good and the crowd all dressed up for cocktail sipping, samba sessions and general bonhomie.

Restaurants & cafés

Gays and lesbians love eating out. They ask for good service – simple, robust but exciting food – and a clientele that will turn heads. It sounds easy, but not everybody gets it right.

Café Erte Internet Café & Cosmic Cocktail Bar

265A Main Road, Sea Point, Atlantic Seaboard (021 434 6624/www.cafeerte.com). **Open** 10am-4am daily. **Credit** MC, V. **Map** p281 D2.
Perfect for sending e-mails, chilling out after the club or eating breakfast. The waiters are friendly and sexy and the clientele mad and wonderful. Take a break: sit outside and doing some people-spotting. A cool glow emanates from the bar area.

Café Manhattan

74 Upper Waterkant Street, De Waterkant Village, Atlantic Seaboard (021 421 6666/ www.manhattan.co.za). **Open** 11am-midnight Mon-Thur; 10am-2am Fri-Sun. **Credit** AmEx, DC, MC, V. **Map** p282 G3.
This venue offers solid plates of food in the gay district. The outside area has a cruisy bar. It's situated in the gay village, so sit outside and enjoy the view.

Evita se Perron

Darling Station, Arcadia Road, Darling, 50 mins north of Cape Town on the R27 (022 492 2851/022 492 2831/www.evita.co.za). **Open** 9am-5pm, 6-11pm Tue-Sun. **Tickets** R75 Pieter-Dirk Uys shows; R50 others. **Credit** AmEx, DC, MC, V.

This is a dinner-theatre venue with fantastic political satire. The food is local, although unpredictable. When there are shows on, the bar and restaurant are open until midnight. It's well worth the short drive out of Cape Town. *See also pp242-3.*

Lola's

228 Long Street, City Centre (021 423 0885). **Open** 7.30am-midnight daily. **Credit** AmEx, DC, MC, V. **Map** p282 G4.

Lola's is a funky '50s-style eatery with a very good vegetarian menu. It is also the place to spot the hip-and-happening people of Cape Town. Packed with the underground gay mafia, fashion industry types, unemployed actors and lipstick lesbians. It's open for coffee, cocktails and drinks.

On Broadway in Green Point

Green Point, 21 Somerset Road, Atlantic Seaboard (021 418 8338/www.onbroadway.co.za). **Shows** 9pm Tue-Sat; special performances Sun. **Tickets** R45-R60. **Credit** AmEx, DC, MC, V. **Map** p282 G3.

On Broadway has great cabarets, and also the longest-running drag show in town, Mince, which will have you in tears of laughter and poignancy all at the same time. You can eat here, too.

My kind of town Pieter-Dirk Uys

Cape Town is... our womb with a view.
Capetonians are... rude, lazy, opinionated, dull and unadventurous.
Table Mountain is... moerse ('helluva') big.
Fabulous food is found at... Madame Zingara's (*see p97*).
I buy take-aways at... a samosa stall in Salt River.
Sundowners are best spent... on Radisson's deck (*see p126*).
Lazy mornings are spent... in my dreams.
The strange thing about this town is... there's nowhere to go 'south-wise', you can only go up.
Ever wondered why... they didn't dig a canal to join Table Bay and False Bay and force Transvaalers to carry passbooks?
I soak up culture at... District Six Museum (*see p47*).
I'm frustrated by... the bridges on the Foreshore that go nowhere (*see p49* **Roads to nowhere**).
Spiritual nourishment is found... in Johannesburg.
The landmark I love... Robben Island, lest we forget (*see p14* **SA in an island**).
The landmark I loathe... most of the buildings on the Foreshore that look pure mid '50s Soviet East European Baroque.
My community is... in Darling.
Creativity flourishes... when politicians forget to laugh.
I bare my body... to my best friend.
I go shopping... at Exclusive Books and Wordsworth (*see p131*).
I show off... to my cats.

I listen to... the President for my next show.
I find local politics... exactly what the voters deserve.

Pieter-Dirk Uys, actor and AIDS activist, and his alter ego Evita Bezuidenhout ('the most famous white woman in Africa') have pushed the political boundaries of South African society for as long as anyone can remember. Pieter-Dirk is an outspoken and fearless critic who, pre-1994, fought the National Party's apartheid policy and now has taken the African National Congress to task on its HIV/AIDS stance. He is a tireless fighter against injustice, a brilliant satirist and a wonderful host – a visit to his headquarters, Evita se Perron, in Darling, is a must, *see above*.

Sauna & massage

The Barracks
Corner of High Field Road & Waterkant Street, Green Point, Atlantic Seaboard (021 425 4700/ www.thebarracks.co.za). **Open** 11am-1am Mon-Sat; 4-11pm Sun. **No credit cards. Map** p282 G2.
The Barracks has become well known for being a discreet and stylish venue in which to meet men. The Barracks is the city's foremost M2M studio, and close to numerous gay venues.

Hothouse Steam & Leisure
18 Jarvis Street, City Centre (021 418 3888/ www.hothouse.co.za). **Open** noon-2am Mon-Wed; noon-6am Thur; 24hrs Fri, Sat. **Admission** R45. **Credit** AmEx, DC, MC, V. **Map** p282 G3.
Hothouse Steam and Leisure is a world-class venue with a relaxed atmosphere and stunning interior – leather couches, TV lounge, cocktails and outside balcony area. This is an ideal place for a special night out. You will find a like-minded sort chilling in the saunas here as this serves as home away from home for a variety of men.

Steamers
www.steamers.co.za.
This sauna has moved and its new address was unknown at time of going to press (check out the website). Crowds are generally uninhibited, young and wild. The sauna and jacuzzi facilities offer relaxation and rejuvenation for tired bodies, while the clientele creates a frisson of excitement for those who want to have some fun.

Shops & services

My Beautiful Laundrette
Shop 1, Villa Rosa, 267 Main Road, Sea Point, Atlantic Seaboard (021 434 3485). **Open** 7am-7pm daily. **No credit cards. Map** p281 D2.
Better than the movie. Cleanliness is next to godliness, should you wish to wash your dirty linen in public. Same-day laundry service, dyeing and alterations are all done with a smile.

Rainbow Trade
29A Somerset Road, Green Point, Atlantic Seaboard (082 359 4343/www.rainbowtrade.co.za). **Open** 4pm-2am daily. **No credit cards. Map** p282 G3.
A fun one-stop shop that stocks gay and lesbian tourist memorabilia such as rainbow stickers and key-rings. T-shirts declaring 'I can't even think straight' are displayed alongside furry handcuffs, adult toys and very grown-up magazines.

Sea Point Dispensary
Shop 126C Main Rd, Sea Point, Atlantic Seaboard (021 434 7616/www.designerunderwear.co.za). **Open** 9am-8pm daily. **Map** p282 E2.
It looks like a chemist and it smells like a chemist, but don't be fooled. It's more than that. If you need designer underwear, sports supplements, exotic fragrances or any sex aids, this is your one-stop-shop. And oops, before we forget, it's also for your legal pharmaceutical needs.

Steven Rom Liquor Merchants & Exporters
Stanley Place, Three Anchor Bay, Atlantic Seaboard (021 439 1112). **Open** 9am-8pm Mon-Fri; 9am-5pm Sat. **Credit** AmEx, DC, MC, V. **Map** p282 E1.
Drink like a fish at the Atlantic seaboard's top gay liquor store. It exports wine worldwide and imports some interesting bottles, too.

Help & information

Cape Town Tourism
The Pinnacle, corner Castle & Burg Streets, City Centre (021 426 4260/www.cape-town.org). **Map** p283 H3.
Lost or bored? For more information on how to find something, what to do and where to stay, contact the gay-friendly tourist board.

Gay Men's AA Group
Catholic Welfare & Development Centre, 37A Somerset Road, Green Point, Atlantic Seaboard (082 899 2525). **Map** p282 G3.
For those who need support for any drinking or drug problem, the Gay Men's AA Group meets every Wednesday evening at 6pm, opposite Bronx in the Pink District and is welcoming to all new comers.

Joy for Life
1 Molteno Road, Oranjezicht, City Bowl (021 423 7413/7452). **Map** p282 F6.
If you're living with AIDS and need looking after (or information about HIV), Joy for Life is a hospice caring for people with HIV. Alternatively, Life Line Aids (0800 0123 22) is a 24-hour helpline. Other helplines include, Triangle Project (021 448 3812/3) for counselling, testing and holistic health, as well as Gay & Lesbian Helpline (021 422 2500).

Tours

Club Travel Gay Travel Service
120 Bree Street, 6th Floor, De Oude Schuur Building, City Centre (021 487 4300/www.gay traveller.co.za). **Map** p282 G4.
This gay travel service will cater for all your gay travel needs, including booking flights all over the world. This service is also proudly gay owned, and lays claim to being the largest independent travel company in the country.

Friends of Dorothy Tours
021 465 1871/www.friendsofdorothytours.co.za.
This exclusively gay tour group offers the following tours: Cape Peninsula, Winelands, City Bowl, Whale-Watching and West Coast Floral Tour. Special custom tours can be organised by arrangement, with tailormade trips around the city's nightlife, cuisine scene, gay village and much more.

Arts & Entertainment

Music

From classical to jazz and local African genres, this is the home of live music.

Groote Kerk.
See p184.

Classical & Opera

The Mother City boasts a philharmonic orchestra, various chamber orchestras, choirs, a reputable ballet company... and not so long ago Cape Town actually had two classical orchestras. But post-1994, government arts funding was allocated elsewhere and classical music culture in Cape Town seemed under serious threat. Petitions and campaigns eventually prompted big businesses to step in with offers of sponsorship, providing the means for a new, more streamlined orchestra that was more sustainable in the long term.

The Cape Philharmonic Orchestra was formed in 2001 and is South Africa's most active, playing around 100 concerts a year.

The premier venues used by the Cape Philharmonic Orchestra are the **City Hall** (*see p182*) and the **Artscape Theatre Centre** (*see below*). Other venues for classical music include the **Baxter Concert Hall** (*see p182*), **St George's Cathedral** (*see p183*), the **Groote Kerk** (*see p184*) and in summer even the great outdoors – **Kirstenbosch Botanical Gardens**, **Oude Libertas Amphitheatre** and **Spier** (for all *see p184*).

Cape Town attracts many international musicians – Omri Hadari, Simon Preston and the late Yehudi Menuhin, to name a few. Look out for South African soloists on tour – Anton Nel (pianist), Petronel Malan (pianist) or Gérard Korsten (conductor).

TICKETS AND INFORMATION

Performances are advertised on posters on Adderley Street and around, at major shopping malls and on local radio. Pick up brochures and book tickets at **Computicket** (083 915 8000/083 915 8100/www.computicket.co.za; open 9am-5pm Mon-Fri; 9am-5pm Sat, Sun). Booking is always essential.

Venues

Major venues

Artscape Theatre Centre

DF Malan Street, Foreshore, City Bowl (021 410 9801/box office 021 421 7839/www.artscape.co.za). **Open** *box office* 9am-5pm Mon-Fri; 9am-12.30pm Sat; and 1hr prior to performances. **Tickets** R100-R300. **Credit** AmEx, DC, MC, V.
In 1971, the NICO Theatre Centre officially opened and became the home of the Cape Performing Arts Board (CAPAB) and the heart of Cape Town's

Hugh Masekela is one of the jazz greats you might see at the annual **North Sea Jazz**

cultural activities. In 1999, the name of the venue changed to the Artscape Theatre Complex. It consists of the Opera House; the theatre; the Arena theatre; the chandelier, marble and theatre foyers; garden, piazza and coffee shop; and various conference and function rooms. The Fine Music radio station is also housed within it. The Opera House seats 1,187; the acoustics are fine and sightlines good.

Throughout the year, opera, ballet, symphony concerts, performances by Jazzart dance studio, light classical music, musicals, popular music and drama are on offer. Operas in foreign languages have subtitles running on a digital screen overhead. It can put strain on your neck, especially if you're in for the long haul with a Wagner opera, but full marks for offering this service. You'll be hard-pressed not to find something that you like. Dress code is eclectic… so whether you don a little black number and heels, or jeans and a T-shirt… you'll feel comfortable.

The Baxter Theatre Centre

Main Road, Rondebosch, Southern Suburbs (021 685 7880/box office 021 680 3989/021 685 7880/ www.baxter.co.za). **Open** *box office* 9am to start of performance Mon-Sat. **Tickets** R50-R150; discounts for concessions. **Credit** AmEx, DC, MC, V.
The Baxter Theatre Centre at the University of Cape Town hosts the best of South African performing arts and reflects the cultures of all the people of South Africa. The Theatre Centre opened in 1977 and has continued to draw on indigenous talent, creating a uniquely South African music, opera, drama, ballet and theatre experience. The Baxter consists of the main theatre, the concert hall and the intimate

Sanlam Studio theatre. The concert hall seats 638 patrons and boasts a Von Beckerath organ. Classical music on offer throughout the year is performed by the Cape Philharmonic Orchestra, the Cape Sinfonia, various string quartets, octets and chamber orchestras, ensembles and orchestra groupings from the University of Cape Town (UCT) and the South African College of Music. Other performances include organ recitals, choir festivals and competitions. World-renowned South African musicals such as *District 6* and *Kat and the Kings* by David Kramer and Taliep Petersen return to the Baxter regularly for a season of performances. Not to be missed. Other offerings are activities for young people and children, dance, comedy, popular and African music. The atmosphere of the Baxter Theatre Complex is more informal and the setting more intimate. Ticket prices are very reasonable. Lunch-hour concerts given by students and staff from UCT on Thursdays at 1pm during the university term are free of charge.

City Hall

Darling Street, across from the Grand Parade, City Centre (Cape Philharmonic Orchestra: 021 410 9809/www.capephilharmonic.org.za). **Tickets** R40-R95; R40 concessions, 30min before concert, if available. **Credit** AmEx, DC, MC, V. **Map** p283 H4.
The City Hall was built in 1905 and is a Cape Town landmark. The most impressive feature of the building is the opulently decorated marble façade, which combines Italian Renaissance features with English Colonial style. Apart from the main concert hall, home to the Cape Philharmonic Orchestra, it also

Arts & Entertainment

Festival, an essential stop on the local jazz trail. *See p187.*

houses the town library. The acoustics of the hall are remarkable. Remember to avoid booking a seat underneath the main balcony – all the sounds get stifled there. The best seats in the house are in the middle section of the balcony. Bear in mind when you book a seat that you can sit on the choir benches behind the orchestra for a lot less money (provided a choir does not perform on the night, of course). It makes for a completely different experience – you can actually look the conductor in the eye. If you love to see a pianist's hands flying over the ivories, get yourself a seat on the left side of the hall.

The Cape Philharmonic performs throughout the year in spring, summer, autumn and winter sessions and has ad hoc performances in between. Concerts are usually held on Thursday nights (occasionally on Sundays nights, too) with repeat performances of some programmes at the Endler Hall in Stellenbosch on Friday evenings.

Other venues

Endler Hall

The Conservatoire, Victoria Street, Stellenbosch, Winelands (021 808 2355/www.sun.ac.za/drama).
Tickets prices vary; phone to check; free lunch-hour concerts. **No credit cards**. **Map** p278 R2.
The new Konservatorium, which houses the music department of the University of Stellenbosch, was erected in 1978. The building is ultra-modern with exceptional acoustics. The concert hall, the Endler, has 556 seats and is equipped with a Marcussen organ. A feature of the foyer is the music murals by

the late Professor Larry Scully. The Stellenbosch University Choir, the University Symphony Orchestra and the Stellenbosch Wind Ensemble are closely associated with the Konservatorium. Repeat performances of the Cape Philharmonic Orchestra take place on Fridays during the concert seasons. The atmosphere of the Endler is formal and a bit stiff but the amazing sound quality of the concert hall does make up for it. The Konservatorium has its own CD label, Conserve Digital Stellenbosch, and CDs are always on sale in the foyer.

St George's Cathedral

Wale Street, City Centre (021 424 7360/ www.stgeorgescathedral.com). **Map** p282 G4.
It was the vision of Robert Gray, the first Bishop in Cape Town, to have a cathedral 'worthy of the glory of God' built in the city. The church's foundation stone was laid in 1907, the design was by British architect Sir Herbert Baker. Over the years, through three wars, a worldwide depression and numerous recessions, various sections were added. But the cathedral is still incomplete. Apart from the regular religious activities of the Anglican Ministry the cathedral is known for its superb music programme throughout the year. Since 1964, Dr Barry Smith has been the organist, and he has started regular choral and orchestral concerts as part of the outreach programme. The liturgical performances of the great orchestral masses by composers such as Haydn, Mozart, Schubert, Beethoven, Bruckner and Stravinsky, given on the last Sunday of each month, have become an important part of the cathedral's music tradition. Full choral evensong is sung on

You'll find the likes of Jimmy Dludlu at **Kirstenbosch Botanical Gardens**. *See p187.*

Sunday evenings. The Hill Organ in St George's Cathedral has been praised and admired by organists and organ-builders from all over the world and is one of the most precious musical treasures of the city. Dr Smith will gladly show you around the organ should you wish to see it up close and and try this magnificent instrument yourself.

Groote Kerk

Adderley Street, City Centre (021 461 7044).
Map p283 H4.
The oldest Dutch Reformed Church in South Africa, dating back to the very start of the Cape colony. The church is known for its distinctive pulpit by Anton Anreith, the elegant stucco work on the ceiling and the crown piece, and the organ, built by Pels & Zoon in 1953. It is the largest church organ in South Africa – 5,917 pipes, four manuals and a console of 102 drawstops. Ensure that you attend an organ recital and book your seat on the organ gallery. A note of caution, though: choir and orchestral performances should be avoided as the acoustics of the church do not lend themselves to these sounds. The pews are built quite high, are most uncomfortable and at some angles you cannot see over the pew in front of you.

Summer concerts

Kirstenbosch Botanical Gardens

Kirstenbosch, Rhodes Drive, Southern Suburbs (021 799 8783/box office 021 799 8782/021 761 2866/www.kirstenbosch.org.za). **Open** *box office Apr-Aug 8am-6pm daily. Oct-Mar 8am-7pm daily.*
Tickets R30; R10 concessions, subject to change.
Credit AmEx, DC, MC, V.
No longer just the venue for summer concerts (Jan-Mar, Dec) where you pack a picnic basket, lie back on the lawn with a glass of the best the winelands can offer and enjoy and all kinds of music under the African skies. Now you do more or less the same thing inside in the Visitor's Centre from June to September. There's jazz, concert brass, opera, traditional African music and rock to choose from.

Oude Libertas Amphitheatre

Oude Libertas Farm, Adam Tas Road, Stellenbosch, Winelands (021 809 7473/box office 021 809 7380/ www.oudelibertas.co.za). **Open** *box office Nov-Mar 9am-5pm Mon-Fri.* **Tickets** R40-R90. **Credit** AmEx, DC, MC, V.
This theatre under the southern skies in the winelands is popular in summer. The auditorium seats 430 and forms a quarter circle surrounded by massive oak trees, ensuring an intimate experience. The season runs from December to March each year; booking opens mid November. Tickets are refunded when the weather refuses to play along.

Spier

Spier Amphitheatre, Spier Wine Estate, R310, Stellenbosch, Winelands (021 809 1177/ www.spierarts.org.za). **Tickets** prices vary.
Credit AmEx, DC, MC, V.
The Spier Summer Arts Festival is a must on the arts and cultural calendar of the Cape. The amphitheatre seats 1,111 and previous star-studded performances have included national as well as international musicians and dancers.

Jazz

If it's jazz you're after, you've come to the right place. From smoky cafés and cigar bars to restaurants and clubs, Cape Town is home to more dedicated jazz venues than you can stroke a chin at. And many of these offer live music seven nights a week. Equally numerous are the jazz styles you'll be able to hear: from the smooth, commercial sounds of a contemporary jazz duo to the local-flavoured experimental jam sessions in the outlying venues. The most intense of these flavours can be experienced in the townships surrounding Cape Town, which harbour several legendary jazz venues. It's not advisable to venture to these areas on your own; call a township tour operator (*see p61*) to find out about outings. For more on the jazz scene *see also p186* **Music to run countries by.**

TICKETS AND INFORMATION

To keep up to date with jazz happenings in Cape Town, check out the listings in the daily newspapers. On Wednesdays the *Cape Argus* 'Tonight' supplement (www.tonight.co.za) features an in-depth jazz gig guide. The cost of these gigs depends entirely on the venue, although you shouldn't pay more than a R40 cover charge to catch a local act at a club or restaurant. Most eateries will want you to book in advance to guarantee a table. Dining isn't always compulsory, though, and most restaurants will let you watch from the bar.

For club gigs, you'll have to buy the tickets at the door, while première and international events can usually be booked through Computicket (*see p181*).

Venues

Cape Town International Convention Centre

Convention Square, 1 Lower Long Street, City Centre (021 410 5000/www.cticc.co.za). **Tickets** R160-R400. **Credit** AmEx, DC, MC, V. **Map** p283 I3.
Within two months of arriving on the scene in June 2003, the new convention centre played host to a concert by international jazz muso Jon Sample. A massive, state-of-the-art venue, it features several halls and two auditoria suited to live jazz performances. Decent acoustics, first-class facilities and secure parking – always a bonus in Cape Town.

Good Hope Centre

Corner Oswald Pirow Street & Sir Lowry Road, City Centre (021 465 4688). **Credit** varies. **Map** p283 I4.
Once the venue of choice for international rock concerts, the abysmal acoustics in the main hall signed its death warrant in that department. Better suited to the quieter nature of jazz shows, the centre features the occasional jazz concert among the usual expos and wrestling line-ups.

His People/Cape Events Centre

Corner Joe Hattingh & Solly Smedt Streets, Goodwood, Northern Suburbs (021 595 1340/ www.cape-events.co.za).

An unusual story: an old warehouse is converted into a church, and then used as a combined religious centre and events complex. The main auditorium, used for Sunday services but strangely devoid of religious symbols, is the sometime venue for classical, jazz and light adult cotemporary concerts. Despite its size, this 5,000-seater provides pretty good sound. The line of sight could be better, though, the result of a floor that isn't banked.

Clubs, restaurants & bars

Cape Colony Restaurant

Mount Nelson Hotel, Orange Street, City Bowl (021 483 1000/www.mountnelson.co.za). **Open** 6pm-midnight daily. **Music** 8-11pm. **Cover** none, but dining compulsory. **Credit** AmEx, DC, MC, V. **Map** p282 G4.
The Cape Colony is very swanky with its colonial blend of arched ceilings, columns and chandeliers – exactly what you'd expect from this historic, five-star hotel. It's also no surprise that, in keeping with the venue's muted atmosphere, the live jazz is best described as contemporary, pleasing and polished. Bring your dancing shoes on Saturday nights.

Drum Café

32 Glynn Street, City Centre (021 461 1305/ www.drumcafe.com). **Open** *Workshops* 9pm-midnight Mon, Wed, Fri. **Cover** R20 Mon; R30 Wed, Fri. **Credit** AmEx, DC, MC, V. **Map** p283 H5.
Although this venue looks like it was once a warehouse, the dim lighting, bean-bag lounge and stars dangling from the ceiling make it pretty inviting. Try your hands at beating an African djembe during the mass drum circles held during the week. Saturday nights (8pm, R20) feature live bands playing everything from straightforward rock to the likes of South African band Stark Raving Sane playing 'world music meets acoustic funk'.

Green Dolphin

V&A Waterfront, Atlantic Seaboard (021 421 7471/ www.greendolphin.co.za). **Open** noon-4.30pm; 6pm-midnight daily. **Music** 8.15pm. **Cover** R20. **Credit** AmEx, DC, MC, V. **Map** p283 H1.
If you want live jazz, you'll find it here every night of the week. Essentially a restaurant, jazz is always first on the menu with the large stage forming the focal point of this inviting venue. The downstairs bar and dining area provide the best view and sound (you need to book), but the music can be heard from any table within the venue's face-brick walls. Not the kind of place where you can get up and boogie, but jazz fans will appreciate the consistently good line-ups – from mainstream to cutting-edge artists.

The G Spot (Generations Café)

Viking Business Park, Showgrounds Avenue, Epping Industrial, Northern Suburbs (021 535 1873). **Open** 3pm-late Mon-Sat; *music* 10pm Mon, Wed, Fri, Sat; 4.45pm Fri. **Cover** R20-R40. **Credit** AmEx, DC, MC, V.

This comfortable venue, with its raised bar area and red, plush couches along one wall, looks rather like an upmarket pub. It is the large stage (with a voluminous sound system to match) that indicate this is not just the local. You'll see over-25s drinking and boogieing to contemporary jazz bands on Wednesday, Friday and Saturday evenings. But on Mondays, you'll find a seated, captive audience listening intently to the evening's jam session.

Hanover Street

Grandwest Casino, 1 Vanguard Drive, Goodwood, Northern Suburbs (021 505 7777/www.grand west.co.za). **Open** 9pm Wed, Fri, Sat. *Music* 10pm Fri, Sat. **Cover** R30. **Credit** AmEx, DC, MC, V.
Situated in the Grandwest Casino, Cape Town's answer to Las Vegas, Hanover Street specialises in commercial jazz. This venue is great for a party on the dancefloor, even if the jazz cannot exactly be described as challenging. So expect lots of talking during the sets. If serious jazz heads find that too much, there is the 'glitz and glamour' of the casino floor or one of the theme restaurants.

Kennedy's Restaurant & Cigar Lounge

251 Long Street, City Centre(021 424 1212). **Open** noon-1am Mon-Fri; 6pm-2am Sat. **Music** 9.30pm Mon-Sat. **Cover** R10 during live performances. **Credit** AmEx, DC, MC, V. **Map** p282 G4.
In a word: opulent. Situated in the trendy part of Cape Town, this cigar lounge is all red walls, wood panelling, chandeliers, comfortable armchairs, leather couches and Persian rugs. The jazz ain't half bad either. Which means that the music can fade into the background a little, making the well-stocked bar the best place to watch and hear the bands.

Music to run countries by

Cape Jazz is not just Cape Town's unique contribution to the world of music. It is a spiritual manifestation of the often troubled soul of a city that has endured the most bizarre forms of political machination over the last 400 years, from colonisation to apartheid to freedom. This song of our city, though, is not a melancholic refrain. Often it is a rousing, almost gospel-like anthem for a people that refuses to lie down and knows how a good party can always put an oppressor's nose out of joint.

Its roots come from the colourful but controlled riot that is the Cape Minstrels' Carnival, which celebrates the emancipation of the slaves. Every New Year and Tweede Nuwe Jaar, they re-assert their right to the ownership of the city with a vibrant parade that rivals New Orleans and Rio for enthusiasm (*see p151* **Sunny Christmas cheer**). Goema, the infectious carnival music that is the progenitor of Cape Jazz, can still be heard from such expert practioners as the **Goema Captains**, **Mac Mackenzie** and **Alex van Heerden**. Afribeat (www.afribeat.com), which has done so much to preserve this historical but living legacy, organises regular live concert series and weekly interactive tours that include intimate performances.

Abdullah Ibrahim, the pianist and composer who almost single-handedly took Cape Jazz to massive international acclaim, was heavily influenced by the goema of his youth. By fusing it with an almost gospel-like divinity and an emotional yet structured technique he took the music out of the streets and homes into the clubs and eventually the concert halls around the world. Born and bred in District Six, Abdullah typifies the bond that Cape Jazz has with this sad yet symbolic part of Cape history. The District Six Museum (*see p47*) has fascinating exhibitions on this interlinked relationship, and stages Cape Jazz-infused events at its home in Buitenkant Street.

One of Abdullah's best and most renowned compositions, *Manenberg*, has become such a Cape standard that you are almost certain to hear it at some point in your stay. It's about one of the dry and dusty Cape Flat suburbs into which the apartheid government re-settled the residents. It is a haunting but surprisingly uplifting melody that never leaves you. Other legendary Cape Jazzers are the late sax man **Basil Coetzee**, whose rendition of *Manenberg* is legendary, and **Robbie Jansen** and Winston Mankunku, who still gig on the festival circuit.

Cape Jazz has become such a national institution that many of its new stars are actually from the north. Names to watch out for include guitarist **Jimmy Dludlu**, pianist **Paul Hanmer**, vocalist **Judith Sephuma**, **Vusi Mahlasela**, **Moses Molelekwa**, **Alvin Dyers**, **McCoy Mrubata**, **Sipho Gumede** and up-and-coming youngsters **Breakfast Included** or the more experimental **Tribe**.

For a relaxed, informal and traditional Cape knees-up go to **Swingers** (*see p187*) or the **G Spot** (*see p185*). Also worth a look are **Manenberg's Jazz Café** (*see p187*), **West End** (*see p187*) and **Kennedy's Restaurant & Cigar Lounge** (*see p186*).

Mama Africa

178 Long Street, City Centre (021 424 8634).
Open *Bar* 5pm-late. *Restaurant* 7pm-late Mon-Sat.
Music 8pm Mon-Sat. **Cover** R15, or R10 when
dining. **Set meal** R130-R160. **Credit** AmEx, DC,
MC, V. **Map** p282 G4.
Yes, it does try a little too hard to capture that
'essence' of Africa – witness the bar counter painted
to look like a snake, the djembes and wire art, and
the sticks lining the walls and ceiling to create the
impression of a Zulu *boma* (enclosure). But, regard-
less of your opinion about the decor, this popular
restaurant features a nightly dose of uncomplicated
African music, from Congolese bands of drummers
to marimba players. Once in a while you'll be able
to hear some African jazz or kwaito.

Manenberg's Jazz Café

*Clock Tower Centre, V&A Waterfront, Atlantic
Seaboard (021 421 5639).* **Open** noon-late Mon-Sat.
Music 8.30pm Mon-Thur; 4.30pm, 9.30pm, 12.30pm
Fri, Sat; 4.30pm, 8.30pm Sun. **Cover** R30-R50.
Credit AmEx, DC, MC, V. **Map** p283 H1.
This refined venue has live jazz seven nights a week.
With a combination of subtle lighting, pastel-
coloured walls, and tables bedecked in pristine white
tablecloths, it may even be slightly clinical. But
that's soon forgotten when the bands take to the
large corner stage. And, judging from the handwritten messages of past performers decorating the
walls, this venue has had its fair share of stars from
various corners of the jazz universe.

Marco's African Place Restaurant

*15 Rose Street, Bo-Kaap, City Bowl (021 423 5412/
www.marcosafricanplace.co.za).* **Open** noon-11pm
Mon-Thur, Sun; noon-midnight Fri, Sat. *Music*
8-11pm Mon-Fri; 8.30-11.30pm Sat, Sun. **Cover**
R20; R10 if dining. **Main courses** R44. **Credit**
AmEx, DC, MC, V.
Hard to miss – both because of its size and distinct
exterior of uniquely African patterns and colours.
Inside the vast, double-storey restaurant, the decor
is more subtle and sophisticated. Try the African
dishes on offer or have a home-brewed African beer
at the bar while watching the live music, which
ranges from afro-jazz and generic traditional African
styles to kwassa kwassa. Charged-up, extremely
rhythmic and originally from the Congo, this draws
tourists and locals to the dancefloor.

Marimba

*Cape Town International Convention Centre,
1 Lower Long Street, City Centre (021 418 3366/
www.marimbaSA.com).* **Open** 7am-midnight daily.
Music 8-11pm Mon-Sat; noon-3pm Sun. **Cover** R25.
Main courses R90. **Credit** AmEx, DC, MC, V.
Map p283 H3.
Named after the traditional African instrument better known as a xylophone, this comfortable restaurant and café takes its music seriously. Mondays,
understandably, are for the blues, while the rest of
the week features African-flavoured jazz and, of
course, marimbas. Be sure to check out the 19-piece

marimban big band. On Fridays and Saturdays
you'll hear mainstream, upbeat sounds; laid-back
jazz on Sundays. Best seats in this chic venue (dark
wood, silver columns and marimba-adorned walls)
are at the dining tables. The bar also provides a
decent vantage point. And if you don't like the
music, retire to the cigar bar next door.

Swingers

*1 Wetwyn Road, off Wetton Road, Landsdowne,
Southern Suburbs (021 762 2443).* **Open** 11am-late.
Music 9.30pm Mon; 12.30am Fri, Sat. **Cover** free-
R20. **Credit** AmEx, DC, MC, V.
This place has character. From the low, beaten-up
stage and plastic patio chairs to the shabby ceiling
fans and mirror ball, the venue isn't exactly what
you'd call trendy. But who cares? Add cigarette
smoke, some excellent music, the occasional star
guest appearance and you have a genuine jazz
bar – a late-night affair. The free, Cape-flavoured
jam sessions on Monday nights are something to
write home about – as long as you don't have claus-
trophobia. Popular mainstream jazz is featured
on Friday and Saturday nights.

West End

*Cine 400 Building, College Road, Rylands,
Cape Flats (021 637 9132).* **Open** 8pm-late Fri,
Sat. *Music* 9pm. **Cover** R30 (subject to change).
Credit AmEx, DC, MC, V.
Expect to hear live bands specialising in jazz with
fusion, African or commercial elements. A touch of
R&B may be thrown in too. Pity this Rylands landmark is only open on weekends. For a break from
jazz, head to the Galaxy nightclub downstairs (*see
p193*). Slightly confusingly, the downstairs venue
hosts the odd Saturday afternoon jazz party too.

Festivals

Jazzathon

*V&A Waterfront Amphitheatre, Atlantic
Seaboard (021 683 2201/www.jazzathon.co.za).*
Map p283 H1. **Date** Jan.
Get a feel for the South African jazz scene at these
jazz concerts featuring top-drawer acts alongside
young upstarts. As they are free shows, 'popular' is
an understatement. Don't expect to get a seat or even
a view of the band, unless you're early.

Kirstenbosch Botanical Gardens

See p184. **Date** Jan, Mar, Dec.
The botanical gardens' sunset concerts often feature
legendary jazz musicians, including the likes of
Jimmy Dludlu and the Soweto String Quartet. Take
a picnic basket and rug, and enjoy the music with
pâté and a bottle of wine.

North Sea Jazz Festival

*Cape Town International Convention Centre,
Foreshore, City Bowl (www.nsjfcapetown.com).*
Date Mar. **Performance** 5pm-3am Fri; 6pm-3am
Sat. **Tickets** R260 day pass, R399 wknd pass.
Credit AmEx, DC, MC, V. **Map** p283 H3.

Arts & Entertainment

The annual Cape Town version of the famous North Sea Jazz Festival has become something of a high-light on the local jazz scene. This is unsurprising, since past artists have included the likes of Hugh Masekela, Youssou N'dour, Herbie Hancock, Miriam Makeba and Tower of Power. Now in its fifth year, the festival is set to up sticks to the new Cape Town International Convention Centre. Its programme still represents Africa and the rest of the world in equal measure, and is a wonderful opportunity to catch some 30 international and local acts. Split over four stages, the bands perform everything from contemporary R&B, soul, jazz and blues to more experimental and progressive styles.

Spier Summer Festival

See p184. **Date** Dec-Mar.

Between December and March, the Spier Wine Estate in Stellenbosch hosts a fabulous Summer Festival of classical music, dance and drama. Traditionally there's also plenty of jazz on the bill. It's fun to eat at one of the estate's restaurants first, and make an event of the evening.

Rock

Face it. DJs are cheaper for venues to hire and attract more of the mindless masses. And, as a result, Cape Town's live rock music scene has been struggling – despite the amount of outstanding talent out there. Bands themselves are notoriously short-lived and live venues even more so. So, you'll you won't find places where live original rock bands perform every night of the week. Instead, most live rock venues double as clubs (with DJs) or restaurants.

But don't despair. There are venues that regularly host Cape Town's rock musicians and, without too much effort, you'll find a number of (mostly pretty decent) bands performing on any given night – although you'll have the most luck on Wednesdays, Fridays or Saturdays.

INFORMATION AND BOOKING

The best way to find out who's playing where is to check out the local papers. The *Cape Argus* 'Tonight' supplement features a weekly rock gig guide on Thursdays. The *Mail & Guardian* and *Cape Times* carry more general live music guides the following day. Otherwise you can go to www.sagigs.com, www.tonight.co.za or www.capetowntoday.co.za.

Most of these gigs take place at smaller venues where no advance booking is possible. So arrive on time with about R30 to R50 in your pocket for admission. When a major event (international band, major South African group, or festival) comes around, booking can be done through Computicket (*see p181*).

Drum Café.
See p185.

Venues

Major venues

A paltry three or four major international artists perform in South Africa each year. When these rare appearances do occur, it is usually by an R&B or hip hop artist/outfit. Most big tours use one of the venues listed below. Tickets for these events average around R200; for more information on booking *see p188*.

Bellville Velodrome

Willie Van Schoor Road, Bellville, Northern Suburbs (021 949 7450).

A bicycle-racing track by day, this is Cape Town's most-used venue for international acts. Tip: you can partly avoid the traditional post-concert traffic mêlée by leaving your car at the Tygervalley Centre down the road.

Green Point Athletics Stadium

Fritz Sonnenberg Road, Green Point, Atlantic Seaboard (021 434 4510). **Map** p282 F1.

The beat of the African soul

Without a doubt the kings of African music in Cape Town are **Amampondo**. This percussion and marimba collective has been deep-rooted in the local musical consciousness for more than 20 years. The band was infectious at the free Mandela Concert in 1988 and again at Mandela 46664 in 2004, and it continues to inject an energetic African soul into this all-too-often Eurocentric city. Amampondo's performances at the Kirstenbosch Botanical Gardens summer concerts are unmissable (*see p184*). Also look out for **Ibuyambo** – the new African music project from Amampondo founder Dizu Plaatjies, which incorporates musical styles from all over southern Africa. Another well-entrenched South African band is **Tananas**, which plays a unique fusion of South African and Mozambique styles that has been in demand on the world music circuit the world over.

The influx of refugees and immigrants from all over the continent since 1994 has brought more diverse beats to the city in the form of kwasa-kwasa, kizomba, marrabenta and ju ju. The kwasa-kwasa scene is notable for its followers' dance moves, a kind of rhythmic pelvic shimmy that would put Beyoncé to shame. The City Centre's African restaurants Marco's African Place (*see p187*), Mama Africa (*see p187*) and Marimba (*see p187*), all have a nightly line-up of Afro-flavours, which more than complement the exotic menus, and the performances can continue till long after the dishes have been washed. **Tucan Tucan**, who play regularly at Marimba, have forged a unique blend of many African forms and is a perfect jumping-off point for a foray into indigenous styles.

On the local Cape scene, the national kwaito phenomenon (a kind of slowed-down chunky house beat with afro hip hop flavours) failed to take off, but watch out for national stars **Mzeke-zeke**, **Mdu**, **Arthur**, **Mandoza** and **Bongo Maffin** on festival line-ups. The UWC (University of the Western Cape) stages big-hitting festivals every year; for more information go to www.uwc.ac.za.

Balladeers Ringo Madlingozi and Lungiswa are big local faves in a soulful world music kind of vein, but the queen of the Cape and probably the whole Afro-pop world is the larger-than-life **Brenda Fassie**. She spends more time on newspaper front pages than on the stage or in the studio, which is all the more reason to catch her if you can. Also look out for **Freshly Ground**, whose genre-bursting music is fast finding fans across all musical divides.

The music of the diaspora is also doubling back very successfully locally. The **African Dope Sound System** (www.africandope.com) is the latest addition to an active roots, dub and reggae scene that is flourishing in the city, mostly around club Uhuru (*see p196*).

Ironically, apartheid and the Group Areas acts (separating black and white into different residential zones) created perfect conditions for a flourishing hip hop scene in the Cape flats. Since then, the '80s collectives such as Black Noise and Prophets of the City (POC) have staged seriously supercharged events showcasing breakdancing, turntable-ism, graf art and MC skills that are on a par with the best in the world. **DJ Ready D**'s (POC) mixing exhibitionism is worth twice any cover charge. All-girl **Godessa** and jazz funktsers **Moodphase 5** are taking the scene to the next level.

To find out more about the latest gigs, keep a watchful eye on the *Cape Argus* newspaper listings on Thursdays, and the *Mail & Guardian* on Fridays. It's also worth tuning into the radio – Bush Radio (98.5FM) and Metro FM (88.6-93FM) are both informative. For information online go to www.afribeat.com.

Arts & Entertainment

Cape Town's largest outdoor venue has, in its day, played host to a number of iconic artists, from U2 to Michael Jackson. It's best to get golden circle or standing tickets as the cheap seats are either miles away or at right angles to the stage. Park at the V&A Waterfront nearby.

Ratanga Junction

Canal Walk, Century City, Milnerton, Northern Suburbs (086 120 0300/www.ratanga.co.za).
This theme park's centre court is occasionally used for live music events. Despite a state-of-the-art sound and light system, the acoustics are less than great so try to get as close to the stage as possible. There you'll get the most out of the muddy sound – and avoid the crowds buying munchies from the surrounding fast-food outlets.

Intermediate venues

Where does a band go when it's too popular to play a club but doesn't have enough fans to fill a stadium? In the case of Cape Town, it's the local town hall. Venues such as Bothasig Town Hall, and the Civic centres in Fish Hoek, Parow and Claremont are increasingly being used for major South African artists and a smattering of international groups. These places have all the atmosphere you'd expect from a town hall, with the acoustics to boot.

Dockside

Century City Complex, Milnerton, Northern Suburbs (021 552 7303/ www.docksidesuperclub.com).
Cover from R40. **Credit** AmEx, DC, MC, V.
The main arena of this huge nightclub usually hosts dance DJs, but bands do make occasional appearances. The venue boasts great sound and lights but artists lacking a dynamic presence can be overpowered by the arena's sheer size.

Studio One

186 Bree Street, City Centre (021 426 1887).
Music 1st Fri/mth. **Cover** from R20. **No credit cards**. **Map** p283 H3.
In keeping with Cape Town's flexible attitude, this venue's day job is as a photo studio. Once a month (on average) the expansive space dons its party gear for glitzy album launches and special live music events. Genres? Pretty much anything goes, as you might well expect.

Clubs

While discussing the tiny venues he played before joining Nirvana, Dave Grohl observed that it was a badge of honour to get 'the singer's spit' in your face. This can certainly happen in Cape Town. Ranging from venues that can take 500 punters to those that would struggle to hold the members of S Club 7, the Mother City's club venues are generally, for lack of a better word,

intimate. And a sorely mismatched bunch they are too. Below you'll find the most regularly used venues with the most consistent line-ups. Although the local pub may have an original live band from time to time, beware of cover groups and the ubiquitous one-man-with-guitar-and-drum-machine 'bands'.

Dorp Street Theatre

59 Dorp Street, Stellenbosch, Winelands (021 886 6107/www.dorpstraat.co.za). **Open** from 5pm daily. *Music* 9pm most evenings. **Cover** R10-R50. **Credit** AmEx, DC, MC, V. **Map** p278 P3.
A warm, red-walled 'theatre restaurant', this cosy venue specialises in Afrikaans popular music. Judging by the autographed pictures adorning the walls, most leading Afrikaans artists have performed here. Cabaret acts and jazz, blues, and rock bands are featured from time to time.

Hidden Cellar

90 Dorp Street, Stellenbosch, Winelands (021 883 3512). **Open** 8pm Wed-Sat. *Music* 9pm. **Cover** R20. **Credit** AmEx, DC, MC, V. **Map** p278 P3.
If this venue were a band it would be the Rolling Stones. It's popular, has been around forever and shows little sign of slowing down. But unlike the Stones, it's not massive. Although not generously girthed, the most well-known live music venue in Stellenbosch is often packed beyond belief. So, if a big-name Afrikaans artist such as Koos Kombuis is playing, get there early and stock up on your drinks before the student masses arrive. De Akker downstairs is also likely to be packed.

The Independent Armchair Theatre

135 Lower Main Road, Observatory, Southern Suburbs (021 447 1514/www.armchairtheatre.co.za). **Open** 8pm-late daily. **Cover** R20-R30. **Credit** AmEx, DC, MC, V.
Don't let the name put you off. This is not a theatre where you'll find painful amateur performances of Shakespeare and Kafka. Instead, this laid-back venue offers cult and manga movies on the big screen, assorted DJs, and live music in a setting that's all couches and red drapes. Which is not to say that the appealing blend of musicians will put you to sleep. Sure, you won't hear any Metallica wannabes, but in their place are cutting-edge alternative and acoustic rock groups, jazz bands and experimental genre-warping outfits.

Lemon Connection

Mettle Building, Willie van Schoor Road, Bellville, Southern Suburbs (021 946 3501/ www.thelemonconnection.co.za). **Open** 6pm-late daily. *Music* 9pm. **Cover** R20-R60. **Credit** AmEx, DC, MC, V.
Another theatre restaurant, this new venue places less emphasis on cabaret. Your chance of seeing rock bands is also far greater here – if you can find it (inside De Kelder inside the Mettle Building along Durban Road, turn into Willie van Schoor Road, between the N1 and Tygervalley Centre).

Mercury Live & Mercury Lounge
43 De Villiers Street, Zonnebloem, City Bowl
(021 465 2106/www.mercuryl.co.za). **Open** 9pm-late
Mon-Sat. **Cover** free-R40. **Credit** AmEx, DC,
MC, V. **Map** p283 H5.
When the country's leading rock bands hit Cape
Town, you'll invariably find them playing at
Mercury Live on a Friday or Saturday night. So, if
you judge a venue by the quality of its line-ups, this
is the best in town. Ditto for sound quality. The plain
decor's not about to win any awards and it's quite
easy to spill your beer as you walk down a couple
of fire-escape-type stairs to the small Mercury
Lounge. With its own bar, the ground-floor venue
hosts smaller up-and-coming acts (some, frankly,
mediocre), acoustic performances and jam sessions.

Purple Turtle
Corner Shortmarket & Long Streets, City Centre
(021 423 6194). **Open** 10am Mon-Sat. *Music* 9pm
Wed, Sat. **Cover** R20. **No credit cards. Map**
p282 G4.
'If it's too loud, get used to it,' is the tag line of one
famous alternative radio DJ. It might as well be used
to describe this large venue, housed in a purple behe-
moth of a building on Greenmarket Square. At the
live gigs you'll hear punk, rock, alternative or metal
bands turning up the volume to Spinal Tap proportions. It can get hectic, but escape is possible by
retreating to the smaller upstairs bar, playing some
pool or staring at the fish tank near the entrance.

Velvet Underground
Shop C10, Eikestad Mall, 43 Andringa Street,
Stellenbosch, Winelands (021 883 8448). **Open**
8pm-late daily. **No credit cards. Map** p278 Q2.
The new kid on the block, this promising venue is
still finding its feet. Hosting live music on varying
evenings throughout the week, the emphasis at the
Velvet is on up-and-coming bands. Some are phenomenal, others aren't. The quality of the venue
itself is not contested, though – from the murals of
'60s rock stars and large stage to the expansive
dancefloor and raised chill-out area.

The Whammy Bar
10 Marine Circle, Tableview, Northern Suburbs
(021 557 5692). **Open** 6pm-late Wed-Sat. *Music*
10pm Fri, Sat. **Cover** R10-R25. **Credit** AmEx, DC,
MC, V.
The bar hides among all the neon signs that are the
Tableview nightlife, and the interior is unobtrusive.
But the bands are an in-your-face mix of anything
from rock, punk and metal to jazz and kwaito. Stand
on the small dancefloor to get eyeball to eyeball with
the lead singer or try to have a conversation while
relaxing in the couches at the entrance.

The following festivals are outside Cape Town;
if you want to make a trip of it *see p234-41* for
accommodation and restaurant ideas.

Kaktus op die Vlaktes
Klein Karoo Nasionale Kunstefees, Oudtshoorn,
Route 62 (044 203 8600/www.kknk.co.za).
Date Apr. **Tickets** R70-R175 (subject to change).
Part of the annual Afrikaans Arts Festival in
Oudtshoorn, it's a bit of a trek (400km/248 miles).
But the open-air concert's line-up is traditionally as
hot as the semi-desert location: mainly Afrikaans
artists and anything from established rock 'n' rollers
to break-out hip-hoppers.

Savannah Up the Creek
Swellendam, Route 62 (021 670 1300/
www.upthecreek.mweb.co.za). **Date** Feb.
Tickets R325 (subject to change).
Held on the banks of the Breede River, some three
hours' drive from Cape Town, this weekend
festival lets you escape from civilisation for a while.
Jump around to a healthy line-up of bands playing
everything from hip hop and kwaito to rock and
blues; laugh or cringe at the stand-up comedians,
relax in the wine lounge or jump in the river. Bring
your tent and camping stuff.

Acoustic & Folk

True to tradition, Cape Town's folk set is
made up of troubadours trailing their travelling
bands from venue to venue. The two tribes
are the long-established Barleycorn (083 235
7245/cotto@pnp.co.za), which has been playing
on Monday nights since Gandalf was a bairn;
and the new Harbour Music Club (021 788
6330), which appears every Wednesday…
a bit like Brigadoon. At the time of going to
press the Barleycorn was resident at the River
Club. The Harbour Music Club at the quaint
Acoustic Café (for both, *see below*). But it's
best to phone the Barleycorn and Harbour
before setting out to check that either of them
hasn't moved to a different venue.

The Acoustic Café
Corner Main & Camp Roads, Muizenberg, False Bay
(021 788 1900). **Open** Music 8pm Wed. **Cover** R10.
No credit cards.
Not just home to the renowned Harbour Music Club
every Wednesday, this quaint little café also has
Saturday jam sessions and more often than not
'plugged-in' bands on Friday and Saturday. Arrive
in good time or book by phoning.

River Club
Liesbeek Parkway, Observatory, Southern Suburbs
(021 686 3478). **Open** *Music* 8pm Mon. **Cover** R10.
No credit cards.
This venue was once a railway workers' recreation
club and then a rave venue before settling down as
a golf driving range and convention centre. It seems
a pretty strange location for the Barleycorn folk
night and, quite frankly, it is.

Nightlife

Clubbing in Cape Town never felt so good.

Sutra Groove Bar. *See p196.*

The Cape Town nightlife scene has seen a resurgence of late. A host of new venues, a posse of new promoters and the honour of being host city for the 2002 Red Bull DJ Academy has put the Mother City back on the international beat map. Proof of a thriving local electronic-music scene (offsetting the less-than-illustrious live scene) are the many local dance music producers (African Dope, Platform, Algorythm and Nano records to name a few) enjoying considerable international success in their respective genres. Though urban R&B and commercial-leaning house are staples of the local scene, you'll find a floor to fit every fancy if you keep your ears to the ground.

The thing that distinguishes Cape Town's clubs from one another is not the music but the door policy – often clubs with identical music (and sometimes the same DJs) have completely different crowds. The clubs cater for everybody from visiting fashionistas and summering Europeans to the 'trainers and caners' brigade, so it's worth checking out the dress code, membership requirements and door damage before you venture out.

Having a long summer season means that Cape Town clubs suffer from the 'now you see 'em, now you don't' phenomenon, especially at peak season; so make sure to check that a club is still open before you set out. Also, many of the more alternative and eclectic beat events happen in unusual venues – everything from airport hangars to old cinemas and art galleries. Check out the press and websites listed below for up-to-the-minute information.

Although the majority of the clubs listed here are situated in the City Centre, there are also some good venues a short drive away in towns like Durbanville and the further reaches of Hermanus. If you plan a trip out of town, stay over and make a night of it, *see pp218-246*.

INFORMATION

To stay in touch with the latest happenings, keep a lookout for flyers, check out Bianca Coleman's column in the *Cape Argus* on Tuesdays, the *Mail & Guardian* on Fridays, and scan the following websites: www.thunda.com www.clubbersguide.co.za and www.e-vent.co.za for general information; www.africandope.com for breaks and hip hop; www.algorythm.co.za for drum 'n' bass; www.dbass.net and www.the breakdown.co.za for drum 'n' bass, hip hop and breaks; www.3am.co.za for hard house and trance; www.psykicks.net for psychedelic trance www.sleaze.co.za and www.recom mended.co.za for house, funk and disco.

Always tip bar staff, especially if you want to get served again. Be nice to the door staff, too. When you leave a club, make sure to order a taxi to pick you up. For reputable taxi companies, *see p248*.

South Africa's bizarre licensing laws mean that, officially, Cape Town closes at 4am – but with the right local connections you can bop till the sun comes up. South Africa also has strict (though inconsistently enforced) laws against recreational substances, so make sure to stay out of trouble. Most clubs open Wednesdays, Fridays and Saturdays, but opening nights change all the time, especially in season when some clubs may be open all week. Because of the changing nature of Cape Town's club scene, always check ahead before setting out.

Clubs

Bossa Nova

43 Somerset Road, Green Point, Atlantic Seaboard (021 425 0295/www.bossanova.com). **Open** 8pm-2am Tue-Sat. **Admission** free. **Credit** MC, V. **Map** p282 G3.

Cape Town's only bona-fide Latino club is so authentic it even offers twice-weekly salsa classes to train the uninitiated. There's a very slick lounge section for the timid, but the focus of the place is the dancefloor, which pulsates with salsa, tango and other Latino flavours all night.

Chilli & Lime

23 Somerset Road, Green Point, Atlantic Seaboard (021 421 3755). **Open** 9pm-5am Wed, Fri, Sat. **Admission** free. **Credit** MC, V. **Map** p282 G3.

A student-orientated venue, which packs the youngsters in with a blend of commercial house, R&B and hip hop. It's famous for its not-so-subtly-labelled 'pigs' night, when you pay R40 and drink as much as your liver can take. From time to time they throw large-scale parties using the outside area.

Cinnamon

Corner Voortrekker & Durban Road, Durbanville, Northern Suburbs (021 948 6000). **Open** 8.30pm-6am Tue-Sat. **Admission** free. **Credit** MC, V.

Cinnamon is a new venue situated in the northern suburbs. Playing a blend of R&B, smooth jazz and house, it is strictly for the laid back only.

Corner House

Glyn Street, City Centre (no phone). **Open** 9pm-4am Wed, Fri, Sat. **Admission** varies. **No credit cards**. **Map** p283 H5.

This tiny little club on the city's fringe has been quietly chugging away for more than 15 years. Its playlist of indie, rock, ska, punk and a little disco does not draw the most glamorous of crowds, but its basic facilities seem to make the punters happy. Watch out for the super-dark dancefloor, surely the closest you'll get to a dark room in a straight club.

Deluxe

Unity House, corner of Long & Longmarket Street, City Centre (021 422 4832). **Open** 10pm-4am Fri, Sat. **Admission** R20. **Credit** MC, V. **Map** p282 G4.

Sophisticated francophonic, deep and tribal house are the order of the night at this sleek, mid-town venue. Models and an over-25 crowd flock here to get down to the latest sounds from Europe. 'Return to the Deep', an ultra-deep house night, takes place here monthly. Retire to the wood-panelled lounge if the dancefloor gets too hectic.

The Fez

38 Hout Street, Greenmarket Square, City Centre (021 423 4889/www.fez.co.za). **Open** 10pm-4am Wed-Sat. **Admission** R30-R40. **Credit** MC, V. **Map** p283 H3.

One of the most popular clubs in Cape Town, this Moroccan-themed venue serves up commercial house and funky anthems to a good-looking, trendy crowd. In summer the club is very popular with young English tourists, drawn by its link to the English chain and the girls in mini skirts. Well known for its great street parties.

Fuse

21 Somerset Road, Green Point, Atlantic Seaboard (021 421 4019). **Open** 10.30pm-6am Wed-Sat. **Admission** R20. **No credit cards**. **Map** p282 G3.

An intimate and sophisticated den, playing the best in soulful and deep house grooves. Its policy of booking DJs for four hours or longer makes for long, sensual journeys. The venue starts slow, but by the wee hours it's cooking. Since the local house scene made it the late-night venue of choice, you'll have to know a local if you want to get in after 4am.

Galaxy

College Road, Rylands Estate, Athlone, Cape Flats, City Bowl (021 637 9132). **Open** 9pm-4am Thur, Fri; 4pm-4am Sat. **Admission** R40. **Credit** MC, V.

Galaxy has been a Cape Flats institution for more than 20 years, situated in the basement of the excellent West End live music jazz venue (*see p187*).

The dance scene

Legend has it that the club used to be used by underground groups plotting against the apartheid government. Nowadays the place is always heaving with punters jiving to hip hop, commercial house and smooth R&B (ask a local to show you how to jazz Cape Town-style).

The Gallery
84 Sir Lowry Road, City Centre (021 461 9649). **Open** 9pm-9am Wed, Fri, Sat. **Admission** R50. **Credit** MC, V. **Map** p283 I4.

The Gallery is home of hard house in Cape Town. If raving till sunrise and beyond is your bag, you're sure to wind up in this banging venue at some point during your visit. It's certainly not as glamorous as large European venues, but has a slightly dodgy charm that, combined with hordes of up-for-it punters, has made it the last port of call on many a legendary night out. Watch out for the Liquid Dream events put on at the Good Hope Centre across the road, and feel free to bring glow-sticks, whistles and other accessories. You won't feel the odd one out.

Gandalf's
299 Lower Main Road, Observatory, Southern Suburbs (no phone). **Open** 9pm-2am Mon-Sat. **Admission** varies. **No credit cards.**

Don't be mislead by the hippie name: this is home of the thrash metal and skate-punk crowd with ridiculously priced drinks specials to boot.

Hanover Street
Grandwest Casino, Goodwood, Northern Suburbs (021 505 7777/www.grandwest.co.za). **Open** 9pm-3am Wed, Fri, Sat. **Admission** R30.

A club in a casino that is better known for its slot-addicted grannies than visits from agents on Her Majesty's Secret Service. Bland R&B and smooth jazz.

Hectic on Hope
69 Hope Street, Gardens, City Bowl (no phone). **Open** 9pm-2am Wed, Fri, Sat. **Admission** varies. **No credit cards. Map** p282 G5.

This venue is a converted pool hall, although you wouldn't think it, now that it houses 'scar' clothing parties that are so popular that even Cape Town's

Arts & Entertainment

Sadly for a region blessed with such stunning natural scenery and a summer season that lasts and lasts, Cape Town still hasn't got a dance festival such as a Homelands or a Tribal Gathering off the ground. However, the city does have some of the best psychedelic trance parties in the world, less than an hour's drive from Cape Town. **Vortex** (021 794 4032/vortexct@mweb.co.za) is now known worldwide for its stunning venues, great productions and international acts at its huge outdoor events. The success of Vortex has resulted in Cape Town mushrooming (if you will excuse the pun) as a venue for psy-trance, when, from December to May, hardly a weekend will go by when you will not be able to lose yourself barefoot in a field. Like all trance promoters, Vortex only reveals its venues once you have purchased your ticket. The first is generally in December, followed by the legendary three-day festivals at New Year and at Easter. To check out the full trance-party calendar for the coming year go to www.psykicks.net.

For the more glamorous among us, namely those of us who like to dress up to go out, there is the **Mother City Queer Project** (021 426 5709/083 309 1553/www.mcqp.co.za). The biggest annual costume party in the world, this has become an institution in Cape Town. It is immensely popular with both gay and straight punters who outdo each other

each year with even more outlandish costumes. The 2004 event is happening in December at the Cape Town International Convention Centre, and the theme is Kitsch Kitchen. For more information on MCQP *see p176* **Dancing queens**.

On the more traditional 'superstar' DJ scene, big names like Roger Sanchez, Erik Morillo, Paul Van Dyk and Hed-kandi are regulars on the scene, particularly in the summer months (for more information, mail rayb@mweb.co.za). Also, look out for big productions from the likes of MTV (www.mtv mash.com) and Thirst (www.heineken music.com). Throw in the Synergy event (jonathan@synergyevents.co.za) that traditionally heralds in the New year for local dance fans and there will be plenty to keep you busy this summer.

electro-clash fashionistas are determined to help this out-of-the-way location find its niche in the Cape Town scene. One of the hippest clubs on the circuit.

Ivory Room
196 Loop Street, City Centre (021 422 3257).
Open 4.30pm-late Wed, Thur; noon-late Fri; 10pm-late Sat. **Admission** free. **Credit** AmEx, DC, MC, V. **Map** p282 G4.
This is another upmarket venue aiming at models and wannabe millionaires. It's a members-only club, supposedly, but if you have the right look – and the right cash – you should get in. There's a sophisticated bar and lounge with a tight dancefloor and an even tighter 'look at me everyone' veranda area.

The Lounge
194 Long Street, City Centre (021 424 7636).
Open 9pm-1am Wed, Fri, Sat. **Admission** R10. **Credit** MC, V. **Map** p282 G4.
Some might say characterful, some might say grungy. But this small upstairs venue, with a long veranda over Long Street, has made an extended

and interesting contribution to the local scene. Tight and intimate breaks (interesting and innovative) and house nights happen here.

Mercury Live & Mercury Lounge
43 De Villiers Street, Zonnebloem, City Bowl (021 465 2106/www.mercuryl.co.za). **Open** 9pm-late Mon-Sat. **Admission** free-R40. **Credit** MC, V. **Map** p283 H5.
Sean Wienand and Kevin Winder are running this new venture, which, they say, aims to be 'clean, fresh, retro, warm and open'. Mercury holds a jam session every Tuesday; Wednesday and Thursday are for live bands; and club nights 'Shaken not Stirred' and 'Straight no Chaser' complete the week on Friday and Saturday. Both of these nights feature a mix of alternative lounge, acid jazz, soul, blues, Latin and Motown.

169
169 Long Street, City Centre (021 426 1107).
Open 10pm-5am Wed-Sat. **Admission** free-R40. **Credit** MC, V. **Map** p282 G4.

This is a rocking first-floor venue that throbs with bump and grind, bling bling and more than a smattering of mean characters every weekend. A rough and ready affair that's not for the fainthearted.

Onverklaar.bar

Main Road, Hermanus, Whale Route (028 312 1679). **Open** 7pm-2am Mon-Thur; 7pm-4am Sat, Sun. **Admission** free-R10. **No credit cards.**

This funky little DJ-bar is situated on our own little Riviera on the other side of the Overberg. In summer, during the whale festival and every weekend, this intimate, atmospheric venue rocks to tunes from some of the biggest names in Cape Town. From Sundays to Thursdays out of season it is a chilled pool bar – and still worth a visit.

Organafix

32 Glynn Street, City Centre (no phone). **Open** 9pm-4am Wed, Fri, Sat. **Admission** varies. **No credit cards. Map** p283 H5.

Organafix is the indoor home of psychedelic trance. This is where serious clubbers come to do long-term preperation for those marathon trance events that Cape Town is so famous for.

New Dockside

Century Boulevard, Century City, Milnerton, Northern Suburbs (021 552 7303/www.dockside superclub.com). **Open** 9pm-4am Wed, Fri, Sat. **Admission** R20-R40. **Credit** MC, V.

Cape Town's 'super-club' is a four-storey, purpose-built 'entertainment palace'. It has multiple venues with state-of-the-art sound and lighting, including everything from a sports pub to a jazz café and an impressive three-floor main arena; New Dockside is being increasingly used for hard-house events from the likes of Nucleus and Tidy Trax. One-stop entertainment mecca or cheesy shopping mall experience? The jury is out, though bar prices are the lowest you'll find in clubland.

Rhodes House

60 Queen Victoria Road, City Centre (021 424 8844/ www.rhodeshouse.com). **Open** 10pm-4am Thur-Sat. **Admission** R50. **Credit** AmEx, DC, MC, V. **Map** p282 G4.

This converted mansion is the venue of choice for the rich and infamous of the summer set. Models, B-grade actors, mafiosi, Euro trash, millionaires and more models rub shoulders and wallets in this beautifully styled, multi-roomed venue. The dancefloor appears to be something of an afterthought – but with all the beautiful people to stare at, who cares? In summer, dress up, bring a tan, platinum card and as many models as you can carry; in winter, the place keeps punters busy with its Thursday R&B nights and some surprisingly original theme events.

Snap

6 Pepper Street, off Long Street, City Centre (no phone). **Open** 9am-1am Wed, Fri, Sat. **Admission** varies. **No credit cards. Map** p282 G4.

The only place in the City Centre where you are likely to hear the sound of the townships – kwaito – played regularly. With a playlist that stretches into R&B, hip hop, house and African flavours, Snap attracts a cosmopolitan crowd from all over Africa. With visiting DJs from Jo'burg stations like Metro and Y, Snap is probably the most authentic urban African club in Cape Town.

Sutra Groove Bar

86 Loop Street, City Centre (021 422 4218). **Open** 10pm-4am Wed, Fri, Sat. **Admission** R20. **Credit** AmEx, DC, MC, V. **Map** p282 G4.

A stylish, two-floored, Eastern-themed ('it's karma, baby') venue. The two lounge areas have an opulent, opium-den feel – a class above the sadly concrete-floored dancefloor. Quality sound, beautiful staff, good line-ups and some very sexy locals (especially at Wednesday night R&B sessions) make it a must for the young urbanite on the town.

Uhuru International

88 Shortmarket Street, City Centre (no phone). **Open** 9pm-2am Wed, Fri, Sat. **Admission** varies. **No credit cards. Map** p282 G3.

An reggae, ragga and dub club that is not always open. But when it is, it never fails to pull the fans of this ever-growing, local dance-music community. *See also p189* **The beat of the African soul.**

Upstairs

Pepper Street, off Long Street, City Centre (082 218 9943). **Open** 10pm-4am Wed-Sat. **Admission** free. **Credit** MC, V. **Map** p282 G4.

The former 'architects bar' above Mama Africa is a very cute and casual, friendly groove bar that plays host to all kinds of beat events – everything from techno to deep house. It has two great outside terraces that are perfect spots to chill and listen to the sirens and sounds of the city at night.

The Valve

Ou Kerk Gebou, 32 Parliament Street, City Centre (no phone). **Open** 8pm-2am Wed, Fri, Sat. **Admission** varies. **No credit cards. Map** p283 H4.

More of a venue than a club, but used on such a regular basis it deserves a mention. The acoustics in this old art deco cinema are, well, pretty shocking, but the grandeur of the place makes up for it. It's named after its centrepiece, a huge, three-metre speaker valve that is still in use.

VUDU lounge

79 Church Street, Heritage Square, City Centre (021 426 0275/www.dbass.net/vudulounge). **Open** 10pm-6am Wed-Sat. **Admission** free. **No credit cards. Map** p282 G4.

This new kid on the block has been struggling to find its identity, trying out a number of varied crowds and musical styles for size. But its intimate dancefloor, funky outdoor patio and inner-city location means that it will be around for at least one more summer season (no mean feat in Cape Town).

Sport & Fitness

The perfect wind, waves and weather for extreme fun.

Active sports

Athletics

Cape Town has such beautiful surroundings that it also boasts some of the most scenic running in the world, the highlight being the epic **Two Oceans Marathon** in April (www.twooceansmarathon.org.za), arguably the most spectacular ultra-marathon in the world. You'll need to enter early, but, if you do miss out, the road-running calendar is a year-long affair. Contact **Western Province Athletics** (021 699 0614) to find details of what's happening where; also try the **Celtic Harriers Athletic Club** (021 705 1461).

Badminton

This is not a mainstream sport in the Western Cape, but try the **Western Province Badminton Association** (021 671 5233) if you're into shuttlecocks.

Bowling

No longer the sole domain of senior citizens, lawn bowls is growing in popularity across the Cape. It's nothing if not relaxing.

Milnerton Bowling Club *Bridge Road, Milnerton, Northern Suburbs (021 551 6452).*
Mowbray Bowling Club *Cecil Road, Mowbray, Southern Suburbs (021 689 1617).*
Western Province Bowling Association *Fountain Medical Centre, Adderley Street, City Centre (021 421 1894).* **Map** p283 H3.

Cricket

Club cricket is particularly popular in Cape Town, but the more social form of the game is also strongly supported. Call the **Western Province Cricket Association** (021 657 2003/ www.wpca.cricket.org) for a club in your area – most clubs are more than happy to let you join in net sessions, and you may well have the chance of getting a game.

Cycling

Capetonians love their cycling, and at the weekend the city is swarming with bicycles. Contact the **Pedal Power Association** (021 689 8420/www.pedalpower.org.za) for details of the next race or organised ride.

Commercial operators supply bikes and back-up to and from Cape Point at a rate of about R500 per person for a half day. Try **Baz Bus** (021 439 2323/www.bazbus.com) or **Downhill Adventures** (021 422 0388/ www.downhilladventures.com). A number of tours are also run by **Day Trippers** (021 511 4766/www.daytrippers.co.za).

Golf

The Western Cape is home to some really fantastic golf courses with, we like to think, some of the best views and settings of any clubs in the world. Caddies, golf carts and clubs are available for hire at most clubs. Note that tee-off times are often booked well in advance, so be sure to phone ahead.

Arabella Golf Club

Just outside the coastal town of Hermanus, 1hr from Cape Town (028 284 9383). **Fees** per 18 holes R425. **Credit** AmEx, DC, MC, V.

This is a splendid setting for a very demanding course. The Arabella hosted the Nelson Mandela Invitational in 2003, and it remains one of South Africa's foremost courses.

Atlantic Beach Golf Club

Birkenhead Drive, Melkbosstrand, West Coast (080 465 3258). **Fees** per 18 holes R245 (no caddies allowed on the course). **Credit** AmEx, DC, MC, V.

This links-style course has a distinguishing feature in its very narrow fairways. This can become quite a challenge to even experienced golfers when gusts of wind come up off the Atlantic Ocean, which runs parallel to the course.

Erinvale Golf Estate

Lourensford Road, Somerset West, Winelands (021 847 1906). **Fees** per 18 holes R495. **Credit** AmEx, DC, MC, V.

This unforgiving course hosts the South African Open, and also hosted the Golf World Cup in 1996. The overall layout is beautiful.

Fancourt, Montagu, Outeniqua, Bramble Hill & The Links at Fancourt

Just outside the town of George, Garden Route (044 804 0010/www.fancourt.co.za). **Fees** per 18 holes R525. **Credit** AmEx, DC, MC, V.

This complex can easily claim to be the jewel in South Africa's golfing crown. Home to Ernie Els among others, Fancourt has four world-class courses, including the Links at Fancourt, which hosted the 2003 President's Cup.

Paarl Golf Club

Wemmershoek Road, Paarl, Winelands (021 863 1140). **Fees** per 18 holes R250. **Credit** AmEx, DC, MC, V.

The Paarl club offers all the necessary amenities in a lovely, wind-protected setting alongside the Berg River. The fairways are lined with lovely old trees.

Pezula Golf Course

Sparrebosch, Knysna, Garden Route (044 384 1222). **Fees** per 18 holes R1,000 (including mandatory golf cart – no caddies on the course). **Credit** AmEx, DC, MC, V.

Is there a more spectacular setting on the continent? Located on the heads at Knysna, with the cliffs dropping away to the ocean below, it's worth it for the views alone – and the course is magnificent.

Rondebosch Golf Club

Klipfontein Road, Rondebosch, Southern Suburbs (021 689 4176). **Fees** per 18 holes R290. **Credit** AmEx, DC, MC, V.

This picturesque course sits at the foot of Table Mountain; its landscape is not too tough to negotiate and is very centrally located. Give it a try.

Cycling. *See p197 and p199.*

Royal Cape Golf Club

174 Ottery Road, Wynberg, Southern Suburbs (021 761 6551). **Fees** per 18 holes R500. **Credit** AmEx, DC, MC, V.

The Royal Cape is one of South Africa's finest courses, and it makes regular appearances on the country's professional tour schedule.

Stellenbosch Golf Club

Strand Road, Stellenbosch, Winelands (021 880 0103). **Fees** per 18 holes R250. **Credit** AmEx, DC, MC, V. **Map** p278 P3.

Stellenbosch is a tree-lined course just outside the town of Stellenbosch. It's not overly challenging and is conveniently close to a number of wine estates – a combination which can make for a great day out.

Hockey

Hockey is one of South Africa's fastest-growing sports, and a number of AstroTurf surfaces have been built in the last few years. Contact the **Western Province Hockey Association** (021 448 2656/www.wphockey.org.za) for a local club if you're interested in playing.

Horse riding

With the Cape's beautiful weather (as long as the wind isn't blowing) and gorgeous landscapes, we would thoroughly recommend horse riding while you are here. Call a riding centre to organise an outride for you and your friends, in vineyards, forests or on the beach.

The Dunes *Noordhoek, False Bay (021 789 1723).*
Horse Trail Safaris *Schaapkraal Road, Philippi, Southern Suburbs (021 703 4396).*
Noordhoek Beach Rides *Kommetjie Road, Noordhoek, False Bay (082 774 1191).*
Riding Centre *Main Road, Hout Bay, Atlantic Seaboard (021 790 5286).*
Sleepy Hollow Horse Riding *Sleepy Hollow Lane, Noordhoe, False Bay (021 789 2341).*

Arts & Entertainment

Ice-skating

Ice-skating in Africa? It is possible. The **Ice Station at Grandwest Casino** (021 505 7777) offers an international-quality ice rink, with skates available to hire and plenty of space.

Rugby

Rugby is religion in South Africa, and the Cape is certainly no different. Contact the **Western Province Rugby Association** (021 659 4500/ www.wprugby.co.za), who will point you in the direction of a suitable club.

Sailing

Sailing on a balmy summer's evening is an understandably popular Cape Town pastime, with all manner of boats taking to the waters – and frequently looking for competent crew. To sign up your services just check out the yacht club noticeboards. Wednesday night is racing night at the Royal Cape Yacht Club. You can either go to watch or take part.

False Bay Yacht Club *Simonstown Harbour, Simonstown, False Bay (021 786 1703).*
Royal Cape Yacht Club *Table Bay Harbour, Foreshore, City Centre (021 421 1354).*
Western Province Sailing Association *Milnerton, Northern Suburbs (021 511 0929).*

Sports & leisure centres

The well-appointed **Sports Science Institute** (Boundary Road, Newlands, Southern Suburbs, 021 659 5600) offers full gym, indoor track and heated swimming pool, and expert training advice. Likewise, Richard Branson's global chain of fitness centres, **Virgin Active**, is represented at various sites throughout Cape Town. To find the gym nearest to you, call the head office on 021 710 8500. Both centres offer daily, weekly and monthly rates.

Squash

You'll find plenty of squash courts around the Cape, but you'll generally need to provide your own rackets and balls. Call the **Western Province Squash Association** (021 686 7462) to find the courts nearest to you.

Tennis

Tennis courts abound in the Western Cape (mostly hard courts) – contact the **Western Province Tennis Association** (021 686 3055) to find the one that is closest to you.

Ten-pin bowling

Not a real sport? Wait till the competition gets going. Drop by the **Stadium Bowl** (Stadium-on-Main, Main Road, Claremont, Southern Suburbs, 021 671 1893). And yes, those cool shoes are available for hire.

Spectator Sports

Cricket

International cricketers regularly identify the Newlands Cricket Ground, under the shadow of Table Mountain, as a favourite. The domestic season runs from September to March, and the Western Province team (which includes national stars Graeme Smith, Jacques Kallis, Herschelle Gibbs, Gary Kirsten and Paul Adams) offers quality action. Four-day games see minimal crowds, but day-night matches draw several thousand spectators, particularly to the grass bank, where the beer flows and the atmosphere is particularly festive.

Provincial cricket is also played in the Boland, local rivals to Western Province, at the small but delightful Boland Park in Paarl, which is situated an hour out of Cape Town in the heart of the winelands.

The international cricket circuit also stops in at Newlands regularly – look out for the England team at the end of the year. One-day internationals usually see a full house, so it's essential to get your tickets early.

Boland Park *Langenhoven Street, Paarl, Winelands (021 862 4580).*
Newlands Cricket Ground *Camp Ground Road, Newlands, Southern Suburbs (012 657 3300).*
Newlands Ticket Hotline *Newlands, Southern Suburbs (021 657 2099).*

Cycling

The highlight of the cycling calendar is the **Pick 'n' Pay Cape Argus Cycle Tour** (021 083 910 6551/www.cycletour.co.za) held in March. With some 35,000 riders participating, it is the biggest timed cycle race on the planet. Stake out your vantage point early, and enjoy a buzzing day in the sun as the city shuts down and goes wheely crazy. The route returned to Chapman's Peak in 2004, making an already beautiful ride more so – check out the website for details of the race in 2005.

Those keen for regular action should contact the **Pedal Power Association** (021 689 8420/ www.pedalpower.org.za) for information about meetings at the **Bellville Velodrome** (Carl Cronje Drive, Bellville, 021 949 7450).

Geared up for the game

World-class stadiums, quality matches and some of the most enthusiastic fans you'll meet – Cape Town is a great destination for the holidaying sports fan. Cape Town fans are cheerfully singleminded, particularly when it comes to the Sharks (Durban's rugby side) or anything Australian, so supporting the local side is always a good move.

Still with rugby, **Newlands Rugby Stadium** (*see p201*) is home to the regional Stormers (dress in black) in the Super 12 tournament, and Western Province (blue and white) for the Currie Cup – the crowds tend to be a little parochial, but if 'our' team is on a winning streak, expect a buzzing crowd of 50,000 screaming supporters.

South African rugby goes hand-in-hand with *boerewors* (local sausage) and Castle lager beer, so stock up for the complete experience. The same carb-heavy diet applies to cricket, with a *braai* (barbecue) on the grass bank at **Newlands Cricket Ground** a time-honoured Cape tradition (*see p199*).

The grass bank is the centre of attention, usually home to noisy students, colourful supporters, and plenty of Mexican waves.

Listen out for the most amusing impromptu sports commentary in the country from within the ranks of supporters – and persistent attempts by the locals to engage and distract opposition fielders in conversation when they come near to the boundary (particularly when trying to take a catch).

Soccer (football) is a different affair entirely – unless Kaizer Chiefs or Orlando Pirates are in town (and if they are, don't miss the most vibrant fans in the country), the crowds are fairly small, but make up for it with a barrage of noise. The plastic trumpets will probably drive you crazy, but the locals love them. Dutch fans may wish to follow Ajax Cape Town (in red and white), and the Greeks Hellenic (blue); for everyone else there's Santos (yellow), who're known as 'The Peoples' Team' (*see below*).

Generally in Cape Town, you'll encounter a love of the game (whichever it may be) and robust sporting debate to go with it. But wandering around in an Australian jersey isn't advisable – two Cricket World Cups are hard to forget, and Capetonians have longer memories than most.

Football

Cape Town has three teams in South Africa's national Premier Soccer League, which is the top division in the country. **Santos** (who were national champions in 2001/2002) and **Hellenic** both play at the Athlone Stadium, while **Ajax Cape Town** (directly affiliated to the Dutch club Ajax Amsterdam) plays home games at Newlands Rugby Stadium.

Unlike the often astronomical expense of seeing a game in England, ticket prices here are fixed nationally at R20, making matches excellent value for money. The season runs from August to May.

Soccer is an incredibly popular sport in the Cape, with many of the stars becoming heroes to the young hopefuls in the townships who practise their hearts out to get to the same level.

Ajax Cape Town *Frans Conradie Drive, Parow, Northern Suburbs (021 993 0601).*
Hellenic *324 Lansdowne Road, Lansdowne, Southern Suburbs (021 697 1104).*
Santos *Klipfontein Road, Rondebosch, Southern Suburbs (021 685 7172).*
Western Province Soccer Association *Harleyvale Stadium, Observatory, Southern Suburbs (021 448 1648).*

Golf

Look out for two major golf tournaments in the Western Cape. The **SAA (South African Airways) South African Open** is played in January at Erinvale Golf Estate (Lournesford Road, Somerset West, Winelands, 021 847 1906) and forms part of the European Tour. The event attracts a host of top international golfers. The **Vodacom Players Championship**, held in December at Royal Cape (174 Ottery Road, Wynberg, Southern Suburbs, 021 761 6551), is a highlight of the South African tour. It features the cream of SA's up-and-coming talent. Contact **Sunshine Tours** (021 850 6500/www.sunshinetour.co.za) for more info.

Horse racing

The horses go racing every Wednesday and Saturday in Cape Town at two race courses, Kenilworth and Durbanville. The highlight of the year is the **J&B Met** (February).

Durbanville Race Course *Bowlers Way, Durbanville, Northern Suburbs (021 975 2524).*
Kenilworth Race Course *Rosmead Avenue, Kenilworth, Southern Suburbs (021 700 1600).*

Ice-skating

Contact the **Western Province Figure Skating Association** (021 557 8520) for information about when local Torvills and Deans are hitting the ice.

Motor sport

The majority of motor sport in the region happens at the **Killarney Motor Racing Circuit** (Rotsdam Road, Killarney Gardens, Tableview, 021 557 1639/www.wpmc.co.za), with everything from drag racing to karts to saloons slugging it out.

Rugby

A packed house at Newlands Rugby Stadium is a truly thrilling sight, and one you have a fair chance of catching during the year. The Stormers, the Western Cape franchise outfit, play at Newlands in the Super 12 tournament from February to May alongside the best sides from South Africa, Australia and New Zealand, and draw regular crowds of 50,000.

Then, from July to November, the Currie Cup is contested, as South Africa's provinces battle it out for the country's most coveted domestic trophy. The Western Province is a traditional powerhouse, and regularly fields a number of national players in their side. Elsewhere in the region, the Boland Cavaliers and South West Districts Eagles play in the same competition. The two sides are based in Wellington and George respectively.

Look out for this year's international at Newlands, when South Africa will be taking on Ireland. Contact the **Western Province Rugby Association** (021 659 4500) or go to www.superrugby.co.za for details, as well as information on the Super 12 and Currie Cup.

Where to watch

South African sports channel SuperSport covers an almost embarrassing amount of sport (English visitors often comment with some surprise that there seems to be more Premiership football shown in South Africa than in England). Most international cricket, rugby, football, golf, tennis and motor sport gets shown live, and much more. So if your hotel doesn't have what you're looking for, check out a local sports bar – they're sure to have what you're after.

River Club *Observatory Road, Observatory, Southern Suburbs (021 448 6117).*
Sports Café *V&A Waterfront, Atlantic Seaboard (021 419 5558).* **Map** p283 H1.

Extreme sports

With two seas and a mountain spine, hot summers and plenty of wind, Cape Town is not short of options on the extreme-sports front. Just remember that weather is the key. If Capetonians are renowned for not making up their minds till the last minute, it's because, meteorologically speaking, anything can happen – and probably will.

The trick is to make this work for you, so start by learning how to tell where the wind is blowing from by how the clouds form over Table Mountain. And then just hop, skip and jump across to whichever side is best for the sport you want to do that day. For example, is summer's good old 'Cape Doctor', the south-easter, howling just when you want to go sea-kayaking? No problem: head for Three Anchor Bay, which sits neatly in the lee of the wind, and paddle out for a stunning sundowner off Camps Bay and Clifton. Is the north-wester giving the Atlantic Seaboard a beating? Well, there'll be a great swell if you're into surfing. Otherwise, pop over to Smitswinkel or one of the other cool dive spots on the False Bay coast, where the sea will be flatter than you can imagine, and underwater visibility good. A gentle breeze? It's paragliding time. If the wind comes up a bit more, quickly whip out that kiteboard or windsurfer. If it rains? Hop on the mountain bike and into the forest. When it gets dark, head to Lion's Head from where the sunset view over the sea is fabulous.

Cape Town's extreme-sports community generally has all the right credentials to ensure you're safe and well looked after – there are lots of competitors and generally only the best operators survive. In fact, recent regulations have ensured that even the more specialist adventure guides need to have basic tourism qualifications, so while the dude with the dreads is busy clipping in your harness, feel free to quiz him about the pretty little red flower next to your foot before you step over that cliff. And ask him a bit about the who's who of his sport in the Cape. This city is home to some real legends – guys and girls who are at the top of their game, have pulled off some pretty impressive firsts all over the world, been there, won some hot contests, done that and never flaunted the T-shirt. But start asking a few questions, and you'll find it's not hard to be invited to the inner circle.

ONE-STOP SHOPS

For some great motivation and an easy way to book any adventure, the **Adventure Village** (021 424 1580/www.adventure-village.co.za) at the top of Long Street in Cape Town, is worth

Quad-biking with **Downhill Adventures**. *See p197.*

a visit. Otherwise, try the **No Limits Centre** (021 434 3175/www.capetownnolimits.com) where Tanya will also fill you in on what's happening in the movie industry. For tailored group events, **180 Degrees Adventures** are your guys. Contact them at 021 712 6960/www.180.co.za. And, further afield, namely the Garden Route, it's Knysna's **The Heads Adventure Centre** (044 384 0831/www.headsadventurecentre.co.za).

Abseiling

This activity is perfectly safe and absolutely thrilling. Devised when the first climbers realised they could safely slide down a rope when they'd got to the top, rather than having to laboriously crawl to the ground, abseiling only recently became popular as an activity in its own right. Very strict safety regulations are enforced by the commercial operators, requiring all equipment to have extremely high breaking strains (no worries about that spare tyre you're carrying – their ropes can take a few tons more) and back-ups in place. The operator has the skill; you just do as you're told, step off the cliff and don't look down.

Great venues abound all over Cape Town, but top of the pops has to be the big-view number (said to be the highest commercial abseil in the world) off Table Mountain, which costs R350 and is run by **Abseil Africa** (021 424 4760/www.abseilafrica.co.za).

Further afield, you can also abseil the **Knysna Heads** (044 384 0831/ www.headsadventurecentre.co.za) for R200.

Adventure racing

You may have seen the TV coverage of Raid Gauloises, Eco-Challenge and the like. Footage of teams (usually four people, at least one

woman) navigating their way by day and by night, non-stop, on foot, by bike, paddling, climbing, swimming... an endless repertoire of agony. Well, the sport is alive and kicking in Cape Town, with one of the world's best teams, Team Mazda Drifter, putting the SA scene on the map by coming fourth in the Fiji Eco-Challenge (the highest-ever slot for a rookie team). They reckon the variety of training terrain here gives them the edge, so hey, if it's good enough for them... The AR people here are a garrulous bunch, so if you're keen to get into the sport and need some contacts or advice, go to www.ar.co.za. Webmaster Lisa de Speville will spare you nothing: races, venues, reports, advice, contacts and much more.

Island Eco Adventures

Stilbaai, Southern Cape (082 455 2875/ www.outthere.co.za).
This offers a number of longer, tougher races through stunning parts of the Cape, such as the Karoo's Swartberg in April and the Wilderness Wildman race through the Garden Route in June.

On Track Club

Stellenbosch, Winelands (021 976 6898/ www.ontrackclub.co.za).
The On Track Club offers a good short-course series that makes a great introduction to the sport of adventure racing.

Angling

The Cape is renowned for its tuna, yellowtail and snoek, but your offshore options include dorado, marlin, swordfish and a whole range of biggies. The tuna season is from September to June. You can expect to pay about R750 for half a day's fishing on a boat.

In the cold winter months, the fishermen themselves make for good entertainment, with the rocks and beaches of the entire Peninsula dotted with light tackle enthusiasts trying for snoek – often on fly. After all, even novices can catch five-kilogram (11-pound) beauties here with a bit of luck on their side.

On the other side of False Bay, the Rooikrans cliffs are famous for all the crosses marking the final fishing spots of those who got caught by the dangerous currents themselves. Inland, the fast-running mountain streams are home to wild rainbow and brown trout. Franschhoek is best known for its 'salmon trout'– the fishing's great but the eating is even better.

Adventure Village *229 Long Street, City Centre (021 424 1580/www.adventurevillage.co.za).* **Map** p282 G4.
Hooked on Africa *Hout Bay, Atlantic Seaboard (021 790 5332/ www.hookedonafrica.co.za).*

Bungee-jumping & bridge-swinging

Because jumping off a perfectly good bridge into thin air with nothing but a big elastic band for support goes against all our most basic survival instincts, bungee-jumping is perceived to be extreme. It's actually not dangerous at all – it's an extremely safe big thrill. No skill is required, even for the world's highest commercial jump: **Face Adrenalin**'s (042 281 1458/www.faceadrenalin.com) 216-metre (708-feet) leap off Bloukrans Bridge just the other side of the Garden Route, which costs R550. Gourits River bridge near Mossel Bay, also on the Garden Route, offers a quarter of that height (but almost as much thrill) for R170, as well as a 'swing' from the parallel road bridge for R120. If you're game you can try them in tandem for R150 in total. **Wildthing Adventures** can also organise a jump for you. Contact them on 021 423 5804/www.wildthing.co.za.

Climbing & mountaineering

Some of the climbing world's legends live in Cape Town. The rest come to visit, for the mountain chain offers an extraordinary range of routes, both sports (where some kind soul has already placed bolts all the way up the rock for you to safely clip your rope into at regular intervals) and trad (climbing based on the more traditional method of placing 'pro' (protection) in tiny cracks and crevices in the rock, and then clipping your rope through this for safety).

Once again, the weather brings all sorts of options and limitations: when one side of the Peninsula is wet or salt-blasted and slippery, simply head for the other side. There are crags all the way above Muizenberg, Kalk Bay and beyond, as well as great lines on some of the

Twelve Apostles. And if it's all wet, head up to the famous Cedarberg, a rocky semi-desert renowned for its bouldering (imagine the rock as a jungle gym, with a cushion placed underneath it to fall onto). Montagu is home to classic crags such as 'Lego Land' and 'Chocolate Speedway', which both offer good entry-level routes and plenty of company.

If you're the big-wall type, head for the Klein Winterhoek mountains and seek out the Milner Amphitheatre, where Andy de Klerk and Pete Samuelsson climbed 'Oceans of Fear' and then jumped from the top, parachutes in hand, for a charming and exhilarating film by the Fresh Air Crew that won an award at the Banff Film Festival a few years back.

Closer to home, **City Rock** (Woodstock, Southern Suburbs, 021 447 1326) is the indoor climbing gym to see and be seen hanging out in. If you are into these sports, make contact with the **Mountain Club of SA** (City Centre, 021 465 3412/www.mcsa.org.za) as well as with the **Cape Town School of Mountaineering** (Pinelands, Southern Suburbs/www.ctsm.co.za).

Diving

Cape Town does not offer the best diving in the country, but it's far better than its reputation would have you believe. And full of surprises too – imagine looking up to find out why the water suddenly became so dark, only to find a whale cruising by just inches above you. Or try swimming through kelp forests with seals, or searching a shipwreck for silver and cutlery (not to be removed, of course). The Cape waters generally deem a five-millimetre (0.2-inch) wetsuit a must, with hood and gloves not just for the softies and beginners. Great diving sites include Coral Gardens near Oudekraal (not strictly coral, but beautifully colourful nonetheless), past Camps Bay on the Atlantic seaboard; shipwrecks just off Hout Bay; and Smitswinkel Marine Reserve. Snorkellers should try getting in just beyond Simonstown's Boulders Beach to have a swim with the lovely penguins, or under the Thesens jetty in Knysna for close encounters with the rare, but increasingly well-protected, seahorses.

Remember once again that the Atlantic and False Bay sides will offer very different sea conditions – with the former generally the better summer option during south-easters, and the latter frequently a fantastic (and surprisingly warm) winter option.

Of course, with the exchange rate currently on the side of tourists (not to mention the industry's cut-throat competitiveness), South Africa is a great spot to get your scuba qualification, if you haven't already done so.

Arts & Entertainment

Shark-cage diving. *See below.*

For a general idea of prices, you can expect to pay R190 for boat dives; R90 for shore entry; R210 equipment rental.

Champion Divers *Diep River, Southern Suburbs (021 706 1595/www.championdivers.co.za).*
Orca Industries *Claremont, Southern Suburbs (021 671 9673).*
Pisces Divers *91 Kloofnek Street, Tamboerskloof, City Bowl (021 422 4026/ www.piscesdivers.co.za).*
Pro Divers *Shop 88b, Main Road, Sea Point, Atlantic Seaboard (021 433 0472/ www.prodiverssa.co.za).*
Scuba Shack *Glencairn Shopping Centre, Glencairn, False Bay (021 782 7358/ www.scuba-shack.co.za).*

And did we mention the shark-cage diving? You don't actually have to be a qualified scuba diver to get up close and personal with the infamous jaws of a Great White. The increased numbers of shark attacks and incidents in recent years are frequently blamed on this industry, which 'chums' with bloody or oily fish to attract the sharks to their boats, in so doing – goes the argument – familiarising these fearsome creatures with humans. The debate has been heated, but the industry is now strictly regulated: very few permits are issued, and a great deal has been achieved by the operators themselves in the name of research. You decide. It costs about R1,000 – including transport, meals and all equipment.

Ecoventures *Gansbaai, West Coast (021 532 0470/www.white-shark-diving.com).*
Shark Africa *Mossel Bay, Garden Route (044 691 3796).*
Shark Diving Unlimited *Gansbaai, West Coast (028 384 2787/www.sharkdivingunlimited.co.za).*

4x4

'Tread lightly' has become the refrain in 4x4 circles after the brash minority caused so much trouble that driving on the beach was banned in South Africa a couple of years ago. While anglers, divers and others who relied on their vehicles to give them sea access are still up in arms and petitioning Environmental Minister Valli Moosa, you can see the positive results all along the Cape shoreline, where the threatened African Black Oystercatcher and other birds that lay their eggs in scrapings in the sand are making a dramatic comeback.

Ignoring those who see 4x4s merely as motorised toy boxes to get their boats to the water or bikes to the mountains, there are generally two motivations in stepping up into these trendy, comfortable and generally rather stylish vehicles – you want to put your driving skills and cool-under-fire attitude to the test, over a tough, technical course. Or you see the vehicle as a sweat-free way of getting deep into the great outdoors, with the luxury of a cooler-box set to continual chill. Either way, the Western Cape has the options.

Klipbokkop Mountain Resort Trail
Outside Worcester on the N1 (082 579 4515/ www.klipbokkop.co.za). **Rate** R200/vehicle.
No credit cards.
This is widely regarded as the best trail in the country. It's renowned for the excellence of its training, and another incentive to visit is the high-speed, expert driver training offered by SA rally legend Sarel van der Merwe.

MontEco 4x4 Adventure Trails
Near Montagu (0800 628 873/www.monteco-nature-reserve.com). **Rate** R180/vehicle. **Credit** AmEx, DC, MC, V.
These trails include seven options to test your abilities in a wilderness environment, as well as giving you a taste of Cape fynbos and Karoo succulent flora types, with rock-art viewing, hiking and mountain-biking to fill in those remaining waking hours.

Vleesbaai Dune Route
Just off the N2 not far from Mossel Bay, Garden Route (044 699 1107). **Rate** R130/vehicle.
No credit cards.
The Vleesbaai route really tests sand-driving abilities, dishing up some wonderful dune and beach scenery along its 12-km (seven-mile) course.

Hiking

Table Mountain just has to be your first choice. Clearly marked routes include Platteklip Gorge which heads up from Tafelberg Road, just past the cable station, and Nursery Ravine, also straight up, behind Kirstenbosch.

The way of the winds

Any surfer visiting Cape Town should know that there are three main wind directions that will determine where you will find the best waves: the off-shore south-easter, which comes directly over Table Mountain; the north-wester, which blows onshore from the direction of Robben Island into the city; and the south-wester.

The south-easter – aka the 'Cape Doctor' – is most prevalent in the warmer months, but all it does is blow the swell flat and the water seriously cold... unless it happens immediately after a spell of the north-wester, which is most prevalent in winter and sinks container vessels like they're dry leaves. The south-wester is just plain annoying. The bottom line is that if there is any swell around, a gentle south-easter will clean up most spots on the Atlantic seaboard from Melkbosstrand and Blouberg to the north, down to Kommetjie in the south. When the north-wester starts to blow, you will need to travel further south, towards Witsand and Slangkop, and east to Muizenberg and False Bay, where it will be blowing offshore.

You'll have noticed, no doubt, that Cape Town straddles the Atlantic and Indian oceans. Although there is a slight difference in water temperatures between them, don't expect the Indian side to be warm enough to surf in baggies. Surfing in Cape Town requires a minimum of four millimeters (0.1 inches) of neoprene. Especially in summer.

Popular spots in the northern regions include Big Bay and Derde Steen along the M14 between Blouberg and Melkbosstrand. Closer to town, you could try your luck along the reefs off Beach Road Boulevard in Sea Point, although we'd recommend you stick around to befriend some of the locals first, if only to glean where the channels are. Clifton isn't really an option, and neither is Camps Bay, but further south along the M6 you'll find Llandudno beach, which can get crowded and ball-achingly cold, but usually sports a wave because of its steep banks.

Dungeons is our big wave break, but you'll need a boat and any balls you haven't frozen off yet because it is a genuine growler. If you have brought your gun, the thing to do would be to bring it to the harbour in Hout Bay where – if the conditions are right, and buddy you'll know when they're right – you'll spot some lunatics as crazy as you loading their

gear into a boat. They'll probably be either mad or impressed enough to fit you in.

If you're up to it, Noordhoek beach is a worthwhile effort, but it will mean a 15-minute hike along the expansive sands towards the middle, where the better waves will be found. Further south is Kommetjie, where the most popular spot in Cape Town is. You can't miss Long Beach (or, as the locals have somewhat bitterly dubbed it, Throng Beach). Five minutes away, on the other side of the town, is the world-famous Outer Kom, a big wave left. It's important to be careful over the rocks – they can be dangerous.

The M65 around the cliffs will bring you to Witsand, a spectacular beach which works in a north-west wind. This goes all the way around into the reserve and out along the yellow Indian Ocean beaches of False Bay: Fish Hoek, Muizenberg and the entire expanse along Baden Powell Drive. Take your pick. The waves in False Bay aren't only slightly warmer, they're also much friendlier.

For the most part, South African surfers are chilled, but isolated incidents of localism have been known to occur. Fortunately, any unpleasantness can usually be diffused with a nod of greeting upon paddling into the line-up and a friendly 'Howzit!'

The Cape of Good Hope Trail

Cape Peninsula. Bookings Cape Peninsula National Park, False Bay (021 701 8692 /www.cpnp.co.za).
Rate R35; R10 children. **Credit** AmEx, DC, MC, V.
This trail is an under-utilised, two-day, 34-km (21-mile) circular route with accommodation at an overnight hut. It's flat walking, though not always easy, depending on tides.

Postberg Flower Trail

Near Langebaan, on the West Coast (bookings 022 772 2144).
Not at all tough, this is a great way to really immerse yourself in the season's surprising floral display. It's only open during spring when the flowers are out.

Kitesurfing (kiteboarding)

Some of the world's best have hit Cape Town, and they're bringing all their mates – with water both sides of the mountain, the Cape offers great spots in almost all winds, with Bloubergstrand's Dolphin Beach and Muizenberg's Surfers' Corner favourites.

Kitesurfing is really only for those with strong ambidextrous, multi-tasking abilities: while swooping a very powerful kite through the air to generate pulling and lift-off power, you allow yourself to be flung into the air with a board attached to your feet. Now do some tricks – somersault, for example. Then work out what's up and what's not. Now land safely on the water at just the right angle to ensure you skid along the surface at nonchalant speed. One of the newest adventure sports around, this one is certainly the Next Big Thing – a radical 3D game, but there's still time to get in on the action now. Sure, you can try teaching yourself, but the board and kite are going to set you back around R4,000 at least, so it's probably worth investing in some lessons first. The experts reckon they can show you the basics in a day or two (expect to pay about R1,500).

Capesport Main Road, Langebaan, West Coast *(022 772 1114/www.capesport.co.za).*
Downhill Adventures *Corner of Kloof, Long and Orange Streets, City Bowl (021 422 0388/ www.downhilladventures.com).* **Map** p282 G4.
The Kite Shop *V&A Waterfront, Atlantic Seaboard (021 421 6231/www.kiteshop.co.za).* **Map** p283 H1.
Windsports *1 Athens Road, Tableview, Northern Suburbs (021 556 2765/www.windsports.co.za).*
Windswept *25 Viola Street, Tablview, Northern Suburbs (082 961 3070/ www.windswept.co.za).*

Kloofing (canyoning)

Cape creeks are epic and dangerous – it's as simple as that. The nature of our rainfall and geomorphology means canyons are generally dry as a bone in summer, and prone to flash

Sandboarding. *See p207.*

floods in the winter-rainfall season. All of which makes the act of following that stream through the mountains so tantalising. The 'pool and drop' nature of most of the Cape's rivers means that you are consistently jumping into pools from great heights, sliding down over waterfalls, or slipping and stumbling along rocky river courses. Bruises are inevitable.

Generally a winter option and thus a rather chilly adventure experience, 'kloofing' in the Cape has all the raw sense of pioneering, but without the deep freeze of European canyoning, which is usually done in glacial melt.

Kamikaze Canyon, just outside Gordon's Bay, offers a great kloofing-and-abseiling duo that helped to put **Abseil Africa** (021 424 4760/ www.abseilafrica.co.za) on the map and still remains one of the best adventure days on offer in the Cape (costs R550).

The so-called Suicide Gorge near Swellendam is a world-renowned epic. Its jumps have been conservatively estimated at a scary average of 14 metres (45 feet). Permits can be obtained through **Cape Nature Conservation** (021 426 0723/www.cnc.org.za).

Further north is a slightly more secretive spot, where the local Super 12 rugby side, Investec Stormers, were put through their gruelling paces at the start of the season by **180 Degrees Adventures** (*see p202*).

The deep and secluded wilderness kloof known as Die Hel forms part of the Groot Winterhoek reserve. Surviving this kloof requires at least six intense hours of your life.

You can book kloofing trips through **Cape Nature Conservation** (021 426 0723/ www.cnc.org.za). Commercial trips can be booked either through **Gravity Adventures** (021 683 3698/www.gravity.co.za) or **Eugene Nel** (082 658 3078).

Mountain-biking

A very active cycling community ensures miles and miles of mountain-biking terrain – much of it 'legal' under the more holistic approach of Cape Nature Conservation.

Deer Park takes in the face of Table Mountain below Tafelberg Road – access is from the top of Deer Park Drive, Vredehoek, or at various well-worn points on Tafelberg Road both before and after the cable station. Entry is free. Alternatively, pay R350 and get a bike, guide and transport there and back with Downhill Adventures (*see below*) on its 'Table Mountain Double Descent'.

Grabouw Forest is a pine plantation with a world-class singletrack. Park at the **Elgin Grabouw Country Club** (Worcester Street, Grabouw, 021 859 3651) and just ride.

Another big attraction is Tokai forest, which was host to the most recent All African MTB championships. It's approximately eight kilometres (five miles) to the radio mast on top of the mountain. Singletrack down. Park behind Tokai Manor House. You pay R8 at the gate, from sunrise to sunset.

Downhill Adventures (*see p197*).
180 Degrees Adventures (*see p202*).
Pedal Power Association *Mowbray, Southern Suburbs (021 689 8420/www.pedalpower.org.za)*.

Paragliding

Imagine taking off from Lion's Head, dangling comfortably under a huge parachute-like canopy for the best possible sightseeing trip of the Atlantic Seaboard, swooping low over the heads of the climbers on Table Mountain, and then landing gracefully on the lawn in front of Camps Bay's La Med restaurant. (Tip: pick up all the gear and walk off nonchalantly, as if oblivious to the admiring gazes of onlookers.) Tandem jumps make great one-offs (R750); otherwise, a course of instruction is a longer-term commitment and more weather-dependent. But what a place to learn.

Paragliding is a surprisingly safe sport for the average participant. The guys who lend it its death-and-destruction notoriety are those who are pushing the envelope. But it's a sport that attracts exactly that type of person. A standard glider is designed to pop back into shape in seconds if it collapses for some reason – it's only the expert-level competition ones that don't. And it's a sport that's regulated – nobody simply has the freedom of the skies. You can only fly at more technical spots such as Table Mountain if you have sufficient appropriate experience. Certainly, anybody who can legally offer you a tandem flight or a course of instruction has to have all the right paperwork and a proven track record. But they also certainly have some gory stories to tell. And if they sense you're not averse to a little bit of adrenaline, they'll yank on one of those toggles to spin you in tight circles at face-contorting G-forces – all for the joy of being out of touch with the ground. Enjoy.

Airborne Paragliding *Sea Point, False Bay (021 434 2011/www.paraglidingkapstadt.de)*.
Paraglide Cape Town *(082 727 6584)*.
Para-Pax *(082 881 4724/www.parapax.com)*.
Parapente Cape *Wynberg, Southern Suburbs (021 762 2441/ www.wallendair.co.za)*.

Sailing

Cape Town sailors consistently appear in the world's top rankings: there's no shortage of training grounds and hectic conditions here to prepare them. False Bay's Fish Hoek beach and Hout Bay, round the corner, are decorated with Hobie Cats every weekend, and when you take in the sightings of whales and dolphins, it's not hard to see the attraction.

Drum Africa

Wynberg, Southern Suburbs (021 785 5201/ www.drumafrica.co.za). **Credit** AmEx, DC, MC, V.
This company offers sailing trips for beginners at R250 per hour, including equipment, or R950 for two-day beginner or advanced courses.

Ocean Sailing Academy

West Quay Road, V&A Waterfront, Atlantic Seaboard (021 786 2436/www.oceansailing.co.za). **Map** p283 H2.
This academy runs courses for all levels. to give you an idea, it costs R4,790 to do your competent crew course. That amount covers five days' accommodation on board the yacht, with all food, tuition and practical experience included.

Sandboarding

With 'what goes up, must come down' as your mantra, you trudge up some hellish sand dunes and then fly down in style on converted snowboards. Atlantis (just north of Cape Town) and Betty's Bay (at the other side of False Bay) are two prime destinations, with operators offering transport-, snack- and equipment-inclusive day trips for approximately R500.

Arts & Entertainment

Axel Zander of **Downhill Adventures** (*see p197*) was the guy who got it all going a few years back, winning the world champs to boot. Also try **Guidance Adventures** (021 783 3622/www.safarinow.com).

Sea-kayaking

Rounding the 'Cape of Storms' has always been one of the greats on any seafarer's CV. The truth is, catch the right day and it's a doddle – even in a small canoe. These days sea kayaks are extremely safe, and (with a life jacket on, of course) it's not necessary to be hugely experienced to head out into the great blue yonder. The best bet for first-timers is to hook up with an existing group from any of the contacts listed below. They'll put you in a nice stable boat (opt to sit in a double with one of the instructors if you really don't have faith in your own abilities) and you'll be amazed at how quickly you're out comfortably sightseeing from the other side of the beach.

Don't just assume the trip's off when it's windy: head for Three Anchor Bay on south-westerly days, or False Bay in gentle north-westers and conditions should be perfect.

If speed is your game, you'll want to try a surf-ski for a balancing act (these sleek speed machines are far more 'tippy' than sea kayaks). Surf-ski hotspots are Hout Bay and False Bay, where the competitive scene is extremely active and the eye-candy real sweet. Further along the coast, check out Langebaan, Knysna Lagoon and Plettenberg Bay.

Coastal Kayak Trails *179 Beach Road, Three Anchor Bay, Atlantic Seaboard (021 439 1134/ www.kayak.co.za)*.
Dolphin Adventures *Knysna, Garden Route (083 590 3405/www.dolphinkayak.com)*.
Mike's Ocean Kayaks *Hout Bay, Atlantic Seaboard (021 790 2359/ www.mikesoceankayaks.co.za)*.
Ocean Blue Adventures *Plettenberg Bay, Garden Route (044 533 5083/www.oceanadventures.co.za)*.
Real Cape Adventures *Hout Bay, Atlantic Seaboard (082 556 2520/www.seakayak.co.za)*.

Skydiving

'Accelerated exhilaration' is what one operator calls skydiving, rather euphemistically. But those heightened senses guarantee that the scenes seen from up there are all the more appreciated. Yes, it will be scary, but you can go from groundling to jumper in the space of a weekend. A Friday evening and full Saturday of instruction will have you leaping from the plane by Sunday, taking in the view from on high, and sleeping like a log that night.

While Citrusdal's drop zone is considered possibly the most beautiful in all the world, especially in September when the spring flowers are out, the field at Stellenbosch can hardly be described as shabby.

More experienced parachutists should consider doing their Accelerated Freefall Courses in South Africa – it's cheaper than almost anywhere else on the planet: R6,300 for the full progression.

Skydive Cape Town *Melkbosstrand, West Coast (082 800 6290/www.skydivecapetown.za.net)*.
Skydive Citrusdal *(021 462 5666/ www.skydive.co.za)*.

Whitewater rafting & kayaking

The bottom line is that neither whitewater rafting nor kayaking is the Cape's strong point. The area simply does't have the snowmelt of Europe and North America, or the sheer volume of the Nile or KwaZulu-Natal. However, the Doring River is still a great option for the winter, and after good rains it can get pretty hairy (around R895 for two days, including food and guides). However, the hands-down winner in terms of Richtersveld mountain beauty and wide-open desert space is the Orange (now known as the Gariep). Although its actual rapids are few and far between, and rate as nothing more than a Grade Three, it has a magical quality that makes it worth the drive all the way up to the Namibian border. Hellishly hot in the summer months, it makes an unbeatable New Year trip and is ideal at Easter. Almost every operator uses the Doring or the Orange. Expect to pay in the region of R1,800 for a four-day trip of around 20 kilometres (12 miles) per day.

African Paddling Association *Kenilworth, Southern Suburbs (021 674 1645)*.
Felix Unite River Adventures *Kenilworth, Southern Suburbs (021 670 1300/ www.felixunite.com)*.
Gravity Adventure Group *Kenilworth, Southern Suburbs (021 683 3698/www.gravity.co.za)*.
Intrapid Rafting *(082 555 0551/ raftsa@iafrica.com)*.
Kalahari Adventure Centre *Northern Cape (054 451 0177/www.kalahari.co.za)*.
Rivers Inc *Bonnievale (082 823 6703/ www.riversinc.co.za)*.
Wildthing Adventures *V&A Waterfront, Atlantic Seaboard (021 423 5804/ www.wildthing.co.za)*. **Map** p283 H1.

▶ For more information, go to www.wavescape.co.za

Theatre & Dance

A diverse mix on any evening, from the Bard outdoors to ballet theatre.

Theatre

Going to the theatre in Cape Town can find you one evening in your pearls and on your best behaviour, lapping up *Les Mis* or *Aïda* and the next in jeans interacting with the performers on stage. From the conventional to the experimental, Cape Town's talent shines under glitzy spotlights and in smoky basements alike.

TICKETS AND INFORMATION

Most of the major venues feature in-house productions as well as visiting shows, so there is no consistent ticket-pricing policy. Mainstream venues generally offer online bookings via Computicket (*see below*), but there's no centralised city outlet for discounted tickets. Ask at booking offices about student/senior concessions, low-priced previews and two-for-one performances, as not all options are advertised. Artscape main theatres and the Baxter do not allow drinks to be taken into theatre, though mineral water in plastic bottles is permitted by the latter.

Tickets for most events can be bought from **Computicket** (083 915 8000/083 915 8100/www.computicket.co.za, 9am-5pm daily).

Avant-garde theatre

Magnet Theatre/The Magnet Theatre Educational Trust

2 Morley Road, Observatory, Southern Suburbs (021 480 7173/www.magnettheatre.co.za).
Engaging and innovative work from this 16-year-old, award-winning physical theatre company. Directors Jennie Reznek and Mark Fleishman focus on community outreach projects aimed at developing young people's skills, and Magnet collaborates regularly with dance companies such as Jazzart.

The Mothertongue Project

Based in Woodstock, Southern Suburbs (021 686 5441/072 183 7866/www.mothertongue.co.za).
The Mothertongue Project envelops all the senses. This dynamic women's collective creates and performs original works using various media: physical theatre, storytelling, ritual, yoga, sound and beadwork to name a few. Rehane Abrahams, Andrea Dondolo, Sara Matchett and Faniswa Yisa also conduct educational and therapeutic storytelling workshops. They can be seen at the Baxter, Artscape, at festivals and on tour.

Picture show: **Evita se Perron**. *See p210.*

Odd Enjinears

The Odd Workspace, Transwerk Industrial Park, Voortrekker Road, Salt River, Southern Suburbs (021 447 5745/www.oddenjinears.co.za). **Tickets** R50; R30 concessions. **No credit cards**.
Inventive industrial theatre practitioners, the Odd bunch are actors, technicians, musicians and sculptors from South Africa and Holland. They create theatre in locations such as old factories and abandoned warehouses, 'exploring the terrain between arts and technology'. No space or medium is off-bounds.

Third World Bunfight

Spier Wine Estate, Stellenbosch, Winelands (082 372 9869/www.thirdworldbunfight.co.za).
A non-profit theatre company that is headed by controversial and provocative writer-director Brett Bailey, 'using an eclectic blend of African and other theatrical forms, music and dance, in a country fixated on Eurocentric theatre'. Bailey loves to shock audiences, and his company made national headlines when, on the final performance of its recent Baxter production of Imumbo JUMBO, a chicken was slaughtered on stage.

Major venues

Artscape Theatre Centre

DF Malan Street, Foreshore, City Centre (021 421 7839/www.artscape.co.za). **Open** Box office 9am-5pm Mon-Fri; 9am-12.30pm Sat; 1hr prior to performances. **Tickets** R100-R300. **Credit** AmEx, DC, MC, V. **Map** p283 I3.

Formerly known as the Nico Malan Theatre, this complex has come a long way since the days of apartheid. It now offers a potent mix of music, drama, opera, comedy, local and international artists, community arts activities, arts education and training programmes. Artscape is home to **Cape Town City Ballet** (021 410 980l/www.capetown cityballet.org.za); **Jazzart Dance** (021 410 9848/ www.jazzart.co.za); the **Cape Philharmonic Orchestra** (021 410 9809/www.capephilharmonic. org.za); and **Cape Town Opera** (021 465 6691/ www.capetownopera.co.za). Gritty, single-act or musical pieces are put on at Artscape on the Side – the smallest Artscape venue (which allows drinks). Theatresports (021 465 6691/www.sports.co.za), based on Drew Carey's TV production *Whose Line is it Anyway*, runs at 8.30pm on Tuesdays and Thursdays (R30; R25 concessions). Peter Toerien and The Really Useful Company's production of Andrew Lloyd Webber's *Phantom of the Opera* opened at Artscape Opera House in April 2004.

Baxter Theatre Centre

Main Road, Rondebosch, Southern Suburbs
(021 680 3989/021 685 7880/www.baxter.co.za).
Open *Box office* 9am to start of performance Mon-Sat. **Tickets** R50-R150. **Credit** AmEx, DC, MC, V.
This vibrant Theatre Centre in the southern suburbs sizzles with drama (home-grown and international), comedy, opera, festivals and events for seniors and children. There's the Main Theatre (665 seats), Concert Hall (638 seats) and Studio Theatre (166 seats), lovely big foyers and the mezzanine level – great for pre- or post-theatre socialising. No smoking inside. The restaurant is open for breakfast, lunch and dinner daily and private functions, and the fully-stocked bar is open from 6pm daily.

Evita se Perron

Darling Station, Arcadia Road, Darling, West Coast,
50 min north of Cape Town on R27 (022 492 2851/
022 4922831/www.evita.co.za). **Open** 9am-5pm,
Tue-Sun. **Tickets** R50-R75. **Credit** AmEx, DC,
MC, V.
Some witty and intriguing Boere-baroque decor characterises these two cabaret venues. The site also has a restaurant, bar, art gallery and conference facilities. There are regular shows by brilliant satirist Pieter-Dirk Uys and his alter ego Evita Bezuidenhout, plus visiting cabaret, dance and drama performers. When there are shows on, the bar and restaurant stay open until midnight.

Theatre on the Bay

1 Link Street, Camps Bay, Atlantic Seaboard
(021 438 3301/www.theatreonthebay.co.za).
Open *Box office* 9.30am-5pm daily (until 8pm on show days). **Tickets** R80-R85. **Credit** AmEx, DC, MC, V. **Map** p284 B8.
Pieter Toerien's comfy and intimate 220-seat theatre hosts Eurocentric comedies, dramas and musicals and attracts incredibly varied audiences, from young and hip to cultured and laconic. You can take

Of **Mince** and men, **On Broadway**. *See p213.*

drinks into the performances (the chairs even have nifty drinks holders), and there's a bar, coffee bar (serving fab cake) and an à la carte restaurant.

Other venues

Bloemendal Cellar Theatre

Racecourse Road, Durbanville, Northern Suburbs
(021 975 2525/www.bloemendal.co.za).
This cellar-like theatre-restaurant offers buffet-style traditional Cape food and theatrical performances that don't need professional lighting and sound.

Cape Town International Convention Centre

Convention Square, 1 Lower Long Street, Foreshore,
City Centre (021 410 5000/www.cticc.co.za/
www.capetownconvention.com). **Tickets** R160-R400.
Credit AmEx, DC, MC, V. **Map** p283 I3.
Past performances in the CTICC auditorium (with theatre seating and stage) have been the musical *Fame* and *Lord of the Dance*.

Dorp Street Theatre

59 Dorp Street, Stellenbosch, Winelands (021 886
6107/www.dorpstraat.co.za). **Map** p278 P3.
Fully licensed and à la carte dining in this informal cabaret venue, which features mainly Afrikaans theatre, music and poetry readings.

HB Thom Theatre

Victoria Street, University of Stellenbosch, Winelands (021 808 3216/ www.sun.ac.za/drama). **Map** p278 R2.

A 430-seat university theatre that hosts Drama Department shows, including children's theatre. Tickets must be bought at the door.

Independent Armchair Theatre

135 Lower Main Road, Observatory, Southern Suburbs (021 447 1514/www.armchairtheatre.co.za).

This informal lounge-theatre setting comes complete with its own bar and has assorted comfy chairs and floppy cushions. The venue hosts comedy, theatre and music. On Sundays, R30 gets you a pizza and a classic movie.

Kalk Bay Theatre

52 Main Road, Kalk Bay, False Bay (bookings 073 220 5430/www.theatreforafrica.co.za). **Tickets** R150 for 3-course meal, coffee and show. **Credit** AmEx, DC, MC, V.

Dine in the kitchen of the bakery and watch a show in the rather petite, 47-seat theatre. The theatre has plenty of character but the wooden seats are austere: take a cushion for the sake of your posterior. All shows are written by Nicholas Ellenbogen and performed by him, his wife Liz, and others. Their shows are infused with humour and perspicacity.

Klein Libertas Theatre Club

Corner Bird & Merriman Streets, Stellenbosch, Winelands (021 883 8164). **Shows** 8.15pm nightly. **Tickets** R30-R50. **No credit cards**. **Map** p278 Q2.

This 110-seater specialises in community and experimental theatre, as well as offering previews of new professional shows. There's an outside veranda for smoking and drinking (wine only).

Lane Theatre

Corner Port & Alfred Road, V&A Waterfront, Atlantic Seaboard (021 418 4600). **Tickets** R30; R20 concessions. **No credit cards**. **Map** p283 H2.

Waterfront Theatre School students show what they can do in their own theatre, putting on about seven productions a year – expect anything from drama to musicals and dance.

Little Theatre & Arena Theatre UCT Drama Theatre

Hiddingh Campus, 37 Orange Street, Gardens, City Centre (021 480 7129/www.uct.ac.za/depts/drama). **Map** p282 G4.

UCT Drama Department's productions under the direction of Associate Professor Christopher Weare are held here. The Little Theatre seats 245 and the cute Arena Theatre holds 72. As these are theatres for hire, quality can range from brilliantly cutting-edge to embarrassingly bad; highlights include

Independent Armchair Theatre.

My kind of town David Kramer

Cape Town is... the place for me.
Capetonians are... ready for the *jol* ('party').
Table Mountain is... old, mysterious, reassuring and to be treated with respect.
Fabulous food is found at... every turn. Visit restaurants in Kloof Street, Camps Bay for variety and ambience. Don Pedro's (113 Roodebloem Road, Woodstock, 021 447 4493) for a laid-back Cape Town experience.
I buy take-aways at... Chef Pon's Asian Kitchen (*see p101*).
Sundowners are best spent at... the top of Lion's Head.
Lazy mornings are spent... walking from Camps Bay to Bantry Bay. Or on the mountain. How lazy are you?
The strange thing about this town is.... why anyone ever wants to leave.
Ever wondered why... people say we're laid-back? Some things are best in a horizontal position.
I soak up culture... in the streets. Visit Wale Street after midnight on New Year's Eve. (The Cape Minstrel Carnival, which celebrates the emancipation of the slaves, is an annual event during

which colourful troubadours compete for honors in this musical extravaganza. New Year's eve sees thousands of spectators jostling for space in the streets to celebrate the New Year and welcome the minstrels who march up from District Six, through Adderley and Wale streets before ending up in Rose Street in the Bo-Kaap.)
I'm frustrated by... the lack of decent public transport.
Spiritual nourishment is found... on the mountain. Or on the beach when the sun rises or sets.
The landmark I love... Lion's Head.
The landmark I loathe... the statue of a constipated Smuts at the top of Adderley Street. (General Smuts was a prominent statesman and soldier).
My community is... gaining confidence.
Creativity flourishes... after a glass of Sauvignon Blanc.
I bare my body on.... a Monday, a Tuesday, a Wednesday. Remember that song?
I go shopping... reluctantly.
I show off... often.
I take tourists to... see the lights from Signal Hill at night.
I listen to... my heart.
I find local politics... the worst aspect of this fascinating city.

David Kramer, singer/songwriter/ playwright/producer, is possibly one of the most recognisable South African celebrities. He portrays himself as a rural everyman, in red leather shoes and with a cheap guitar, who travels through small-town South Africa. His simple yet powerful lyrics about South African situations and characters have earned him a large fan base as well as the respect of all South Africans who are touched by his sensitivity towards the marginalised communities. More recently, his collaborations with fellow artist Taliep Petersen have won him more international respect as well as awards. Three of these musicals have toured internationally and the more recent *Kat and the Kings* has been performed on Broadway in New York and London's West End. Go to www.davidkramer.co.za.

superb productions written and/or directed by drama lecturers, and, every year, UCT Drama stages at least two school set works.

Off Moroko Café Africaine

Adderley Street, City Centre (021 422 1129/ www.offmoroko.co.za). **Credit** AmEx, DC, MC, V. **Map** p283 H4.
This City Centre venue has poetry readings every Monday at 8pm. Comedy, open-mic sessions and jazz evenings are also fun to attend.

On Broadway

On Broadway Green Point, 21 Somerset Road, Atlantic Seaboard (021 418 8338/www.onbroad way.co.za). **Shows** 9pm Wed-Sat. **Tickets** R50-R60. **Credit** AmEx, DC, MC, V. **Map** p282 G3.
There's a great vibe at this theatre and dinner venue, home to established performing artists and a platform for emerging performers. On Broadway offers cabaret, musical, comedy and drag shows (Mince), and its tribute and best-of shows always go with a swing. You might very well find yourself dancing on the tables by the end of the performance. There's simple food available. If you want to have dinner, you should be seated by 7.30pm.

Outdoor theatre

Kirstenbosch Open-Air Theatre

Kirstenbosch Gardens, Rhodes Drive, Newlands, Southern Suburbs (021 799 8783/021 761 2866/www.nbi.ac.za). **No credit cards**.
Beautiful productions are staged in the open-air theatre against the slopes of Table Mountain. Although considerably smaller, Kirstenbosch's venue replicates the conditions of the Ancient Greek theatres. Lovely wines are available.

Maynardville Open-Air Theatre

Corner of Church & Wolf Streets, Wynberg, Southern Suburbs (bookings 021 421 7695/ www.artscape.co.za). **Shows** mid Jan-end Feb 8.15pm Wed-Sat; school performances 7.45pm Mon, Tue. **Credit** AmEx, Dc, MC, V.
During the summer, Artscape's Shakespearean productions are the principal users of this parkland open-air theatre. They tend to serve up the Bard with a contemporary, energetic and funky spin, hoping to appeal to young audiences. Fabulous lighting makes use of the beautiful park setting. Throughout the year, dance, jazz and theatre groups appear here. In the adjacent park, there is a popular annual Community Chest Fair.

Oude Libertas Amphitheatre

Oude Libertas Farm, Adam Tas Road, Stellenbosch, Winelands (021 809 7473/www.oudelibertas.co.za). **Open** Box office Nov-Mar 9am-5pm Mon-Fri. **Tickets** R40-R90. **Credit** AmEx, DC, MC, V.
Situated in a stunning rural vineyard nestling under the Papegaaiberg (Parrot Mountain), this amphitheatre makes for a pleasant theatre experience. The summer festival of music, theatre and dance has

been going for 25 years, and features local and international artists. Theatre-goers are given a complimentary glass of Distell wine; Sundays host popular Twilight Picnic concerts.

Paul Cluver Amphitheatre

Paul Cluver Farm, Elgin/Grabouw, take the N2 Kromco exit (021 859 0605/www.cluver.co.za). **Credit** AmEx, Dc, MC, V.
This idyllic forest amphitheatre is situated next to rolling apple orchards and vineyards. The line-up for 2004 included the iconic Nataniel weaving his riveting cabaret, comedy, and singer Steph Bos from the Netherlands. Taste some Paul Cluver Wines such as the heady Pinot Noir or sinfully sweet Late Harvest desert wine. Eats available. Pre-order your picnic basket (from R65) on 082 320 2060.

Spier Amphitheatre

Spier Estate, R310, Lynedoch, Stellenbosch, Winelands (021 809 1111/bookings 021 809 1158/ www.spier.co.za). **Performances** Dec-Mar 8.30pm. **Tickets** R40-R120. **Credit** AmEx, DC, MC, V.
Outdoor amphitheatre with the majestic Helderberg mountains as a backdrop. The 2003-2004 Spier Arts Summer Season included musical theatre – *The Rocky Horror Show, Queen* and *ibali loo Tsotsi, The End is Naai* – and the world premiere of Pieter-Dirk Uys's Mammoth 10-Year Retrospective with Searing Social Commentary. All festival shows start at 8.30pm, but turn up early and you can enjoy a glass of wine or eat at one of the venues on Spier Estate.

Circus

South African National Circus School

Hartleyvale Stadium, Observatory, Southern Suburbs (021 692 4287/072 100 3509).
Founder Dimitri Slaverse grew up in Hanover Park ('a crime- and gangster-ridden township'). He has worked for over 22 years in the circus arts and became trapeze world champion. The show includes aerial rope acts, juggling, human pyramids, unicyclists, acrobatics, trapeze… The main attraction, *The Man in the Bottle*, is apparently the only act of its kind: a huge man contorting himself into a little bottle. The school currently performs in the open air at the stadium, but is raising money for its own tent.

ZipZap Circus School

Montague Gardens Industrial Park, Montague Gardens, Northern Suburbs, 10min from Cape Town City Centre (021 551 9901/www.zip-zap.co.za). **Tickets** prices vary. **No credit cards**.
From the underprivileged to the affluent, this non-profit school, founded 11 years ago, is made up of youngsters from all walks of life. ZipZap is an outstanding venture, and it's no wonder that the internationally acclaimed Cirque du Soleil gives it training support. ZipZap recently appeared in the *Bartered Bride* opera at the Baxter along with dancers from Dance for All.

Spier. *See p213.*

Dance

Hip hop, classical ballet, jazz, tap, millennium
funk, modern… you name it, Cape Town's got
it. For information about dance studios and
shows all over the Cape, contact Daphne Jubber
at the Western Province Dance Teachers
Association (021 762 3141).

Elements of dance also find their way into
all forms of theatre: tango teacher and dancer
Mark Hoeben has performed in Cape Town
Opera's *Faust*, for example, and Jazzart
collaborates regularly with the **Magnet
Theatre** and **Cape Town Opera**. There
was also a strong dance component at the
Oude Libertas Festival Summer 2004 season.
And Dance for All wowed audiences when its
members danced in the opera *Bartered Bride*
at the Baxter. Look out for performances by
this outstanding group.

TICKETS AND INFORMATION

To make bookings, call Dial-a-Seat (021 421
7695; 9am-5pm Mon-Fri, 9am-12.30pm Sat;
1hr prior to performances) or the
comprehensive Computicket (*see p209*).

Dance companies

Ballet Theatre Afrikan

*Johannesburg (011 880 3099/
www.ballettheatreafrikan.co.za).*
This Gauteng-based professional company sometimes performs at Cape Town venues such as
Artscape and the Baxter Theatre complexes.
Blending classical ballet techniques, contemporary
dance and afro-fusion, it trains its dancers from
start to professional finish.

Cape Dance Company

*Christy Centre, Kendal Road, Diep River,
Southern Suburbs (021 712 9445/www.capedance
company.bizland.com).*

This contemporary dance company runs in close association with an accomplished dance studio (modern, tap and classical) called the Academy of Dance; both are under the directorship of well-known dancer Debbie Turner. The Company performs annually at the Grahamstown Festival (July) and has successfully performed at the Edinburgh Festival.

Cape Town City Ballet (CTCB)
Artscape Theatre Centre, DF Malan Street, Foreshore, City Centre (021 410 980l/ www.capetowncityballet.org.za). **Tickets** R100-R300. **Credit** AmEx, DC, MC, V. **Map** p283 I3.
This 70-year-old non-profit company dances ballet classics such as *Swan Lake*, the *Nutcracker* and *Don Quixote* as well as popular contemporary international and indigenous works. The company's home is the Artscape Opera House, but it also performs at the Maynardville Open-Air Theatre (Sunday evenings in summer season), the Masque Theatre in Muizenberg, and in the Spier Summer Festival. Its ridiculously cheap matinées sell out fast.

Dance for All
Joseph Stone Auditorium, Klipfontein Road, Athlone, Southern Suburbs (021 633 4363/ www.danceforall.co.za).
Run by Philip Boyd, former principal dancer with Capab Ballet, this innovative company offers classical, contemporary and traditional dance tuition to more than 200 underprivileged children in Gugulethu, Khayelitsha, Nyanga and the Joseph Stone Theatre and Alexander Sinton High School in Athlone. The results are outstanding.

The Free Flight Dance Company
021 433 2838.
Headed by choreographer Adele Blank, Free Flight is an active collaborator with the Cape Town City Ballet, Ballet Theatre Afrikan and others. The company's style is 'organic and eclectic'. Adele offers dance classes; fees depend on the type of lesson.

Jazzart Dance Theatre
Artscape Theatre complex, DF Malan Street, Foreshore, City Centre (021 410 9848/ www.jazzart.co.za). **Map** p283 I3.
Jazzart is a well-respected, contemporary African dance company that performs widely, from television to theatre to schools. It also holds classes at all levels (R30; R25 concessions) in contemporary dance, funk, street dance, improvisation, ballet and creative dance for children and teens.

Dance venues

Bossa Nova
43 Somerset Road, Green Point, Atlantic Seaboard (021 425 0295/www.bossanova.co.za). **Admission** R20 women; R50 men. **Credit** AmEx, MC, V. **Map** p282 G3.
This latin-style lounge and club offers salsa lessons where students get to practise their moves.

The Valve
32 Parliament Street on Church Square, City Centre (021 461 1535/www.gentleembrace.co.za). **Admission** free. **Map** p283 H4.
The Valve is a sumptuous venue that's loaded with history. For dancers, Mark Hoeben holds general classes, plus weekly tango socials – called Milongas – on Tuesdays (8.30-10.30pm for R20). Every six weeks Mark holds a Grand Tango Salon, where participants dance to live tango music supplied by the Cape Town Ensemble (083 601 5751). There's a free beginners' lesson beforehand.

Dance studios

Aerobic Dance
Bergvliet Congregational Church Hall, Hiddingh Road, Bergvliet, Southern Suburbs (Moira 021 715 3908). **Fees** R380/term. **No credit cards.**
Dance, exercise and stretch routines from mother-and-daughter team Gwen and Moira Marshbank. Gwen has been teaching for 28 years and Moira, a former South African aerobics champion, has been in the business for 18 years. Moira once danced in Sun City extravaganzas.

Freestyle Fusion
Room 28, Heathfield Primary School, 16 Chadwin Road, Diep River, Southern Suburbs (082 512 1750/ 083 966 0017). **Fees** R135/mth. **No credit cards.**
This is a creative and diverse studio for men and women – from the physically fit to 'the unfit and the bored'. Here you can learn capoeira, t'ai chi, African and Native American drumming, belly-dancing, yoga and modern and jazz.

Nia
Our Space, The River Club, Liesbeek Parkway, Observatory, Southern Suburbs (021 674 3747). **Fees** R40. **No credit cards.**
This is a good cardiovascular workout that combines dance, martial arts, healing, stretching, relaxation and meditation done to a mix of world music. Classes run every day from 9.15am.

La Rosa Spanish Dance Theatre
Waverley Business Park, Wycroft Road, Mowbray (021 448 7718/021 448 4124/ www.larosa.co.za). **Fees** R300/term. **No credit cards.**
Spanish dance is taught through the Spanish Dance Society syllabus and flamenco technique; children and adults; beginners to professionals. The La Rosa Spanish Dance Theatre also performs regularly at venues such as On Broadway (021 418 8338/ www.onbroadway.co.za).

UCT School of Dance
University of Cape Town, Woolsack Drive, Rosebank, Southern Suburbs (021 650 2398/www.uct.ac.za).
This is the 'feeding ground' for Cape Town City Ballet aspirants. On offer are degree and diploma courses; junior ballet school (extra-mural classes for ages six to 16) as well as evening classes for adults.

www.sunstays.com

ACCOMMODATION IN CAPE TOWN AND SOUTHERN AFRICA
ONLINE: BOOKING, AVAILABILITY AND CHOICE.
FLIGHTS, TOURS, PROPERTY SALES.
TEL: +27 82 377 7777   Email: info@sunstays.com

SUN
STAYS

Trips Out of Town

Features

Getting Started

Beaches, fishing villages, whales and wine – sound like paradise?

There are traveller's routes in all directions outside Cape Town. Well, all directions except west, which will take you – after a long swim – to the middle of the Atlantic Ocean and on to South America... Heading north takes you up the West Coast, where sleepy fishing villages and miles of unspoiled beaches await. South won't take you far (only as far as Cape Point), but eastwards along the Cape South Coast lie two of the Western Cape's favourite drives: the Whale Route, and a little further along, the gorgeous Garden Route. Also going east, into the Winelands, you'll reach the start of Route 62, the world's longest wine route and the gateway to the Wild West semi-desolation of the Klein Karoo (think of it as a semi-semi-desert). All these excursions allow for a comfortable amount of driving in a day – none of them should exceed 450km (280 miles), and in many cases (like the Whale/Garden Routes) you can mix and match. If driving's not your thing, there are alternative means of transport as well.

GETTING AROUND

The Western Cape's roads are well tarred and well maintained, with clear signposts for towns (blue) as well as local places of interest (brown) – if you're on a gravel road, the chances are you're either at a small wine farm or you're lost. The only major toll roads to watch out for are through the Huguenot Tunnel on the N1 between Paarl and Worcester, and at the far end of the Garden Route at Tsitsikamma (just before Storms River). Remember that travelling distances can be deceptive – especially on the long, empty stretches of tar in the Klein Karoo and along the sandy West Coast. Touring the Western Cape is generally a car-driven exercise: apart from the risky business of catching a minibus taxi in the urban areas, Capetonians don't have much of a culture of getting on and off public transport.

But, there are still plenty of ways to get around for non drivers. Even though buses and trains have reduced their services over the past

Paternoster. *See p244.*

few years, they still offer good value and convenience if you plan your trip in advance. The backpacker-style Baz Bus (021 439 2323/www.bazbus.com) is the closest you'll get to a stop-off drop-off tour bus, and it's a perfect way to travel if you're a backpacker or individual traveller. Baz follows two-way routes up and down the southeast coast between Cape Town and Port Elizabeth, Durban and Johannesburg/Pretoria (via Swaziland or the Drakensberg). You simply buy a ticket to your destination and hop on and off the bus as you feel. For something more structured, coaches run up and down the Garden Route between Cape Town and Port Elizabeth. Most coaches leave from Cape Town Station (*see p249*).

Intercity trains (044 801 8202) run between Cape Town and Port Elizabeth, while Shosholoza Meyl (the transporter formerly known as Spoornet) offers safe train trips around the country (021 449 3871/0860 008 888/www.spoornet.co.za). The luxurious Blue Train (021 449 2672/www.bluetrain.co.za) has unrivalled (but expensive) comfort on its routes to Pretoria. And for a unique local travelling experience, stop at George Station and hop aboard the Outeniqua Choo-Tjoe (044 801 8288) – an old steam train that travels between to and from Knysna, hugging the coast on one of South Africa's most scenic railway lines.

The best Destinations

For the great outdoors
Knysna is a true paradise, with its lagoon, forests and mountains (*see p231*). The coastal town of **Wilderness** (*see p230*) has beautiful views and a national park, and **Montagu** has some awe-inspiring rock formations (*see p238*).

For whale watching
They're as close to Cape Town as False Bay, but **Hermanus** is the self-styled whale universe (*see p221*). At **Gansbaai** you might even see some sharks (*see p223*).

For wild flowers
In early spring (August and September) the whole of the West Coast is carpeted in brightly coloured wild flowers. And if you are there in September, **Darling**'s wild flower show is a must (*see p242*).

For wine & brandy
Robertson Wine Valley (*see p236*) has its fair share of wines, as does **Worcester**, which is also home to the largest brandy cellar in the world (*see p235*).

Vineyards abound.

While self-drive tours or the Baz Bus allow you to travel at your own pace, guided tours obviously remove the stress of getting lost or – on Route 62 – getting too tipsy to drive yourself back to your hotel. Hylton Ross (021 511 1784/www.hyltonross.co.za) offers five-star, half- or full-days tours in Cape Town's surrounding areas. Their Whale Route and Cape Grand Slam (Cape Point and the Winelands on the same day) tours are top class. African Eagle Day Tours (021 464 4266/www.daytours.co.za) have multilingual (French, German and Spanish) tours of the Whale Route, the Wine Route and the West Coast Wild Flowers, among others. Five-day tours, taking in the Whale Route, Garden Route and Route 62 are offered by the patriotically named BokBus (20 Houghton Road, Camps Bay, 082 320 1979/www.bokbus.com).

TOURIST INFORMATION
Cape Town Tourism (corner of Castle and Burg streets, 021 426 4260/www.cape-town.org) has stacks of brochures and information on booking agencies for trips and accommodation out of Cape Town. The national parks board, SANParks (012 428 9111/www.parks-sa.co.za) also offers a reservation facility.

Trips Out of Town

Whale Route

The best place to see whales doing aquabatics (among other things...).

It's hard to imagine 60 tons of solid matter doing anything as frivolous as frolicking, but when the Southern Right whales launch their massive bodies into the air, only to crash down with a thunderous splash, it appears to be simply because it's a whole lot of fun.

From July to December each year our seas turn into a gigantic nursery for hundreds of playful whales who swap their chilly Antarctic feeding grounds for our warmer, protected bays where they mate, calve, breach and lobtail, sometimes just metres from the shore. This spectacle has even the grumpiest among us perched – on rocks or in boats – gasping at the aquabatics, and scanning the water without daring to blink.

We weren't always this lucky – whale hunters took a devastating toll on numbers from the 1800s onwards. Of all the whales in these waters, worst off were the Southern Rights which, incidentally, are so named as they were the 'right' ones to hunt. They're extremely rich in oil, plus – once killed – they're obliging enough to float, making

them easy to get to shore. Thankfully, the Southern Right became a protected species in 1935 and now the whales are back, with more and more returning to our shores each year.

The warm-water whale route actually starts as close to Cape Town as Cape Point, following the curve of False Bay through Muizenberg to Gordon's Bay, and on the magnificent drive that clings to the coastline, winding through Rooi Els, Pringle Bay, Betty's Bay and Hawston to Hermanus and Walker Bay. But the South Coast seaside town of **Hermanus** (located only about 90 minutes from Cape Town down the N2) is the self-styled centre of the whale-watching universe, as well as being home to some excellent wine farms.

But it's not the only place you're going to see whales. About 25 kilometres (15 miles) east of Hermanus you'll pass the sleepy inland town of **Stanford** and the seaside village of **De Kelders** (which offers excellent whale-watching spots of its own), before eventually reaching **Gansbaai**. Here's where you can share some quality time with the area's other

Whale-watching in **Hermanus**.
See p221.

famous sea-dwellers: Great White Sharks.
And if you're feeling really brave, Gansbaai
offers caged shark diving (from Ecoventures,
021 532 0470/www.white-shark-diving.com or
Gansbaai harbour, 084 414 3809/www.shark
bookings.com)… and remember that you're
the one in the cage.

Leaving Gansbaai, you'll pass through a
number of blink-and-you'll-miss-'em towns
(zzzz… Pearly Beach… zzzz… Bredasdorp…
zzzz) before the turn-off to **L'Agulhas**, the
southernmost tip of the African continent. Here
– far, far away from Ra's al Abyad in Tunisia
at the other end of the continent – L'Agulhas's
Eqyptian-inspired lighthouse watches over
Africa's southern coast… and over the few
whales that aren't showing off in Hermanus.

And while you're about it, a lovely diversion
away from the whales takes you to **Greyton** –
a quaint village situated beneath the
Riviersonderend mountains.

This is a comfortable weekend getaway, and
if you have more time, you can head further
along the N2 to stop off in **Struisbaai** and
Arniston before hitting Witsand on the coast.

Waenhuiskrans Cave, **Arniston.**
See p225.

Hermanus (Walker Bay)

The World Wide Fund for Nature (WWF) has
recognised Walker Bay as one of the world's
top-12 whale-viewing sites. In fact in season
you're virtually guaranteed a good sighting
somewhere within the bay, and often you can
count up to 20 whales at play at once.

Hermanus is a tourist mecca – here you can
shop till you drop at the whale-view market or
any number of gift shops offering whale-
themed goodies of every description, or whale-
watch over your plate of seafood at several
sea-view restaurants, all of which overlook
the Old Harbour. To get the big picture, take a
spin up Rotary Way, which winds up into the
mountains above the town, where you can
watch paragliders and hangliders leap into the
air, and get 180-degree views across the bay.

You can get up close and personal, too.
The whales often come within ten metres of
the shore, so taking a picnic (and a pair of
binoculars) along the cliff paths or down to
the rocks will give you a front-row seat.

But if you really want to know precisely
where to go, just listen. Hermanus is the only
town in the world that employs a whale-crier,
Wilson Salukazana, who blows a kind of Morse
code on a kelp horn to indicate exactly where
the whales are. (Or you can phone the 24-hour
Whale Hotline, 083 910 1028/083 123 2345.)

The best (and, of course, the busiest) time
to visit Hermanus is during the annual whale
festival, which takes place in September each
year. And while your here, take to a trip to the
wine estates around Hermanus to stock up on
some of excellent local wines.

What to do

Beaumont Wines

*In Bot River, 25km (15 miles) from Hermanus
(028 284 9733).* **Open** 8.30am-12.30pm, 1.30-5pm
Mon-Fri; Sat by appointment. *Tours* by appointment.
Tastings free if fewer than 10 people, R20 for 10
or more.

Here you can taste and buy unique wines created by
the Beaumont family. You can tour the historic wine
cellar and then taste almost anything you can possibly think of: Pinotage, Shiraz, blends, Chenin
Blanc, Sauvignon Blanc, Chardonnay, Noble Late
Harvest and a port, to mention a few.

Bouchard Finlayson Vineyards & Cellars

*In the Hemel en Aarde Valley on the R320,
about 5km (3 miles) from the R43 into Hermanus
(028 312 3515/www.bouchardfinlayson.co.za).*
Open 9am-5pm Mon-Fri; 9.30am-12.30pm Sat.
Tastings free.

This small vineyard and cellar, situated in the beautiful Hemel en Aarde ('heaven and earth') Valley, is
dedicated to producing Pinot Noir, Chardonnay and
Sauvignon Blanc. Its excellent Galpin Pinot Noir
2001 Tête de Cuvée has recently won a gold medal
at the International Wine Challenge. Wine is offered
for tasting adjacent to the maturation cellar, which
is built into the hillside above Walker Bay, and is
thus hardly visible at all.

Trips Out of Town

Fernkloof Nature Reserve

Follow the signs from the (only) traffic lights (028 313 8100). **Open** 6am-8pm Mon-Sat. *Nursery* 8am-noon Mon-Sat.

There are more than 40km (24 miles) of graded paths and trails in this reserve, a third of which is along the cliff tops, amid beautiful fynbos and ericas.

Hamilton Russell Vineyards

In the Hemel en Aarde Valley on the R320, about 5km (3 miles) from the R43 into Hermanus (028 312 3595). **Open** 9am-1pm, 2-5pm Mon-Fri; 2-5pm Sat. **Tastings** free.

This vineyard, which specialises in Chardonnay and Pinot Noir, is the closest to the sea in the whole of Africa. There are tastings, but no cellar tours.

Old Harbour Museum

At the Old Harbour, Marine Drive (028 312 1475). **Open** 9am-1pm, 2-5pm Mon-Fri. **Admission** R2; R1 concessions.

Dive into Hermanus history, with a good look at whaling (including the ugly harpoons used), astonishing whale bones, ancient diving equipment and some original fishing boats.

Ubuntu Cultural Tours

Hermanus (028 312 4334/028 312 2629/073 214 6949). **Tours** by appointment. **Tickets** R80/1hr 30mins.

Whale-crier Wilson Salukazana will take you on a guided tour through Zwelihle township, for a taste of African hospitality, shopping at a spaza (African shop) and a quick ale in a shebeen.

Where to shop

Beach House Interiors

Corner Broad & High streets (028 313 0383). **Open** 8.30am-5pm Mon-Fri; 8.30am-1pm Sat.

A stylish step up from the average gift and decor shop, selling books, desirable gifts and ceramics.

Where to eat

Bientang's Cave

Below Marine Drive, near the Old Harbour (028 312 3454). **Open** 11.30am-4pm Mon-Fri; 11.30am-4pm, 6.30pm-8.30pm Sat, Sun. **Main courses** R45.

You can't get closer than this. The restaurant is built into a cave immediately above the rocks and waves – mind the whales don't splash you.

Where to stay

Arabella Country Estate

On the R44 to Kleinmond (028 284 0000/ www.arabellasheraton.co.za). **Rates** on request.

There are hundreds of guesthouses and B&Bs in Hermanus, but for the ultimate weekend breakaway you might as well stay out of town, in immeasurable style, relieving the exhaustion of rounds of golf with pampering in the spa.

Auberge Burgundy

16 Harbour Road (028 313 1201/ www.auberge.co.za). **Rates** R450-R2,200, B&B.

A luxurious boutique hotel, right in the centre of town so everything's in walking distance – including the whales.

Birkenhead House

Corner 7th Avenue & 11th Street (028 314 8000/ www.birkenheadhouse.com). **Rates** R3,800-R5,900/room, all meals included.

Dollar prices, but ultra luxurious and in the most spectacularly beautiful position, perched right on the cliffs above the sea.

Tourist information

Hermanus Tourism Bureau

Old Station Building, Mitchell Street (028 312 2629/ www.hermanus.co.za).

Southern Right whales

The months between August and November make up the whale season in and around Cape Town. And there are so many whales, that you can forget the idea of having an uninterrupted leisurely drive along the coast: you'll find yourself stopping at all the look-out points in awe of the pods of whales cruising along just off the shore.

By far the most common whales to spot are the **Southern Right whales**. Below are a few facts that will have you sounding like a seasoned whale-spotter in no time:

● The Southern Right whale has been a protected species since 1935.

● While they may be the most popular whales to spot, they actually only number around 3,000 so seeing one should definitely count as a 'Kodak moment'.

● You'll know a Southern Right whale when you see one because of the characteristic rough patches of skin, called callosities, found on the head, chin, near the eyes and near the blowhole.

● They can grow to 18 metres long, and weigh up to 80 tonnes.

● Male Southern Right whales have the largest testes in the animal kingdom. Each pair can weigh as much as one tonne.

Wheatfields in the sleepy village of **Bredasdorp**. *See p225.*

Stanford, De Kelders & Gansbaai (Walker Bay)

From Hermanus the R43 heads inland alongside the Klein River to Stanford, a quirky town of arty locals, neat holiday homes and the odd interesting junk shop, with plenty of back-to-nature opportunities along the river. The town stands on the farm once owned by Captain Robert Stanford, who fell out with his neighbours – in fact the entire Cape colony – in 1849 when he agreed to provision a ship bringing British convicts to settle in the Cape. He eventually packed up and went home to England – where he was knighted.

The road then heads once again for the coast at De Kelders where, with the bright lights of Hermanus twinkling far across Walker Bay, the whale route settles again into a gentler rhythm, and at night it's quiet enough to hear the whales moaning and blowing in the bay.

There are excellent whale-watching opportunities all along De Kelders to Gansbaai and Danger Point, the rocky promontory infamous for wrecking the HMS Birkenhead in February 1852, with the loss of 445 lives. On board were British soldiers en route to the Eastern Cape frontier wars, and their stoic bravery in standing on deck as the ship foundered, while civilians climbed aboard the few lifeboats, has gone down in maritime history as the Birkenhead Drill – 'women and children first'.

Today Gansbaai is a more cheerful place, although there's still plenty of call for bravery if you're up for climbing into a metal cage to go diving with the sharks.

What to do

Klein River Cheese

Outside Stanford, on the R326 towards Riviersonderend (028 341 0693). **Open** 9am-5pm Mon-Fri; 9am-1pm Sat.
Once you taste the cheese on offer here, you'll want to buy all of them. The range includes Gruyère, Leiden, Colby and Danbo.

Marine Dynamics

Geelbek Street, Kleinbaai, Gansbaai (028 384 1005). **Open** 10am-4pm Mon-Sun, weather permitting.
Come face to face with Jaws – only you're safely in a cage dangled over the side of the boat. Companies such as *National Geographic, Time* magazine and the Discovery Channel have used Marine Dynamics to make various documentaries.

Where to eat

Birkenhead Brewery

Outside Stanford on R326 to Riviersonderend (028 341 0183/www.birkenhead.co.za). **Open** 11am-5pm daily. *Summer* 11am-11pm Fri-Sun. *Tours* 11am, 3pm daily. **Tickets** R20/person. **Main courses** *Restaurant* R60.
This is a child-friendly micro-brewery with a restaurant and pub attached, where you can taste their home brews – lager, honey blonde (a German wheat beer), malt stout, and black-and-tan (mixture of lager and stout) – after a tour of the brewery. There are big plans afoot for the addition of wine, bottled water, quad bikes and horse riding.

Mariana's Deli & Bistro at Owl's Barn

12 Du Toit Street, Stanford (028 341 0272). **Open** 9am-4pm Fri, Sat, Sun. **Main courses** R32.

These books are made for walking

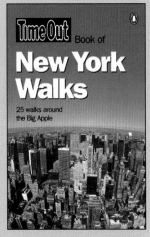

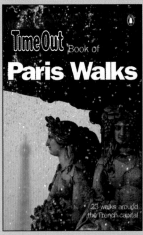

Watch the haggling for fish and get some soul food at **Arniston** harbour.

Believe it or not, this Deli and Bistro's reputation is a lot bigger than the town's. The dishes use home-grown organic ingredients where possible, and – if that's not enough – you can buy fresh-baked breads, pastas, mustards and salad dressings to take home with you. Plan your trip around lunch here.

Tourist information

Gansbaai Tourism Bureau
Corner of Berg & Main Roads (028 384 1439).

Stanford Tourism Bureau
17 Queen Victoria Street (028 341 0340).

Struisbaai, L'Agulhas & Arniston

Keep your eyes on the sea (not you, driver) as you travel the road from Gansbaai through Pearly Beach and on to Quoin Point for more whale aquabatics, but you'll be forced inland again towards Bredasdorp, before turning south once more to L'Agulhas, the southern tip of the continent. The decidedly Egyptian lighthouse, the second oldest in South Africa, looks a little out of place, but it was built to echo the Pharos Tower in Egypt, at the northern end of Africa.

It's worth climbing the lighthouse tower not only for the view, but to glimpse the surprisingly tiny lightbulb that pumps out the light equivalent of 18 million candles. Make time for the museum, too. A plaque down below on the rocks marks the exact southern tip of Africa, the ('official') meeting place of the mighty Indian and Atlantic oceans.

Because it's so rocky here there's no chance of hanging around in the sand, for this you'll have to head to nearby Struisbaai for its long white beach (and holiday homes with some of the most astonishing names on the continent).

But Arniston should be your destination if you want some quiet time in an enchanting fishing village, with raucous haggling for fish at the harbour contrasting with long beach walks for soul food. Named after a British transport ship that was wrecked here in 1815, Arniston is also known as Waenhuiskrans (literally, 'wagon-house cave'), after a huge sea cave that local settlers said was big enough to shelter several wagons and their oxen. It's possible to walk to the cave, but it's only accessible at low tide for a couple of hours.

What to do

Cape Agulhas Lighthouse & Museum
At the southern tip of Africa. Lighthouse tower & museum (028 435 6600/Restaurant 028 435 7506). **Open** 9am-4.45pm daily. *Restaurant* 8am-5pm (or to 11pm if enough bookings). **Admission** R10; R7 concessions. **Main courses** R45.
The museum sheds light on the history of light-houses around the country, not just this one. After your climb up the tower, rest up in the restaurant. (The tower closes 15 minutes before the museum.)

De Mond Nature Reserve
Between Struisbaai & Arniston, about 28km (17 miles) from Bredasdorp (028 424 2170). **Open** 7am-4pm daily. **Admission** R15; R8 concessions.
Home to South Africa's two most endangered coastal birds, the Damara tern and African black oystercatcher, the De Mond Nature Reserve has trails along the river and estuary, and through dune thickets and ancient milkwoods.

EcoQuad
612 Main Road, L'Agulhas (082 854 5078/082 854 5079). **Tours** by appointment. **Tickets** R180-R400/person.
Explore L'Agulhas's fynbos and visit shipwrecks along the coast on a quadbike, which, they promise, has minimal impact on the environment.

The Whale Trail

De Hoop Nature Reserve 028 425 5020/
www.capenature.org.za. **Tickets** R520/person
6 or 12 people. **Rates** *Camping* R95/night;
cottages R285-R550.
The Whale Trail is an unforgettable, five-day, 55-km (34-mile) trail through the De Hoop Nature Reserve, meandering through mountain fynbos with the sea at your side. To add to this, you'll see the biggest concentration of whale calf and cow pairs off this coast during spring and summer.

Where to stay

Arniston Hotel

Beach Road, Arniston (028 445 9000/
www.arnistonhotel.com). **Rates** R530-R865/
person/night, incl breakfast.
There are plenty of holiday homes for hire in Arniston, but the hotel offers peaceful luxury, with balconies overlooking the harbour.

Tourist information

Suidpunt Tourism Bureau

Dr Jansen Street, Bredasdorp (028 424 2584/
www.suidpunttourism.co.za).

Greyton

There are no whales even remotely near Greyton. But it's included here because if you're travelling along the N2 to or from the Whale Route, Greyton makes a delightful and tranquil detour.

Cape Agulhas Lighthouse & Museum. *See p225.*

What to do

Greyton, tucked beneath the Riviersonderend mountains, is a very traditional village, with country stores, tree-lined gravel streets and gardens bursting with blossoms. It's relentlessly (but adorably) quaint. While some of the newer houses on the outskirts are getting a bit big and modern, the more original cottages towards the village centre retain their historic charm and many are National Monuments. Weekend retreats are lazy and tranquil, even though there's plenty to do – horse riding, cycling and it's one end of the spectacular Greyton-McGregor hiking trail. But even better is to indulge in a slow breakfast with the weekend papers, then stroll around the tempting shops (there are seven art galleries), before nipping back to your cottage for a quick pre-lunch nap.

Where to shop

Inside Story

Main Road (028 254 9827). **Open** 9am-1pm,
3-5pm Mon-Sat.
One of those shops where it's difficult to browse without reaching for your wallet – soaps, glasses, gorgeous garden goodies and desirable gifts.

Where to eat

The Oak & Vigne Café

Dr Botha Street (028 254 9037). **Open** 8.30am-6pm daily. **Main courses** R40.
It's worth driving from Cape Town for the 'Cheeky Scramble' alone – a dreamy concoction of scrambled egg, smoked salmon and other interesting goodies.

Where to stay

Greyton Lodge

52 Main Road (028 254 9876). **Rates** R229-R445/
person/night B&B.
This is a real old English country lodge, with the welcome addition of a very convivial pub.

The Post House

22 Main Road (028 254 9995). **Rates** R260/person/
night B&B.
New owners have brought a fresh burst of energy to this historical National Monument. Friendly and cosily stylish, with each room uniquely decorated. There is superb food in the popular restaurant and a good pub in which the locals hang out.

Tourist information

Greyton Tourism Bureau

28 Main Road (028 254 9414/
www.capeoverberg.co.za).

Garden Route

Famous for its hiking trails and stunning valleys, as well as its tourists.

The famous Garden Route is a thin, green, band of forests, rivers and valleys stretching along the south Cape coast from Mossel Bay to Storms River in the Tsitsikamma national park woodlands. This 230-kilometre (143-mile) coastline boasts the largest continuous natural forest area in South Africa, covering a huge 650 square kilometres (250 square miles). The coast is tickled by the Indian Ocean, which is seldom cooler than 20°C and teems with game fish and molluscs.

This is a mecca for lovers of the Great Outdoors: the region offers hiking in the forests of the Outeniqua mountains, canoeing in the Wilderness wetlands, diving off the Knysna heads, mountain-biking in the Knysna forests and whale-watching all along the coast.

The Garden Route is also a gold mine of tourism opportunities. Knysna's annual Oyster Festival is worth an estimated R77,000,000 to the local economy, and the Garden Route as a whole has inspired countless armchair travel books and picture guides.

Mossel Bay is regarded as the start of the Garden Route. Overlooked by the Langeberg and Outeniqua mountains, Mossel Bay still offers the same postal system it offered to its first foreign visitors (15th-century sailors): an old boot – or a boot-shaped box at least – under the Post Office Tree.

The next stop along the coast is **George**. Certainly not the prettiest town on the Garden Route (it's actually a bit ugly, if truth be told), George nonetheless offers enough outdoor activities to keep its visitors' attention away from its dull, industrial appearance.

Just 15 kilometres (nine miles) east of George is the gorgeous, tiny coastal town of **Wilderness**. A quiet dorpie ('little village'), Wilderness offers excellent views, walks in the tranquil forest, a beautiful wetlands National Park... and very little else.

The real 'Jewel of the Garden Route' (and reigning champion of the tourism PR cliché) is the next stop, **Knysna**. Located on the banks of a beautiful lagoon and protected from the

Looking towards **Plettenberg Bay**.
See p232.

Indian Ocean by the towering Knysna Heads, Knysna is a real paradise – and consistently tops polls as South Africa's favourite town.

If you don't get stuck in Knysna (and it's a beautiful town, so it's likely that you will), **Plettenberg Bay** up the coast is well worth a visit. It's the last Garden Route town before Storms River, and offers a gorgeous beach, set in the shadow of the imposing Beacon Isle Hotel.

Although it's undeniably beautiful, parts of the Garden Route are tacky and overdeveloped. Overpriced holiday homes have sprung up all along the coast, and as far west as Swellendam you'll start seeing B&Bs proclaiming themselves to be the 'Heart of the Garden Route'. Accommodation prices rise by about 30 per cent in mid-season, while some establishments more than double their rates during the summer. In season the area (especially Knysna) can become overcrowded and subsequently unpleasant, but for every crowded shopping centre there's a quiet beach or a secluded forest.

GETTING THERE

All the major towns on the Garden Route are located on the N2 National Road, which connects Cape Town to Durban. There is an airport at George (which has international status) and at Plettenberg Bay.

Bus companies offer daily services to the Garden Route from Cape Town (about 500 kilometres/312 miles away) and Port Elizabeth (about 250 kilometres/155 miles away), and car hire services are available in all major Garden Route towns. If you feel like something a little different, try the Outeniqua Choo-Tjoe: an old steam train that runs between George and Knysna.

The main roads that lead to and around the Garden Route (especially the N2) are generally in excellent condition – just be aware of winding mountain passes between George and Knysna, and hyperactive traffic speed traps all along the route. Cows and pedestrians have the nasty habit of strolling aimlessly across the N2 at George, while the road into Knysna is notoriously narrow, and can be a gridlock nightmare during the tourist season. It's still extremely scenic, though, so look on the bright side: it's one of the prettiest places to get caught in a traffic jam.

Mossel Bay

You'd have to be really unlucky to get caught out by bad weather during your stay in Mossel Bay: the *Guinness Book of Records* lists the town as having the world's second-mildest year-round climate (after Hawaii). Overlooked by the Langeberg and Outeniqua mountains,

Around **Wilderness**. *See p230.*

Mossel Bay has – curiously for a south-coast town – north-facing beaches on the warm waters of the Indian Ocean.

Although the area was home to the Khoi and San people for thousands of years, Mossel Bay was first discovered by European traders in 1488, when Bartolomeu Dias rounded the Cape while seeking a sea route to the East. From then on, the sailors who stopped in Mossel Bay left letters for home under a milkwood tree in the bay, establishing an early – and surprisingly reliable – form of postal service. The Post Office Tree still stands today, and letters that are posted at the Tree (which now looks less like a wild milkwood and more like a boot-shaped box) all receive a special postmark.

What to do

Places of interest include the Shell Museum (044 691 1067) and Marine World (044 691 9066). The Cultural Museum (044 691 1067) houses an exhibition of artefacts which were used by Mossel Bay's early indigenous inhabitants. For an afternoon excursion you could take a tour to Kwanonqaba (where the wise witchdoctor will tell you the story of the fallen patriot), or embark on a boat trip to Seal Island to see some, er, seals?

Dias Museum

Market Street (044 691 1067/diasmuseum. museum.com). **Open** 8.15am-5pm Mon-Fri; 9am-4pm Sun. **Admission** R10; R3 concessions.
Here Bartolomeu Dias's caravel still has a home (at least, a life-sized replica does). A boarding pass will allow you on board the ship, where you can find out how the sailors and explorers of old lived at sea.

Where to eat & drink

Café Gannet

Corner Church & Market Streets (044 691 1885). **Open** 7am-11pm daily. **Main courses** R55.

Famous for its local seafood specialities – fresh oysters, mussels and Mossel Bay sole – the Gannet is located near the old Post Office Tree.

Two Oceans
Pick 'n' Pay Centre, 10 Market Street (044 690 3787). **Open** 10am-10pm daily. **Main courses** R60.
This restaurant offers exotic dishes for adventurous seafood-eaters. Baby shark, anyone?

Where to stay

Like the other major Garden Route centres, Mossel Bay's accommodation options vary. There are some good deals around, so avoid the temptation to stay at a fancy-looking hotel directly on the beachfront. Look around and ask at the local tourism office for the best deals. Most spots offer rooms with sea views.

On the eastern side of town (following the N2 to George) is the predominantly Afrikaans town of Hartenbos, where the local caravan park is either crowded and noisy (during the summer holidays) or nearly deserted (during the winter) – take your pick.

ATKV Hartenbos
Follow the signposts from George Street (044 601 7200). **Rates** R200/6 people camping.
This holiday resort caters well for families who wish to be in the Hartenbos area. There are plenty of distractions for children.

Diaz Strand Resort
Beach Boulevard (044 692 0050/ www.diazbeach.co.za). **Rates** R500/4 people camping.
Families needing to stay closer to Mossel Bay may want to head for the massive Diaz resort which offers a variety of entertainment.

Mossel Bay Backpackers
1 Marsh Street (044 691 3182).
Rates R70/person.
Mossel Bay Backpackers has everything you would expect from this kind of establishment; it's cheap, convenient and a great place to meet other travellers.

Old Post Office Tree Manor
Corner of Church & Market Streets (044 691 3738/ www.oldposttree.co.za). **Rates** R730/couple, B&B.
A luxurious guest house, the Old Post Office Tree Manor has a traditional years-gone-by ambience. The food is also good here.

Resources

Internet address *www.visitmosselbay.co.za*.
Internet access *Dotcom, corner Church & Bland Streets (044 690 3866)*.
Mossel Bay Tourist Information *Market Street (044 691 2202)*.
Hospital *12th Avenue (044 691 2011)*.
Police *George Drive (10111/044 691 2222)*.
Post Office *55 Mash Street (044 691 1308)*.

George

If Knysna is the flowerbed of the Garden Route, and Wilderness the Feng Shui water feature, George would have to be the moss-covered garden gnome. Not the most attractive of Garden Route towns, George is the sixth-oldest town in South Africa, with probably the dullest name – it was founded in 1811 while the area was still under British Rule and named after King George III. With a population of about 140,000, the town is the main business centre of the Garden Route. Despite its industrial air and, frankly, dull appearance in places, George is one of the highlights of the Garden Route. There are loads of outdoor activities in the surrounding areas, and the town – located on a picturesque coastal plateau – is probably the best base for a long stay in the Garden Route.

What to do

Not far from George (18 kilometres/11 miles) is **Herold's Bay**, George's intimate beach resort. Herold's Bay is popular for its fishing (especially at Voëlklip and Skotsebank), tidal pools and natural rock pools. The steep cliffs and surrounding trees give the charming little bay a woodland feel.

George Museum
Old Drostdy, corner Caledon & Courtney Streets (044 873 5343). **Open** 9am-4.30pm Mon-Fri, Sun; 9am-12.30pm Sat. **Admission** free.
While the main theme of this museum is the area's lucrative timber industry, it also houses – bizarrely – South Africa's largest collection of gramophone records, all in perfect working order.

Outeniqua Choo-Tjoe
Runs from George's Outeniqua Transport Museum, 2 Mission Street (044 801 8288) & the Knysna Station, Remembrance Avenue (044 382 1361).
Fares R55 single, R65 return; R40 single, R45 return children (under-16s).
The last steam-hauled scheduled passenger train operating in southern Africa. It runs Mondays to Saturdays along one of South Africa's most scenic lines, through Wilderness and along the ragged Indian Ocean coastline. Passengers pay the fare and can hop on and off at their own leisure.

Where to eat & drink

In keeping with the Garden Route tradition, George's pubs and restaurants offer a wonderful range of seafood dishes.

Reel 'n' Rustic
Corner York & Courtenay Streets (044 884 0707).
Open Noon-2.30pm, 5pm-10pm daily. **Main courses** R80.

Trips Out of Town

Tsitsikamma woodlands. *See p127.*

This 'old reliable fishmonger and grill room' is a multi-award-winning restaurant that boasts an ever-changing menu (ranging from fresh seafood to prime-cut meats) and a fantastic wine list.

Where to stay

George's accommodation options range from hotels to holiday resorts. It has to be said that the George Tourist Resort is a bit of a dive but there are some great alternatives.

If you don't want to stay in George, but want to use the area as a base, try to book a spot in nearby Herold's Bay or Victoria Bay. The latter, a surfer's paradise and a small car's nightmare, is nestled in a tiny cove (with room for only 12 ocean-front homes) at the bottom of a ridiculously steep hill. Situated only nine kilometres (six miles) from George's city centre, Victoria Bay has its own (small) caravan park, and it's on the beach (044 889 0081).

Dolphin View
Rooidraai Road, Herold's Bay (044 851 0110/ www.gardenroute.co.za/dolphin). **Rates** R200.
There are some beautiful views of the bay at this laid-back and casual lodge. Among the accommodation available is an apartment or hillside chalet.

Dutton's Cove
21 Herolds Bay Drive (044 851 0155/ www.duttonscove.co.za). **Rates** R360.
Combine luxurious lounging about with dolphin-watching at this rather posh place.

Palm Tree
On the Beach (082 838 4964). **Rates** R200.

Palm Tree is the kind of place where you can sunbathe and surf and swim… and that's about it. Does it sound like paradise to you?

Loerie Guest House
91 Davidson Road, (044 874 4740). **Rates** R290-R480.
A comfortable and charming B&B that is perfectly well-located and friendly accommodation.

Oakhurst Manor
Corner Meade & Cathedral Streets, 044 874 7130/ www.oakhursthotel.co.za). **Rates** R300-R350.
If you prefer accommodation that is a little more snooty than most, this is for you.

Pine Lodge
Knysna Drive (044 871 1974). **Rates** R229-R710.
This is a lovely spot for the whole family.

Resources

Internet address *www.georgetourism.co.za.*
Internet access *Internet Café, Harryman Square, 112 York Street (044 884 0020).*
George Tourist Office *124 York Street (044 801 9295).*
Hospital *Corner of Davidson Road & Langenhoven Drive (044 874 5122).*
Police *37 Courtney Street (10111/044 874 5122).*
Post Office *97 York Street (044 874 1212).*

Wilderness

The quiet seaside town of Wilderness is located just 15 kilometres (nine miles) east of George, but the two towns are so different, that they may as well be light years away.

What to do

The tranquil surroundings make Wilderness a tiny quiet village where most of the excitement is limited to the daily visit of the Outeniqua Choo-Tjoe train. Dolphin's Point, on the cliff at the western end of town, is famous for its whale- and dolphin-watching.

Wilderness National Park

Take the signposted turn-off from the N2 on the eastern side of the lagoon (044 877 1197). **Open** 8am-5pm daily. **Admission** R15; R8 concessions.
The 250sqkm (96.5sqm) of Wilderness National Park is home to a huge wetlands area, which comprises five rivers, five lakes and 20km (12m) of beautiful sandy beach. A joy for those that love the water.

Where to stay

Wilderness offers a wide range of guest houses and B&Bs: it seems every Wilderness property owner has a spare room for guests. Because of Wilderness's limited space, most of the town's larger lodges also house restaurants.

The Boardwalk Lodge & Resort

Young Terrace Road, Wilderness (012 665 5180/ www.boardwalklodge.co.za). **Rates** from R210/ person sharing B&B in the lodge; R810/night for a 2-bedroom self-catering unit.
Nestled deep within the forested slopes of one of the last indigenous forests in the region is this undiscovered gem. Choose between B&B at the lodge or fabulous two-bedroomed, self-catering timber chalets (with privacy and sundecks), all of which overlook the ocean. And to top it all, there's a swimming pool.

Wilderness National Park

Take the signposted turn-off from the N2 on the eastern side of the lagoon (044 877 1197). **Rates** R160 campsite; R560 cabin (4 people).
The park is divided into two camps, both of which offer the high-quality service and self-catering comfort that visitors have come to expect from South African National Parks.

Tourist information

Wilderness Tourism

Leila's Lane (044 877 0045/www.wildernessinfo.co.za).

Knysna

It won't take long to see why Knysna became known as 'The Jewel of the Garden Route'. Set on the banks of a lagoon, protected from the Indian Ocean by the majestic Knysna Heads and flanked in the north by the Outeniqua mountains, Knysna really is a natural paradise. It even has rare birds (the Knysna Loerie) and rarer elephants in the surrounding forests.

Locals are made up of an unusual mix of hippies, businessmen, artists, retired couples and Rastafarians (there's a mini Rasta community at Judas Square), but the most dominant demographics are the smiling locals and curious tourists.

At its best, Knysna is a seaside forest paradise; at its worst it's a snarl of tourist traffic and stressed-out holidaymakers. What you land up with on any given weekend tends to be the luck of the draw. While the summer season is understandably the busiest, Knysna's winter months are just as hectic. The annual Knysna Oyster Festival (044 382 5510/ www.visitknysna.co.za) was designed to attract visitors during the quiet months (back in the days when Knysna actually had quiet months), and now attracts about 120,000 visitors every July. The annual Pink Loerie Mardi Gras is held at the end of May (072 322 2795/www.pinkloerie.com).

What to do

There are shopping centres and shops along Knysna's Main Road, but the widest selection (ranging from overpriced junk to underpriced gems) can be found at the Knysna Waterfront complex (21 Waterfront Drive, 044 382 0955) and at the Woodmill Lane Centre (Memorial Square, 044 382 3045/ www.woodmillane.co.za). For those interested in art, African artwork is usually sold at the western entrance to town, near White Bridge.

Being the creative capital of the Garden Route (or at least the commercial capital), Knysna has a huge selection of art galleries and stores, and the nearby Rheenendal Ramble houses more than 30 studios and attractions, ranging from ceramicists and painters to woodcarvers.

Adventure nuts can try diving and snorkelling at Thesen's Jetty and off the eastern Head, or hiking in the nearby forests. Other attractions include boat charters and a visit to the gold-mining ghost town of Millwood (which, like most ghost towns, is little more than a lonely row of empty buildings in the middle of nowhere). The forest is your best bet for a quiet getaway – unless of course you happen to encounter one of the famous (but extremely rare) Knysna elephants while you're strolling through the trees.

Where to stay

In keeping with a seaside town geared for the tourist market, Knysna offers everything and anything when it comes to accommodation: from backpacker lodges to caravan parks,

Trips Out of Town

B&Bs to luxurious, tree-top hideaways. The lagoon area is home to two cosy caravan parks. Woodbourne also offers self-catering cottages up on the eastern Head, while the western edge of town has intimate lodges and guest houses.

There are so many commendable options to choose from, and there's little point in mentioning them all here. Ask the Knysna tourism offices for a list of accommodation to suit your needs – they're unbiased, and their recommendations can be trusted.

Lightley's Holiday Houseboats

Knysna (044 386 0007/www.houseboats.co.za). **Rates** *4-sleeper* R6,925 5 days; *6-sleeper* R9,950 5 days.
Be daring, be different – hire a houseboat and have a chilled out holiday on the water.

Monk's Caravan Park

Main Street (044 382 2609). **Rates** R70/2 people, R45 each extra person.

Woodbourne Caravan Park

George Rex Drive (044 384 0316/ www.gardenroute.co.za/woodbourne). **Rates** R180/campsite.
Cheap and cheerful, the caravan parks are a great option if you simply need a base at which to dump your things and sleep.

Where to eat & drink

For many South Africans, the words 'Knysna' and 'oysters' are two ways of saying the same thing. Fortunately, oysters are usually available all year round, so you don't have to brave the crowds during the manic Knysna Oyster Festival (in July) if you want to sample this local delicacy. If you're not a fan of seafood, Knysna also offers plenty of steakhouses and carveries. For takeaways and fast-food franchises, try Knysna's busy Main Street.

Grill Room

51 Main Street (044 382 5553). **Open** 7am-10pm daily. **Main courses** R50.
The name says it all – basic and delicious grills, mostly meat but also seafood, are found here.

Harry B's

42 Main Street (044 382 5065). **Open** 7am-8pm daily. **Main courses** R50.
When you feel like a good steak or linefish, but are not in the mood for dressing up, watch the world go by at Harry B's.

Knysna Oyster Company

Long Street, Thesen Island (044 382 6941). **Open** 9am-5pm daily. **Main courses** R55.
This famous restaurant is the best place for oysters. You simply cannot say you have been to Knysna and not eaten them here.

Oysters Restaurant

Pledge Square, 48 Main Street (044 382 6641). **Open** 6-9pm Mon; noon-2pm, 6-9pm Tue-Sun. **Main courses** R60.
If the Oyster Company (*above*) is fully booked, this is a good second bet for oysters. A bustling, busy, friendly restaurant that is welcoming to all.

Pezula Grill

Pezula Golf Club, Lagoon View Drive, Sparrebosch (044 384 1222). **Open** 7am-8pm daily. **Main courses** R65.
Lunch or dinner here is the perfect end to a game of golf… or any other activity for that matter.

34º South

The Market (044 382 7268). **Open** 9am-10pm daily. **Main courses** R58.
This is an unpretentious and comfortable restaurant that serves everything from salads to seafoods and grills. Recommended for lunch or dinner.

Resources

Internet address *www.visitknysna.com.*
Internet access *Africa Adventure, corner of Grey & Waterfront Drives (044 382 4959).*
Knysna Tourism Bureau *Main Road (044 382 5510/www.visitknysna.com).*
Hospital *Main Road (044 382 6666).*
Police *Main Road (10111/044 302 6608).*
Post Office *Main Road (044 382 1211).*

Plettenberg Bay

Named Formosa ('beautiful') by the Portuguese explorers, Plettenberg Bay was later renamed in honour of a Dutch governor. But the name 'Beautiful' is definitely more appropriate: the town lies to one side of the picture-postcard bay, overlooking the endless white beach and the woody Keurbooms River. Plettenberg Bay is absolutely gorgeous… and, in season, completely over-run by visitors.

The pristine beach at the foot of the imposing Beacon Isle Hotel is the summer-time playground of the rich and famous (or simply rich). These days, 'Plett' is populated by retired couples, wealthy holidaymakers and rowdy end-of-year school-leavers.

What to do

Arts-and-crafts enthusiasts will enjoy a visit to Old Nick Village, just three kilometres (1.8 miles) down the hill from the turn-off to Plett. Housed in an historical Cape settlement, Old Nick boasts a wide range of crafts and fine art, perfect for stocking up on gifts.

For nature lovers, the Plett area also boasts elephant and primate sanctuaries, along with about 15 nature reserves.

Monkeyland

16km/10 miles east of Plett on the way to Storms River (044 534 8906/www.monkeyland.co.za). **Open** 8am-6pm daily. **Admission** R80; R40 3-12s.

The primates in this wildlife sanctuary aren't caged – they're free to swing around the forest as they wish. To see the monkeys in action, visitors have to search for them in their natural habitat – and this is done by guided safari only.

Robberg Nature Reserve

8km/5 miles south of Plettenberg Bay on Garden Route (044 533 2125/www.capenature.org.za). **Open** 7am-8pm daily. **Admission** R15; R8 concessions.

The red sandstone of the Robberg peninsula is home to a wealth of wildlife: seals, sea birds and (during the Spring) Southern Right whales.

Tsitsikamma coastline. *See p127.*

Where to eat & drink

Being the playground of the jet set, Plett obviously boasts many fine restaurants – some of which, believe it or not, are perfectly affordable. Added value is that most of the town's restaurants place as much emphasis on ambience as on appetite, making a night out feel like a journey to another world.

Rafiki's

Kettle Beach, Keurboomstrand (044 535 9813/www.rafikis.co.za). **Open** 9am-10pm daily. **Main courses** R60.

A dramatic venue where you can enjoy oysters, local catches and local wines while trying to catch a sight of the local dolphins and whales.

Weldon on Kaya

Piesang Valley Road – off N2 highway (044 533 2437/www.weldonkaya.com). **Open** 8.30am-10pm daily. **Main courses** R48.

Weldon on Kaya offers African-style food in an African-style venue. If you're lucky, you might even witness African drumming, dancing and singing.

Midships Restaurant

Beacon Island Hotel, Crescent Drive (044 533 1120/www.midships.co.za). **Open** 7am-10.30am, 7pm-10.30pm Mon-Fri, Sat; 7am-10.30am, 12.30-2pm, 7pm-10.30pm Sun. **Main courses** R60.

Situated in the Beacon Isle Hotel, Midships offers a daily themed buffet and breakfast restaurant in hotel surrounds. The beach views are beautiful.

Where to stay

As far as accommodation in Plettenberg Bay goes, you can choose either from the wide range of guest houses, or go big. Here are two recommendations, one at either end of the scale.

Aventura Plettenberg

Off the N2 between Plettenberg and Keurboom, (044 535 9309). **Rates** *Chalet* R455. *Camping* R48.

Relaxed accommodation in chalets or tents.

Beacon Isle Hotel

Beach Road, Central Beach (044 533 1120). **Rates** R1,580/room B&B.

This stunning hotel overlooks the magnificent bay. If you need a break from camping and caravan parks, take it here.

Resources

Internet address *www.plettenbergbay.co.za.*
Internet access *The Computer Shop & Café, Main Street (044 533 6007); Plettenberg Bay Tourism Shop 35, Main Street (044 533 4065).*
Police *Main Street (10111/044 533 2100).*
Day Hospital *Marine Drive (044 533 4421).*
Post Office *Main Street (044 533 4422).*

Trips Out of Town

Route 62

The world's longest wine route.

Running parallel to the Whale and Garden routes, Route 62 was once the inland traveller's route that linked Cape Town and Port Elizabeth, but was quickly forgotten when the coastal N2 highway was built. In recent years Route 62 has been dusted off like an old Woodstock-era LP, and given a new spin. Nowadays it's the meandering alternative to the hasty, sometimes crowded Garden Route – and it has also gained fame as the world's longest wine route. Leading eastwards from Paarl and Franschhoek, Route 62 (www.route62.co.za) passes through the vineyards of Worcester, McGregor, Robertson, Montagu, Barrydale, Calitzdorp and Oudtshoorn. It combines lush Winelands scenery with the harsh Klein Karoo landscape, hiding away small villages that seem to have been in hibernation since the N2 first got its Tarmac.

The diverse and fertile **Breede River** valley is home to Utopian Ceres (one of the world's richest agricultural areas), Dutch-influenced Tulbagh (an earthquake survivor: the town was hit by a quake as recently as 1969) and the main economic centre of Worcester. All three towns are near enough to Cape Town to offer quick getaways, and the gorgeous setting should be temptation enough to take up that offer.

As Route 62 winds its way from the Breede River Valley, it reaches the **Robertson Valley**, which is home to dairy farms, wine co-operatives and some bizarre – and entirely out of place – cactus vegetation. While the Winelands and the Breede River have definite French and Cape Dutch architectural heritages, the Robertson Valley, which has anglophile town names like Bonnievale and McGregor, has a more Victorian and Georgian feel.

After the fertile valleys, you will reach a land of Wild West one-horse towns, dry landscapes and empty roads (rolling tumbleweed enters stage to the left). The **Klein Karoo** (literally 'little karoo') is a dry, sobering microcosm of South Africa's famous semi-desert… little wonder, then, that the locals thought it best to establish wine farms and brandy boomtowns here. Montagu offers a matchless combination of historical heritage, awesome rock formations and challenging off-road driving trails (for the more adventurous among you). And after a long and relaxing (or dull, depending on what kind of mood you're in) drive you'll reach Oudtshoorn – a former ostrich feather boomtown (back when those extravagant accessories were all the rage).

Gamka Valley, **Calitzdorp**. *See p238.*

Trips Out of Town

Breede River Valley

This diverse region, which serves as the starting point for the Robertson and Worcester wine valleys, offers panoramic landscapes and magnificent cliffs, with charming and interesting farm towns nestling in the cool valleys. And in case you feel you're turning into too much of a cellar-dweller after all the wine-tasting, the Breede River offer loads of outdoor activities – the most enticing of which is a dip in the river itself.

Ceres

Ceres lies in one of the Cape's richest agricultural areas, on the western side of a fertile basin surrounded by mountains. When it was established in 1854, Ceres was named after the Roman goddess of agriculture, and when diamonds were later discovered in the interior, the road through Ceres became the main route to the north. The Ceres Valley, with its near-Alpine climate, is famous for its apple orchards and other fruits and during cold winters there is often enough snow for skiing in the higher mountains.

Tourist information

Ceres Tourist Information
Corner of Voortrekker & Owen Streets (023 316 1287/www.ceres.org.za).

Tulbagh

Situated on the northern edge of the exquisite Breede River Valley, Tulbagh is surrounded by mountain ranges. It also happens to lie right on top of a dislocation of the underground rock systems. Consequently, in 1969 the town was rocked by an earthquake which did extensive damage to the Cape Dutch buildings on its main drag, Church Street. Tulbagh was subsequently restored and 32 of the buildings in the street were declared National Monuments – this is now the biggest concentration of buildings of this kind in one street in South Africa. Earthquakes and monuments aside, Tulbagh's other curious claim to fame is that its surrounding valleys produce 70 per cent of South Africa's prunes.

Where to eat

Paddagang Restaurant & Wine House
23 Church Street, Tulbagh (023 230 0242). **Open** 8.30am-4pm daily. **Main courses** R75.

Tulbagh's most famous restaurant is Paddagang, situated in historic Church Street. The menu is packed with traditional Western Cape cuisine, and the wines are well worth a taste.

Reader's
12 Church Street, Tulbagh (023 230 0087). **Open** 12.30-11pm Wed-Mon. **Main courses** R70.

Another of Tulbagh's quaint Church Street restaurants, Reader's is nestled in a row of National Monuments. The menu is straight forward but tasty – and the choice of dishes varies daily depending on the availability of fresh produce. A nice addition to the restaurant, located in an 18th-century surgeon's home, is that it also houses an art gallery.

Where to stay

Kagga Kamma
About 80km (50 miles) north of Ceres: follow the directions to Prince Albert Hamlet & Citrusdal, then follow the signs after Op-die-Berg (021 872 4343/ www.kaggakamma.co.za). **Open** 7.30am-6.30pm Mon-Thur, Sat; 7.30am-9pm Fri. **Rates** R1 400/night/person, incl meals & 2 excursions.

The remote bush retreat of Kagga Kamma is quite a detour from Route 62, but it's well worth the extra miles if your wanderlust gets the better of you (be prepared to stay overnight, though – day trips aren't recommended). The area boasts San rock paintings dating back 6,000 years, and the guided 4x4 excursion and San Cultural Tour allows guests to appreciate the ancient sites first-hand.

Mont Rouge
12km (12 miles) from Tulbagh towards the Winterhoek mountains (082 332 8124). **Rates** R200/night for cottage.

Beautifully situated, Mont Rouge is surrounded by fruit trees, rolling vineyards and the magnificent Winterhoek mountains. While the accommodation itself is quite basic (a self-contained cottage on the river front), there are plenty of activities in and around the area to keep you occupied. These range from 4x4 trails for the more adventurous, to orchard and vineyard tours for the more sedate.

Tourist information

Tulbagh Tourist Information
4 Church Street (023 230 1348/www.tulbagh.com).

Worcester

Serving as the main economic centre of the Breede River Valley and the western gateway to the Klein Karoo, Worcester is the centre of the Western Cape's largest fruit- and wine-producing area. It boasts a large number of historically-important old houses in the Cape Dutch and Cape Georgian styles which are well worth visiting. In terms of volume, the

Worcester district is the most extensive and one of the most important wine-making areas in the country. It takes in as many as three co-operative cellars and four private estates, stretching as far as Wolseley, Slanghoek and the Hex River Valley in the north, Villiersdorp in the south and the Nuy Cellar in the east. Varieties from the Worcester Winelands include Chardonnay, Colombar, Chenin Blanc, Pinotage, Cabernet Sauvignon and Sauvignon Blanc. The Worcester region is also the country's most important brandy-producing area, and is home to the world's largest brandy cellar, around which it is fascinating to take a tour.

Montagu: seeped in history. *See p238.*

What to do

Karoo National Botanical Gardens
The turn-off is on the N1 highway, just outside Worcester (023 347 0785). **Open** 8am-5pm daily. **Admission** free.
The Karoo Gardens are one of Africa's only true succulent gardens, boasting beautiful landscaped green spaces and 1.4 square kilometres (half a square mile) of natural, semi-desert vegetation. In spring the gardens burst into a riot of colour, with countless Karoo blooms exploding to life with the first rainfalls. Beautiful, and a must for all green fingers.

Kleinplasie Open-Air Museum
1km (less than half a mile) outside Worcester on the way to Robertson (023 342 2225/www.klein plasie.co.za). **Open** 9am-4.30pm Mon-Sat. **Admission** free.
Kleinplasie offers a slice of life of the early pioneer farmers of the Cape, and features working displays of the agricultural activities that made this country great: witblits (a kind of schnapps) distilling, tobacco rolling and melktert ('milk-tart') baking.

KWV Brandy Cellar
Turn right at the T-junction after Kleinplasie (023 342 0255). **Tours** 10am (Afrikaans) & 2pm (English) Mon-Fri; tours during weekends & in foreign languages can be arranged in advance. **Tickets** R15; R8 under-18s.
Worcester's KWV Brandy Cellar is the largest cellar of its kind in the world, housing about 120 copper pot stills under one roof. A guided tour will allow you to visit the massive maturation cellar, and sample a taste of the superb selection of brandies.

Where to stay

Esperance Guest Farm
Follow the Nonna de Wet turn-off on the R60 between Worcester & Robertson (023 342 1416/ www.esperance.co.za). **Rates** R130-R200/person.
Esperance offers some welcome comfort and seclusion in a Cape Dutch Homestead (complete with Oregon-pine floors, doors and furniture), set in a typical farm environment.

Nuy Valley
Werda Nuy turn-off on the R60 (023 342 1258/ www.nuyvallei.co.za). **Rates** R160/person.
Nuy Valley is a working wine estate, so guests in the farm's rooms and guesthouses have hiking trails, 4x4 trails, angling and wine-tasting directly on their doorstep. The estate, with its divine restaurant, is a popular venue for weddings and conferences.

Rustig Chalets & Holiday Resort
7km (4 miles) off the N1 at Worcester (023 342 7245). **Rates** R320-R360/chalet.
Rustig ('restful') nestles right on the slopes of the Worcester's Brandwacht Mountains. The self-contained chalets offer utter tranquility as well as magnificent scenery, providing a perfect base for exploring the surrounding area… or just sitting back and taking it easy.

Tourist information

Worcester Tourist Information
23 Barring Street (023 348 2795/ www.worcester.org.za).

Worcester Winelands
023 342 8710/www.worcesterwinelands.co.za.

Robertson Valley

Representing 32 members (including 11 co-operatives, 14 estates and seven private producers), the Robertson Wine Valley embraces the four districts of Ashton, Bonnievale, McGregor and Robertson. The **Robertson Wine Valley** (023 626 3167/ www.robertsonwinevalley.co.za) is famous for its Cap Classique sparkling wines, as well as its exceptional examples of Chardonnay, Colombar and Sauvignon Blanc.

Ashton & Bonnievale

Ashton and Bonnievale are in cheese-and-wine country: the quiet villages are home to several cheese and dairy factories, while the outlying farmlands are rich in vineyards.

What to do

Lys se Kombuis

7km (4 miles) from Bonnievale on the road to Swellendam, just after the Merwespont Wine Cellar (023 616 2806). **Open** *by appointment.*
After Ronnie (he of the infamous Sex Shop, *see p239*), Lys (pronounced 'lace') is one of the most charming characters you'll meet on Route 62. A former farm labourer, Lys now serves vetkoek (a freshly-baked local speciality) from her kitchen near the Merwespont Wine Cellar, 7km (5 miles) outside Bonnievale on the road to Swellendam. Her vetkoek is served with a huge dollop of rich storytelling about life in the Breede River farming communities.

Sheilam Cactus Garden

Along the R60 between Robertson & Ashton (023 626 4133).
On the road from Robertson to the fruit-growing town of Ashton, this garden and nursery houses one of the biggest collections of succulents in the world (more than 3,000 specimens), and is well worth a visit – if only for the sheer entertainment value of comparing the silhouettes of the misshapen cacti to the familiar figures of people you know.

Tourist information

Ashton Tourist Information

Main Road (023 615 1100/www.ashton.org.za).

Bonnievale Tourist Information

Main Road, (023 616 2105/www.bonnievale.co.za).

Robertson & McGregor

Nestling in the heart of the Breede River Valley, and with the imposing Langeberg Mountains to the north and the Riviersonderend Mountains to the south, the sleepy farming town of Robertson is home to some of the area's most distinctive wine, fruit and stud farms. The streets are lined with old Victorian and Georgian cottages, shaded by brilliantly purple jacaranda trees. As the biggest town in the valley, Robertson can be used as the base for exploring the surrounding area's smaller towns, like McGregor with its quaint 19th-century charm, colourful characters and country walks.

Where to eat

Branewynsdraai Restaurant & Wine Shop

1 Kromhout Street, Robertson (023 626 3202). **Open** *Wine sales* 9am-5pm Mon-Sat. *Restaurant* 10am-3.30pm, 7-10pm. **Main courses** R80.
Enjoy an excellent and traditional, à la carte or light meal at the restaurant before picking up a bottle of local wine at the wine shop. Perfect.

Rooiberg Winery

Situated on the R60 between Worcester and Robertson (023 626 1663/www.rooiberg.co.za). **Open** 8am-5.30pm Mon-Fri; 9am-3pm Sat.
For any wine enthusiasts, Rooiberg Winery is well worth a stop on your way to or from Robertson. This farm stall will offer snacks and local delicacies to keep the hunger pains at bay. Nestled below the Langeberg range, Rooiberg draws on wines and grapes from 34 farms in the surrounding area.

Where to stay

Deer Creek

Off the R60 between Robertson & Montagu (023 626 5851/www.deercreek.co.za). **Rates** R60-R135/person.
Boasting stunning views across the Breede River Valley to the Langeberg and Riviersonderend Mountains, Deer Creek is a working fruit-and-wine farm with a renovated old farmhouse, which has been converted into three luxurious, fully-serviced, self-catering cottages.

Toy Cottages

7km (4 miles) east of Bonnievale on the road to Swellendam (023 616 2735). **Rates** R50-R75/person.
Set on the outskirts of Bonnievale, Toy Cottages offers two fully-equipped luxury chalets, both of which overlook the beautiful Breede River. Central enough not to be in the middle of nowhere, Toy Cottages are also secluded enough to offer some well-needed rest and recreation.

Tourist information

McGregor Tourist Information

Voortrekker Road (023 625 1954/ www.mcgregor.org.za).

Robertson Tourist Information

Corner of Piet Retief & Swellendam Streets (023 626 4437/www.robertson.org.za).

Klein Karoo

Long, empty roads... small, one-horse towns... the Klein Karoo is a microcosm of the dusty semi-desert that dominates the South African interior. And there's nothing for miles. Considering the 'sobering' and unforgiving climate of the Klein Karoo, it's hard to imagine the area serving as the backdrop to a wine route. But towns like Calitzdorp and Barrydale wouldn't survive if they didn't make a roaring trade in fine wines and papsak ('wine-in-a-bag') plonk. The region's wine culture began back in the 18th century when casks of brandy were transported through the area on their journey to the mining boomtowns of the interior. The Klein Karoo Wine Route (028 572 1284/

Ronnie's Sex Shop. See p239.

www.kleinkaroowines.co.za) now stretches
all the way from the Cogmanskloof outside
Montagu in the west, to the tiny hamlet of
De Rust in the east.

Calitzdorp

Calitzdorp works hard to earn the title of
South Africa's port capital (as in fortified wine,
not harbours and docks). The town is home to
five wine cellars – Axe Hill, Boplaas, Calitzdorp
Wine Cellar, Die Krans and Withoek – and
hosts a Port Festival and the Kannaland Food
and Wine Festival every year. Don't despair,
if you are a teetotaller: sleepy Calitzdorp also
offers the lovely Gamka Mountain Nature
Reserve and the Calitzdorp Spa (044 213
3371/www.calitzdorpspa.co.za) situated
22km (13 miles) from Calitzdorp on the old
cement road to Oudtshoorn.

Tourist information

Calitzdorp Tourist Information
*Shell Garage Building, Van Riebeek Street (044 213
3408/www.calitzdorp.co.za/www.calitzdorp.org.za).*

Montagu

Montagu combines interesting historical
landmarks with outdoor adventure activities.
The town is home to 22 National Monuments
(14 of them are found on one street), while its
awe-inspiring rock formations are fast turning
it into a mountaineering hotspot for rock
climbers. One of the entrances to Montagu leads
over Cogmanskloof Pass, which passes through
a hole in the rock face guarded by an old
English fort from the Boer War.

What to do

Barrydale Wine Cellar
1 Van Riebeeck Street (028 572 1012). **Open** 9am-
5pm Mon-Fri; 9am-1pm Sat.
Although Barrydale is a classic blink-and-you'll-
miss-it town, the Barrydale Wine Cellar is well worth
a visit. The cellar boasts a selection of red and white
wines, as well as the Joseph Barry Brandy, named
after a famous local trader from the 1800s. This Cape
pot-still brandy is distilled in Woodberg stills, before
maturing in French oak for five years. The cellar is
open to the public for tastings, but tours need to be
arranged by phoning in advance.

Montagu Tractor Trips
*Starting at Neil Burger's protea farm, 30km
(15 miles) from Montagu on the road to Touws
Rivier (023 614 2471).* **Tours** 10am, 2pm Wed
(depending on demand); 10am, 2pm Sat. **Tickets**
R45; R10-R30 concessions.
Among Montagu's most popular outings are Neil
Burger's three-hour tractor/trailer rides to the summit of the Langeberg mountains, followed by a typically South African potjiekos (pot-au-feu) meal. For
many South Africans, tractor rides and potjiekos
were an integral part of childhood summer holidays,
so if you're hoping to sample the local culture (or
recapture your youth), hop on board.

Mont Eco 4x4 Trail
*Mont Eco reserve, follow the brown tourism signs
from the R62 between Montagu & Barrydale (0800
62 8873/028 572 1922/www.monteco-nature-
reserve.com).* **Tours** R160 for rock art & fossil tour.
Tickets R80/vehicle/day.
This is rated by those-in-the-know as one of the
toughest in the country. The Mont Eco 4x4 trail is
highly recommended for any tough off-road driver.
The terrain is mostly rough and rocky, but the views
are spectacular, and any 4x4 driver will love to sink
his teeth into the challenge of the tricky trail.

Where to eat & drink

Preston's Restaurant
17 Bath Street (023 614 3013). **Open** 10.30am-2.30pm, 5.30-9pm daily. **Main courses** R60.
This traditional, à la carte restaurant offers a very comfortable dining experience in either the cosy Thomas Bain Pub (smoking section) or the main dining area, or even alfresco on the sheltered garden patio. A must if you feel peckish.

Ronnie's Sex Shop
In the middle of nowhere, about 25km (15 miles) east of Barrydale on the R62 (028 572 1153/ www.ronniessexshop.co.za). **Open** 10am-9pm Tue-Sun. **Main courses** R35.
Watch out for a lonely white building with the words 'Ronnie's Sex Shop' painted on the side. This well-stocked bar (it's not really a sex shop) came about completely by accident. It's the result of a failed farm stall called 'Ronnie's Shop', which was then spiced up with a touch of risqué vandalism – and has become an oasis for bored and thirsty travellers.

Where to stay

Fraai Uitzicht Historic Wine & Guest Farm
Klaas Voogds East, on the gravel road between Robertson and Ashton/Montagu (023 626 6156/www.fraaiuitzicht.com). **Rates** R385-R730/person.
Fraai Uitzicht offers four-star accommodation in a farmhouse that dates back to 1798, surrounded by vineyards and fruit orchards.

Tourist information

Montagu Tourist Information
24 Bath Street (023 614 2471/www.montagu.org.za).

Oudtshoorn

If you can't be bothered to explore every town in the Klein Karoo, go directly to Oudtshoorn. The Cango Caves, the ostrich farms and the Cango Wildlife Ranch are enough to keep you occupied for a good few days. If you're in town in April, prepare for the flood of up to 10,000 visitors to Oudtshoorn's famous art festival, the Klein Karoo Nasionale Kunstefees (044 203 8600/www.kknk.co.za).

What to do

Cango Caves
28km (17 miles) outside Oudtshoorn, located on the R328 (044 272 7410/ www.cangocaves.co.za). **Open** daily. **Tours** *Standard tours* 9am-4pm every hr on the hr daily. *Adventure tours* 9.30am-3.30pm every hr on the half-hr daily.
Tucked away in the foothills of the Swartberg Mountains lie the incredible Cango Caves. The caves extend for more than 5km (3 miles) in a series of huge chambers connected by low passages (most of the darker reaches are off limits to the public, though). The rocks and limestone have been sculpted and scoured by 20 million years' worth of rainwater, which flowed through fissures and crept through cracks in the earth's surface, gradually forming the Cango Cave's dramatic subterranean halls and winding tunnels.

Cango Wildlife Ranch
North of town on the R328 to the Cango Caves (044 272 5593/www.cango.co.za). **Open** 8am-5pm daily. **Admission** R42; R28 concessions.
At Cango Wildlife Ranch, you can see hippos, crocodiles and snakes, not to mention white Bengal tigers. The ranch is known for its conservation efforts, especially its cheetah-breeding programme.

Where to eat

Headlines Restaurant & Coffee Shop
Baron von Rheede Street (044 272 3434). **Open** 8.30am-2.30pm daily; 8.30am-2.30pm & 6-10pm Mon-Sat. **Main courses** R30.
If you're in Oudtshoorn you're in ostrich country – and you can't leave without trying a dish of ostrich omelette. And the best place to sample it is Headlines, which claims to be the only restaurant in the whole world that specialises in ostrich cuisine.

Jemima's Restaurant
94 Baron von Rheede Street (044 272 0808). **Open** 6-10pm Tue-Sun. **Main courses** R55.
This is a wonderful restaurant run by two sisters, where diners will find a sizeable bite of local flavour. Jemima's offers a broad selection of excellent Oudtshoorn delicacies – with the local wines taking pride of place on the menu.

Trips Out of Town

WWW.OUDTSHOORN.COM

Linking the *Garden Route* & ROUTE 62

Oudtshoorn, the ostrich capital.

Where to stay

Cango Mountain Resort
22km (13 miles) out of Oudtshoorn on the R328 (044 272 4506). **Rates** R238-R440/chalet.
Voted among one of the top-100 self-catering resorts in South Africa, Cango Mountain Resort is located in dense bushveld in the heart of the Swartberg. And with the Cango Caves only 7km (4 miles) away, this is the perfect base for exploring Oudtshoorn without actually staying in Oudtshoorn.

Caves Country Lodge
3km (2 miles) out of town on the R328 towards the Cango Caves (044 272 2511/www.ostrich showfarm.co.za). **Rates** R150-R205/person.
With the Oudtshoorn Ostrich Show Farm right on its doorstep, Caves Country Lodge offers visitors a vibrant farm atmosphere. And if seeing the ostriches makes you hungry, the lodge serves various ostrich dishes at the Old Vic's restaurant (open for lunch, noon to 2.30pm daily). A fun place to stay.

De Hoek
35km (21 miles) out of Oudtshoorn, off the Swartberg Pass road on the way to the Cango Caves (044 272 8214/www.dehoekmountainresort.co.za). **Rates** R40-R280.
Some distance out of Oudtshoorn, De Hoek offers camping, caravan and self-catering accommodation, with plenty of adventure activities for the outdoor types, from rock climbing to abseiling.

La Plume Guesthouse
Follow signs to Volmoed from the R328, heading in the direction of Safari and Highgate Ostrich farms (044 272 7516/ www.laplume.co.za). **Rates** R350-R525/person.
This is a four-star guesthouse set in a charming turn-of-the-century Victorian homestead on a working ostrich, alfalfa and vineyard farm. La Plume offers good views of the Olifants River Valley and the Swartberg Mountains.

Oulap Country House
Drive through Oudtshoorn heading for De Rust. After De Rust take the Willowmore turn-off on the R341 & 15km (9 miles) later you will see the turn-off to Oulap Country House. Take the road that leads you up the mountain (044 241 2250/ www.classicafrica.com/portfolio/oulap.htm). **Rates** R750/person, incl breakfast & dinner.
This private country home sits in splendid isolation in the magnificent Swartberg Mountains. Friendly owners Jans and Elmari Rautenbach are truely delightful company, taking on different roles: while Elmari serenely spoils her guests with excellent traditional dinners, Jans, a master storyteller, regales visitors with stories of the region – its magic and people. It's a wonderful place.

Oudtshoorn's ostriches

Oudtshoorn is the ostrich capital of the world – nowhere else are these funny-looking feathered creatures found in such great numbers. Thanks to ostrich feathers becoming hugely popular, Oudtshoorn became a boom town in the early twentieth century. The fad for oversized feathers died out eventually, but the ostrich ranches remain – and now offer guided tours and the chance for visitors to interact with – and ride on – these enormous birds.

Cango Ostrich Farm
14km (8 miles) out of town on the R328 heading towards the Cango Caves (044 272 4623/ www.cangoostrich.co.za).

Highgate Ostrich
Farm 2km (1 mile) off the R328 heading west out of town (044 272 7115/www.highgate.co.za).

Oudtshoorn Ostrich Show Farm
3km (2 miles) out of town on the R328 towards the Cango Caves (044 279 1861/www.ostrich showfarm.co.za).

Safari Ostrich Farm
5km (3 miles) south of Oudtshoorn on the R328 (044 272 7311/www.safariostrich.co.za).

Tourist information

Oudtshoorn Tourist Information
Baron von Rheede Street (044 279 2532/ www.oudtshoorn.com).

Trips Out of Town

West Coast

Wind down in the West Coast: famous for its beaches and fabulous flowers.

Spring flowers in **Darling**.

While the touristy south coast (with its Whale Route and Garden Route) is famously foresty and green, the West Coast is all sand, sea and sleepy fishing villages.

It's no wonder surfers so enjoy the Weskus (as its known in Afrikaans): with its long stretches of white sand, it seems specially designed for leisurely walks along the beach.

Strictly speaking, South Africa's west coast stretches all the way from Cape Town to Oranjemund at the Namibian border – for visitors, though, the touring route known as the West Coast only goes as far as Lambert's Bay.

Travelling north on Route 27 – the West Coast road – you follow the rugged coastline, looping from one quiet fishing village to the next. The landscape is always beautiful, but the best time to visit is early Spring (August and September), when the entire area is carpeted in brightly coloured wild flowers. Plan your route to travel north in the morning and south in the afternoon, as the flowers tilt their faces during the day to face the warm West Coast sun

Darling, your first stop on the West Coast route, isn't really a 'stop along the coast', but this inland village is well worth the quick detour – especially in the springtime when the flowers are blooming.

Just as the remoteness of the West Coast is starting to get you down, along comes **Langebaan** – a popular coastal resort town (still not nearly as crowded as the spots along the Garden Route) that offers excellent kite-surfing and rock angling... as well as the bright lights of the local casino.

If you've still got the energy, retrieve your peace of mind at the popular fishing village, **Paternoster**, before catching a stunning sunset at **St Helena**. And lastly, you'll reach **Lambert's Bay** – where the working fishermen will show you how it's really done.

Darling

It's not actually on the coast, but any trip up the R27 has to include a quick detour to Darling to visit Evita Bezuidenhout and her sidekick, Pieter-Dirk Uys, for a humorous update on the progress of democracy in South Africa. Revues at Evita se Perron, the theatre situated on the old Darling station platform, are so sharply funny they cut right to the bone, and a long warm afternoon (or evening) with Evita on the stage and a plate of wholesome *boerekos* ('farm food') on your table is what draws people to Darling in droves.

It's a heady mix of Azania and gazanias for, of course, people also visit for the flowers – in spring, Darling becomes a floral mecca, and has hosted a spectacular wild flower show almost every September since 1917.

What to do

Darling Cellars
On the R315, 15km from Darling (022 492 2276). **Open** 8am-5pm Mon-Thur; 8am-4pm Fri; 9am-noon Sat.
This wine cellar produces a wide range from vineyards in the area, under the Darling Cellar, Onyx, Flamingo Bay and Zantsi labels. Take a cellar tour to see how the wine is made then finish up with a generous tasting of Merlot, Pinotage, Cabernet Sauvignon, Chardonnay and Sauvignon Blanc.

Evita se Perron
Darling Station, Arcadia Road, Darling, 50 min north of Cape Town on the R27 (022 492 2851/ 022 492 2831/www.evita.co.za). **Open** 9am-5pm Tue-Sun; bar & restaurant till midnight on show nights. **Tickets** R75 for Pieter-Dirk Uys shows; R50 for others.
If you must do anything, you must see Tannie ('Auntie') Evita's state-of-the-nation performances, in this theatre that is almost a museum. She'll 'praat kaktus' on stage, giving the audience a 'dekaffir-nated' take on racism and life in South Africa.

Where to eat

Tannie Evita's Pantry
Evita se Perron, Darling Station, Arcadia Road, Darling, 50 min north of Cape Town on the R27 (022 492 2851/022 492 2831/ bookings@evita.co.za/www.evita.co.za). **Open** 9am-5pm Tue-Sun; *bar & restaurant* until midnight on show nights. **Main courses** R45.
Delicious, traditional South African breakfasts and lunches, and, when there are evening shows, dinners, all washed down with lashings of satire.

Tourist information

Darling Tourism Bureau
Corner Pastorie & Hill Streets (022 492 3361/ www.darlinginfo@mweb.co.za).

Langebaan

It's always playtime in Langebaan, even when the weather's lousy and the wind threatens to blow the world away. 'Perfect!' shout the wind- and kitesurfers, who turn the lagoon into a colourful frenzy of soaring sails. When it's calmer, the kayakers take over, the anglers hit the rocks and the more restful among us sit back and watch from a lagoonside restaurant,

a glass of chilled Chardonnay in hand. For golf fans, there's a golf course nearby, and, if you're missing the city's bright lights, you can get your fix at the casino.

The first Dutch settlers called the deep channel at the southern end of the lagoon the baan, and so Langebaan got its name. Today the lagoon is a magnet that draws people in hordes, and supports more than 250 species of birds, some from as far as Siberia. But peak season is when the floral fiesta lights up the earth in August and September.

One other good thing about Langebaan is that the water in the lagoon is warmer than the ocean – although that's not saying much.

What to do

Cape Sports Centre
Right on the beach (022 772 1114/www.capesport. co.za). **Open** 9am-5pm daily.
Join the human butterflies who take to the air on windy days at the lagoon. But if kitesurfing isn't your thing, choose from guided kayaking, windsurfing, mountain biking and dirt bike tours. Accommodation is also available.

West Coast Fossil Park
On the R45 (West Coast Road) near Langebaan (022 766 1606). **Open** 8am-4pm Mon-Fri; 9am-1pm Sat, Sun. *Tours* 11.30am daily. **Rates** R20; R10-R15 concessions.
At the West Coast Fossil Park you can tour the excavation site that's unearthing evidence of the African bears, three-toed horses and short-necked giraffes that roamed the coast between two and five million years ago. You can even sift for bones yourself. The guided tour includes a slide show and talk. Great for kids, big and small.

West Coast National Park & Postberg Reserve
Off the R27 near Langebaan (022 772 2144). **Open** 7am-7pm daily. **Admission** R20 locals; R60 international visitors.
This beautiful reserve that embraces Langebaan lagoon is famous for its kaleidoscope of wild flowers that carpet the land in late winter and into spring. There are also several bird hides that get you up close to the hundreds of species of birds. Postberg Reserve, a beautiful section of the park, is open 9am to 5pm in August and September only, and is well worth visiting if you are in the area during those months. There's accommodation within the park.

Where to eat

Die Strandloper
On the beach, on the road to Club Mykonos (022 772 2490/ 083 227 7195). **Open** Lunch & dinner daily in season, otherwise by reservation. **Main courses** R130 eat-all-you-can buffet.

Trips Out of Town

Here's why we love the West Coast – for the beach restaurants where you leave your shoes in the car and take a dip in the waves between courses. Arrive at noon, grab a tin plate and a mussel shell for a spoon, and you're set for a feast where, just as you think you've had enough, they slap more seafood on the fire. Plenty of *potjies* (pots au feu) for carnivores.

Where to stay

The Farmhouse Hotel
5 Egret Street (022 772 2062/ www.thefarmhouse langebaan.co.za). **Rates** R280-R460.
Stay at the Farmhouse Hotel for superior luxurious comforts and spectacular views over the stunning Langebaan Lagoon. A real treat.

Houseboats on Langebaan Lagoon
Moored at Kraalbaai in the West Coast National Park (022 492 3944/082 882 9001/South African National Parks boat: 021 552 0008). **Rates** R650 4 persons/night.
There's nothing more idyllic than bobbing gently in the lagoon, aboard a fully equipped houseboat. Find the peace you came here for.

Cape fish

While driving along the West Coast, you'll come across rows of tiny fish strung up on ropes on the roadside. Don't be afraid – these are a local delicacy called *bokkoms. Bokkoms* come from a fish called 'Harders', which are caught, pickled and wind-dried, making, in other words, fish biltong – to be enjoyed with a glass or two of something ice cold on a sweltering day. And if that's not enough to tempt you, think of them as poor man's anchovies. Other fish favourites include:

Snoek
A game fish that can be eaten fresh or pickled. It's not usually found on restaurant menus and is best eaten straight off the *braai* (barbecue).

Tuna
A summer gamefish – and some of the cheapest sashimi in the world.

Cob (Kabeljou) & Geelbek (Cape Salmon)
Both are white fish, fairly firm and best eaten fresh from the sea.

Kingklip
A firm white fish, with a neutral flavour, that can be cooked in all sorts of ways.

Tourist information

Langebaan Tourism Bureau
Bree Street (022 772 1515/www.langebaaninfo.com).

Paternoster

Many of Paternoster's original fishing cottages above the beach are being bought up quickly, because of their position and their charm. Cutesy bed-and-breakfasts are mushrooming everywhere, some excellent, some little more than a place to sleep, but there's still an air of West Coast wildness, simplicity and charm as you walk the long beach.

'Paternoster' is Latin for 'Our Father', and one story goes that the village was so named after a Portuguese ship was wrecked on these treacherous rocks. Luckily, all the sailors were rescued, and they gave special thanks by reciting many 'paternosters'.

The Cape Columbine headland, about five kilometres (three miles) from Paternoster, is named after another forsaken ship, the Columbine. The Columbine was claimed by this treacherous coast in 1829 during a voyage from London to Australia.

The Cape Columbine lighthouse is now the first thing sighted by ships coming from Europe, warning them with the equivalent of the light of nine million candles.

What to do

Cape Columbine Lighthouse
In the Cape Columbine Nature Reserve (021 449 2400). **Open** 10am-3pm Mon-Fri. **Admission** R10; R5-R7 concessions.
Visit this lighthouse for an insider's view of all the workings. Before a stroll in the nature reserve.

Cape Columbine Nature Reserve
5km (three miles) from Paternoster (022 752 2718). **Open** 7am-7pm daily. **Admission** R9; R6 concessions.
This is a wild and rocky shoreline strewn with seashells and seaweed. Camping is available.

Flower-spotting
Paternoster (022 752 2632). **Date** Aug-Sept.
Find out where the flowers are blooming most prolifically in the Paternoster area.

Where to shop

Die Winkel op Paternoster
St Augustine Road (022 752 2632). **Open** 10am-4.30pm daily.
Weave your way through mountains of bric-a-brac and home-made preserves, plus the unavoidable *bokkoms* or dried fish.

The Oystercatcher's Haven
48 Sonkwasweg (022 752 2193/www.oystercatcher shaven.com). **Rates** R320/person sharing.
Experience West Coast solitude at its best at this beautiful (and intriguingly named) home on a headland, with its stunning and endless views of the sea. And to top it all, the house is tastefully decorated. The only drawback is that there are three double rooms, so you may be expected to share.

St Helena
You're guaranteed fantastic sunsets over the sea all along the West Coast, but St Helena has a unique claim to fame. Due to the configuration of the bay, it's the only place anywhere along this coast where you can watch the sun rise over the water.

The bay is also a favourite with migrating Southern Right whales, which use its calm waters for mating and calving.

St Helena was named by Portuguese explorer Vasco da Gama, who touched South African soil here for the first time – you can visit a monument that marks the spot on the right as you head towards Britannia Bay. St Helena itself is centred on the commercial fishing industry, and factories enjoy the most stunning locations right on the beach. The rugged natural beauty returns as you head west towards Stompneus Bay and Paternoster, but only once you've passed all the luxury housing estates that are swallowing up the coast.

What to do

Flower-spotting
Langebaan (022 752 1944). **Date** Aug-Sept.
Phone to find the best displays in the area.

Where to eat

Oystercatcher Cattle Baron
At Shelley Point, Britannia Bay (022 742 1042). **Open** Lunch and dinner Tue-Sat; lunch on Sun. **Main courses** R60.
Whatever you order is 'on the rocks'– the restaurant perches beautifully right above the beach. Perfectly placed so that you can watch the whales while enjoying meaty fare, with lots of seafood, too.

Where to stay

Dolphin B&B (or self-catering)
22 Ecklonia Street, Britannia Bay (022 742 1944/ www.dolphinsa.com). **Rates** R150-R185/person sharing.
This B&B is right on the beach at Britannia Bay – watch the dolphins from your bed.

Fresh fish in **Paternoster**. *See p244.*

Where to eat

Voorstrand Restaurant
Right on the beach (022 752 2038). **Open** 10am-10pm daily. **Main courses** R60.
Book a table on the verandah and let lunch last until the sun sinks lazily into the sea.

Where to stay

The Beach Camp
In the Cape Columbine Nature Reserve (082 926 2267/www.ratrace.co.za). **Rates** R95-R175 tented accommodation.
An alternative to B&Bs, this is a tented (but cosy) camp right on the beach within the reserve, with hot showers and seafood straight from the water.

Trips Out of Town

Doring Bay.

Lambert's Bay

Lambert's Bay is definitely not one of those quaint little fishing villages you'll find reproduced in a thousand watercolours. But it is the real thing. The town's hub is the harbour, where you can smell the fish factories and watch the tough fishing trawlers heading out for another battle with the Atlantic. Aside from deep-sea fishing and boat trips, the main attraction for travellers is Bird Island, a slab of rock that's home to about 14,000 Cape gannets and is the world's only gannet-breeding colony that's accessible on foot – it's just a short walk along the harbour wall.

Aside from the gannets, the island also hosts large numbers of cormorants and penguins, all clustered together in their own, fiercely separate groups. And judging by the decibel level, they're all shouting at each other. But suffer the noise, because the sight of several thousand densely packed and squabbling gannets is unforgettable (as is the smell!).

Also worth a visit is Doring Bay, a short drive (on a gravel road) from Lambert's Bay: not only is it a charming fishing village, but it is also visited by dolphins and whales during August and September.

What to do

Bird Island Nature Reserve
Follow the marked signs from Lambert's Bay (022 931 2900). Visitors' complex & bird hide. **Open** *Summer* 7am-7pm daily. *Winter* 7am-5pm daily.
This amazing island reserve is simply a must-see for bird lovers and tourists alike. The bird hide puts you right where the action is, in full view of the beautiful creatures. But it can get very noisy, so you might want to take earplugs with you! There's also a coffee and curio shop for browsing.

The Dunes 4x4 Route
On the R364, 50km (30 miles) from Lambert's Bay (027 432 1244).
This is a major sand pit for 4x4 lovers. Routes can be tailored to suit your skills and your vehicle, with guides on hand if you get stuck.

Where to shop

Sandveld Organics Suurfontein Farm
On the R364 outside Lambert's Bay (027 432 1244). **Open** 9am-6pm daily.
Aside from a range of organic veggies, shelves groan with garlic cloves in oil, pickles, chillies and all sorts of preserves like carrot and radish jam.

Where to eat

Isabella's Coffee Shop
Lambert's Bay Harbour (027 432 1177). **Open** 8am-10pm daily. **Main courses** R55.
You don't get fresher than this. Isabella's is right on the wharf inside the commercial harbour, just metres from the nearest ship. Very casual, with a floor of sea shells, offering light meals and loads of fish.

Muisbosskerm
On the Eland's Bay road, 5km (three miles) south of Lambert's Bay (027 432 1017). **Open** Lunch & dinner daily, depending on reservations. **Main courses** R120 eat-all-you-can buffet.
Allow several hours for this endless feast of fish, mussels, calamari and crayfish prepared on open fires, bread straight out of the *bakoonde* (oven) and *potjies* (pots au feu) of venison. And it's all eaten on the beach, toes in the sand.

Tourist information

Lambert's Bay Tourism Bureau
Church Street (027 432 1000).

Directory

Directory

Getting Around

Arriving & leaving

By air

Cape Town International Airport
021 937 1200/www.airports.co.za
The airport is 22 kilometres
(15.5 miles) east of Cape
Town along the N2 highway.
International airlines serving
Cape Town International
include South African Airways,
British Airways, KLM,
Lufthansa and Virgin Atlantic.

Avis, Budget, Eurocar and
Hertz are the car hire operators
at the airport. Desks are
located inside the Arrivals
terminals. If you hire a car that
needs to be returned to the
airport, make sure to refuel
beforehand, as there is no
petrol station at the airport.

There are no train or bus
services from the airport,
therefore it is recommended
– if you haven't hired a car –
that you get a taxi or shuttle
bus. The authorised airport
taxi company, **Touch Down
Taxis** (021 919 4659), prides
itself on getting passengers to
the City Centre in about 20
minutes, costing R150 to R160.

Shuttle services are available
on demand or by prebooking
at the Arrivals terminals.
Shuttle companies **Way 2 Go**
(021 934 2503), **Magic Bus**
(021 934 5455) and **City
Hopper** (021 934 4440) drive
passengers, on request, to their
required destination. Schedules
vary according to flight arrival
times; passengers can prebook
their return trip to the airport.

Domestic airlines serving
Cape Town are SAA,
SA Airlink, BA/Comair,
Nationwide and Intensive

By Air. There are daily flights
from Johannesburg, Durban,
Port Elizabeth, Bloemfontein
along with several other cities
and large towns.

Airlines
South African Airways
*reservations 021 936 1111/arrival
& departure times 021 934 0407/
www.flysaa.com.*
British Airways *reservations &
passenger enquiries 0260 011747.*
KLM Royal Dutch Airline
*reservations 086 024 7747/021
670 2500.*
Lufthansa *086 184 2538.*
Virgin Atlantic *021 797 7512.*

Public transport

Public transport is sorely
lacking in Cape Town.
Using a car is therefore the
recommended, and sometimes
the only, option. If you don't (or
don't want to) drive, you can
hire a car with driver or use a
shuttle service (*see below*). If
you're in a group, this is a safe
and economical option.

Taxis
We recommend that you take
taxis if you are on your own or
travelling at night, but they're
expensive, at R7 to R8 per
kilometre. Check the fare in
advance and make sure your
driver is familiar with the area
you're going to. There's a taxi
rank at the Adderley Street
end of the Grand Parade in the
City Centre.

Reliable taxi services
Sea Point Taxis *021 434 4444.*
Marine Taxis *021 434 0434.*
Unicab *021 448 1720.*

Minibus taxis
Minibus taxis are the
main form of transport for
people commuting from the

townships. Consequently they
are very cheap (a trip from
Cape Town all the way to the
Southern Suburbs will set you
back between R3 and R5), but
routes are predetermined
(however informal), so make
sure they are going where you
want to go before hiring one.
Major routes are covered – for
example, from Adderly Street,
City Centre, to Sea Point on the
Atlantic Seaboard and then
along Main Road from Sea
Point all the way to Wynberg
in the Southern Suburbs. You
can either go to a designated
taxi rank (there's one at Cape
Town Railway Station deck,
see p249) or flag one down.
The only way to determine
the route is to ask the driver,
and you should always do so:
you don't want to end up in
Khayelitsha or the Cape Flats
(not the safest of places). Be
alert to your personal safety
in the crowded minibuses,
especially if you're travelling
on your own (this applies
particularly to women).

Minibus taxis may be cheap,
but they are not right for
everyone: they can get very
crowded at peak hours and
are not always roadworthy;
drivers often drive very fast,
offering hair-raising rides. If
nothing else, you will be
exposed to a side of Cape
Town that few tourists get to
see – the quirky humour,
optimism and resilience of the
Cape Flats people who operate
and travel on these taxis.

Rikkis
Rikkis (call 021 423 4888 or
hail one on the street) are
open vans holding up to eight
passengers. They offer speedy,
convenient transport within

the City Bowl and surrounds, going as far as Camps Bay in Atlantic Seaboard, and Observatory in the Southern Suburbs. Prices are low, ranging from R10 to R50. Rikis operate from 7am to 7pm Monday to Friday and 7am and 2pm on Saturday.

By bus

Alternatively, there are a few bus routes in Cape Town: **Golden Arrow**'s buses (0800 656 463) run from Cape Town Station to most of Cape Town's suburbs. They travel between 6am to 6pm from Mondays to Saturdays and 8am to 5pm on Sundays, though timetables are erratic, so it is best to phone first to confirm. Fares are cheaper during off-peak hours (8am to 4pm). As an example, it costs R8.90 for a single ticket from Cape Town to Hout Bay and you can buy a weekly clipcard ticket for R42.

The double-decker **Cape Town Explorer Topless Bus** (021 511 1784) offers a whirlwind two-hour see-the-city tour for R90 with a hop-on-hop-off facility. It leaves from outside Cape Town Tourism at the V&A Waterfront (*see p259*), and runs in a loop, with major stops at the City Centre, Table Mountain and Camps Bay.

Train

Cape Town Railway Station serves mainly long-distance destinations, although **Metrorail** (0800 656 463) has four routes to the Cape Town suburbs, including a scenic route from Cape Town to Simonstown, for R12 one-way (a weekly clipcard is R82).

Trains are usually packed during rush hour (7-8am and 4-6pm). For a more leisurely experience, the sedate Biggsy's Restaurant Carriage and Wine Bar (021 449 3870) – operating daily on the Cape Town/Simonstown route – offers breakfast, lunches, snacks and magnificent False Bay views.

For timetables, route maps, train traffic reports and contact numbers, consult www.capemetrorail.co.za.

Spoornet/Shosoloza Meyl (021 449 3871, 086 000 8888/www.spoornet.co.za) trains run from Cape Town to the major Winelands towns, including Stellenbosch, Paarl and Franschhoek.

If you want your rail experience to be pleasant, it's vital you follow these rules:
● Always travel first class (Metroplus). A third-class (Metro) ticket might cost you half the price, but you stand to gain twice the trouble: pickpocketing, broken

windows, standing room only.
● Always travel during peak times when there is more security. Off-peak, security becomes almost non-existent, allowing drunkenness and lawlessness to take over.

Cape Town Railway Station
Adderley Street, City Centre (021 449 2991/booking office 021 449 3871). **Open** *booking office* 7.30am-3.55pm Mon-Fri; 7.30-10.30am Sat. **Credit** AmEx, DC, MC, V.

Driving

South Africans drive on the left side of the road, so the opposite side from the US and Europe (excepting the UK). On multiple lanes it is advised to overtake on the right-hand side. The speed limit in South Africa is around 120 kilometres per hour (75 miles per hour) on open roads and 60 kilometres per hour (37 miles per hour) in urban areas.

South Africa has a very high road accident rate, with the annual death toll around 10,000. A further 15,000 are injured. Many accidents take place during public holidays.

Vehicle hire

If you want to hire a car, you must be over 25 years old and have a valid driver's licence.

Travel in style

Le Cap Motorcycle Hire
43 New Church Street (021 423 0823/ www.lecapmotorcyclehire.co.za). **Rates** from R200/day.
Lots of models of motorcycles for hire, plus longer tours and accommodation packages.

African Buzz
202 Long Street, (021 423 0052). **Rates** from R175/24hrs.
African Buzz rents out scooters for two. You'll need a motorcycle licence (or an international driving licence with the 'A' category checked).

Harley-Davidson Cape Town
45 Buitengracht Street (021 424 3990). **Rates** from R1,000/day 9am-5pm, R1 150/24hrs.
You'll need to pay a fairly sizeable deposit to rent a Harley here, and be over 23.

Cape Limousine Service
Muizenberg (021 785 3100/082 927 9320). **Rates** from R850/hr, R,000/2hrs.
Imported Lincolns can be hired out (complete with chauffeur). Rates get cheaper the longer you rent for.

Some agencies require five years' driving experience. Call around to get a good deal; some agencies do not hesitate to rip off foreigners.

The Automobile Association (0800 010101 www.aasa.co.za) advises foreign drivers to obtain an international driver's licence (available through local auto associations) for driving in South Africa. However, car hire companies only require a valid overseas licence.

Avis *021 424 1177.*
Budget *021 418 5232.*
Hertz *021 400 9650.*
Khaya Car Hire *021 936 2255.*
National Car Hire *021 425 1755.*

Fuel stations

Petrol (gas) stations can be found throughout Cape Town (particularly along main roads, in the V&A Waterfront and along Buitengracht Street). Most are open 24 hours a day, with a convenience store, but aim to keep the petrol tank full to avoid running out late at night or in remote areas. At the time of writing petrol cost around R4 a litre. Tip your 'petrol jockey' your change up to ten per cent.

Insurance

Driving on gravel roads can be very dangerous: go very slowly, and be aware that your hire car insurance might not cover road damange.

When you rent a car check your agreement for details of both both damage and liabililty insurance, as levels of cover vary. If you don't have a home policy that covers you for every eventuality, it might be best to pre-book via a multinational company in your home country.

Parking

A new parking plan has been adopted in the City Centre. In some shopping areas,

uniformed attendants are stationed to help you park, either for a fee or a tip, during office hours from Monday to Saturday.

On the streets, authorised parking marshals, in uniform, can help operate meters and sell parking cards, which are also available from shops and kiosks. Parking marshals are allowed to accept tips but can't solicit them.

There are also hordes of 'unofficial' car guards (not in uniform), which can make parking an unsettling experience. These car guards, usually in competition with each other, direct you to a vacant parking bay, or ask for money to mind the meter for you. The city authorities are keen to control this practice and recommend that you decline the services of such 'parking attendants'. But be aware that some of them do not take kindly to being snubbed and, fuelled by liquor, can become abusive, especially towards women. It's better to keep your windows up, ignore their blandishments and find a parking garage or official parking lot. At night, park in a secure, well-lit area.

Vehicles are removed if parked illegally – another reason to avoid the illegal parking spots offered by the 'car guards'. To locate your missing car go to a police station or call the traffic department tow-away section on 021 406 8700. You might have to cough up around R500 if your car has been impounded plus R200-R500 for a parking ticket. You will be charged R22 per day storage fee after the fourth day.

When you go along to pick up your car, take along your rental agreement and passport to show officials. Payment is by cash or (local) cheque only.

For more information about parking in the City Centre call 0800 220 017.

Walking

Cape Town is so spread out that it's really a driver's town: walking is only a viable means of transport within certain focal areas – once you've got there by car. These include the beach-side promenades and the City Centre, which the authorities make a big effort to keep safe and attractive through local initiatives and business partnerships. The areas containing its main attractions are both practicable and enjoyable to explore on foot, with plenty of street life.

Cape Town is a car town both because of the distances involved but also because it can feel safer sitting in your vehicle than out on the streets, where you may well feel at your most vulnerable. Walking is not safe city-wide, and as a stranger not tuned in to the cues and clues you should err on the safe side and always take the following precautions:

● Avoid dark, isolated areas.
● Do not walk alone.
● If you get lost, a stranger may not be your best source of help. Try and find a police or traffic officer.
● A camera around your neck marks you as a tourist. Carry it in a shoulder bag.
● Don't carry large sums of money. Keep small change in your wallet or purse and bank notes and credit cards in an inside pocket.
● Never carry your wallet in the back pocket of your trousers.
● Don't wear valuable/ ostentatious jewellery.
● Carry your bag close to your body.
● Don't be fooled by con artists or strangers who offer you the opportunity to get rich quickly.
● If in doubt, call a cab. Always carry the number of a reliable company; *see p248* or ask at a hotel or tourist office.

Resources A-Z

Age restrictions

The legal age for drinking and buying alcohol is 18. You have to be 16 to smoke or purchase tobacco products. The age of consent for sex is 16.

Attitude & etiquette

South Africa has an informal atmosphere and people usually introduce themselves by their first names, even in business relationships. Capetonians are, according to their hardworking Gauteng cousins, notoriously laid-back. Most organised events start punctually in the Mother City, but be warned: no Capetonian worth their salt will be less than an hour late for an informal engagement. Blame it on the gorgeous sunsets over our beaches – such influences make it hard to be punctilious.

Business

The Cape Town Regional Chamber of Commerce and Industry, founded in 1804, is a one-stop shop for business information and advice.

Funded by its more than 4,500 members, 70 per cent of which are small businesses, the Chamber offers a host of networking opportunities, an interactive website that includes a searchable database, contacts locally and overseas, international trade information and advice. It provides a comprehensive library, events and exhibition management facilities, specialist advice and links to local, regional and central government.

The *Cape of Good Hope Business Guide*, published by the Cape Town Regional Chamber of Commerce and Industry, is available at the Cape Town Tourism Visitor Information centres (*see p259* **Visitor information**). It lists business associations, local financial institutions, property brokers and other services vital to setting up business.

Business organisations

Cape Chamber House

19 Louis Gradner Street, Foreshore, City Bowl (021 402 4300/ www.caperegionalchamber.co.za). **Open** 8.30am-2.45pm Mon-Fri.

The Cape Town Regional Chamber of Commerce and Industry (Cape Regional Chamber) is the leading source for business information and services. Cape Town is regarded as the hub of South African commerce and is a major convention destination.

Wesgro

021 402 8600/www.wesgro.org.za. Wesgro is the official Trade and Investment Promotion Agency for the Western Cape Province. It is the first point of contact for foreign importers, local exporters and investors wishing to take advantage of the Cape's investment opportunities.

Conventions & conferences

Cape Town International Convention Centre

Convention Square, 1 Lower Long Street, City Centre (021 410 5000/ www.cticc.co.za/www.capetown convention.com).

The Cape Town International Convention Centre opened in June 2003. All facilities are accommodated under a single roof, including a deluxe hotel, dedicated exhibition space and generous banqueting and meeting facilities.

For older and less glamourous facilities, the Good Hope Centre (021 4002507) or Civic Centre (021 400 4196) are spacious venues.

Couriers

Use the trusted names when you want to courier your parcel: **DHL Worldwide Express** *086 0345000*; **XPS** *021 380 2400*.

Shipping

Britannia (021 551 3676/ www.britannia.co.za) will ship anything from one box to an entire container or more.

Translators & interpreters

For translation and interpretation services contact **Folio Translation Consultants** on 021 426 2727 or the **SATI** (South African Translators' Institute) on 021 976 9563.

Travel advice

For up-to-date information on travelling to a specific country – including the latest news on safety and security, health issues, local laws and customs – contact your home country government's department of foreign affairs. Most have websites that are packed with useful advice for would-be travellers.

Australia
www.dfat.gov.au/travel

Canada
www.voyage.gc.ca

New Zealand
www.mft.govt.nz/travel

Republic of Ireland
www.irlgov.ie/iveagh

UK
www.fco.gov.uk/travel

USA
www.state.gov/travel

Consumer affairs

South Africa has recently experienced an upsurge in awareness of consumer rights. Call the companies below for any consumer-related problems, enquiries and complaints: **Consumer Affairs Office** (021 483 3256/3049/3910/ 5497/5735); **Consumer Complaint Line** (0800 007 081).

Customs

There is a huge list of prohibited goods and it is in your best interest of visit the following website if you are in any doubt: www.sars.gov.za (and go to the Customs link), or phone 021 413 5000.

Personal effects (used, not new) are admitted duty free. Other allowances for visitors to South Africa are as follows (per adult):

● 1 litre of spirits.
● 2 litres of wine.
● 400 cigarettes.
● 50 cigars.
● 50ml perfume.
● 250ml eau de toilette.
● Gifts and souvenirs to the value of R500.

A permit is required for firearms. Available at entry points, it's valid for 180 days, and can be renewed at any South African police station.

Disabled

Most attractions and hotels in Cape Town are disabled-friendly (for details on the outlying areas, contact the relevant tourism bureaux). Passenger Aid Units (PAU) are on call at all major airports. Larger car rental companies can provide vehicles with hand controls.

The following companies can provide services for disabled travellers:

Flamingo Tours
*021 557 4496/www.flamingo
tours.co.za.*

Titch Travel & Tours
021 686 5015/www.tichtours.co.za.

Drugs

Cannabis (or dagga), while the drug of choice and freely available, is still illegal and its possession a punishable offence. Hard drugs are also available, but once again, not legal and could land you in prison. Among locals, the rave generation favours the likes of ecstacy, while the real problem lies with drugs like mandrax (or buttons), heroin and crack.

Electricity

The power supply is 220/230 volts AC. The standard plug in South Africa is the 15-amp round-pin, three-prong plug. The European-type two-pin plug can be used with an additional adaptor plug (which can be bought at shops). Remember to bring transformers along for larger appliances where necessary. Most hotels have 110-volt outlets for electric shavers.

Embassies & consulates

Belgium Consulate General
Vogue House, Hans Strijdom Avenue, Foreshore, City Bowl (021 419 4690).
British Consulate
Southern Life Centre, 8 Riebeeck Street, City Centre (021 425 3670).
Canadian High Commission
Reserve Bank Building, 60 St George's Mall, City Centre (021 423 5240).
French Consulate *2 Dean Street, Gardens, City Bowl (021 423 1575).*
German Consulate General & Embassy *St Martini Gardens, Queen Victoria Street, City Centre (021 464 3000).*
New Zealand Hon. Consulate General *2 Lente Road, Sybrand Park, Rondebosch, Southern Suburbs (021 696 8561).*
USA Consulate General
Broadway Centre, Heerengracht Street, City Centre (021 421 4280).

Emergencies

Ambulance *10177.*
Poison Crisis Centre *Red Cross Children's Hospital 021 689 5277.*

Police flying squad *10111.*
Sea Rescue *021 405 3500.*

Gay & lesbian

For gay and lesbian services, *see p180*; for entertainment *see p177* Gay **& Lesbian**.

ATIC Aids information and counselling centre *021 797 3327.*
Galacttic *www.galacttic.co.za.*
Tourism & business *021 439 4649.*
Gay Film Festival *021 465 9289.*
Gay, Lesbian & Bisexual Helpline *021 448 3812.*
Open 1-5pm Mon-Fri; 1-9pm Sat, Sun.
Triangle Project Health *021 448 3812*
Information, counselling and support.
Wolanani HIV/Aids Service Agency *021 423 7385.*

Health

There is no national health scheme in South Africa. Be sure to purchase good travel insurance which will cover full medical expenses.

Travel clinics situated at Tourism Visitor Information centres can advise you on health matters (021 426 4260/ 021 405 4500/021 419 1888).

South Africa has excellent medical and dental services with highly trained doctors and fully equipped hospitals; standards of hygiene are high throughout Cape Town and the towns of the Western Cape. As a result many foreign visitors combine tourism with dental procedures, laser eye surgery or cosmetic surgery, which cost much less here because of the favourable exchange rate.

Contraception & abortion

All mother-and-child health services – family-planning advice, contraception and abortions – are free to all South African citizens and tourists. A fee of R7 is charged for pregnancy tests. The 'morning after' pill, effective up to 72

Directory

hours after unprotected sex, is now available over the counter in South Africa. This peace of mind will cost you R60.

Cape Town Station Reproductive Health Clinic

Cape Town Railway Station, City Centre (021 425 2004/www.capetown.gov.za). **Map** p283 H-I4. **Open** 7am-3.45pm Mon-Fri; 8am-11am Sat.

Chapel Street Clinic

Corner of Chapel & Balfour Streets, Woodstock, Southern Suburbs (021 465 2793/4/www.capetown.gov.za). **Open** 7.30am-4pm Mon-Fri.

Civic Centre Clinic

Ground Floor, Civic Centre Building, City Centre (021 400 2083/www.capetown.gov.za). **Open** 8am-3.30pm Mon-Fri.

Marie Stopes Clinics

91 Bree Street, City Centre (0800 11 77 85). **Map** p282 G4.

Dentists

Government facilities have come under tremendous

budgetary pressure and tourists are likely to face long queues and bureaucratic formalities. Use one of the major private clinics in the event of an emergency (but check your health insurance will cover you). Dental charges are very reasonable by international standards.

Doctors

Your hotel can call a doctor for you; alternatively get a list of approved doctors from your embassy. Doctors are listed in the phone book under 'Medical', Hospitals under 'H'.

Hospitalisation is generally arranged through a medical practitioner but in the event of an emergency, visitors may telephone or go directly to the casualty department of any general hospital. To call an ambulance dial 10177.

Outpatient treatment may be obtained at hospitals for a reasonable fee.

Hospitals

Cape Town Medi-Clinic *021 464 5500.* **Christiaan Barnard Memorial Hospital** *021 480 6111.* **Durbanville Medi-Clinic** *021 980 2100.* **Libertas Medical Centre & Hospital** *021 591 3018.* **Panorama Medi-Clinic** *021 938 2111.* **Red Cross Children's Hospital** *021 658 5111.*

Pharmacies

Most pharmacies trade at normal shopping hours. **Lite-Kem** (Scotts Building, 24 Darling Street, City Centre, 021 461 8040) and **Glengariff Clicks Pharmacy** (2 Main Road, Atlantic Seaboard, 021 4348622) are open until 11pm.

STDs, HIV & AIDS

Chapel Street Clinic *Corner of Chapel & Balfour Streets, Woodstock, Southern Suburbs (021 465 2793/4/www.capetown.gov.za).* **Open** 7.30am-4pm Mon-Fri.

Slanging match

You would think that in a city where everyone speaks English you'd find your way around easily. But with 11 official languages that all feed off each other, you might just get some friendly local telling you 'check you at the *braai*, it's gonna be a jol' or 'it's good weather to catch a tan, we're leaving now-now'. So, to avoid any confusion, here's a helpful guide to the most common South African slang words.

Braai A barbecue, an extremely popular South African past-time, where you're likely to eat things off the grill, accompanied by lots of beer and maybe bread and salads.

Bru/boykie/bra/china A friend, buddy, mate, used for men and, strangely, sometimes women.

Catch a tan To suntan, mostly carried out on the Clifton beaches when you should be at work.

Dankie Not so much slang, it's Afrikaans for 'thank you'.

Dop An alcoholic drink.

Eish! Expression of disbelief.

Howzit/Hoesit Very nifty, a greeting and 'how are you' combined.

Izzit An expression of disbelief, as in 'Is it?'. Add it to the end of sentences to mean 'You're kidding'.

Jol A very good time, anything from a party to a good shopping spree.

Just now/now now This can mean anything from 'in a little while' to 'when I get around to it' to 'the next day'.

Lekker Cool, nice, sounds good (the opposite is *vrot*, *kak* or *sif*).

Lank Very. As in 'it's lank cool'.

Sweet/kiff See *lekker (see above)*.

Robot Don't be alarmed, this is a traffic light.

Slap chips French fries. 'Slap' means floppy, even though they're just as rigid as anywhere else in the world.

Moerse An over-used swear word, used liberally as an adjective, implying a lot or huge, or even great. As in 'A *moerse* party' ('the mother of all parties'), 'A *moerse* hangover'('a mother of a hangover').

Kak Afrikaans for 'shit'. Used often.

Civic Centre Clinic *Ground Floor, Civic Centre Building, City Centre (021 400 2083/www.cape town.gov.za).* **Open** 8am-3.30pm Mon-Fri.

Helplines

The following helplines all operate 24 hours daily.

Alcoholics Anonymous *021 592 5407/www.alcoholicsanonymous. org.za.*
Gay, Lesbian & Bisexual Helpline *021 448 3812.*
Lifeline/Childline *021 461 1111/www.lifeonline.co.za.*
Narcotics Anonymous *0881 30 03 27/www.na.org.za.*
National AIDS Helpline *0800 012 322/aidshelpline.org.za.*
Rape Crisis Centre *021 447 9762/www.rapecrisis.org.za.*
Stop Women Abuse *0800 150 150.*

Internet

Internet cafés are springing up like mushrooms in the city, and most large shopping malls (*see p128*) have them. Charges are reasonable. Many hostels and hotels now also have internet facilities, as do the City Centre and V&A Waterfront offices of the Cape Town Tourism Visitor Information Centre (*see p259*).

ID

You have to be 18 or over to get admission to a club, but the door people will not ask to see your ID unless they think you still look like a teenager. Leave your passport in a safe at your hotel if you're just sightseeing for the day.

Language

South Africa has 11 official languages: English, Afrikaans, Ndebele, North Sotho, South Sotho, Swazi, Tsonga, Tswana, Venda, Xhosa and Zulu. In the Western Cape, English, Afrikaans and Xhosa are the most commonly spoken. Staff at some establishments and attractions speak German

(there is a large German community in Cape Town), French or Italian.

Left luggage

Left Luggage is a company that will hold your baggage when you cannot. Contact them on 021 936 2884 at Cape Town International's domestic terminal and on 021 936 2494 for the office at the International terminal.

Legal help

Law Society of the Cape of Good Hope
Waalburg Building, Burg Street, City Centre (021 424 8060). Map p283 H4.

Legalwise Leza Legal Insurance
3 Medical Centre, Adderley Street, City Centre (021 419 6905). Map p283 H3.

Legal Resources Centre
Greenmarket Place, Greenmarket Square, City Centre (021 423 8285). Map p283 H4.

Libraries

Visitors may register as temporary members at any Cape Town City Library branches (see the telephone directory under Municipality of Cape Town). City Library Head Office 021 467 1500 can also help.

Lost property

Check the 'lost and found' section in the classified section of the daily newspapers. Report your loss at the local police station and leave a contact number and address.

Media

Newspapers

Local newspapers focus on local content, engaging in the usual slugfests with politicians

and sportspeople. There are also community weekly newspapers such as the *Atlantic Sun,* which informs on a very local level. *Mail & Guardian* comes out every Thursday and has an excellent entertainment section.

Morning: *Cape Times & Business Day* (English), *Die Burger* (Afrikaans).
Afternoon: *Cape Argus* (English).
Sunday: *Sunday Cape Argus* (English), *Sunday Times* (English), *Rapport* (Afrikaans).

Radio

An excellent audio guide comes via talk radio station Cape Talk (567AM), which gives detailed weather information by area, news, traffic reports, arts and entertainment updates. Other local, largely music FM radio stations such as 5FM (89.9FM), KFM (94.5FM), P4 (104.9FM) and Good Hope FM (94-97FM) pepper their line-ups with South African music and include information on live performances along with news. Fine Music Radio (101.3FM) has a more classical line-up to soothe the ears.

Magazines

Monthly magazines vie for space on groaning shelves. Imports tend to be ridiculously overpriced. *Cosmopolitan, Elle, Marie Claire* and *Glamour* all have local versions. If you're after a bit of gossip and TV entertainment, look out for *TVplus* or *Heat.*

TV

SABC (South African Broadcasting Commission) owns SABC 1, 2 and 3. SABC 1 caters almost exclusively for the black market and has local shows and news plus older dubbed programmes in the main local languages and soaps. SABC 2 also has multi-lingual programmes, including

Afrikaans. SABC 3 is in English with much US and some British programming. E.tv is a privately owned station that tries to push the limits in its line-up: some not so great local shows along with big US series. M-net is a subscriber channel, big on sport, series and movies.

Money

Banks

ABSA Bank *LTD Adderley Street, City Centre (021 480 1911).*
First National Bank *82 Adderley Street, City Centre (021 487 6000).*
Nedbank *85 St George's Mall, City Centre (021 469 9500).*
Standard Bank *Provincial Head Office, Standard Bank Building, Heerengracht, City Centre (021 401 2111).*

Bureaux de change

Foreign exchange facilities can be found at larger commercial banks, along with the Cape Town Tourism Visitor Information centres (*see p259*), the airport and bureaux de change such as Rennies Travel and American Express.

American Express *V&A Waterfront 021 419 3917; Thibault House, Thibault Square, City Centre 021 408 9700.*
Rennies Travel *Riebeeck Street, City Centre (021 410 3600/www. renniestravel.co.za).*
Other locations: check phone book.

Credit cards & ATMs

South Africa has a modern and sophisticated banking system, and most shops and hotels accept credit cards, including international cards such as AmEx, Diners Club, Visa, Mastercard and their affiliates. In country areas the use of cards might be restricted. Standard credit cards cannot be used to pay for petrol (gas); only special 'garage cards' or cash are accepted.

Automatic Teller Machines (ATMs) are widespread and accept most international cards.

Lost or stolen cards

American Express *0800 991021 traveller's cheques/011 710 4747 cards.*
Diners Club *011 358 8406.*
MasterCard *0800 990 418.*
Visa International *0800 990 475.*

Currency

The local currency is the South African Rand. The Rand tends to be weak on the international currency markets, making Cape Town a great destination for bargain luxury. (At press time there were R6.5 to the dollar and R11.6 to the pound.)

● R1 = 100 South African cents.

● Coins in circulation: 1c, 2c, 5c, 10c, 20c, 50c, R1, R2, R5.

● Banknotes in circulation: R10, R20, R50, R100, R200.

Tax

South Africa has adopted a Value Added Tax system of 14 per cent on purchases and services. If you are a foreign visitor, you can reclaim VAT on purchases you're taking out of the country if their prices total more than R250. Go to the VAT office at the airport, in the international departure hall, leaving yourself plenty of time before your plane leaves. You'll need your original tax invoiced receipts and your passport, along with the purchased goods. Once you've filled in a form and had your application accepted, you can pick up a refund in your home currency from one of the banks in the departure lounge.

You can also do the paperwork at the VAT Refund Offices at the Tourism Visitor Information centres (*see p259*).

Natural hazards

Visitors may drink tap water anywhere unless a notice specifically warns otherwise.

The sun in South Africa is much stronger than in Europe

and it is essential for visitors to use a good sunscreen for protection. Skin cancer has become a serious concern in sun-worshipping Cape Town.

Venomous snakes and spiders might occasionally be encountered. If you are bitten, try to get a good look at the animal so that you can identify it and call 10177 for help.

Opening hours

Most shops in the City Centre and suburbs are open between 9am and 5-5.30pm weekdays and on Saturdays till 1pm. Major malls may open at 9am and close at 6pm (or even 9pm, Sundays and most public holidays included, sometimes with a 10am start).

Government agencies keep to traditional weekday-only hours. Most banks close at 3.30pm weekdays, and are open on from 9am to 11am on Saturday mornings.

Muslim-owned businesses close between noon and 1pm on Fridays.

Police stations

If you have been the victim of a crime that you don't deem serious enough to summon the Police Flying Squad (10111), go to your nearest police station (in the phone book under Regional Offices of National & Provincial Government, or call Directory Enquiries on 1023).

Cape Town Charge Office *021 467 8077.*
Cape Town International Airport Police Station *021 934 0707.*
Cape Town Railway Station Charge Office *021 419 1673.*
Police Tourist Unit *021 418 2852.*
Tourist Safety Unit *021 421 5115/5116.*

Postal services

Post from Cape Town is remarkably inexpensive. For R3.30 you can send a postcard to Europe or the US; letters cost R3.30 for a standard envelope up to 50g in weight.

Local and international mail can be handled by all post offices (open 8.30am-4.30pm weekdays; 8am-noon Saturdays). The main branch is on Parliament Street, City Centre (021 464 1700). This office has an enquiry desk. Look in the *White Pages* under 'Post Office' for a full list.

Religion

Anglican: St George's Cathedral *corner of Queen Victoria & Wale streets (021 424 7360).*
Buddhist: Information Plantation Centre *Plantation Road Wetton (021 685 3371/021 671 7443).*
Bahai: Bahai Centre *2 Vine Street, Woodstock (021 448 1102).*
Dutch Reformed Church *Groote Kerk Adderley Street (021 461 7044).*
Evangelical: Lutheran Church *Strand Street (021 421 5854).*
German Evangelist *St Martins 240 Long Street (021 423 5947).*
Greek Orthodox *Church 75 Mountain Road, Woodstockm Southern Suburbs (021 447 4147).*
Hindu: Temple Siva *Aalayam 42 Ruth Street, Rylands (021 638 2542).*
Jewish: Cape Town Hebrew Congregation *88 Hatfield Road, Gardens (021 465 1405).*
Methodist: Metropolitan Church *corner of Longmarket & Burg streets, Greenmarket Square (021 422 2744).*
Mosque: Palm Tree *185 Long Street (021 447 6415/021 448 4723).*
Mosque: Shaafie *Chiappini Street, Schotche Kloof (021 423 4569).*
Roman Catholic: St Mary's Cathedral *At the bottom of Roeland Street; the pink cathedral opposite parliament (021 461 1167).*
Salvation Army *Corner of Vrede & Tuinplein Streets (021 686 7511).*

Safety & security

Cape Town's City Centre and major malls have made considerable efforts to safeguard tourists and

residents against crime. Surveillance cameras monitor activities in the City Centre and security guards watch over major shopping centres. Nonetheless, tourists should take the sensible precautions they would in any major city.

For your safety, stick to the beaten path – especially after dark. If you visit a township, it should be with a guided tour during the day, and steer clear of anywhere near the Cape Flats.

Being safe is very much a case of using your common sense and being alert. Always chat to the staff at your lodgings about local safety, and take their advice seriously. If you're staying in the City Bowl and visiting the V&A Waterfont in the evening, take a taxi. If you do walk anywhere at night, make sure it is in a busy area, filled with restaurants and clubs. Safety in numbers applies, and women should try not to walk alone.

In addition to this, avoid carrying large sums of cash, having cameras or video cameras hanging loose and leaving your belongings unattended. Take special precautions at lonely lookout points, especially at dusk or after dark. For more precautions, *see p251*.

Street children and beggars may approach you for a handout. Many social workers counsel against giving money to the children as it usually gets handed over to an older figure or is spent on sniffing glue. If you wish to do good, give food, or donate to a local organisation (*see p22* **Kids who live on the streets**).

Smoking

Smoking is prohibited in all public places. Some restaurants and bars, however, provide specially demarcated smoking sections for their smoking patrons.

Study

You can learn a local language, or a foreign one, at one of the many language schools dotted around town. Call Cape Town International School of Languages on 021 674 4117.

Telephones

Dialing & codes

The international dialing code for South Africa is 27 followed by the area code (minus the first zero) and the subscriber's number. Nationally, the area code is used with the zero in front; within an area the zero is dropped. South Africa's telephone system is run by Telkom, which, up to now, has had no competition. Legislation, however, is underway to introduce some privatisation into the market. Numbers prefixed with 086 are generally recorded information numbers and do not always work from outside the country.

Useful local codes

Beaufort West (0)23
Bloemfontein (0)51
Caledon (0)28
Durban (0)31
George (0)44
Johannesburg (0)11
Kimberley (0)53
Langebaan (0)22
Oudtshoorn (0)44
Pietersburg (0)15
Port Elizabeth (0)41
Pretoria (0)12
Upington (0)54
Worcester (0)23

Mobile phones

If you're visiting from abroad, you can hire a cellphone (mobile phone) at the airport or at one of the Cape Town Tourism Visitor Information centres (*see p259*). You then purchase pay-as-you-go airtime from your local provider. South Africa operates on the digital GSM900 network. Standard dual-band UK phones will operate, but only tri-band US phones.

Public phones

Blue public phones work on coins (50c, R1 and R2 coins are best) while green public phones work on local Telkom phone cards, which you can purchase in a variety of shops and post offices – most public phones advertise the closest sale point. International calling cards (R50 or R100) are available from Cape Town Tourism Visitor Information centres (*see p259*).

Time

South Africa is two hours ahead of GMT, seven ahead of Eastern Standard Winter Time and ten ahead of Pacific Standard Time. South Africa does not have daylight saving time in summer.

Tipping

Many waiters and waitresses are students who rely on tips to supplement their wages. A ten per cent tip is acceptable although up to 15 per cent may be given if service is outstanding. Groups of over eight often have an automatic ten per cent service charge added to their restaurant bill. Tip porters in hotels and at airports R5 to R10 per piece.

Toilets

Most public toilets in shopping malls and restaurants are clean and should be used rather than the public facilities in the City Centre and surrounds, which, although you may be lucky and find a clean one, are not always sanitary.

Tourist information

Tourism Visitor Information Centres

Corner of Burg & Castle Streets, City Centre (021 426 4260/www.cape-town.org). **Open** 8am-5pm Mon-Fri; 8.30am-1pm Mon-Sat; 9am-1pm Sun, public holidays.
This is your first stop for maps and brochures, and to book guided tours (*see p43*). Plus currency exchange, internet access and other services.
Other locations: V&A Waterfront (021 405 4500).

Visas & immigration

Visa requirements

Citizens of the UK, the Republic of Ireland and Australia do not need visas,

Climate control

Spring

After the cold, miserable indoor months of winter, September comes springing onto the scene in suitably colourful, springtime style. Take a drive up the N7 highway into the Namaqualand for a look at the stunning spring flowers (call 022 752 1944 to find out the best spots), and head down the N2 to Hermanus for the Whale Festival (*see p150*). Beware, though: spring brings with it the first puffs of Cape Town's most infamous wind, the south-easter, and while this is good for kite-fliers, it's not so good for windswept city dwellers, girls in loose-hanging skirts or blustered, flustered newspaper vendors. Hold onto your hat, though: the south-easter only really starts howling in summer.

Summer

The most important thing to remember if you are visiting in the summer is to pack high factor sunscreen. It's so tempting to spend the days strolling through the streets and enjoying the many beaches, and to forget that you must keep protected. The sun is blistering hot. But it also cools down into long and warm evenings – perfect for the many outdoor events and festivals. The week around Christmas and New Year is the busiest (*see p151* **Sunny Christmas cheer**).

Autumn

Forget your season of mists and mellow fruitlessness, with spring lingering like the guest who just won't leave, Cape Town's weathermen have been known to cancel autumn all together. With most locals taking a long break for the Easter Weekend, April is a busy – and dangerous – month on the roads. This time of year is usually a washout, and by the time the rains really roll round sometime in May, the stormy winter will have arrived in force.

If you're travelling by car, take special care on the roads around Easter – South Africa's shameful road death statistics make horrifying reading… and the local drivers never seem to learn.

Winter

Q: What comes after two days of rain in Cape Town? A: Monday. The city's prime seaside location at the bottom end of Africa comes at a price: it's first in the firing line when the barrage of cold fronts moves in from the Antarctic, and the winters can be especially nasty. The early settlers used to call it the Cape of Storms, and these days it's only insane surfers and hungry fishermen who brave the waters in winter.

as long as they have a passport valid for 30 days beyond the length of their trip, a return ticket, proof of accommodation and, if travelling for business, a letter from the inviting organisation. If they stay for longer than 90 days (up to a year is allowed without a visa), they also need a letter from a chartered accountant offering proof of funds.

The requirements for trips of up to 90 days are the same for US travellers, but for longer trips a visa is required.

For more information, consult www.southafrica house.com/Consulate.htm (UK citizens), www.saembassy.com (US citizens) or http://home-affairs.pwv.gov.za (South Africa's home affairs department).

Entry requirements can change at any time, so check carefully on the above sites and with your airline/travel agent well in advance of your planned departure date.

Weights & measures

South Africa uses the metric system. Useful conversions are given below.

1 centimetre (cm) = 0.39 inches (in)
1 inch (in) = 2.54 centimetres (cm)

1 yard (yd) = 0.91 metres (m)
1 metre (m) = 1.094 yards (yd)

1 mile = 1.6 kilometres (km)
1 kilometre (km) = 0.62 miles

1 ounce (oz) = 28.35 grammes (g)
1 gramme (g) = 0.035 ounces (oz)

1 pound (lb) = 0.45 kilogrammes (kg)
1 kilogramme = 2.2 pounds (lb)

1 pint (US) = 0.8 pints (UK)

1 pint (UK) = 0.55 litres (l)
1 litre (l) = 1.75 pints (UK)

50°F = 10°C
68°F = 20°C
86°F = 30°C
15.5°C = 60°F
24°C = 75°F
32°C = 90°F

When to go

Cape Town's climate is in general Mediterranean, with warm, dry summers and mild, moist winters. On the coast during summer (November to February) the temperature ranges from 15°C (59°F) up to 27°C (81°F). Inland it increases by 3-5°C (37-41°F). During winter (May to August) it ranges between 7°C (45°F) and 18°C (65°F). Inland the mornings are 5°C (41°F) and midday around 22°C (72°F).

Cape Town's long, balmy summer nights are invariably filled with some or other festival, fun run, concert or carnival. The weeks around Christmas and New Year are especially hectic. Pack tons of sunscreen, though (factor 30 and up): the summer days are blistering torture, and it's easy to lose track of the sunburn when you're enjoying the city's beaches and mountain walks. Beware also of the forceful 'Cape Doctor' that appears as if from nowhere in summer. This south-easterly wind helps to clear the air, and drapes Table Mountain with a snow-white tablecloth of clouds.

The season starts changing around April, with a certain

briskness to the air. The lovely autumn colours draw people to out of town to forests in Newlands and Constantia, as well as the winelands.

Wintertime is synonymous with rain. Occasional storms wreak havoc on telephone poles and there are often floods, especially in townships.

The vagaries of Cape Town's weather, however, mean that winter storms can be followed by mild sunny days, and Christmas (summer) can be cool and rainy.

Public holidays

New Year's Day (1 Jan); Human Rights Day (21 Mar); Good Friday; Family Day (21 Apr); Freedom Day (27 Apr); Workers Day (1 May); Youth Day (16 June); National Women's Day (9 Aug); Heritage Day (24 Sept) Day of Reconciliation 16 Dec); Christmas Day (25 Dec); Day of Goodwill (26 Dec).

Working

Find information from your nearest Department of Home Affairs office if you're in South Africa. If you're abroad, do so on the websites given under the Visa section (*see above*).
Department of Home Affairs Subdirectorate *Temporary Residence, Private Bag X114, Pretoria 0001, South Africa (012 314 8911).*

Weather averages

	Max (°C) temperature	Min (°C) temperature	Rainfall (mm)
January	26	16	15
February	27	16	17
March	25	14	20
April	23	12	41
May	20	9	68
June	18	8	93
July	18	7	82
August	18	8	77
September	19	9	40
October	21	11	30
November	24	13	14
December	25	15	17
Annually	22	11	515

Further Reference

Fiction & literature

Boyd, William
A Good Man in Africa, 1982
Entertaining farce of a lowly British
diplomat grappling with colonial
arrogance, local corruption and
sexual frustration in a fictitious
African state.

Brink, André
*Rumours of Rain, A Dry White
Season,* and *An Act of Terror*
Intriguing politicised novels written
in a haunting voice.

Coetzee, JM
*Disgrace, Waiting for the
Barbarians, The Life and Times of
Michael K* and *Dusklands.*
Winner of the Nobel Prize for
literature in 2003, this remarkable
writer's novels go to the very heart
of the South African psyche and
question the political and social
landscape of the country.

Fugard, Athol
*Blood Knot, Boesman and Lena, A
Lesson from Aloes, 'Master Harold'...
and the Boys, The Road to Mecca,
The Islans, My Children! My Africa!,
Playland*
Works by one of South Africa's most
esteemed playwrights, most famous
as a campaigning dramatist, tackling
issues of apartheid.

Galgut, Damon
The Good Doctor
Shortlisted for the 2003 Man Booker
prize, Galgut's novel explores post-
apartheid South Africa, where deep-
rooted social and political tensions
threaten shared dreams for the future.

Gordimer, Nadine
*July's People, Burger's Daughter,
Sport of Nature.*
Nobel prize-winning novelist dealing
with the tensions of her racially
divided country.

Jooste, Pamela
*Frieda and Min,Dance with a Poor
Man's Daughter, People Like
Ourselves.*
Contemporary fiction skimming on
the realities ordinary people face in
the new South Africa.

Matthee, Dalene
Circles in a Forest, Fiela's Child
Beautiful historical novels with the
lush Knysna Forest as a backdrop.

Mda, Jakes
Heart of Redness, Ways of Dying
Magic realism gets a contemporary
African twist.

Michener, James
The Covenant
Epic tale of empire building and the
creation of a country full of turmoil.

Paton, Alan
Cry the Beloved Country
A South African classic about
families, racism and ultimate
reconciliation.

Schreiner, Olive
The Story of An African Farm
Written in the late 19th-century,
Schreiner's novel applies a
Dickensian cast to radical ideals
about women and society. A book
that is widely acclaimed as an early
South African classic.

Schonstein, Patricia
A Time of Angels, Skyline
New on the scene with magical
realism touches to create a sense of
timelessness in Cape Town.

Sharpe, Tom
Indecent Exposure, Riotous Assembly
A blazing satire of apartheid, written
with typical best-selling aplomb.

Van Niekerk, Marlene
Triomf
Novel of post apartheid South Africa
seen from the eyes of a poor white
Afrikaans family.

Non-fiction

Breytenbach, Breyten
*The True Confessions of an
Albino Terrorist*
Memoir of his seven-year
imprisonment in South Africa.

Du Preez, Max
Pale Native
Roving, liberal reporter writes of his
times in troubled SA.

Elion, Barbara &
Strieman, Mercia
Clued up on Culture
An excellent source of local customs
and political correctness.

Gilliomee, Herman
The Afrikaners
Traces the history of the Afrikaner
from Dutch settler to apartheid's
master. Where does the Afrikaner
stand in the 21st century?

Harlan, Judith
*Mamphela Ramphele: Challenging
Apartheid in South Africa*
A biography of Mamphela Ramphele,
a woman who, as a doctor, teacher
and advisor to the Mandela
government, challenged racial and
gender inequities in South Africa.

Kanfer, Stefan
*The Last Empire: De Beers,
Diamonds and the World*
History of the De Beers diamond
empire. A story of cutthroat
capitalism, and the economic and
racial development of South Africa.

Krog, Antjie
*Country of my Skull, A Change of
Tongue, Down to my last Skin*
Krog analyses the country and its
people in an erudite and
contemporary manner.

Malan, Rian
My Traitor's Heart
Malan, a writer from a well-known
Afrikaner family, explores the
brutalities of apartheid.

Mandela, Nelson
Long Walk to Freedom
Autobiographical account of his life.
It should be next to everyone's bed.

Merwe, Hendrik
W.Van Der
*Peacemaking in South Africa:
A Life in Conflict Resolution*
A political memoir by this
internationally known peacemaker.

Mutwa, Credo
Indaba, My Children
Be enchanted by myths and legends
from all over Africa.

Pakenham, Thomas
*The Boer War, The Scramble for
Africa*
Quintessential Brit-based history.

Russell, Diana E.H.
*Lives of Courage: Women for a
New South Africa*
South Africa-born sociologist records
24 oral histories of white and black
women activist leaders, struggling
against oppression.

Tutu, Desmond
No Future Without Forgiveness
Essential reading to gain a sense of
empathy.

Welsh, Frank
History of South Africa
This single volume covers it all.

Food & wine

Cheifitz, Philippa
Cape Town Food
Vibrant food in a glorious setting.

Platter, John
SA Wine Guide
A new version comes out every year to stay up to date on all the quaffing possibilities in SA.

Platter, John and Erica
Africa Unkorked
The Platters go in search of weird wine around the continent. Fun romp through unexpected wine country.

Stevens, Ursula
Cape Town on Foot: A Walk through Town and History

Williams, Faldela
The Cape Malay Cookbook
Practice your new favourite flavours.

Amandla!
(Lee Hirsch 2002)
Stunning documentary telling the story of protest music in South Africa, which was inextricably linked to the struggle against apartheid.

Country of My Skull
(John Boorman 2003)
Adapted from Antjie Krog's book on the TRC, this follows a foreign journalist tracking the TRC.

Cry, The Beloved Country
(Zoltan Korda 1951 and Darell Roodt 1995)
Famous film adaptation of novel of the same name by Alan Paton.

Cry Freedom
(Richard Attenborough 1987)
True story of an inspiring friendship in an impossible time.

Ghandi
(Richard Attenborough 1982)
Insight into Ghandi's experiences as a young lawyer in South Africa.

Mapantsula
(Oliver Schmitz 1989)
A stirring film set shanty towns and a white middle-class shopping centre in Johannesburg.

Promised Land
(Jason Xenopulos 2002)
Adapted from the Afrikaans novel by Karel Schoeman, this is a story about hidden truths and near impossible quests.

Road to Mecca
(Athol Fugard, Peter Goldsmid 1992)
A moving story of Helen Martin's Owl House.

Sarafina
(Darell Roodt 1992)
Adapted from Mbongeni Ngema's stage musical. Whoopi Goldberg plays an idealistic teacher who helps an impressionable teenage girl to throw off the shackles of apartheid.

Shot Down
(Andrew Worsdale 1986)
Banned for ten years, Worsdale describes this film as 'the only record of young white leftie anxiety amid the turmoil of the eighties'.

Abdullah Ibrahim
Knysna Blue (1994)
Story of this jazz pianist's return to Cape Town.

Brenda Fassie
Memeza (2001), *Mina Nawe* (2002)
Cape Town's queen of pop.

Ladysmith Black Mambazo
The Ultimate Collection (2001)
A band that embodies the musical traditions suppressed in old SA.

Lucky Dube
Soul Taker (2001)
South Africa's greatest reggae star.

Lungiswa
Ekhaya (2000)
Fresh talent from Cape Town's Langa township.

Mzwakhe Mbuli
Born Free but Always in Chains (2000)
The pro-democracy 'people's poet' now imprisoned for a crime he claims he didn't commit.

Rebecca Malope
Free at Last: South African Gospel (1997)
This is Nelson Mandela's favourite gospel singer.

Winston Mankunku Ngozi
Abantwana Be Afrika (2004), *Molo Africa* (2000)
A leading jazz saxophonist from Cape Town.

Yvonne Chaka Chaka
The Best of Yvonne Chaka Chaka Vol.1 (2001), *Bombani* (1999)
A leading figure in South African popular music.

Arts & Entertainment
Cape Town Today
www.capetowntoday.co.za
Lively entertainment guide.
Cape Town Events
www.capetownevents.co.za
Plan your events calendar.
Wots News
www.wotsnews.co.za
Events all over South Africa.

Children
Cape for Kids
www.capeforkids.com
Plenty of ideas for family fun.

Food & Wine
Eating Out
www.eating-out.co.za
Restaurant guide for the whole of South Africa.
Wine Routes
http://wine.capetourism.org
Wine routes and estates in Cape Town and the Western Cape.

Sport & Fitness
Golf South Africa
www.golfinginsouthafrica.co.za
News, courses, tours and a link to the official South African golf association site.
Hike Cape Town
www.hikecapetown.co.za
Hike your way around the Cape Town Peninsula.
Western Cape Tourism
http://sport.capetourism.org
The latest on sports in and around Cape Town.

Useful information
Airports Company South Africa
www.airports.co.za
Up-to-date information on flights, weather conditions and airport news.
Cape Town Tourism
www.cape-town.org
All the information you need about the city's resources – from golf courses to plastic surgeons.
City of Cape Town
www.capetown.gov.za
Keep abreast of council projects and developments.
Cyber Cape Town
www.cybercapetown.com
Information on top-class hotels, car hire, safaris, tours and holiday packages.
South African Weather Service
www.weathersa.co.za
Check out the forecast.
Western Cape Tourism
www.capetourism.org
Official tourist board site, with plenty of practical detail.
Yellow Pages Online
www.yellowpages.co.za
Comprehensive business directory.

Index

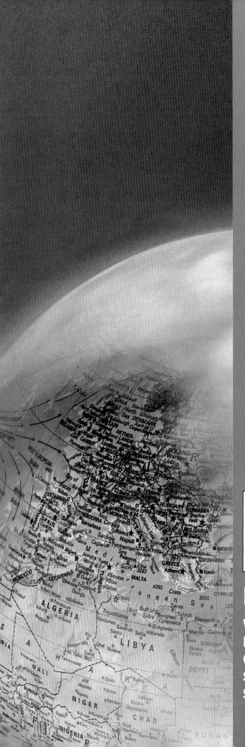

Place of interest and/or entertainment	
Railway stations	
Parks	
Hospitals	
Area name	CLIFTON

Maps

ATLANTIC OCEAN

INDIAN OCEAN

Cape Town

Johannesburg Pretoria

Republic of South Africa

1024 m

875 m

Bitterfontein

Nuwerus

Landplaas

Brandkop

Lutzville

Vanrhynsdorp

Papendorp

Vredendal

Doringbaai

Klawer

Rooiduinepunt

Heerenlogement

Lambert's Bay

Graafwater

Leipoldtville

Clanwillam

Wuppertal

Elandsbaai

Baboon Point

N7

CEDERBERG

Soetkuil

Paleisheuwel

Cederberg

*St Helena
Bay*

Aurora

Citrusdal

PIKETBERG

KOUE BOKKEVELDBERGE

SWARTRUGGENS

Stompneusbaai

Velddrif

Paternoster

Vredenburg

Piketberg

Porterville

Saldanha

*Great Winterhoek
Wilderness Area*

Laingsbur

Matjiesfontein

*Saldanha Bay
Postberg NR*

Hopefield

Langebaan

*Churchhaven
West Coast NP*

Moorreesburg

Tulbagh

Prince Alfred
Hamlet

N1

27

Yzerfontein

Darling

Wolseley

Ceres

Touwsrivier

WITBERG

HEXRIVIERBERGE

Matroosberg

*Dassen
Island*

Malmesbury

De Doorns

Mamre

Atlantis

Wellington

Worcester

Robertson

Montagu

Melkbosstrand

N7

Paarl

Rawsonville

Robben Island

Milnerton

Winelands
Area

*Marloth
NR*

Barrydale

Table Bay

See pp276-7

Franschhoek

*Vrolijkheid
NR*

Ashton

CAPE TOWN

Stellenbosch

Genadendal

Swellendam

Suurbraak

Hout Bay

Somerset West

N2

Simonstown

Strand

Grabouw

Riviersonderend

Malga

*Cape of Good
Hope NR*

Botriver

Caledon

*De Hoop
NR*

*False
Bay*

Kleinmond

*Cape of
Good Hope*

Betty's
Bay

Hermanus

Napier

Bredasdorp

*Cape
Point*

Hawston

Stanford

Elim

Walker Bay

De Kelders

Arniston
(Waenhuiskrans)

Danger Point

Gansbaai

Struisbaai

Pearly Beach

*Quoin
Point*

*Cape
Agulhas*

L'Agulhas

ATLANTIC OCEAN

The Western Cape

0   100 km

0   50 miles

© Copyright Time Out Guides 2004

Sneeukraal

Murraysburg

Nelspoort

Karoo
National
Park

1913 m

Beaufort West

NUWEVELDBERGE

N1

Wiegnaarspoort

Merweville

KOMSBERG

Leeu-Gamka

Kruidfontein

N12

Seekoegat

Prince
Albert

Klaarstroom

GROOT-SWARTBERGE

Matjiesrivier

KLEIN-SWARTBERGE

De Rust

Ladismith

Calitzdorp

Oudtshoorn

Dysselsdorp

KAMMANASSIE MTNS

Uniondale

Volmoed

62

Van Wyksdorp

N12

Haarlem

OUTENIQUA MTNS

N9

George

Barrington

Blanco

Wilderness

Knysna National
Lake Area

Tsitsikamma
NP

LANGEBERG

Herbertsdale

Wilderness
National Park

Knysna

Plettenberg
Bay

Heidelberg

Riversdale

Groot-
Brakrivier

Slangrivier

Albertinia

N2

Mossel Bay

Witsand

Still Bay

Vleesbaai

Gouritsmond

Infanta

St
Sebastian
Bay

Cape
Infanta

INDIAN OCEAN

Taking time off?
Take Time Out.

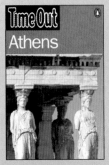

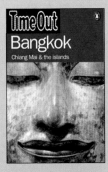

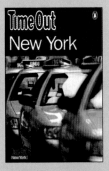

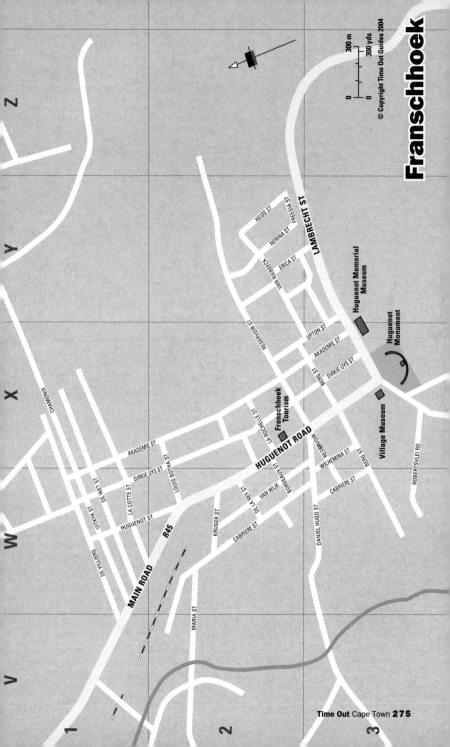

Franschhoek

300 m
300 yds

© Copyright Time Out Guides 2004

HEIDE ST

NERINA ST

FREESIA ST

ERICA ST

VAN RIEBEECK ST

LAMBRECHT ST

RESERVOIR ST

UPTON ST

AKADEMIE ST

BERG ST

DIRKIE UYS ST

Huguenot Memorial Museum

Huguenot Monument

CHAMONIX

AKADEMIE ST

DIRKIE UYS ST

LA COTTE ST

DE WET ST

UITKYK ST

HUGUENOT ST

LOUIS BOTHA ST

LA RICHELLE ST

Franschhoek Tourism

HUGUENOT ROAD

RESERVOIR

WILHEMINA ST

BERG ST

Village Museum

ROBERTSVLEI RD

DE VILLIERS

R45

MAIN ROAD

KRUGER ST

DE LA REY ST

VAN WIJK

BORREAUX ST

CABRIERE ST

DANIEL HUGO ST

CABRIERE ST

MARIA ST

CABRIERE ST

Z

Y

X

W

V

1

2

3

Robben
Island

ATLANTIC OCEAN

Table Bay

Blouubergstrand
West Beach
Table View

NORTHERN SUBURBS

Durbanville

N7

N1

Milnerton
Milnerton Beach
Montague
Gardens
Century City
Goodwood
Bellville
Ysterplaat
Parow
N7

Mouille Point
V & A
Waterfront
See pp282-3
See p281
Green Point
Three Anchor Bay
Sea Point
Cape Town
Fresnaye
Tamboerskloof
Paarden Eiland
Salt River
Observatory
Bantry Bay
Zonnebloem
Woodstock
Clifton Bay
Pinelands
Clifton
Gardens
Vredehoek
Camps Bay
Oranjezicht
Groote Schuur
Estate
Mowbray
Rondebosch
TABLE MOUNTAIN
Newlands
See p284
Claremont
M5
SOUTHERN
SUBURBS
Cape Town
International
Bishopscourt
Kenilworth
N2
Llandudno
Alphen
Rust-en-Vrede
Wynberg
Sandy Bay
Constantia
Plumstead
CAPE FLATS
Hout Bay
High Constantia
Diep River
Parkwood
KARBONKELBERG
Mitchell's Plain
M3
Zeekoevlei
Noordhoek
Muizenberg
Sunnydale
Kalk Bay
St James
Kommetjie
Fish Hoek
Sweetwater
(Soetwater)
Glencairn
Simonstown
Schusterskraal
False Bay
SWARTKOPBERGE
Smitswinkel Bay
Cape of Good
Hope Nature
Reserve
0   5 km
0   3 miles
© Copyright Time Out Guides 2004
Cape of
Good Hope
Cape Point

276 Time Out Cape Town

Greater Cape Town

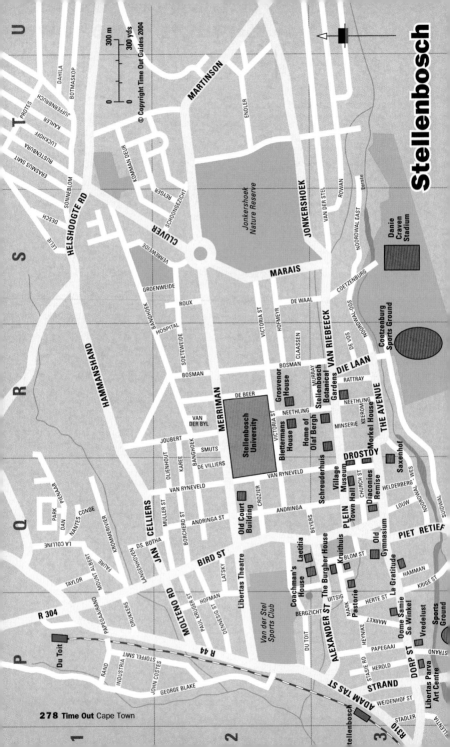

Stellenbosch

Street Index

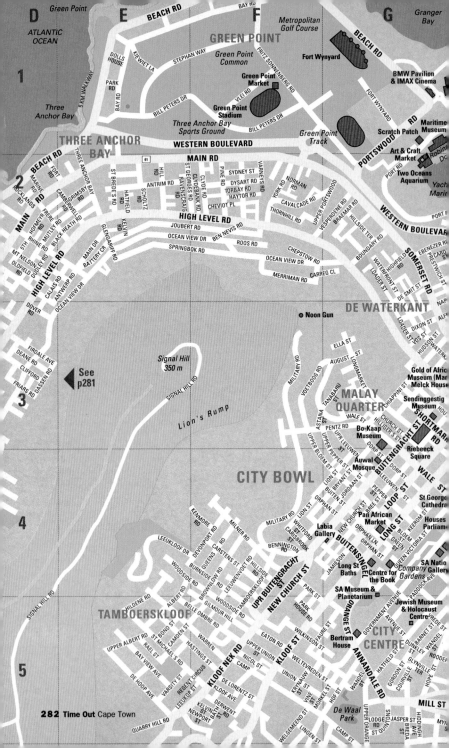

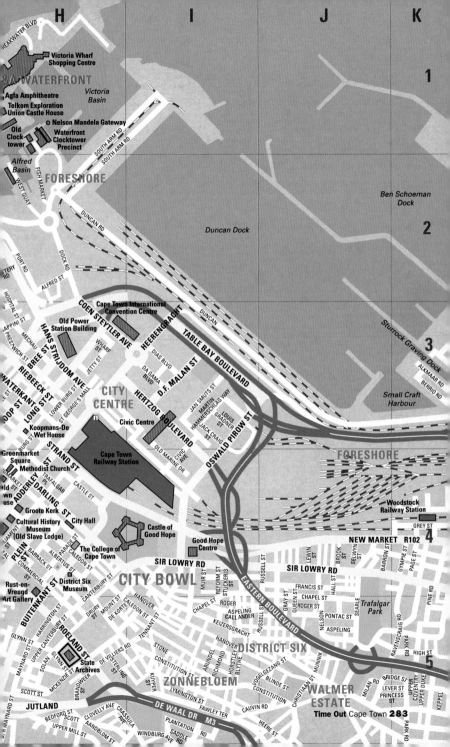

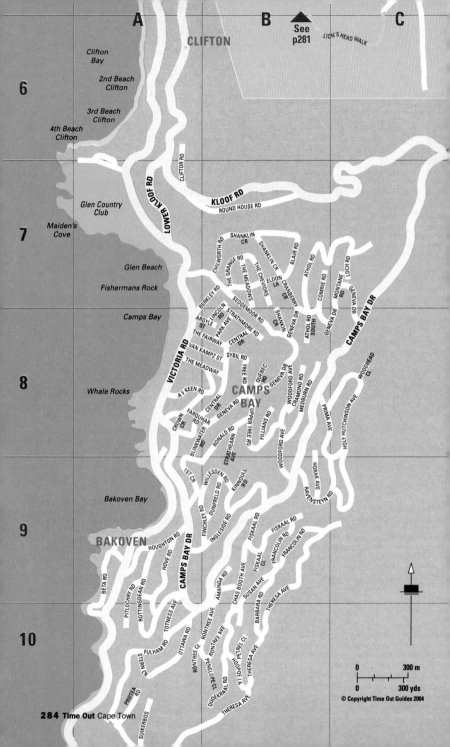

CLIFTON

See p281

LION'S HEAD WALK

Clifton Bay

2nd Beach Clifton

3rd Beach Clifton

4th Beach Clifton

6

CLIFTON RD

LOWER KLOOF RD

KLOOF RD

ROUND HOUSE RD

Glen Country Club

Maiden's Cove

7

SHANKLIN CR

CHILWORTH RD

SHANKLIN CR

THE GRANGE RD

THE MEADOWS

THE CHEVORS

ELDON LA

CRANBERRY CR

BLAIR RD

ATHOL RD

COMRIE RD

MONTANE RD

LOCH RD

GENEVA DR

Glen Beach

Fishermans Rock

Camps Bay

BERKLEY RD

SEDGEMOOR RD

LINCOLN RD

STRATHMORE RD

SHANKLIN CR

GENEVA DR

GENEVA DR

ATHOL RD SOUTH

GENEVA DR

CAMPS BAY DR

ARGYLE ST

PARK AVE

CENTRAL DR

THE FAIRWAY

VICTORIA RD

VAN KAMPZ ST

SYBIL RD

THE MEADWAY

TREE RD

QUEBEC RD

GENEVA DR

WOODFORD AVE

CRAMOND RD

MEDBURN RD

WOODHEAD CL

8

A F KEEN RD

CENTRAL DR

GENEVA RD

UPPER TREE RD

FILLIANS RD

PRIMA AVE

HOLY HUTCHINSON AVE

CAMPS BAY

Whale Rocks

CROWN CR

FARQUHAR RD

BLINKWATER RD

RONALD RD

STRATHEARN AVE

WOODFORD AVE

1ST CR

WILLESDEN RD

DUNFIELD RD

KINNOULL RD

HORAK AVE

RAVENSTEYN RD

Bakoven Bay

FINCHLEY RD

INGLESIDE RD

FISKAAL RD

FISKAAL RD

9

BAKOVEN

HOUGHTON RD

CAMPS BAY DR

HOVE RD

FISKAAL CL

FRANCOLIN CL

FRANCOLIN RD

BETA RD

PITLOCHRY RD

ROTTINGDEAN RD

TOTNESS AVE

AMANDA RD

CHAS BOOTH AVE

SUSAN AVE

FISKAAL RD

THERESA AVE

BARBARA RD

THERESA AVE

FULHAM RD

RONTREE AVE

RONTREE AVE

OTTAWA RD

OUDEKRAAL RD

HOP PETREL CL

THERESA AVE

10

STERN CR

PROTEA RD

SUIKERBOS

THERESA AVE

0   300 m
0   300 yds

© Copyright Time Out Guides 2004